Religions in America

*a completely revised and up-to-date guide
to Churches and Religious Groups
in the United States*

edited by Leo Rosten

The famous *LOOK* magazine series
on Religion, greatly amplified and rewritten,
plus the most complete and authoritative compilation
of facts, figures, tables, charts, articles
and reference material on Religion
in any published volume

A Touchstone Book Published by
Simon and Schuster / New York

Copyright © *1952, 1953, 1954, 1955, 1963*
by Cowles Magazines and Broadcasting, Inc.

A TOUCHSTONE BOOK
PUBLISHED BY SIMON AND SCHUSTER
ROCKEFELLER CENTER, 630 FIFTH AVENUE
NEW YORK, N. Y. 10020

COPYRIGHT © 1952, 1953, 1954, 1955, 1963
BY COWLES MAGAZINES AND BROADCASTING, INC.

ELEVENTH PAPERBACK PRINTING

SBN 671-21272-9 CASEBOUND EDITION
SBN 671-21271-0 TOUCHSTONE PAPERBACK EDITION
LIBRARY OF CONGRESS CATALOG CARD NUMBER: 55-7133
MANUFACTURED IN THE UNITED STATES OF AMERICA
PRINTED BY THE MURRAY PRINTING COMPANY, FORGE VILLAGE, MASS.

Editor's Note to the Revised Edition

A Guide to the Religions of America, *first published in 1955, has won so gratifying a response and has elicited so many requests for a revised edition, that we are pleased to present now a book which has been re-edited from the first to the last page and has been greatly amplified by the addition of much new and, we think, fascinating material.*

Part One, Religious Beliefs, *contains twenty chapters, in question-and-answer form, by twenty distinguished spokesmen for their faiths—including the personal testaments of a humanist, a scientist and a world-famous agnostic. "What Is a Greek Orthodox?" has been added to our collection of articles. The regrettable absence from the original edition of an article on the Eastern Orthodox faith was simply the consequence of our inability to obtain an authoritative article from a spokesman approved by the proper church officials; we are happy now to include Mr. Arthur Douropulos' excellent delineation.*

Part Two, Facts, Figures and Opinions on Religion in the United States, *has been entirely changed and vastly augmented by a wealth of new facts, statistics, public opinion surveys and data not in existence in 1955. This part contains new excerpts from significant books, and recent articles in journals of sociology and religion.*

Part Three, Selected Reading List and Reference Aids, *has been designed to help those who wish to widen their own explorations in the field of religion. We are especially grateful to the American Library Association, which prepared a special bibliography of recommended readings for this edition, including histories of each religious group, biographies of church fathers and leaders, and superior fiction which dramatizes the lives of men and women who played an important part in the founding of their religious order or the perpetuation of their faith.*

We have, in short, tried to create as clear, meaningful and useful a volume as can be fashioned from the massive and often confusing figures, writings and research on the religious creeds and institutions in the United States.

—LEO ROSTEN

Contents

part two / Facts, Figures and Opinions on Religion in the United States

part three / *Selected Reading List
and Reference Aids*

part one

Religious Beliefs

What Is a Baptist?

WILLIAM B. LIPPHARD

Mr. Lipphard writes from an editorial background of nearly fifty years of professional association with the American Baptist Convention, which consists of more than 6,500 churches. He was president of the Associated Church Press from 1947 to 1949, served for ten years as its executive secretary, and is now an honorary life member of that fellowship of 160 Protestant church press editors. He was for twenty years editor of the Baptist publication *Missions Magazine,* and on his retirement in 1953, was appointed editor emeritus for life. In the course of his work with the American Baptist Convention, he has served as a delegate to Baptist World Congresses in Sweden, Canada, Germany, the United States, Denmark and England.

Mr. Lipphard was born in Evansville, Indiana, in 1886. He was educated at Yale University from which he received a B.A. and an M.A. degree, and at Colgate-Rochester Divinity School, where he earned his B.D. His honorary degrees include a D.D. from Franklin College and a Litt.D. from Ottawa University, Kansas.

From 1940 to 1943, Mr. Lipphard was secretary of the World Relief Committee of the American Baptist Convention. He was a member of the Joint Commission on Missionary Education of the National Council of Churches of Christ and is presently a member of the American Friends of the World Council of Churches, the Foreign Policy Association, and the Baptist National Committee on Public Affairs. He is a former vice-president and director of the American Baptist Historical Society.

In 1951 Mr. Lipphard received an award from the Associated Church Press for eminence in editorial writing. He served as Director of the Church Press at the second assembly of the World Council of Churches at Evanston, Illinois, in 1954. Mr. Lipphard is the author of four books.

WHAT IS A BAPTIST?

A Baptist is a faithful follower of Jesus Christ, who sincerely endeavors to establish His way of life among mankind, is a stanch believer in the historic Baptist principle of religious liberty, has been baptized by immersion, and is a member of a parish church which is identified by the name Baptist.

Baptists believe that religion is a personal relationship between the human soul and God. In this realm, nothing may intrude—no ecclesiastical system, no government regulation, no ordinance, no sacrament, no preacher, no priest. The saving grace of Christ and the infinite mercy of God are available to every individual, without the mediation of any priest or minister or church or system. Baptists believe in the "priesthood of all believers."

WHAT ARE THE BASIC TENETS OF THE BAPTIST CREED?

Baptists have no single, official creed. Periodically, efforts have been made by extreme conservatives to secure the adoption of a statement which would become a test for service or fellowship. Each time, such a proposal has been defeated. The nearest statement to a formal creed is the so-called "Grand Rapids Affirmation," adopted on May 23, 1946, by the American Baptist Convention, which declares:

RESOLVED: That we reaffirm our faith in the New Testament as a divinely inspired record and therefore a trustworthy, authoritative and all-sufficient rule of our faith and practice. We rededicate ourselves to Jesus Christ as Lord and Savior and we call all our churches to the common task of sharing the whole gospel with the whole world.

A relatively small organized group of conservative Baptist churches in the United States has adopted an official creed which all missionaries, faculty members and trustees of its colleges and divinity schools are required to sign. Despite their wide differences of theological interpretation, Baptists *are* united in one fellowship and committed to a common purpose. They are motivated by a transcending loyalty to Jesus Christ, as Lord and Savior. For Baptists, Christ stands at the door of every human heart and knocks, waiting to be invited in to take possession of that person's life, to make him a living reincarnation of Christ Himself. As the apostle Paul expressed it: ". . . I live; yet not I, but Christ liveth in me." To that concept of the reincarnation of Christ, every Baptist gives wholehearted assent.

WHAT ARE THE DISTINCTIVE CHARACTERISTICS OF THE BAPTIST FAITH?

The answer can best be expressed in two words: religious liberty. Throughout their history, Baptists have contended for full, complete, unrestricted religious freedom. And the freedom they demand for themselves they just as zealously demand for those of all other religions— Catholic, Moslem, Hindu, Jew, Buddhist, Shintoist or pagan—as well as for the adherents of no religion.

Baptists claim that an atheist has just as much right to cherish his views, and to persuade others to accept his views, as any advocate of any religion —provided only that nobody in the profession of his convictions interferes with the right of all others to do likewise.

Baptists believe that religious error can never be suppressed or eradicated by legislation, force or persecution—whether by state or church. The Baptist contention is not for mere "tolerance" but for absolute liberty. Tolerance means concession and expediency; liberty means inalienable right. The English philosopher John Locke said: "The Baptists were the first propounders of absolute liberty, just and true liberty, equal and impartial liberty."

WHY DO BAPTISTS CALL THEMSELVES A DENOMINATION AND NOT A CHURCH?

Because most Baptists do not admit that they constitute a "church"— but are organized into local "churches." The local parish church is the sovereign, all-powerful ecclesiastical unit. The term "Baptist Church" is used for convenience; "denomination" is preferred by most Baptists.

Baptists have no hierarchy, no centralized control of religious activity, no headquarters' "oversight" of churches or liturgies, practices or regulations. The local parish church is a law unto itself. Its relations with other churches, its compliance with recommendations from national church headquarters, its acceptance of any resolutions formulated at a convention—all these are entirely voluntary, without the slightest degree of compulsion.

DO BAPTISTS ACCEPT THE LITERAL INTERPRETATION OF THE BIBLE?

Yes and no. All Baptists believe in the inspiration of the Bible, but only the extreme fundamentalists accept it literally or regard it as infallible in every detail. All Baptists accept the Bible as infallible in religious teachings and as a trustworthy record of the progressive revelation of God, climaxed by the supreme revelation of Himself in Jesus Christ. Progressive and liberal Baptists regard some sections of the Bible as written in the thought patterns of Biblical times—allegorical, figurative, legendary, yet conveying eternal religious truths. No official dogma prescribes how an individual Baptist shall interpret the Bible.

WHY DO BAPTISTS BAPTIZE ONLY BY IMMERSION?

For two reasons: (1) Immersion was the mode of baptism in the New Testament; John the Baptist immersed his converts in the Jordan River; Christ Himself was so immersed. (2) Baptists regard baptism as a public confession of Christian faith and a symbol of the burial and resurrection of Christ, as stated by Paul in his Epistle to the Colossians. Hence, Baptists look upon immersion as realistic symbolism, through which the life of sin is buried in baptism and the new life of faith emerges.

Immersion is limited to adults and to such children as have reached an age where they can understand the meaning of baptism. "Baptize" is a transliteration of the Greek work *baptizein* (meaning "to immerse"), not a translation. To say that Baptists baptize by immersion is redundant, since baptism originally was immersion.

WHY DON'T BAPTISTS BAPTIZE INFANTS?

Since baptism is a voluntary public profession of Christian faith, only persons old enough to understand its significance and its symbolism should be accepted for baptism. Moreover, Baptists give their children the right to decide for themselves whether or not they wish to be baptized as a public profession of Christian faith. Such a decision makes religion and the ceremony of baptism more meaningful.

DO BAPTISTS ACCEPT THE DOCTRINE OF THE VIRGIN BIRTH OF CHRIST?

A great majority undoubtedly do. A substantial minority do not. For the majority, the doctrine of the Virgin Birth is essential to faith in the deity of Christ. The minority need no such support, since they find no reference to the Virgin Birth in the writings of Paul or in the gospels of Mark and John.

Since Baptists have no authoritarian creed to control their faith and practice, each local parish church has the right to decide whether or not to make acceptance of the doctrine of the Virgin Birth a condition of church membership.

Baptists pay no special homage to Mary but respect her as the noblest of women. They have never accepted the doctrine of *her* immaculate conception or the doctrine, announced in 1950 by Pope Pius XII, of the Assumption of Mary.

DO BAPTISTS ACCEPT THE DOCTRINE OF THE TRINITY?

Yes. This is a basic doctrine of Christianity. The trinitarian formula, "in the name of the Father, and of the Son, and of the Holy Ghost," is used at every baptism. The sublime mystery of the Trinity, of the eternal and infinite essence of God manifested in three persons, the Baptist leaves to the theologians to interpret. He simply accepts it.

WHAT IS THE BAPTIST POSITION ON SIN AND SALVATION?

A Baptist affirms the competency of the individual, under God, in matters of religion. Every true believer in Christ as personal Savior is saved—without the intervention of preacher or church. Each individual must give evidence of his personal redemption by faith, good works and the Christian way of life. The confession of sin is a personal matter between the individual and God. Hence no priestly mediation or resort to the confessional is needed.

With most Protestants, Baptists believe that man sins against the holiness and righteousness of God, that he willfully disobeys God's commands, allows his selfishness to motivate his life, and is therefore in need of salvation. A good Baptist definition of sin explains it as "lack of conformity to the moral law of God, either in act, disposition or state." Man cannot save himself. He needs and finds in Jesus Christ a divine redeemer who unites in Himself both the human nature and the divine. By His death on the Cross, man was reconciled to God and God to man. Through faith in this reconciling ministry of Christ, man is saved from his sins.

DO BAPTISTS BELIEVE IN HEAVEN AND HELL?

A categorical answer, applicable to all Baptists, is impossible. Most Baptists believe in some form of life beyond the grave. They cannot conceive of the total annihilation of spiritual values; nor can they imagine the continued existence of spiritual values without the continuing existence of personalities to express them. As to the precise nature of life hereafter, Baptists cherish a vast range of ideas, from some nebulous, indefinable existence to some definite place, like a city of golden streets or a region of everlasting torment as envisaged by the extreme literalists. Some Baptists find it difficult to reconcile the fact of an all-merciful God with endless punishment for sins committed within the short span of a lifetime on earth. Still others, with sublime confidence and trust, simply accept the assurance of Christ: "Where I am, there ye may be also."

DO BAPTISTS HAVE SACRAMENTS?

No. What are known as sacraments are regarded by Baptists as simple dignified ordinances with no supernatural significance and no sacramental values. The Lord's Supper, or communion service, is usually observed on the first Sunday of the month. It is a reminder of the death of Christ and is observed in obedience to His command the night before He was crucified. Whatever grace a Baptist derives from participating in the Lord's Supper depends on his own awareness of what the Supper signifies as a memorial service. No grace is supernaturally bequeathed to him by the officiating clergyman or by his partaking of the bread and of the cup. Whatever blessing he receives comes through some new rededication by the participant in the communion service to a life of righteousness and of service to his fellow men.

DO BAPTISTS APPROVE OF DIVORCE?

No, except for adultery. But there is no regulation among Baptist churches regarding divorce. Annual conventions of Baptists have often condemned the rising divorce rate in the United States. Each Baptist clergyman depends on his conscience in deciding whether or not to officiate at the marriage of divorced persons. No church law prescribes what he must do.

DO BAPTISTS SANCTION BIRTH CONTROL?

No parish Baptist church and no ecclesiastical convention of Baptists has ever by resolution expressed approval or disapproval of birth control or planned parenthood. Even if it had, such resolution would not be binding on any Baptist. Most Baptists would resent and repudiate any such resolution as an unwarranted intrusion into the private life of husband and wife.

HOW DO BAPTISTS PROPAGATE THEIR FAITH?

The historic Baptist view holds that *every* church member, and every professing Christian, is an evangelist. By word, deed and character, he is committed to proclaim his Christian faith and to seek to win others to its acceptance. Throughout their history, Baptists have engaged in very active missionary effort, at home and abroad. Foreign missions have been successful on every continent.

HOW MANY BAPTISTS ARE THERE IN THE WORLD? IN THE UNITED STATES?

In 1962, there were nearly 25,000,000 Baptists in the world. An accurate tabulation is impossible because religious statistics cannot be compiled in countries behind the Iron Curtain. It is estimated that there are 2,000,000 Baptists in Soviet Russia. How many Chinese Baptists have survived the Communist regime is unknown. *The World Almanac* for 1962 records 21,374,126 Baptists in the United States, divided among the four larger national groups and eighteen smaller bodies, all of whom identify themselves as Baptists. Since Baptists do not baptize infants or children until they have reached the age when they understand the meaning of baptism, the figures for church membership do not include children. About one-third of the Protestants in the United States are Baptists.

HOW DID THE BAPTIST MOVEMENT BEGIN?

Most Baptists like to trace their ancestry directly back to John the Baptist. But there is no historical evidence of any definite, organized body of Baptists before the year 1611 when groups in England began to maintain that only believers in Christ, not infants, could be baptized and that baptism had to be by immersion.

Baptist *principles,* however, go back to the teachings and practices of the churches in the New Testament, before they became organized and controlled under the hierarchical system known as Roman Catholicism. Professor Hans von Schubert of Heidelberg acknowledged that "in the ancient church, it was not the general custom to baptize children; preparation for baptism and the baptismal ceremony were designed for grown persons."

During the early centuries and through the Middle Ages, small groups of Christians sought to maintain the purity and simplicity of the early churches. Later groups emerged who became known as Anabaptists, because they insisted on rebaptism. They regarded their original baptism as infants as not in accord with the New Testament and therefore invalid.

Among them was Balthazar Hubmeier, who died at the stake on March 10, 1528, and his wife, who was drowned in the Danube a few days later, because of their unswerving fidelity to three basic Baptist principles: (1) the supremacy of the Scriptures, rather than the Church, in matters of faith and doctrine; (2) religious liberty; and (3) the baptism of believers rather than infants.

Anabaptist groups flourished for nearly four centuries, mostly in Switzerland, Germany and the Netherlands. They were the ecclesiastical ancestors of the Baptists of today. Since 1611 in England, and since 1639 in the United States, when Roger Williams, who was exiled from Massachusetts because of his insistence on religious liberty, founded the first Baptist church on American soil, in Providence, Rhode Island, the Baptist denomination throughout the world has grown in the number of its local parish churches, its adherents, its religious prestige and its moral and spiritual influence.

What Is a Catholic?

JOHN COGLEY

John Cogley was executive editor of *The Commonweal*, the distinguished weekly journal edited by Catholic laymen, when this article was written. He has since become associated with the Fund for the Republic as a member of its executive staff. As a director of the Fund's center for the Study of Democratic Institutions in Santa Barbara, California, he has been in charge of studies of religion in American life and of the American character.

Mr. Cogley was born in Chicago in 1916, studied at Loyola University in that city, and completed graduate work in philosophy and theology at the University of Fribourg, Switzerland.

He is the author of numerous articles for a variety of periodicals and has edited two volumes on religion, *Catholicism in America*, a series of articles that appeared in *The Commonweal*, and *Religion in America*, a collection of essays written by Protestant, Catholic and Jewish spokesmen. He is also the author of *Report on Blacklisting*, a two-volume study of civil liberties in the entertainment industries. Mr. Cogley was chosen for the Christian Culture Award in 1960. He is a trustee of the Council on Religion and International Affairs, a Carnegie endowment, and has worked closely with the National Conference of Christians and Jews.

NOTE TO THE READER: This article was submitted to the proper authorities in the New York Archdiocese, who declared that it presents a correct understanding of Catholic doctrinal and moral teachings. The author alone is responsible for non-doctrinal opinions.

DO CATHOLICS BELIEVE THEIRS IS THE ONLY TRUE RELIGION?

Yes. The fact that there are many religions, all holding different—often contradictory—doctrines about God and man strikes the Catholic as tragic. The idea that they are all equally true (those that hold Christ was divine and those that hold He was merely human, for instance) seems absurdly illogical.

Catholics believe that Christ, the Son of God, founded the Church and promised to remain with it, "even unto the consummation of the world." But when they say theirs is the only true religion, Catholics do not mean that they alone are the children of God or that only Catholics are righteous and God-fearing. Many non-Catholics are saints; some Catholics are scoundrels. Nor do Catholics believe that only Catholics go to heaven. Pope Pius IX wrote: "It is to be held as of faith that none can be saved outside the Apostolic Roman Church . . . but, nevertheless, it is equally certain that those who are ignorant of the true religion, if that ignorance is invincible, will not be held guilty in the eyes of the Lord." Catholics believe that in the sight of God, all who love Him and sincerely desire to do His will are related in some way to the Church which His Son founded and so can be saved.

WHAT ARE THE CHIEF DIFFERENCES BETWEEN THE CATHOLIC AND JEWISH FAITHS? THE CATHOLIC AND PROTESTANT?

The Catholic Church claims four distinctive marks: it is *one* (in doctrine, authority and worship), *holy* (perfect observance of its teachings leads inevitably to sanctity), *catholic* (it is unchanging in its essential teachings and preaches the same gospel and administers the same sacraments to men of all times in all places), and *apostolic* (it traces its ancestry back to the apostles and, like them, carries the message of Christ to all, regardless of race, nationality, station or class).

Judaism: Pope Pius XI at the time of the Hitler persecutions wrote: "Spiritually, we are Semites." In the Mass, reference is made to "our father Abraham." The Catholic recognizes the unique religious role of the Jewish people before Christ. He shares their belief in God the Father, in the brotherhood of man, and in the moral teachings handed down by the patriarchs and prophets. Christianity, as he sees it, is the fulfillment of Judaism. "I came not to destroy the law but to fulfill it," Christ said.

The big difference is that Catholics believe that Jesus Christ was the promised Messiah, true God and true Man. They believe that mankind was redeemed by Christ's atonement, though individual men must still work out their own personal salvation by faith and good works. Catholics accept the New Testament with its "new law" of charity—by which is meant the love of God for His own sake and of all men (even of enemies) because they too are children of God. The Catholic believes that with the coming of Christ, all races and nations became "chosen people."

Protestantism embraces a variety of doctrines. Some Protestants are closer to Catholic belief than others. Two of the chief differences seem to be these:

THE BIBLE: Protestants believe in private interpretation. Catholics believe that the Church is the divinely appointed custodian of the Bible and has the final word on what is meant in any specific passage. The Church guards orthodoxy (including interpretation of the Scriptures) and passes down essential Christian tradition from one generation to another.

UNIVERSAL PRIESTHOOD: Most Protestants affirm the "priesthood of all believers," in opposition to the Catholic idea of a specially ordained priesthood. Catholics, too, believe that by virtue of the sacraments laymen share in the priesthood of Christ. But the "priesthood of the laity" is subordinated to that of the clergy, who alone have received the sacrament of Holy Orders.

The Catholic Mass is not the same as a Protestant Communion Service—not only in ceremony but in what each congregation believes is taking place. Protestantism provides for a greater variety of opinion on such matters as divorce and birth control, which the Catholic feels have been settled once and for all either by the natural law or by revelation. The average Protestant thinks of "the Church" as a broad spiritual unity; the Catholic using the same words has a precise institution—the Roman Catholic Church—in mind.

MAY CATHOLIC PRIESTS TAKE PART IN INTERRELIGIOUS SERVICES?

No. The public worship of Catholics, and the priest's exercise of his spiritual office, are subject to the authority of the Church. Since the Church's authority is not recognized by the other participants at an interfaith service, Catholics at such services, be they priests or laity, are placed in an untenable position. They are implicitly called upon to deny their own Church's claims and sometimes, by the wording of prayers and hymns, to assent explicitly to beliefs they do not hold.

DO CATHOLICS BELIEVE THE POPE CAN DO NO WRONG? MUST CATHOLICS ACCEPT EVERYTHING THE POPE SAYS?

Catholics do not believe the Pope can do no wrong. Nor does the Pope. He confesses regularly to a simple priest, like the humblest peasant in the Church. Catholics admit freely that there were popes who were wicked men (I first learned of them in parochial schools), though their number and the enormity of their sins have often been exaggerated.

Catholics do believe that the Pope, be he saint or sinner, is preserved by God from leading the Church into doctrinal error. These are the conditions of a papal pronouncement that Catholics consider infallible: (1) it must come under the heading of faith or morals; (2) the Pope must be speaking as head of the Church with the intention of obliging its members to assent to his definition.

Everything that the Church teaches as infallible doctrine, a Catholic must accept. On questions that have not been defined as articles of faith (the miracles at Fatima, for instance), he is under no such obligation.

WHAT DO CATHOLICS BELIEVE ABOUT THE VIRGIN MARY? DOES THE DOCTRINE OF THE ASSUMPTION, DEFINED IN 1950, MEAN THAT MARY IS NOW IN AN ACTUAL PLACE?

Catholics believe that from the moment of her conception in *her* mother's womb, the mother of Jesus Christ was preserved free from original sin. This is what is known as the Immaculate Conception, often confused with the Virgin Birth—which, of course, refers to the birth of Christ. Mary remained a virgin throughout her life (Catholic Biblical scholars hold that the mention of Jesus's brethren in the scriptures is to be interpreted as referring to His cousins and kinfolk). Because of her stainless life and vast dignity as the Mother of the God-Man, Catholics believe, Mary is the greatest of the saints. Catholics pray *to* God *through* Mary because they believe she is a powerful intercessor and that, in keeping with what Christ said on Calvary, "Behold thy mother!", she is the mother of mankind.

The Assumption (the belief that Mary's body was preserved from corruption and taken to heaven and reunited to her soul) is not a new belief. Fifteen hundred years ago, the feast was celebrated. What took place during 1950 was this: Pope Pius XII solemnly declared that the ancient belief was now a formal doctrine, to which all Catholics must give assent. The Pope made this solemn declaration in answer to a widespread popular request by clergy and laity.

The word "heaven" is used to mean both a place and a state of being. Of the state, Catholics believe that it consists essentially in seeing God "face to face" (I Corinthians 13, 12). Of the place, we have no knowledge beyond the fact that it *exists*. "Eye hath not seen, ear hath not heard, nor hath it entered into the heart of man what God hath prepared for those who love Him" (I Corinthians 2, 9).

DO CATHOLICS BELIEVE THAT UNBAPTIZED BABIES CANNOT GO TO HEAVEN BECAUSE OF "ORIGINAL SIN"?

Though there are Catholic theologians who hold that such babies may achieve salvation through the desire of parents and *their* bond with the Church, the more general belief is that unbaptized babies are forever cut off from heaven.

This belief is not as harsh as it is sometimes understood to be. It is Catholic teaching that no one by nature has a "right" to heaven. Man, just because he is a man, does not have a claim on the *supernatural* happiness he enjoys in seeing God "face to face." That is a free gift of God.

The loss of supernatural life—generally called the fall from grace—was incurred by Adam at the time of his rebellion against God. Because Adam was head of the human race, all mankind was involved in the historic sin of disobedience by which the first man rejected the gifts God had given him that were above and beyond the needs of human nature.

Since the redemption by Christ ("the new Adam"), it has been possible for men to regain the life of grace. Baptism restores supernatural life. Without that life, man simply does not have the capacity to enjoy heaven. In the case of adults, the life of grace may be gained by an act of perfect contrition or pure love of God ("baptism of desire"). Infants are incapable of such an act of the will.

Unbaptized babies (in "limbo"—the poetic designation for an eternal state of purely natural happiness) do not suffer in any way, even from a sense of loss. Saint Thomas Aquinas taught that they, too, have a knowledge of God—but according to a "natural" capacity. Their happiness is greater than any known by man on earth, however limited it may be as compared with that of the saints in heaven.

HOW DO CATHOLICS LOOK ON THE DEVIL?

Catholics believe that Satan (the leader of the fallen angels) and his co-horts are pure spirits with an intelligence of a very high order and a will which is now obstinately bent on evil. The Devil and the other fallen angels can tempt and torment men, though all temptations are not directly attributable to them. Many religious thinkers have said that the Devil's greatest triumph lies in convincing the world that he doesn't exist.

Hell, to Catholics, means two things: a place and a state of punishment. The Devil is not confined to hell as a place, and will not be until the last day; but he exists "in hell"—as a state of eternal punishment.

WHY DO CATHOLICS WORSHIP "GRAVEN IMAGES"?

They don't. Like any religion, Catholicism uses symbols to heighten the meaning of spiritual truths. The Council of Trent summed up the Catholic position on images four hundred years ago: The images of Christ and the Virgin Mother of God, and of the other saints, are to be had and to be kept, especially in the churches, and due honor and veneration are to be given to them; *not that any divinity or virtue is believed to be in them, on account of which they are to be worshiped, or that anything is to be asked of them, or that trust is to be put in images,* as was done of old by the Gentiles, who placed their hopes in idols; but because *the honor which is shown them is referred to the prototypes which these images represent.* [My italics.]

WHY DO CATHOLICS SPRINKLE HOLY WATER ON BUILDINGS, FARM IMPLEMENTS, ETC.?

Water is an ancient symbol of spiritual purification. Holy water in the Church is an adaptation of an old Jewish custom. Catholics do not believe that the water has any power in itself. When it is sprinkled, with appropriate prayers, on buildings, farm implements and the like, the ceremony signifies that the Church is humbly calling upon God to drive away the forces of Satan and accept for His own glory the uses to which the thing blessed will be put. Man is a unity of body and spirit, and the Church has never hesitated to recognize this by using material objects to signify spiritual realities.

WHAT IS PURGATORY?

Like "heaven" or "hell," the word "purgatory" refers to a place and a state. Catholics believe that purgatory exists to *purge* those souls who are not yet pure enough for heaven and its vision of God, but who have not died in a state of serious (mortal) sin. Such near-saints must undergo the pain of intense longing for God until they have paid the debt of temporal punishment due them because of their sins on earth. In a word, purgatory exists to make saints who will be ready for the purity of God's presence. If one does not succeed in becoming a saint on earth but yet escapes eternal hell, he is purified in purgatory. After the Last Judgment, when all men have achieved their final state, purgatory will cease to be.

WHAT IS THE REAL MEANING OF THE MASS?

The Mass is the central act of worship in the Catholic Church. It is the true sacrifice of the Body and Blood of Christ, made present on the altar by the words of consecration (over the bread, "This is my body"; over the wine, "This is . . . my blood . . ."). "In this divine sacrifice," the Council of Trent declared, "the same Christ is present and immolated in a bloodless manner who once for all offered himself in a bloody manner on the altar of the cross; . . . only the manner of offering is different."

Mass must be celebrated by a priest or bishop, with whom the congregation joins in offering to God "a re-presentation and a renewal of the offering made on Calvary."

Catholics believe that after the priest pronounces the words of consecration in the Mass, the whole substance of the bread becomes the Body of Christ, the whole substance of the wine becomes the Blood of Christ. They believe that Christ is truly and substantially present in the Eucharist, body and soul, humanity and divinity.

Mass is said in various tongues—in the West, mainly in Latin. The priest performs an act of social worship; he does not preach or teach in Latin. Catholics use missals (which contain translations) and know, in most cases, what the standard Mass prayers mean.

DO CATHOLICS REGARD THE HUMAN BODY AND THE ACT OF LOVE AS SHAMEFUL?

The Church puts great stress on modesty—but precisely because it disapproves so strongly of any cheapening of sex, which it regards as a sacred trust. How could a Church that teaches the Son of God became flesh and blood regard the human body as shameful? Far from looking upon the act of love as unclean, the Church teaches that it is the means by which men share in the work of the Creator.

IS IT TRUE THAT CATHOLICS CONSIDER ALL NON-CATHOLIC CHILDREN ILLEGITIMATE?

No. It is Church law that the wedding of a Catholic must be performed in the presence of a priest and two witnesses. In the case of non-Catholics, the Church recognizes the sacredness and binding nature of all ceremonies which mark "the conjugal union of man and woman, contracted between two qualified persons, which obliges them to live together throughout life."

DOES THE CHURCH FORBID INTERMARRIAGE?

Yes. But while never approving of mixed marriages, the Church for a serious reason will lift the ban provided: (1) the non-Catholic party agrees in writing not to interfere with the religion of the Catholic; (2) both parties agree to have all children baptized and brought up as Catholics; and (3) there is moral certainty that the promises will be kept.

IS A CATHOLIC PERMITTED TO GET A DIVORCE?

Catholics believe that marriage, by its nature, must be a contract "till death do us part." The Church does not recognize any absolute divorce between a couple who are validly married, where one or the other would be free to marry again. For good reasons (infidelity, cruelty), the Church may approve separation from bed and board. In such cases, a Catholic may be permitted to get a civil divorce in order to satisfy some legal requirement. He may not, however, remarry during the lifetime of the other party. In cases where the Church has decreed nullity—where, according to Church law, there was no marriage in the first place—a civil annulment or divorce may sometimes be necessary.

IN A CASE WHERE DOCTORS AGREE THAT A MOTHER MAY DIE DURING CHILDBIRTH, MUST CATHOLIC DOCTORS SAVE THE CHILD RATHER THAN THE MOTHER?

No. The Catholic doctor is bound to make every effort to save both. Both mother and child have an inherent right to life. *Neither may be killed so the other can live*. This is the answer the Church has to give either to a grief-stricken young husband who needs the help of his wife in raising a family, or to a royal figure who feels a greater need for a son and heir than for his queen. Directly to take the life of an innocent is never permitted—even as a means to a good end.

The question, incidentally, is largely academic. Statistics show that maternity deaths in the nation's Catholic hospitals are as low as any.

WHY DON'T PRIESTS AND NUNS MARRY?

For hundreds of years, the Western Church has required that its clergy remain unmarried. This is a disciplinary matter which could (but undoubtedly won't) be changed overnight. The rule leaves priests wholly free from the responsibilities of family life for pastoral and missionary work. It is wholeheartedly accepted by the clergy and is popular with the Catholic laity.

Nuns and monks take a vow of chastity—not because they despise marriage and human love but in order to dedicate themselves wholly to the service of God in a religious order. Nuns (and those monks who have not received priestly orders) may marry with the Church's blessing any time they are dispensed from their vows by the proper authority. But as long as they choose to remain in the cloister, nuns and monks are obliged to observe the life of poverty, chastity and obedience to which they have freely dedicated themselves.

Such self-chosen celibacy is quite in keeping with the teaching of Saint Paul on the superiority (in the spiritual order) of virginity.

Incidentally, many Catholic priests *are* married. They are members of the Eastern rites, in union with Rome. Among these Catholics, it is customary to ordain married men, though second marriages are forbidden.

WHY DOES THE CATHOLIC CHURCH OPPOSE BIRTH CONTROL?

The Catholic position on birth control is based on the belief that: (1) artificial contraception is against the law of God; and (2) because it is immoral, it cannot be employed as a means, even to a good end.

Strictly speaking, it is artificial birth *prevention* (by means of contraceptive devices, chemicals, etc.) that the Church condemns as intrinsically evil. The proper end of the sex act is procreation. The physical expression of love in marriage is surely good but is subordinated to the ultimate reason for sexual relations. The pleasure connected with sex, like the satisfaction that goes with eating, is good, too, as long as it is taken for what it is—a means to an end.

Basing its objections on the natural law, the Church says that deliberately to frustrate the proper end of the sex act is contrary to reason, is conduct unbecoming to rational beings, and, for this reason, is immoral. Birth prevention is regarded by Catholics as being evil in itself—circumstances cannot change it into something morally good or indifferent.

"Natural" birth control—the so-called rhythm theory—is permitted (as Pope Pius XII stated) in cases where undue economic or medical hardship makes family limitation imperative. His Holiness, along with condemning artificial birth control, urged that the nations make greater efforts to support the present population of the world by opening under-populated areas to immigration, by increasing food production, by sharing technical advances with the have-not nations, and by developing more natural resources.

ARE CATHOLICS CONSCIENTIOUSLY OBLIGED TO SUPPORT ANTI-BIRTH CONTROL LAWS SUCH AS EXIST IN MASSACHUSETTS AND CONNECTICUT?

No. Though most Catholics in these states have zealously supported the laws over the years, some eminent Catholic spokesmen have denounced them as an invasion of privacy and as unwise, unnecessary legislation. For example, the outstanding Jesuit theologian, Father John Courtney Murray, wrote of the Connecticut law:

It was passed in 1879, in the Comstock era, under Protestant pressure. Its text reveals a characteristic Comstockian ignorance of the rules of traditional jurisprudence. . . . Since it makes a public crime out of a private sin, and confuses morality with legality, and is unenforceable without police invasion of the bedroom, the statute is indefensible as law. But the configuration of social power [in New England] has become such that Catholics now defend it—with a saving sense of irony, I hope.

Why have so *many* Catholics been firmly behind laws that some of their own best thinkers regard as untenable? I believe Father Murray is right in concluding that it is a matter of "social power." Catholic prestige is seen to go up or down in accordance with the fate of the laws, if only because they are founded on a moral position that, these days, Catholics are almost alone in upholding. But certainly Catholics have no obligation to "impose" birth control laws on others. (In this connection it is interesting to note that while seventeen states prohibit traffic in contraceptives, subject to various exceptions, the most "Catholic" state in the union, Rhode Island, has no laws at all affecting birth control.)

A brilliant student of jurisprudence, Norman St. John-Stevas, summed up one responsible Catholic opinion on this subject when he wrote:

> The proposition that an act is contrary to the natural law does not imply that the act should be forbidden by the law of the state. Whether legislation is desirable is a jurisprudential rather than a theological question, which must be decided in relation to the conditions prevailing in a given community. While Roman Catholics in a democracy have every right to work for legislation outlawing the sale and distribution of contraceptives . . . the Catholic community would be wise not to attempt to secure a total legislative ban on contraceptives, but should limit its efforts to securing a policy of state neutrality on the issue and the passing of measures to protect public morality that command the general support of the community.

In recent years, Father Murray's and Mr. St.John-Stevas's view of the problem has gained more and more general support in the American Catholic community, though there are still many, both within and outside the Church, who mistakenly believe that because the Church brands contraception immoral, Catholics are obliged in conscience to demand state prohibitions against it.

WHAT ACTUALLY HAPPENS IN CONFESSION? CAN A CATHOLIC GAIN ABSOLUTION FOR A SIN, REPEAT THE SAME SIN, AND RECEIVE ABSOLUTION REPEATEDLY?

Confessions are usually heard in the boxlike "confessionals" found in every Catholic Church. It is dark inside. Sometimes you can see the priest dimly, but often a white cloth is tacked to the grille separating priest and penitent. Before you enter the confessional, you prepare yourself by examining your conscience.

Inside, you kneel and whisper to the priest on the other side of the grille. You tell him how long it has been since your last confession. Then, as completely as you can, you name your sins, giving their number and such details as are necessary to supply a clear idea of what you did that was wrong.

When you finish, the priest usually says a few words of spiritual counsel and encouragement. Then he gives you your "penance." This is a certain number of prayers or prayerful acts that you must perform to signify your genuine sorrow and your resolution to do better. You say the Act of Contrition, a formal prayer which expresses love for God, sorrow for sin and "purpose of amendment." As you recite this prayer, you can hear the priest's words of absolution. The priest sends you out with a "God bless you" and usually asks you to pray for him, a sinner like yourself.

Like other people, Catholics find themselves repeating the same old sins. But no one sins *because* he goes to confession regularly. If one does not intend to make a sincere effort to break sinful habits, there is no point in going to confession. A "bad confession" (where sins are withheld or where genuine sorrow or the "purpose of amendment" are not present) is considered invalid and sacrilegious.

WHAT IS THE ATTITUDE OF THE CHURCH TOWARD DRINKING AND GAMBLING?

Neither is considered evil in itself, though both may become sinful by excess or abuse. The Church approves total abstinence in the same way that it puts its approval upon voluntary celibacy. Both sex and alcoholic drinks are the creation of God; they may be forsworn but must not be condemned as intrinsically evil.

Gambling is regarded as an innocent pastime unless one or all of the following conditions are present: (1) the subject matter of the bet is sinful; (2) one party is *forced* to play; (3) one party is certain of the outcome; (4) one party is left in ignorance of the real terms of the gamble; (5) cheating and fraud are present; (6) the money staked is needed to pay debts or for the support of oneself or family; or (7) the gambling game is forbidden by legitimate public authority.

WHY DO CATHOLICS HAVE THEIR OWN SCHOOLS?

Religious schools antedate the public school system in the United States (which did not get under way until, in 1805, the Free School Society was founded in New York "for the education of such poor children as do not belong to, or are not provided for by any religious society"). Until 1825, American religious schools received help from public funds. In that year, New York City's share of the state school fund went exclusively to the Free School Society, which was re-named the Public School Society.

Catholic schools had existed since colonial times—the earliest was founded by Maryland Jesuits at Saint Mary's City about 1640—but the first parish school was established by Mother Elizabeth Seton at Emmetsburg, Maryland, in 1810. Her system was endorsed by the American Bishops in 1843, when they ordered that all pastors were "to provide a Catholic school in every parish or congregation subject to them, where this can be done."

This step was taken mainly because the public schools of the time were in effect "Protestant" schools. Even Horace Mann, who fought against "sectarian" indoctrination, held that the public school system "found its morals on the basis of religion" and welcomed the Bible into the schools "enshielded from harm, by the great Protestant doctrine of the inviolability of conscience, the right and sanctity of private judgment, without note or interpreter." Catholic pupils were required to join in reading the Protestant Bible, reciting Protestant prayers, and singing Protestant hymns, in accordance with custom. Moreover, the textbooks used, according to the bishops, were biased against Catholicism. "The schoolboy can scarcely find a book," they protested, "in which one or more of our institutions or practices is not exhibited for otherwise than it really is, and greatly to our disadvantage." The Catholic hierarchy of the time were convinced that the Presbyterian clergyman who wrote in the *Freeman's Journal* (July 11, 1840) that "the Bible and the Common Schools [were] two stones that [would] grind Catholicity out of Catholics" knew whereof he spoke.

Later, after the parochial school system was well established, religion and religious practices were gradually removed from public school classrooms. Most Catholics, concerned about the religious education of their children and with a heavy investment in their own schools, found this even less satisfactory. Hence, at great sacrifice, over the years the American Catholic community has built, staffed and supported an ever-growing parochial school system, while continuing to meet in full its obligations to the public schools.

These sacrifices have been made because Catholics believe that no ignorance is as tragic as religious ignorance and that imparting a religious attitude related to life and learning is a seven-day-a-week, not merely a Sunday-morning, task.

AREN'T CATHOLICS NOW SEEKING SUPPORT FROM PUBLIC FUNDS FOR THESE SCHOOLS, ESPECIALLY IF FEDERAL AID IS FORTHCOMING?

Most are. But 28 per cent of the Catholics polled by the Gallup organization in March, 1961, thought that federal aid should go to public schools only. Of the Protestants polled, 63 per cent took this position. Most of these opponents would probably agree with President Kennedy that federal aid to parochial education is unconstitutional.

The controversy is complex. There are several distinct issues to consider: (1) the constitutional issue; (2) the claim that to cut off federal aid from parochial schools represents an injustice; and (3) the importance of raising the standards of parochial schools as part of the general need to improve American primary and secondary education.

On the constitutional issue: One side holds that the juridical issue is clear-cut and was settled once and for all by the First Amendment; the other argues that since the idea of federal aid to education is new, its constitutional implications are yet to be resolved. There are Catholics and non-Catholics on both sides. Both parties can cite eminent jurists in their favor.

On the question of justice: Many Catholic spokesmen, but not all, have argued that if federal aid to education is withheld from parochial schools (even though pupils in these schools are counted in determining how much aid a given state may get), a striking inequality between public and parochial education will result. Their argument boils down to this: those who support both systems have only so much money to contribute to education. If some of the funds which Catholic parents are now giving to their parochial schools must go for the additional taxes which will be necessary for federal aid, they will be called upon to "starve" the school they choose for their children in order to fulfill their obligation to public education. They may even be forced to "starve" the parochial school out of existence, some have said—though this strikes me as a polemical exaggeration. In any case, every dollar added to his taxes is one less dollar the Catholic taxpayer will have to spend on parochial schools and the education of his children in these schools.

On the standards of American education: Those who support federal aid hold that such aid is necessary in order to raise the general level of education, for at least 9 per cent of the nation's children are in parochial elementary and secondary schools. In some cities the percentage runs considerably higher: New York, 26 per cent; Chicago, 34 per cent; Philadelphia, 39 per cent; Detroit, 23 per cent; Cincinnati, 28 per cent; Boston, 30 per cent; Milwaukee and New Orleans, 33 per cent; Buffalo, 40 per cent; Pittsburgh, 42 per cent. This pattern is frequently repeated in the newer suburbs. *Can* the general level of American education be raised if such significant numbers of schools, educating millions of young Americans, fall well below national standards? If, for example, federal aid in a given community means that the public school can afford to hire more teachers, can out-bid the parochial school in getting them, can buy more equipment, employ better teaching aids and in general move ahead, the neighboring parochial school will slip even further behind the standard thereby established for education in that community. If, like other denominational systems, the Catholic schools educated only a small percentage of Catholic pupils, the total resources of the Church might be enough to match the additional revenue which public education would get from federal aid. (In the past, Catholics have tried to match the support given from community taxes to public schools.) But, with approximately half of Catholic children in Catholic parochial schools, the odds are against that solution.

It should be emphasized that the American Catholic community did not press for a share in public funds for parochial schools until federal aid to education became a possibility. Then it became clear that federal aid to public schools *alone* might sound the death-knell for the present parochial school system: through the sheer impossibility of supporting their schools at a higher level to meet the "competition" of public education, Catholic parents might have to give up the goal of a religious education for their children. Those who have no taste for parochial schools, including some Catholics, may think this is a good idea. But most Catholics do not agree. The democratic principle that parents have a natural right to determine the education of their children has been affirmed by various Supreme Court dicta; if Catholics are indirectly forced to abandon that principle through action taken by the federal government, the constitutional implications may be serious. The conscientious jurist may face as many problems as the proponents of no-share-in-federal-aid present in making the case against the aid-to-all schools policy which is proposed by many Catholic bishops and laymen.

WHY DOES THE CHURCH FORBID CATHOLICS TO READ OR SEE CERTAIN BOOKS, PLAYS AND MOVIES?

What a Catholic believes by faith, he believes absolutely. He is ready to take the Church's word on what constitutes a danger to this faith.

Catholics regard their Church as a moral teacher. When books, plays, movies, etc., are forbidden, it is because it is the Church's judgment that, for the ordinary person, such books, plays, etc., may provide either a temptation to sin, a false religious understanding or a challenge to faith which he is not equipped to handle. Many of the works on the index of forbidden books are theological studies written in good faith by devout Catholics; the Church has proscribed them because they contain some theological error.

In the case of clearly obscene books, there is the added obligation not to encourage immorality. Where pornography is not the issue, a Catholic may ask for permission (from a representative of the local bishop) to read a forbidden book or see a proscribed play. If it is felt he is sufficiently well instructed to meet the challenge to his faith, and there is good reason for his request, the permission is readily granted.

DO CATHOLICS BELIEVE IN RELIGIOUS TOLERANCE?

American Catholics believe in and practice religious tolerance, as their Protestant and Jewish neighbors amply testify. There are bigots in the Church, as in every group, but this is a psychological failing of individuals, not something that derives from Catholic belief.

In certain Catholic countries (as in a few Protestant countries), religious tolerance is not wholeheartedly accepted as a political idea. On the other hand, the Catholic can point to a country like Eire, where not long ago a Protestant was elected President. The general American Catholic attitude toward the equality of all faiths before the law is reflected in the views of John F. Kennedy, who once said he preferred to be known as the first President who is a Catholic, rather than the first Catholic President.

Often "religious tolerance" may mean "religious indifferentism"—the idea that "one religion is as good (or as bad) as another." This is a proposition which Catholics cannot accept. It should not be imposed on American citizens as a test of patriotism, especially in the name of tolerance!

If by tolerance is meant living in peace with one's neighbor, making no attempts to interfere with his religious practices, recognizing his civil right to pick his own church (or no church), then the record of American Catholics is second to none.

On this score, Catholics have probably been more sinned against than sinning—if we recall the Know-Nothing Movement, the Ku Klux Klan, the vicious campaign against Al Smith when he was the Democratic candidate for President.

THE CATHOLIC CHURCH IS AN AUTHORITARIAN INSTITUTION. DOES THIS CONTRADICT DEMOCRATIC PRINCIPLE?

The Church *is* authoritarian. So are the family, the school, the army, and various other institutions that thrive in democracies. But the central point is that the Church is a religious, not a political, society.

Democracy is a system of government in which each man is free to serve God—that is, to acknowledge the authority of God—according to his own conscience. The Catholic is convinced that his Church is a divinely-founded institution with the right to speak with God-given authority on matters of faith and morals. How, then, can he "contradict democratic principle" by following the religious dictates of his conscience? Wouldn't it, rather, "contradict democratic principle" to demand that Americans act, not in accordance with their own consciences, but in accordance with some standard of religious orthodoxy derived from a political, not a theological, principle?

What Is a Christian Scientist?

GEORGE CHANNING

George Channing (1888-1957) was known internation-
ally as a Christian Science lecturer, teacher and practitioner. He served as First Reader in the Mother
Church, Boston, and was a trustee of the Christian
Science Publishing Society which publishes the
Christian Science Monitor and the religious periodicals
of Christian Science. He had been editor of the *Christian Science Journal,* the *Christian Science Sentinel*
and the *Herald of Christian Science.* From 1950 to 1953,
he was manager of the Committees on Publication.

Mr. Channing was born in Providence, Rhode Island.
He was a graduate of Brown University and studied
law at Yale and Boston Universities. He had a broad
career in journalism, beginning on the Providence
Journal, and working for the Detroit *Free Press* and
Journal, and as city editor of the Seattle *Star.*

During World War I, Mr. Channing served in France
as a first lieutenant. In 1953 he received the "Brown
Bear Award" from Brown University for distinguished
activities as an alumnus.

NOTE TO THE READER: The views expressed by Mr. Channing in this article were officially approved by the Mother Church, The First Church of Christ, Scientist, Boston, Massachusetts.

WHAT IS A CHRISTIAN SCIENTIST?

A Christian Scientist is one who accepts and practices Christian Science as his religion. Christian Science has been defined by its discoverer and founder, Mary Baker Eddy: "As the law of God, the law of good, interpreting and demonstrating the divine Principle and rule of universal harmony."

WHY DO YOU CONSIDER IT CHRISTIAN?

Because it is based wholly on the teachings of Christ Jesus which make clear the spiritual meaning of the Holy Scriptures. It requires its adherents to be active in obeying all the commandments of Jesus, including healing the sick.

WHY DO YOU CONSIDER IT SCIENTIFIC?

Because it is exact in premise and conclusion and is completely demonstrable.

WHAT IS THE BASIC PREMISE OF CHRISTIAN SCIENCE?

That God is divine Mind, the conceiver of man and the universe, and Mind is all that exists. Mind expresses itself and its expression is man.

Spirit is eternal and real; matter is an unreal illusion subject to decay and dissolution.

Evil has to do with matter—therefore evil is unreal, an illusion.

Spirit and its expression, man, are indestructible. Death is an illusion of mortal sense, which may continue to appear until destroyed by spiritual sense, either on this or the other side of the grave. The individual continues to live even though unseen by persons on our plane of existence.

WHAT IS THE RELATION OF MAN TO GOD?

Man and the universe are made in the image and likeness of the divine Mind, God, which conceives them. Mind is synonymous with Spirit, Soul, Life, Truth, Love, Principle (which means cause or origin).

Man, the idea and image of God, is immortal, perfect, wholly good, untouched and untainted by evil because man expresses God.

WHAT IS HEALTH TO THE CHRISTIAN SCIENTIST?

Health is a spiritual reality; therefore health is eternal. Disease and illness are aspects of falsehood—delusions of the human mind which can be destroyed by the prayer of spiritual understanding. The divinely mental can and does replace the materially mental.

WHO WAS MARY BAKER EDDY?

Mary Baker Eddy (1821–1910) was the discoverer and founder of Christian Science. She is regarded by Christian Scientists as the revelator of truth to this age. She brought the Comforter that Jesus foretold. This Comforter is the Science of Christianity and is available, through Mrs. Eddy's achievement, to all who desire to utilize God's power and God's law as Jesus did.

Each person, of any religion, can find what is satisfying to him as the spiritual meaning in the Bible. But Christian Scientists feel that Mrs. Eddy's book, *Science and Health with Key to the Scriptures,* offers the *complete* spiritual meaning of the Bible. They believe that this full meaning would not have been available to them without Mrs. Eddy's discovery.

DO CHRISTIAN SCIENTISTS CONSIDER THEMSELVES PROTESTANTS?

Yes. Christian Science is a truly Protestant religion, although it embodies several distinguishing characteristics:

Christian Science holds that good is infinite, that sin, death, and disease are unreal, and that evil is a delusion.

Christian Science maintains that healing is a *religious* function.

Christian Science has no ordained clergy or personal pastors. Though Christian Scientists know the pure consecration of Christian martyrs, martyrdom has no place in Christian Science. The Christian Scientist does not die for his religion; he lives in it.

There is no personal preacher in a Christian Science service. The Bible in the King James version and *Science and Health with Key to the Scriptures*, by Mrs. Eddy, are the only "pastors" of the denomination. Texts are read aloud from these books by a first and second reader.

Prayer, to the Christian Scientist, is scientific and achieves healing; Christians who understand such prayer are equipped to fulfill the promise of the Master Christian: "In my name shall they cast out devils; they shall speak with new tongues; they shall take up serpents; and if they drink any deadly thing it shall not hurt them; *they shall lay hands on the sick, and they shall recover*" (Mark 16:17–18).

Christian Scientists do not practice baptism in the material form; to Christian Scientists, baptism means purification from all material sense.

Salvation, to Christian Scientists, consists of being saved from the illusions and delusions of mortal sense—which means the sense of being capable of becoming sick and dying.

Protestantism, it should be remembered, began as a protest against certain organizations or forms of worship. Christian Science also protests—against mortal sense.

WHAT DO CHRISTIAN SCIENTISTS BELIEVE ABOUT JESUS?

Christian Science accepts the divinity of Christ, but does not deify Jesus—which means that to Christian Scientists, Christ Jesus was not God, but was the Son of God. The true mission of Christ Jesus was to redeem mankind from the beliefs of mortality by showing that man in his real nature is spiritual. Man is not God, but bears witness to God's presence.

The healings of Christ Jesus are regarded by Christian Scientists not as miracles, but as the result of the application of natural spiritual law.

Christian Science completely accepts the Virgin Birth.

By the Trinity, Christian Scientists mean the unity of Father, Son and Holy Spirit—but do not accept the Trinity as three persons in one. Life, Truth and Love are "the triune Principle called God" (*Science and Health*).

WHAT ROLE DOES PRAYER PLAY IN CHRISTIAN SCIENCE?

An all-important role. To the Christian Scientist, living is basically praying. "Men ought always to pray" (Luke 18:1). The understanding of God is reached through praying. The true Christian Scientist applies his thought in an effort to attain perfect praying. Real devotion and experience are needed to pray the perfect prayer.

A Christian Scientist may not always pray perfectly. The efficacy of his prayer reflects the degree of his own spiritual understanding. If he has attained high spiritual understanding, and if he applies his understanding honestly and with devotion, results may follow which seem miraculous to others.

Healing is accomplished by spiritual understanding. Christian Science distinguishes faith from understanding: Faith means acceptance before proof. Through faith, degrees of evidence appear which serve to *lift* faith into spiritual understanding.

WHAT IS A CHRISTIAN SCIENCE PRACTITIONER?

A practitioner is one who prays for those who ask his prayers in their behalf.

To be registered as a public practitioner, one must be approved by the Mother Church, the First Church of Christ, Scientist in Boston, Massachusetts. To be a practitioner requires systematic instruction, either self-acquired or under authorized teachers, and satisfactory evidence of successful healing work. Candidates must demonstrate a capacity to apply spiritual understanding to the destruction of human ills and discords.

CAN A PRACTITIONER TREAT A PATIENT HUNDREDS OF MILES AWAY?

Yes. False beliefs are destroyed by spiritual truth, through prayer, regardless of the geographical location of the person who entertains such false beliefs. Jesus healed the Centurion's servant (Matthew 8:5—13) and the daughter of the Greek woman (Mark 7:25—30) while not physically present with them.

DO CHRISTIAN SCIENTISTS DENY THAT SOME DISEASES ARE CAUSED BY GERMS, MICROBES AND VIRUSES?

The Christian Scientist knows that life is divine in origin and that health is a *spiritual* reality. Theories about germs and microbes come from beliefs which hold that life is material and that disease is real. The

Christian Scientist knows by experience that his belief is demonstrable despite theories of disease involving germs, microbes and viruses.

HOW CAN CHRISTIAN SCIENCE MAINTAIN ITS ATTITUDE TO DISEASE IN VIEW OF MODERN MEDICAL KNOWLEDGE?

The Christian Scientist's attitude to disease is supported by reason and by actual demonstration. Christ Jesus demonstrated, as did his followers, what healing and health really mean. Christian Scientists maintain their faith by spiritual intuition and by the proofs they are able to accumulate in their own experience.

Let us remember that the conclusions of material medicine are constantly changing. Recently, the "wonder drugs" (penicillin, aureomycin) were acclaimed almost as panaceas; yet later, their efficacy had to be qualified. Strict warnings had to be issued against too much trust in them. There are countless instances of this kind.

Christian Scientists hold that sickness, sin and death are aspects of falsehood; and falsehood can be destroyed by exposing it to spiritual truth. Christian Scientists feel they have incontestable evidence that in this way their religion destroys, effectively and permanently, the hatreds, doubts, lusts and other discords of the human mind and body.

The objective of Christian Science is not *primarily* to heal physical disease—but to regenerate human thought through spiritual understanding. Healing is the effect of attaining this regeneration in some degree. The achievements of medical research do not present any problem to the Christian Scientist, for the results of such research in no way affect the substance and permanency of spiritual truth.

DO CHRISTIAN SCIENTISTS GO TO HOSPITALS?

The teaching and faith of Christian Science basically reject medical treatment. To the extent that a man or woman relies on material methods of healing, he or she is not relying fully on Christian Science.

DO CHRISTIAN SCIENTISTS REFUSE MEDICAL ATTENTION WHEN THEIR OWN CHILDREN ARE SICK?

Christian Scientists love their children as deeply as other parents. When their children are ill, they want them to have the most effective and reliable help. They employ the method of Christian Science—prayer, or spiritual understanding—fearlessly and with complete confidence, because they have reason to know that Christian Science is efficacious. (No one is forced to rely on Christian Science against what he may regard as his own good judgment.)

Christian Scientists in many schools and colleges ask for and receive exemption from regulations requiring medical means—*yet their health is as good as that of the rest of the student body, and is often better*. The Christian Scientist knows that he takes good care of his children in one particular way: he prays earnestly for himself and his children every day. He prays not only for their health, but for their spiritual progress.

DO CHRISTIAN SCIENTISTS CALL IN A DOCTOR AT CHILDBIRTH?

Yes. The Christian Scientist makes sure that someone who possesses the necessary skills is present at childbirth. The Christian Scientist does not presume to do what he is neither trained nor licensed to do.

HAVE NOT CHRISTIAN SCIENTISTS DIED BECAUSE THEY REFUSED MEDICAL ATTENTION, OR RELIED ENTIRELY ON FAITH AND PRAYER, OR CALLED IN A DOCTOR TOO LATE?

One might as readily ask, without intending to give offense, "Have not many persons died because they refused the spiritual method of Christian Science, and relied entirely on material aid?"

No statistics prove that the healing methods of material medicine are superior to those of Christian Science. We do know that thousands of men and women who were pronounced "incurable," and who spent years in invalidism and suffering, turned to Christian Science and were healed. Such persons are numerous among the members of the Christian Science Church.

Efforts to understand and apply any rule may appear more successful in some instances than in others. The failure to bring certain facts to light does not alter the verity of the facts themselves. The laws of mathematics, for instance, may fail to reveal a correct answer when improperly applied; indeed, many sciences fail to reveal certain answers even when properly applied.

One does not judge the medical profession by the cases it loses, nor by the overcrowded hospitals and graveyards. May not Christian Science ask that it be judged by its potentialities for good and its achievement in canceling the sense of disease, in erasing sin (and the penalties for sin) from the experience of innumerable persons?

DO CHRISTIAN SCIENTISTS REFUSE MEDICAL ATTENTION IN THE CASE OF FRACTURES OR ACCIDENTS?

There are innumerable instances of bone fractures which have been set and healed perfectly under Christian Science treatment—without medical or surgical aid. Results depend upon honest effort, correct understanding and constancy in Christian Science practice.

A Christian Scientist does not surrender his status as a free man or woman under God. He works out his own salvation by following the course which wisdom dictates to him. If the Christian Scientist has not reached the degree of spiritual understanding which is needed for healing by spiritual means and resorts to some other means, he obviously cannot be said to be employing fully the method of Christian Science. He does not undergo condemnation for this; nor does he assume any burden of guilt. He is always free to improve his spiritual understanding and employ it exclusively, thus restoring his status as a Christian Scientist.

IF GOD IS INFINITE AND GOOD, HOW DOES EVIL EXIST?

Evil is hypnotic. It has no more reality than a dream—yet to the dreamer it *appears* real. The nothingness of evil—and of that which sees, feels, or believes in evil—is proved through spiritual awakening.

DOES CHRISTIAN SCIENCE BELIEVE IN SIN?

Man is really sinless and free. Sin is the belief in the real existence of a mind or minds other than the divine Mind, God. Mortal mind, which believes in decaying and dying, is the sinner. Saint Paul called it the "carnal" mind. If a person accepts the carnal mind, *its* sins will appear to be his sins, and its suffering his suffering.

Christian Scientists rid themselves of sin by breaking the false notion that the carnal mind is real, or one's own. Penalty for sin lasts only as long as such false belief lasts. The Christian Scientist tries to live so that the divine Mind is revealed as his mind.

Christian Scientists hold that sin is unreal. But this does not mean that one can sin with impunity. The sinner does not know that sin is unreal; if he did, this would destroy his capacity for sinning.

DO CHRISTIAN SCIENTISTS BELIEVE IN HEAVEN OR HELL?

Yes—but not in a geographical sense. As Mrs. Eddy said: "The sinner makes his own hell by doing evil, and the saint his own heaven by doing right."

WHY DON'T CHRISTIAN SCIENTISTS USE THE WORD "DEATH" OR THE WORD "DIED"?

They do use both words. The words appear in Christian Science periodicals where the context requires them. But the term "passed on" is considered more exact by Christian Scientists, who accept literally the fact that individual life is indestructible. We believe that what is called "death" is not termination, but only an incident in the dream of mortality, an experience of mortal mind, not the divine Mind.

DOES CHRISTIAN SCIENCE MAINTAIN THAT DEATH ITSELF CAN BE ELIMINATED?

Yes. The Christian Scientist believes that material decay and destruction can be stopped by the full realization of divine truth. Through progressive improvement of one's spiritual understanding which alleviates the circumstances of death, the ultimate elimination of death itself can be achieved. In this way, true immortality can be realized.

DO CHRISTIAN SCIENTISTS HOLD FUNERAL SERVICES?

It is perfectly proper for the family to engage a Christian Scientist to read passages from the Bible and from the Christian Science textbook. These passages are intended to remind the hearers that Life, God and man (who is the individual expression of Life) are eternal. It is also proper to have no reading at all.

WHAT IS THE ATTITUDE OF CHRISTIAN SCIENCE TOWARD BIRTH CONTROL?

There is a whole chapter on marriage in Mrs. Eddy's book, in which this statement occurs (*Science and Health,* p. 56:7–8): "Marriage is the legal and moral provision for generation among human kind." Mrs. Eddy explains that marriage will continue subject to moral regulations needed to secure increasing virtue until mankind attains the spiritual understanding which discerns the perfect spiritual creation, untainted by matter. In accordance with this teaching, married couples are free to follow their own judgment as to having children and as to the number they will have.

DO CHRISTIAN SCIENTISTS OPPOSE VACCINATION?

Christian Scientists do not oppose vaccination for those who want it and believe in it. They do oppose compulsory vaccination for Christian Scientists—as a trespass upon their religious convictions.

Mrs. Eddy specifically instructed Christian Scientists to obey the law, but to seek legal exemption from those laws which violate their religious rights or the rights of conscience. To exempt Christian Scientists from vaccination does no harm to others—especially if vaccination is as effective as it is claimed to be for those who believe in it.

Incidentally, Christian Scientists and their children obey all quarantine regulations because they don't want their neighbors to become fearful of their safety because Christian Scientists refrain from material methods.

WHY DO CHRISTIAN SCIENCE STUDENTS REQUEST EXEMPTIONS FROM CERTAIN EXAMINATIONS—IN BACTERIOLOGY, FOR INSTANCE?

The only instruction to which Christian Scientists object is that which tends to set up the method of material medicine as the *only* healing method or system. Christian Scientists object to picturing the processes of disease in ways which visualize the terror which begets disease. They also object to compulsory medical regulations because, in effect, such regulations constitute indoctrination which may undermine the religious teaching of the home.

WOULD CHRISTIAN SCIENTISTS ABOLISH SANITATION AND PUBLIC HEALTH MEASURES?

No. Christian Scientists advocate sanitation because they love cleanliness—inner and outer. They respect the right of the community to take such measures as the community considers essential—so long as these measures do not impose compulsory medication on those who practice their own spiritual method of healing.

Incidentally, Christian Scientists feel that reliance on spiritual means alone, to safeguard public health, is wise *only in proportion to the spiritual understanding of health among the people in the area involved.*

WHAT IS THE ATTITUDE OF CHRISTIAN SCIENCE TOWARD PSYCHIATRY AND PSYCHOANALYSIS?

There is no similarity between medical psychiatry and Christian Science. Christian Science is religion. It treats all ills by prayer. As Mrs. Eddy said: "To heal . . . is to base your practice on immortal Mind, the divine Principle of man's being; and this requires a preparation of the heart and an answer of the lips from the Lord."

Psychiatrists and psychoanalysts investigate the *human* mind; Christian Science is based on the understanding of the divine Mind. Our faith is devoted to the destruction of the false notions of the human mind by exposing them to the spiritual idea of truth. The divine Mind is the only permanent and real remedy for any ill.

WHAT IS THE ATTITUDE OF CHRISTIAN SCIENCE TOWARD OTHER RELIGIONS?

The Christian Scientist does not feel superior to the adherents of any denomination. Every man is free to demonstrate the efficacy of his own faith; each is entitled to encouragement in his pursuit of spiritual objectives. Mrs. Eddy said: "A genuine Christian Scientist loves Protestant and Catholic, D.D. and M.D.—loves all who love God, good; and he loves his enemies."

What Is a Congregationalist?

DOUGLAS HORTON

Douglas Horton is retired Dean of the Divinity School, Harvard University. For seventeen years he was minister of the General Council of Congregational Christian Churches. He is the chairman of the Faith and Order Commission of the World Council of Churches. He has been a trustee of several theological seminaries; and is trustee emeritus of Princeton University. For fifteen years he served as chairman of the board of the American University in Cairo, Egypt.

Mr. Horton was born in Brooklyn, New York, in 1891. He finished his undergraduate studies at Princeton University and went on to graduate work in Edinburgh, Scotland, Oxford, England, and Tübingen, Germany. He has taught at the Newton Theological Institution, the Union Theological Seminary in New York, and the Chicago Theological Seminary. During World War I, he served as chaplain in the United States Navy, He has received eleven honorary degrees.

Mr. Horton was ordained to the ministry of the Congregational Churches in 1915, and has served as minister in Middletown, Connecticut, Brookline, Massachusetts, and Chicago, Illinois. The books he has written include: *Out into Life, A Legend of the Grail, Taking a City, The Art of Living Today, Congregationalism: a Study in Church Polity, The Meaning of Worship,* and *The United Church of Christ;* and he translated from the German the works of the distinguished theologian, Karl Barth, *The Word of God and the Word of Man,* and from the Latin, John Norton's *The Answer* (1649).

NOTE TO THE READER: Since this article was written, the Congregational Christian Churches of America (1,385,000 members) and the Evangelical and Reformed Church (790,000 members) have united to form a new body known as the United Church of Christ. This union was effected on June 25, 1957.

WHAT IS A CONGREGATIONALIST?

He is a member of a Congregational Christian Church, which in turn is a member of the fellowship of Congregational Churches which encircles the earth.

WHAT IS THE CONGREGATIONAL CHRISTIAN CREED?

If a creed be defined as an attempt to define one's faith in the living God, Congregationalists have been among the greatest creed-makers of history—for each particular congregation is accustomed to write its own creed. A few churches use the Apostles' Creed. Other churches have given up the use of this creed, chiefly because one or two of its phrases are believed to be untrue. Congregationalists remain Puritans, with a passionate regard for truth. They do not adopt a creed unless persuaded that it is all true. The Catholic faith which they hold is fundamentally a belief not in any creed but in the living person of Jesus Christ.

IS A CONGREGATIONALIST A CATHOLIC?

Yes, though not in the sense that he recognizes the sovereignty of the Pope. He is a Catholic in the sense that he holds what he regards as the Catholic faith, that universal faith which is common to all Christians and which binds together the "Holy Catholic Church." He holds the Roman to be *one* of the true branches of the Church.

DOES HE BELIEVE IN THE APOSTOLIC SUCCESSION?

Yes. He does not believe that this succession is chiefly visible in the line of popes, nor in the Anglican or other episcopal lines, nor in the lines of elders or other office-bearers of the Church. Rather, he sees the entire Church of Christ as the succession from the apostles. He believes that the humblest church member, as well as the most distinguished of prelates, can carry the riches of the Church's belief to succeeding generations.

WHAT SACRAMENTS DO CONGREGATIONAL CHRISTIANS OBSERVE?

Two: Baptism and the Lord's Supper. Baptism is the rite by which the Church takes a child (or adult) to itself. The mode is usually that of "sprinkling," though other forms may be used if desired. The holy communion is the ritual meal at which Christ is the host and through which the Church's faith is confirmed and increased. In some Congregational Christian churches the people receive the communion at the altar rail; in most, the elements of communion are brought by the deacons to the people in the pews.

DO CONGREGATIONAL CHRISTIANS BELIEVE IN THE VIRGIN BIRTH?

Probably the majority do not. Undoubtedly many do. It is regarded as a subject for historical research. The fact of Christ, and not the manner in which he was born, is held to be of dominant importance. It is, indeed, the reference to the Virgin Birth in the Apostles' Creed which unfits the latter for use in many churches.

DO CONGREGATIONAL CHRISTIANS BELIEVE IN THE HOLY TRINITY?

Fully. They believe in God the Father, Creator and Sustainer of the universe, infinite in wisdom, goodness, and love. They believe that God was in Christ reconciling the world to Himself. They believe in the Holy Spirit to such an extent that they are extremely sensitive to the dangers which lie in unchangeable laws and ceremonies which prevent new responses to the Spirit's call.

WHAT IS THE CONGREGATIONAL CHRISTIAN VIEW OF SIN AND SALVATION?

The view of most Christians. Sin is opposition or indifference to the will of God. God, however, as Jesus revealed Him, is willing to forgive. When, therefore, a person repents in faith, God accepts him—and when God has accepted a person, he need have no fear of any future in this world or the next. He is "saved."

DO CONGREGATIONAL CHRISTIANS BELIEVE IN HEAVEN AND HELL?

Certainly not as *places* of torment and of bliss. They do believe that physical death is not the end of life, that the justice of God cannot finally be escaped, and that it will be heaven to be with God and hell to be without Him.

WHAT IS THE CONGREGATIONAL ATTITUDE TOWARD THE BIBLE?

The Bible is regarded as revealing God in a way which will never be superseded. Once one knows that God is love, as Christ shows Him to be, all subsequent knowledge is simply an elaboration of this fundamental truth—and it is this knowledge that God imparts to men through the pages of Scripture.

Congregationalists apply methods of science wholeheartedly to the study of the Bible. As a result they feel they know what God is saying in the Bible better than their fathers who lived in a pre-scientific age.

DO CONGREGATIONALISTS FAVOR BIRTH CONTROL?

On this matter they have made no official statement. They believe that marriage is a holy estate, whether or not it results in the birth of children. In general, however, they do believe that the use by man of the brains which God has given him to invent means of preventing conception is not contrary to God's will.

WHAT IS THE CONGREGATIONAL ATTITUDE TOWARD DIVORCE?

Though the Congregational Christian Churches have never made a joint official pronouncement on divorce, it is safe to say that they regard the current divorce habits of the American people as a scandal. They are endeavoring to meet this disorder by giving youth better training in the Christian understanding of marriage. They do not oppose legal divorce after a couple have entered into the tragedy of spiritual divorce.

HOW AND WHY DID THE CONGREGATIONAL MOVEMENT START?

The Congregationalists were one of several groups within the Church of England during the controversial days of the early seventeenth century. They desired that the bishops should have less, and the people more, power over the churches. New England offered them an opportunity to stay nominally within the English Church (for they did not wish to separate) and yet be free from what they regarded as the persecution of the bishops. The tie with the Church of England was broken when, with the coming of Charles II, strict conformity to the Book of Common Prayer was demanded.

WHAT TYPE OF WORSHIP IS USED IN THE CONGREGATIONAL CHRISTIAN CHURCHES?

It usually is a moderately formal order of prayers (silent and spoken), hymns, Scripture reading, and preaching designed to express adoration of God, confession of sin, thanksgiving and commitment to God's will.

WHAT DISTINGUISHES THE CONGREGATIONALIST FROM OTHER PROTESTANTS?

His emphasis upon the place of the *congregation* in the life of the Church. It is in congregations that the Church is visible in its succession from age to age. It is in the congregation that the sacrament is celebrated and the preaching of the Word is heard. The congregation is the point at which God is most likely to reveal his will to a worshiping people. In a congregation all hearts are brought close to each other in brotherhood by being brought close to Christ.

WHAT IS THE PLACE OF WOMEN IN CONGREGATIONALISM?

Here the Congregational view differs from many others. So far as ecclesiastical status is concerned, no distinction is made between men and women. In a situation in which an ordained woman can give better service than an ordained man, the Congregational Churches give ordination to a woman of the proper spiritual qualifications. Only about four per cent of the Congregational Christian ministers are women and of these less than one-third are pastors of churches.

HOW ARE CONGREGATIONAL CHRISTIAN CHURCHES GOVERNED?

Ideally, by the mind of Christ through the people who constitute the congregation. When any problem arises, the people seek—through prayer, study and mutual consultation—to understand His mind concerning it. Though their spiritual shortcomings and ignorance too often stand in their way, these obstacles do not excuse them from seeking the will of Christ and following it.

As in most American denominations, there are county and state associations of churches and a national association—the General Council; but these have no power over the internal life of any of the congregations. This is the reason the Congregational Churches are sometimes known as Free Churches. The freedom of the congregation is inviolable, because the congregation is better able to consult the mind of Christ about itself than is any outside group. No minister beloved by his people can be removed by external pressure. No church can be disbanded except by the wish of its people. The relation between Christ and "two or three gathered together" in His name is sacred.

WHAT DISCIPLINE IS USED BY THE CONGREGATIONAL CHRISTIAN CHURCHES?

The chief discipline is brotherly persuasion. Theoretically, public censure is possible and, in extreme cases, the withdrawal of fellowship from an offender. The latter procedure has been invoked only when the well-being of the Church itself seemed at stake. Since the Church's interest is in redemption, a Congregational Christian Church recoils from any discipline which tends to separate an offender from its ministries.

WHAT ATTITUDE DOES THE CONGREGATIONALIST TAKE TOWARD THE JEW?

That of a brother. Congregational ministers and Jewish rabbis in many cities exchange pulpits regularly, and there are happy friendships between them. Both have a strongly ethical emphasis in their religious teaching; both stand for the establishment of justice and human brotherhood. The Congregationalist considers that fraternity with non-Christians expresses his Christian belief.

WHAT IS THE CONGREGATIONAL ATTITUDE TO THE CONDITION OF SOCIETY?

Like other Christian groups, they are committed to helping humanity. They were leaders in the abolition of slavery. They set up and supported hundreds of schools for Negroes south of the Mason-Dixon line, when they were most needed. The Congregational is the oldest foreign missionary society founded in North America—of the sort that have been called "the greatest international peace agencies on earth."

The Council for Social Action of the Congregational Christian Churches educates the people of the churches to the social needs of the day.

Congregationalists as children of the Reformation believe that the Church stands under the constant judgment of God and must be willing to reform *itself,* if need be, in every age.

IN THE CONGREGATIONAL VIEW, FOR WHAT PURPOSE DOES THE CHURCH EXIST?

Congregationalists hold that the mission of the Church of Christ is to proclaim the Gospel to all mankind, to exalt the worship of the one true God, and to labor for the progress of knowledge, the promotion of justice, the reign of peace and the realization of human brotherhood. An official statement of 1913 reads: "Depending, as did our fathers, upon the continued guidance of the Holy Spirit to lead us into all truth, we work and pray for the transformation of the world into the Kingdom of God; and we look with faith for the triumph of righteousness and the life everlasting."

WHAT IS THE CONGREGATIONAL ATTITUDE TOWARD EDUCATION?

Congregationalists have always believed in an educated ministry and an educated laity. Harvard College was founded by the Congregational fathers "to advance learning and to perpetuate it to posterity." Yale had similar beginnings. Congregationalists have set up other institutions of learning across the entire country. The Congregational freedom from imposed forms compels them to do their own thinking in the light of the Gospel—and that makes education indispensable.

DO CONGREGATIONALISTS BELIEVE IN COOPERATION AMONG THE DENOMINATIONS?

Unreservedly. They are sometimes called the interdenominational denomination. No other ecclesiastical group has participated in a greater number of unions with other groups. They will cooperate with any Christian communion which will cooperate with them. In any community they oppose religious isolationism and denominational exclusiveness.

The Congregational Churches accept members from other Christian communions without re-confirming them, and clergy from other communions without re-ordaining them.

HOW MANY CONGREGATIONAL CHRISTIANS ARE THERE IN THE UNITED STATES? IN THE WORLD?

According to the latest census (1960), there are 1,432,486 members gathered in 5,458 churches in the United States. There are over 2,000,000 Congregationalists in the world.

WHAT ROLE HAVE THE CONGREGATIONALISTS PLAYED IN AMERICA?

The Pilgrim Fathers who landed on Plymouth Rock were the first Congregationalists to reach the New World. Shortly thereafter, other shiploads of Congregationalists poured into the Puritan colony of Massachusetts Bay. They gave to New England its early character. They were pious and hardy; they loved learning.

The historian Bancroft calls the Mayflower Compact, which was composed and signed by the Congregational Fathers, "the birth of popular constitutional liberty" in this country. Being itself a pure democracy under God, and summoning all its members to individual responsibility and labor, Congregationalism today conserves, as historically it helped create, American democracy.

Who Are the Disciples of Christ?

JAMES E. CRAIG

James E. Craig, honorary elder for life of the Park
Avenue Christian Church, New York City, has had a
distinguished career in journalism. He was chief editorial writer for the New York *Sun*, editor of its editorial
page, and managing editor of *The Protestant World*.

Mr. Craig was born in Norborne, Missouri, in 1881.
He was baptized into the Disciples of Christ by his
father, a Disciples minister. Mr. Craig studied at the
University of Missouri. As reporter, feature writer, and
editor, he worked on the Kansas City *Journal*, *Star*, and
Post, and the St. Louis *Post-Dispatch*. He was city
editor of the St. Louis *Globe-Democrat* and the New
York *Evening Mail*, and was managing editor of the
Brownsville, Texas, *Herald*. He has written an authori-
tative history of the Freemasons, and won the *Masonic
Outlook* prize essay contest in 1925.

NOTE TO THE READER: While members of this communion use the name "Disciples of Christ," "Churches of Christ," and "Christian Churches" interchangeably, the term "Christian Churches (Disciples of Christ)" is more commonly used by those churches which cooperate through the International Convention of Christian Churches.

WHO ARE THE DISCIPLES OF CHRIST?

The Disciples of Christ constitute the largest purely indigenous American religious group, with about 1,800,000 adult communicants and some 8,000 autonomous congregations. In point of origin, the beliefs of the Disciples are as American as the Declaration of Independence. In point of individual liberty of conscience, they are as American as the Bill of Rights.

Some will say that the Disciples of Christ are a great evangelical, Protestant denomination. Others will say that they are not a denomination at all, but the pure New Testament Church of Christ. Still others will prefer to describe the Disciples as a brotherhood, or a communion. Perhaps the most favored word among Disciples is movement—a movement back to the New Testament, and forward to ultimate unity under God of all who call themselves Christians.

WHAT ARE THE BASIC TENETS OF THEIR CREED?

The Disciples have no creed but Christ and no doctrines save those which are found in the New Testament or are reasonably to be inferred therefrom. The Disciples are God-centered, Christ-centered, Bible-centered, with no creed save one—the answer of the apostle Peter to a question from Jesus himself: "Thou art the Christ, the Son of the Living God." Open confession of this faith, public acceptance of the Nazarene as Lord and Savior, and baptism by immersion are all that may be demanded of a candidate for admission into the fellowship. The Disciples are inclined to regard formal creeds and historical sects as so many milestones on the long highway of an evolving theology. As for themselves, they put aside ancient speculations and dogmas, and content themselves with Peter's simple exclamation that Jesus was the Messiah promised in the Scriptures.

The Disciples believe in the priesthood of all believers—that is, that the individual believer can reach the Throne of Grace without any human intermediary. According to the authorizations they find in the New Testament, the Disciples have evangelists, pastors, elders and deacons. But they look upon these officers as useful instruments sanctioned by the apostles. They never doubt the right of any man to go directly to God, by prayer, for guidance in all problems arising in the forum of conscience. They place absolute trust in the everlasting oversight of Divine mercy and good will. They nevertheless recommend pastoral consultation and guidance.

WHAT DO THE DISCIPLES BELIEVE ABOUT THE BIBLE?

The Disciples share the common Protestant belief that the Bible (except for the Apocryphal Books) is the inspired Word of God, written by different persons at different times under the inspiration of the Holy Spirit. They use the Old Testament for meditation and instruction, a schoolmaster bringing the faithful to Christ.

Many Disciples believe, however, that the Old Testament represents *two* dispensations—one for the patriarchal age before Moses, the other for the age from Moses to the resurrection of Jesus. These Disciples accept the New Testament as a third and purely Christian dispensation, for the guidance of Christian churches and peoples.

In common with other Christian bodies, the Disciples have their fundamentalists and their liberals. The literalists, or fundamentalists, accept every word of the authorized version of the Bible as a final and infallible word of God. The liberals believe that newer translations of the original tongues, and the studies of inspired scholars, have thrown new light upon many passages of the Scriptures. There is nothing to prevent literalists and liberals from sitting down together around the Table of the Lord's Supper, each responsible for his own belief and each serving God according to the dictates of his own conscience.

DO DISCIPLES BELIEVE IN THE HOLY TRINITY?

The Disciples have had little trouble in discarding most of the dogmas which sprang up between the first century and the nineteenth. Hence, speculation about the Holy Trinity and the nature of a triune God has bothered them little or not at all. They baptize into the name of the

Father, Son and Holy Spirit, as Christ commanded. They believe that the Holy Spirit is the Comforter promised in the New Testament, but they do not worry over its constitution or the nature of its operations. They accept its guidance as constantly enlarging the horizons of Christian thought. They are not concerned about such matters as original sin or predestination.

DO THE DISCIPLES BAPTIZE?

They baptize only those who are adult enough to know what they are doing when they stand up to confess Christ. They baptize by immersion, believing it to have been the New Testament way—an act of obedience and surrender, a symbol of the death, burial and resurrection of the Lord Jesus.

DO THE DISCIPLES BELIEVE IN THE VIRGIN BIRTH?

It is probable that a vast majority of them do. It is possible that others have doubts on the subject. But there is no ecclesiastical or denominational authority that can declare one belief to be orthodox and reject the other as heretical.

WHAT DO THE DISCIPLES BELIEVE ABOUT SIN AND SALVATION?

No answer covering all the congregations is possible. The Disciples as a rule reject the doctrine of original sin; but most of them believe that we are all sinful creatures unless and until redeemed by the saving sacrifice of the Lord Jesus.

Early in the history of the movement, the conception gained ground that a reasonable God would not leave His creatures without a rational plan of salvation which any person could understand and follow. Walter Scott was perhaps the first notable exponent of this idea. He suggested a five-fold plan: faith, repentance, baptism, newness of life, gift of the Holy Spirit. By faith he meant a sincere belief in the power and goodness of God, accompanied by complete surrender to His holy will. By repentance he meant not merely sorrow for past misdeeds, but perfect contrition, coupled with resolution not to sin again. By baptism he meant obedience to a command of the Savior and emulation of the example of the apostles. By newness of life he meant such conduct thereafter as would be void of further offense to God and scandal to the Church. By the gift of the Holy Spirit he meant the coming of the indwelling Comforter promised in the Gospels.

It was Walter Scott's belief that when a sinner honestly fulfilled these requirements he had no need to look for some mystical and emotional inner manifestation of saving grace. If you do what God has told you to do, he argued, you may be sure that God will reward you accordingly. Although the accent and terminology may have shifted, the essentials of this plan are still widely accepted among the Disciples.

DO THE DISCIPLES BELIEVE IN HEAVEN AND HELL?

Here again it is difficult to give an answer that will prove satisfactory to all members of this great fellowship. Practically all of them believe in the immortality of the soul and in a blissful reunion hereafter for all the faithful who have died in the Lord. Many doubtless believe in a literal paradise and a literal hell. Many others are content to leave the details of future rewards and punishments in the hands of Divine Mercy, without troubling themselves over theories elaborated in medieval theology. Disciple faith in general is a matter of deep personal conviction, rooted in serene confidence that the Kingdom of God will prove invincible in this world and in the life to come.

HOW DID THE DISCIPLES BEGIN?

The Disciples began by the confluence of two main currents of religious thought: one, the Christian Church, developed in Kentucky and Ohio under the leadership of Barton W. Stone; the other, that of a body which came to call itself Disciples of Christ, developed in western Pennsylvania and western Virginia under the leadership of Thomas Campbell, his son, Alexander Campbell, and Walter Scott, a kinsman of the great novelist.

All these men, who came to be known as the Big Four, were of Presbyterian antecedents; all were well educated according to the scholarship of their time, which laid emphasis upon proficiency in Greek, Latin and Hebrew.

These scholars and religious statesmen cast their lot among pioneers and in pioneering conditions. In the early years of the nineteenth century, a great westward migration was in full swing. Men and women of various church allegiances found church homes among denominations with which they were familiar. Many others were unchurched wanderers, tossed about by every wind of doctrine. Out of this emergency a great opportunity and a great vision came into flower.

The opportunity was that of bringing all these drifters into a single Christian fold. The vision was that of an ultimately united and militant Protestant Church. Here and there earnest men had begun asking themselves whether some way could not be found to break down the sectarian barriers which separated Christians into different corrals of creed. From many proposed answers one began to prevail: that a divided church could lay aside its divisive creeds and start afresh, building once more upon the foundations of the primitive churches as laid down in the New Testament.

This revolutionary idea cannot be ascribed to any one person. As early as 1803, Barton W. Stone and his supporters gave voice to it in Kentucky. In 1809, Thomas Campbell gave it cohesive literary expression in his Declaration and Address, long looked upon as the cornerstone of the edifice about to be built. Walter Scott and such powerful and popular preachers as "Raccoon John" Smith (Baptist) of Tennessee imparted to it an evangelistic fervor. Alexander Campbell, a skillful debater, gave it forensic and theological expression up to the time of his death in 1866.

In their enthusiasm for the cause, Calvinists and Arminians did not hesitate to lay many of their traditional beliefs upon the altar of a conviction that Christ died not for a chosen few, but for all; that the New Testament provided a plan of salvation which any adult of reasonable intelligence could understand and adopt.

Simple as the program may sound, the practical business of putting it into effect encountered enormous difficulties. It was easy enough to say there should be no creed but Christ, and to adopt the ordinance of baptism (by immersion) and weekly observance of the Lord's Supper. After declaring the New Testament to be the guide for Christian faith and practice, it seemed logically possible to ask for strict fidelity to the essentials of faith while allowing complete liberty of opinion regarding the nonessentials. Here, of course, came the rub: how do you decide what the essentials are and who is to make the decision? The distinction has troubled individual Disciples to this very day. Such difficulties are inevitable in a religious system which magnifies individual responsibility and reduces ecclesiastical authority to a minimum.

ARE THE "DISCIPLES OF CHRIST," "CHRISTIAN CHURCH," "CHURCHES OF CHRIST" ALL THE SAME?

In 1832 the Disciples of the East and the Christians of the West came together in a single union. From that day on, the term "Christian

Church" has been more commonly used in the Midwest and South; the term "Disciples of Christ" has been favored in the East. In the International Convention and in many congregations the words are used interchangeably. One of the oldest congregations, on Park Avenue in New York City, calls itself the Park Avenue Christian Church, with "Disciples of Christ" in parentheses.

Two other groups called themselves Christian Churches. One was James O'Kelly's group, which first called itself Republican Methodists and then changed its name to Christian. Another was the fine New England group which has since united with the Congregationalists as the Congregational-Christian Church.

Not long after the Civil War one group of members of the original movement proclaimed independence of the main body and since has gone its separate way. It insists, among other things, that there is no warrant in the New Testament for instrumental music or for missionary societies and the like. This extremely conservative body usually speaks of its congregations as Churches of Christ. (That name is also used by some of the churches cooperating through the International Convention, as well as by individual congregations of other denominations.) This group maintains headquarters in Nashville, Tennessee. Some other conservative congregations are not identified with the International Convention for reasons having to do with New Testament interpretation.

DO THE DISCIPLES OF CHRIST PROSELYTIZE?

They invite but do not proselytize. No Sunday morning service closes without an offering of fellowship to any adult who cares to take his stand by the Cross of the Risen Lord.

DO THE DISCIPLES HAVE AN ORDAINED MINISTRY?

Except in a few remote sections where ordained ministers are not available, practically all of the cooperating churches do have ordained pastors. In an emergency an elder or other layman may fill the pulpit. Elders usually, but not always, conduct the Communion Service.

In the early days, distrust of clericalism was so great that ministers were called "Elder," not "Reverend," and the wearing of gowns or cassocks in the pulpit was looked upon as smacking of "prelacy."

(Both these prejudices have now largely passed away.) No important distinction was made between clergy and laity. Indeed, any elder elected by the congregation could perform any ministerial duty—except that of saying marriage ceremonies, a function usually regulated by the state.

As time wore on, certain weaknesses in this system became obvious. Congregations began to demand ordained pastors. Today there are between thirty-four and thirty-eight Disciple colleges, universities, and Biblical training schools which are trying to fill that demand.

WHAT ARE THE DISCIPLES' VIEWS ON DIVORCE?

There is no central church authority on this subject.

In practice, ministers and congregations of the Disciples of Christ differ in their attitudes to divorce. Some believe that the questions propounded to Jesus by the Pharisees on this subject were "trick" questions concerned with then-current Jewish law, and that what Jesus answered must be viewed in that light. Some ministers and congregations take the Master's answer as binding to this day, and therefore oppose any remarriage of divorced persons. Others are willing to consent to the remarriage of any innocent party to a divorce obtained on the ground of adultery. Still others, perhaps a majority, believe that divorce has become a legal function of the state, and do not hesitate to remarry any person to whom the civil government has accorded the right of remarriage.

WHAT ARE THE DISCIPLES' VIEWS ON BIRTH CONTROL?

The old Disciple rule is that where the Scriptures speak, we speak; where they are silent, we are silent.

There can be no doubt, however, that a majority of Disciple ministers believe that birth control is justifiable under certain circumstances. The one sure test of this attitude rests in the fact that no Disciple minister can be muzzled, either by the Brotherhood at large or by his own congregation. By the terms of his ordination, each considers himself empowered, as were the Prophets of old, to denounce whatever he considers amiss in the life of his people—and silence seems to give at least a modified consent. In general, Disciples are content to leave matters such as birth control to the individual consciences of husband and wife.

Disciples have no catechism and no prescribed rituals of worship.

Disciples do not accept the doctrine of Apostolic Succession. Hence they have no archbishops or bishops or hierarchy of ecclesiastical authority. Disciples interpret the words "bishop" and "elder" as synonyms for one office—a *lay* office, elected by the members of the congregation and in no sense authorized or regulated from above.

Disciples believe that a confession of faith in Jesus as the Christ requires no added metaphysical doctrine.

They regard conversion as a voluntary, rational act which does not require special personal revelation. In receiving a new member, they take the applicant's simple statement of faith at face value. They employ no formula of interrogation or board of inquiry.

Disciples believe that a Christian's right to Holy Communion is entirely a matter for his own conscience. They admit to the Lord's Supper any baptized person, without regard to his sectarian affiliations.

Perhaps the most notable difference between Disciples and other Protestant groups is the emphasis of Disciples upon individual liberty of opinion, upon the right of each man to interpret the Scriptures in his own way.

Disciples base their whole case and their whole appeal on a simple outline of faith and a democratic system of church government. They have no sense of rivalry between the denominations. They hold that as long as a member accepts the simple faith, and the idea of democratic government in the church, he may believe what his mind dictates about many of the tenets of other Christian bodies.

Disciples observe with joy that the differences among Protestants are receiving less and less attention today, while the many things they have in common receive more and more. To Disciples, the rising trend toward a mutual ground of faith marks a steady advance toward ultimate church unity. And in this field the Disciples have made their influence most heavily felt. They have been in the forefront of almost every important Protestant cooperative and ecumenical movement. Thirty-nine Disciples were active in establishing the old Federal Council of Churches; two hundred are enrolled in the National Council of Churches of Christ in America; fourteen Disciple leaders serve the World Council of Churches.

WHAT IS THE CHURCH SERVICE LIKE?

With minor variations, Sunday morning service in Disciple churches follows pretty much the same pattern. With or without processions and with or without organ, the worship begins with the singing of hymns. This is followed by responsive readings, recitation of the Lord's Prayer, reading of the Scriptures, pastoral prayer, an anthem or two, the sermon, an invitation to fellowship, gathering of tithes and offerings, Communion Service, benediction, and final hymn or recessional. Sometimes Communion precedes the sermon. On occasion, the sermon may be omitted, but never Communion. (In the sanctuary of the Park Avenue Christian Church in New York City is preserved a little table at which Alexander Campbell and Walter Scott presided over the Lord's Supper. Incidentally, it is a tradition of this congregation that it has not omitted Communion Service on a single Sunday in over 150 years.) Many Disciples attribute their large gain in membership to the weekly practice of extending the right hand of fellowship to all who may desire to unite with a congregation.

HOW ARE THE DISCIPLES GOVERNED?

The average Disciple church is administered by a pastor, an Official Board of elders and deacons, and perhaps representatives of the Christian Women's Fellowship. Women are taking an increasingly greater part in every branch of Disciple activity—from the pulpit, the prayer meeting and missionary society, to the pew.

Elders look after the spiritual welfare of members; deacons manage incidental business. All matters of fundamental importance must ultimately be decided by the congregation as a whole.

Trials for heresy are almost unknown, although "withdrawals" of fellowship for immoral or scandalous, unchristian conduct are subjects of congregational action. Disciples believe that only the Lord himself can expel any person from the Church Universal.

DO THE DISCIPLES BELIEVE THEIRS THE ONLY TRUE RELIGION?

Certainly not. They believe theirs to be most nearly in accord with the practices of the early Christian churches. They also believe that their greatest mission in life is to bring Christians of all faiths into one Church of Christ. Their ancient retort to an ancient gibe about their name was to say: "We are not the only Christians, but are Christians only."

WHAT IS THE INTERNATIONAL CONVENTION?

The International Convention of Christian Churches (Disciples of Christ) is a voluntary and cooperative fellowship of local churches in the United States and Canada, and their various missionary, benevolent, and administrative agencies. It is a "reporting convention" rather than a legislative body. It receives reports from sixteen major boards and, in turn, submits these to the local congregations.

Though the cooperating churches send representatives, any Disciple may attend and vote.

The International Convention presents recommendations on every subject affecting the movement. These are advisory only, but because of the great prestige of the Convention and its officials most of the recommendations are accepted by the local congregations. What has been said about the International Convention is similarly true with respect to autonomous conventions in cities, districts and states.

What Is an Episcopalian?

W. NORMAN PITTENGER

W. Norman Pittenger, professor of Christian Apologetics at General Theological Seminary in New York, is vice-chairman of the Commission on Christ and the Church, appointed under the World Council of Churches. He was born in Bogota, New Jersey, in 1905, and studied at Columbia University, Ripon Hall in Oxford, England, Union Theological Seminary, and General Theological Seminary, from which he was graduated in 1936. He was made a deacon in the Episcopal Church in 1936 and was ordered priest the following year.

Dr. Pittenger has served as an examining chaplain in the Diocese of New Jersey, as vice-chairman of the Church Congress; and president of the American Theological Society. He is American editor of *Theology*, an English monthly journal, and serves on the editorial boards of *The Anglican Theological Review* and *Religion in Life*. In 1961 he became chairman of the editorial board of *The Witness*, an American religious weekly.

Dr. Pittenger has written twenty-five books. He is the co-author (with the Right Reverend James A. Pike, Episcopal Bishop of California) of *The Faith of the Church*, the authoritative and quasi-official statement of the Episcopal point-of-view. His most recent books are *The Word Incarnate* (1959), *Pathway to Believing* (1960), and *Proclaiming Christ Today* (1962).

WHAT IS AN EPISCOPALIAN?

An Episcopalian is a member of the Protestant Episcopal Church, which is one branch of the Anglican Communion—a religious group spread throughout the world and numbering some forty million Christians. There are "Episcopal Churches" in all parts of the globe. The Church of England is the mother of them all. Many of our churches are self-governing, like the Japanese Church (called the Holy Catholic Church in Japan) or the Canadian. They all use the Book of Common Prayer; they all are in communion with the Archbishop of Canterbury; they all recognize bishops as their chief pastors.

"Episcopalian" is derived from the Greek *episkopos,* which means "bishop." It describes the type of "order" or ministry which the Church maintains—that is, the bishop is looked upon as the symbol of the Church's unity and the chief pastor of the flock.

IS THE EPISCOPALIAN CHURCH CATHOLIC OR PROTESTANT?

In a profound sense, it is both. It is sometimes called "the bridge church." The Episcopal Church preserves the ancient Catholic sacraments and professes the ancient Catholic creeds; this was the intention of its reformers in the sixteenth century. On the other hand, it is a "reformed" church, for during that century, the authority of the Bishop of Rome (the Pope) was rejected and many modifications were made in worship and doctrine. But in no sense did the early reformers in England intend to deny "Catholic truth." The official title of the Church in America, "the Protestant Episcopal Church," was adopted when the word "Protestant" meant "non-Roman" or "non-papal."

WHAT IS THE EPISCOPAL ATTITUDE TOWARD ROMAN CATHOLICISM?

The Episcopal Church has no official position in regard to present-day Roman Catholicism. It believes that the Anglican Communion possesses all the essential marks of historical Catholicism—the apostolic faith, sacraments and ministry. But most Episcopalians would seriously question Roman Catholic centralization of power in the Bishop of Rome, and would regard with disfavor what they conceive to be the Roman Church's suppression of freedom in many intellectual areas, as well as in the understanding of the relation of Church to civil government and education.

DID HENRY VIII FOUND THE EPISCOPAL CHURCH?

No. Under Henry, the freedom of the English Church from the authority of the Bishop of Rome was achieved; but that was the end of a long period of protest and agitation against what were conceived to be the Pope's unwarranted usurpations of authority. Henry's desire for an annulment provided the occasion but was not the *cause* of the independence of the Church of England. It is unfortunate that in many textbooks the mistake of identifying occasion and cause has led to the propagation of what is in fact an untruth.

WHAT ARE THE BASIC BELIEFS OF EPISCOPALIANS?

They are affirmed in the Apostles' Creed and the Nicene Creed. The Apostles' Creed is the ancient baptismal statement of faith. As used in Episcopalian services, it runs:

I believe in God the Father Almighty, Maker of heaven and earth:
    And in Jesus Christ his only Son our Lord: Who was conceived by the Holy Ghost, Born of the Virgin Mary: Suffered under Pontius Pilate, Was crucified, dead, and buried: He descended into hell; The third day he rose again from the dead: He ascended into heaven, And sitteth on the right hand of God the Father Almighty: From thence he shall come to judge the quick and the dead.
    I believe in the Holy Ghost: the holy Catholic Church; The Communion of Saints: The Forgiveness of Sins: The Resurrection of the body: And the Life everlasting. Amen.

The Nicene Creed, used at the service of Holy Communion, is an expanded statement of the Christian faith, essentially the same as the Apostles' Creed.

Both creeds state the main points of Christian belief in a pictorial and dramatic form. Some of the phrases are clearly "symbolic" (as, "sitteth on the right hand of God the Father," which of course could not be *literally* true); some parts are historical in intention (as "born," "crucified," "dead," "buried," "rose again"); and some parts are theological such as "of one substance," in the Nicene Creed, although more often the theological affirmations are phrased in the pictorial language which the early Church took over from its Jewish background.

WHAT DO EPISCOPALIANS BELIEVE ABOUT JESUS CHRIST?

They believe that He is "truly God and truly man, united in one person" for the salvation of mankind. There are different ways of understanding and teaching this doctrine, but it is central and unchangeable for all Episcopalians.

WHAT IS THE EPISCOPAL VIEW OF THE VIRGIN BIRTH?

The creeds and the liturgy of the Episcopal Church assert the traditional belief that Jesus was born of Mary without human father. There is no disagreement within the Church on the *theological* meaning of the Virgin Birth. There has been, and still is, disagreement about the Virgin Birth in its biological detail. Most Episcopalians probably accept it as literally true; some regard it as symbolic in character. The Episcopal Church is able to contain both types of thinking within it, since all Episcopalians accept the Incarnation—the true deity and humanity of Jesus—as the central truth about Christ.

WHAT ABOUT THE TRINITY?

The Trinity is the Christian teaching about God. In the light of man's experience of God's working in the world, Christians have been driven to assert that God *is* as He *reveals* Himself. He is Creative Reality (God the Father); He is Expressive Act (God the Son); He is Responsive Power (God the Holy Spirit). Yet He is *one* God. This is "theology." What matters most, in the Book of Common Prayer, about the Trinity is that we worship God and experience Him in a "trinitarian" fashion.

WHAT DOES THE EPISCOPAL CHURCH BELIEVE ABOUT THE LORD'S SUPPER?

Holy Communion, sometimes called the Lord's Supper or Holy Eucharist (from an ancient Christian word for the service), is the chief service of worship in the Episcopal Church, although it does not always occupy the chief place in the Sunday schedule. The teaching of the Church about this sacrament is expressed in these words: "The Sacrament of the Lord's Supper was ordained for the continual remembrance of the sacrifice of the death of Christ, and of the benefits which we receive thereby"; and the Offices of Instruction (Prayer Book, page 293), from which these words are quoted, goes on to say that "the . . . thing signified" in the sacrament "is the Body and Blood of Christ, which are spiritually taken and received by the faithful."

DO EPISCOPALIANS PRACTICE PRIVATE CONFESSION?

They may, since provision is made in the Prayer Book for private confession of sins to a priest, with the declaration of absolution by him. However, this is not enforced, as in the Roman Catholic Church; it is entirely optional. Many Episcopalians avail themselves of the privilege, some frequently, some occasionally. Many do not desire to use this "means of grace" and find satisfaction in the *general* confessions and absolutions which are provided in the regular services of the Church.

HOW DO EPISCOPALIANS REGARD THE BIBLE?

The Holy Scriptures are, for Episcopalians, the great source and testing ground of Christian doctrine. Nothing may be taught "as necessary to eternal salvation" excepting what can be "proved" (the Elizabethan word for "tested") by Holy Scripture.

But the Episcopal Church does not hold to the literal inerrancy of Scripture. The Bible is considered sacred for its general inspiration, as the record of God's revelation.

The Episcopal Church maintains a balance between gospel and tradition, on the one hand, and the use of reason on the other. Freedom of investigation, restatements of the Christian faith, and incorporation of scientific truths are possible *without* creating violent fundamentalist-modernist controversies. The Episcopal Church has accepted the theory of evolution as an account of man's origin, as well as other new scientific discoveries, without disturbing its central beliefs. In both freedom of inquiry and Biblical criticism, the Episcopal Church's position has been liberal and has left a place for a "modernist" school of thought among its members, as well as a "catholic" and an "evangelical" emphasis.

WHAT IS THE BOOK OF COMMON PRAYER?

At the time of the English reforms, the old service books of the Church were translated into English. Some of the services were combined and edited; many were shortened and simplified. The result was the Book of Common Prayer, completed in 1549. All later Prayer Books, including that used in America today, are re-editings of the 1549 book, whose beautiful, stately language, simplicity and dignity are unparalleled. The regular services, like the Holy Communion or Holy Eucharist, Morning and Evening Prayer, the Litany, are all taken from the Prayer Book. Episcopalians believe that a prescribed form of service, with parts assigned to clergy and people, is the most fitting way to adore God. Frequent revisions are made to meet the needs of succeeding ages; but the principle of ordered worship remains at the heart of Anglicanism.

The worship of the Episcopal Church is not rigid. Many variations are found in the Prayer Book; the special prayers ("collects") and the different readings from the Bible give considerable variety for each Sunday and holy day.

DO EPISCOPALIANS BELIEVE IN HEAVEN AND HELL?

The teachings of the Episcopal Church about death, judgment, heaven and hell are stated plainly in the Book of Common Prayer. Death marks the end of this period of man's life. He is judged in terms of his real character, by a God "unto whom all hearts are open, all desires known, and from whom no secrets are hid." Heaven is a state in which the vision of God is enjoyed in a "life of perfect service" of God. Hell is alienation from God, and therefore the loss of that goal to which man's whole existence is directed.

Episcopalians do not believe in a *physical* heaven or hell; these are "states of being." The departed in whom there is some possibility of goodness are prepared for the full enjoyment of God by such cleansing and purifying as they may require—in a way, this resembles the idea of "purgatory." But Episcopalians do not use the term in their official teaching because they feel that it is often associated with crude ideas of payment of penalty and the like.

By the "resurrection," the Episcopal Church means not the raising of the physical body we now possess but the re-creation by God of the total personality of man with a "spiritual body"—that is, with an instrument of self-expression and a means for continuing fellowship, appropriate to a heavenly life.

WHAT THEN IS MEANT BY SALVATION?

Modern Episcopalians tend to understand by this term "health or wholeness of life." Salvation means that one is given the wholeness which is God's will for man, and is delivered from arrogance and selfishness. Salvation has to do not only with the "hereafter" but also with man's present earthly existence. In man, sinner because he is ridiculously proud and self-centered, there is no real "health"; by fellowship with God in Christ, he is brought into the sphere of healthy and whole life.

DOES THE EPISCOPAL CHURCH HAVE A PRIESTHOOD?

It does. There are three "orders of ministry" included in "Holy Orders": bishops, priests, deacons. The Offices of Instruction state that the bishop's office is "to be a chief pastor in the Church; to confer Holy Orders; and to administer confirmation." A priest's office is "to minister to the people committed to his care; to preach the Word of God; to baptize; to celebrate the Holy Communion; and to pronounce absolution and blessing in God's name." The deacon assists the priest in divine service and other ministrations; he is a minister in the real sense of the word, but without such "higher" privileges as priest and bishop.

The priest is the "ministerial representative" for Christ in his church; he also represents the priesthood of the laity, which is shared by all who are baptized. An Episcopal minister is never called a "preacher," since that is only one aspect of his office; he is also celebrant of the Holy Communion—absolver, teacher, shepherd of his flock.

The ministers of the Episcopal Church may marry or not marry as they see fit, "as they shall judge the same to serve better to godliness."

ARE THERE MONKS AND NUNS IN THE EPISCOPAL CHURCH?

Yes. There are many orders of Episcopal monks and nuns, both in the United States and elsewhere. Some are purely "contemplative"— that is, engaged in prayer; others are "mixed"—that is, engaged both in prayer and in teaching, writing, preaching. These men and women take the vows of poverty, chastity and obedience. They do not marry. They live in communities established for the purpose of sharing a common life of work and prayer.

WHAT IS MEANT BY "HIGH," "LOW," AND "BROAD" CHURCH?

These words are used to describe parishes, but they are misleading. A "high" parish is one which emphasizes sacramental worship, the supreme value of the "Catholic tradition," and a rather elaborate service of worship. A "low" parish is one in which the services are simpler and a stronger emphasis is placed on the gospel and on personal religion. In a "broad" parish, which may be either "high" or "low," the importance of a rational understanding of the Christian tradition is stressed, with a concern for "liberal values." But all these emphases meet in the proclamation of the gospel, sacramental worship, and the reasonable presentation of Christianity. Episcopalians appeal to Scriptures, tradition, and personal experience, as well as reason, for vindication of the truth of the Christian faith. Differences in emphasis are welcomed in the Episcopal Church, as long as the central affirmations are maintained.

DOES THE EPISCOPAL CHURCH PERMIT DIVORCE?

In America, the "canons" (or church law) do not recognize divorce, but do provide a number of grounds for annulment—the ecclesiastical declaration that no marriage has in fact existed because of some factor that made such impossible. A bishop may permit a divorced person to remarry if certain conditions are met. He may also admit to Holy Communion persons who have been divorced and remarried—if they can prove that they are in good faith, are struggling to live a Christian life, and have demonstrated their stability and repentance.

WHAT IS THE EPISCOPALIAN ATTITUDE TOWARD BIRTH CONTROL?

The Anglican Communion has spoken, through its conference of bishops at Lambeth, on birth control, saying that when practiced without selfish motives, it is permissible. There has been much discussion of the "moral theology" of contraception, but no more clearly defined position has yet been taken.

WHAT IS THE CHURCH ATTITUDE TOWARD DRINKING AND GAMBLING?

The Episcopal Church has been nonpuritanical in most respects; it believes that God intends men to enjoy life—if they can do so without such excesses as will harm them and spoil their potentialities as children of God. The Episcopal Church's primary concern has been with abuses. It has not taken an official stand on gambling and drinking, although there have been some quasi-official condemnations of the gambling evil and the perils to character which it involves. As to drinking—like card-playing, dancing, and the like, the Episcopal Church has· on the whole been "liberal" in attitude, feeling that the evils come when the activities are abused.

DO EPISCOPALIANS BELIEVE THAT THEIRS IS THE ONLY TRUE FAITH?

No. We hold that all who are baptized (whether by Episcopalian or other baptism, provided it is with water and in the name of the Holy Trinity) are members of the Church of Christ. Christ is the "head" of His Church (called in the New Testament "The Body of Christ") and those who belong to Him by baptism are His "members." Confirmation by the bishop is necessary to communicant status, but it is not believed to be "joining the Church." It is a sacramental rite by which, Episcopalians believe, the Holy Spirit is given to a Christian reaching communicant status.

Even those who are not actually baptized, but by intention would be baptized if they were able, are believed to be "saved." The Church is Christ's instrument for fulfilling His purpose in the world and the means by which His continuing presence is made available. Of that one Church, Episcopalians believe they are a part; they have never claimed they are the *only* part.

HOW IS THE EPISCOPAL CHURCH GOVERNED?

In different countries the Anglican Communion has different kinds of government. In the United States, there are parishes, with elected laymen to represent the congregation; dioceses, with the "convention" under which the bishop and his clergy carry on the Church's work; and a general convention which meets every three years and represents the entire American Church. The Church is democratic: delegates to the general convention and laymen to diocesan conventions are elected. At the general convention, the House of Deputies, composed of laymen and priests, and the House of Bishops, in which all bishops may sit, must concur in legislative measures. Neither bishops nor parish clergy have any autocratic rights; all must cooperate with the laity.

WHAT IS THE LAMBETH CONFERENCE?

Every ten years, more than three hundred bishops of the Anglican Communion meet at Lambeth in London, under the presidency of the Archbishop of Canterbury. This assembly has no legal power; its decisions have moral authority only. The meetings are the great symbol of the unity of the whole communion. The presidency of the Archbishop of Canterbury indicates that all the churches in the world-wide Anglican fellowship are at one in their common loyalty and in their communion with the see of Canterbury.

HOW MANY EPISCOPALIANS ARE THERE IN THE UNITED STATES?

Statistics from the Episcopal Church Annual for 1962 show that there are 3,269,325 baptized Americans in the Episcopal Church. In addition, approximately a half-million or so persons look to that Church for ministrations but are not formal members. The Episcopal Church has 9,343 clergy in the United States, in some 8,000 parishes and missions.

DOES THE EPISCOPAL CHURCH OWN SCHOOLS AND COLLEGES?

Yes, it either owns or controls such colleges as Hobart, Kenyon, University of the South, Trinity, and such schools as Groton, Saint Mark's, Saint Paul's, and others. The Church has eleven seminaries, plus two diocesan seminaries, where clergy are trained. In addition, it supports five "overseas" seminaries, in Liberia, Puerto Rico, Haiti, Brazil and the Philippines.

DOES THE EPISCOPAL CHURCH BELIEVE IN MISSIONARY WORK?

Yes, it has been active in this field. Apart from any work done by other branches of the Anglican Communion, the Episcopal Church has missionaries in Asia, South America, Africa, and in many parts of the United States. This activity is under the National Council of the Church, whose Director of Overseas Activities is in charge of foreign missions and whose Director of the Home Department is in charge of domestic missions.

WHAT ROLE HAS THE EPISCOPAL CHURCH PLAYED IN AMERICAN HISTORY?

Services of the Anglican Communion were held in North Carolina, San Francisco Bay, and perhaps elsewhere, before the first regular worship of the Church was inaugurated at Jamestown, Virginia, in 1607. For many years, the Episcopalians in the colonies were under the Bishop of London; with the War of Independence, they became self-governing.

A majority of the founders of this nation were Episcopalians— including George Washington, Alexander Hamilton, James Madison, James Monroe, John Marshall and John Jay. From that time to the present, the Church has played a significant part in our national life. Despite its close fellowship with the Church of England, it has been thoroughly American and its members are loyal citizens of this land.

What Is a Greek Orthodox?

ARTHUR DOUROPULOS

Arthur Douropulos is director of the office of information of the Greek Archdiocese of North and South America.

He was born in Baltimore, Maryland, and obtained his A.B. (cum laude) and his M.A. degrees from Harvard. From 1938 to 1942 he taught English at Pennsylvania State University, and from 1942 to 1948 was a member of the English department of Harvard College.

Mr. Douropulos was the representative of the Greek Archdiocese of North and South America in the first official pilgrimage of the Greek Ecumenical Patriarchate of Constantinople, in Istanbul. He is the English editor of *The Orthodox Observer,* official publication of the Greek Archdiocese of North and South America, a member of the General Board of the National Council of the Churches of Christ in the U.S.A., and is on the board of directors of Religion in American Life.

The Greek Orthodox Church considers itself to be the one, holy, catholic and apostolic Church, founded by Jesus Christ in the year of His death, 33 A.D. It is holy because its founder, Jesus Christ, is holy. It is catholic because the whole world is considered its province, and because it is universal in time and place. It is apostolic because it was established on earth by the apostles of Christ.

"Orthodox" means "true belief," from the Greek words *orthe* and *doxa*.

Yes. The term "Greek Orthodox" is historically correct; the early Scriptures were written in Greek, and Christianity originated and spread largely through Greek culture and traditions. For centuries the various national bodies of the Orthodox Church retained the word "Greek" as part of their titles; some still do; but with the rise of nationalism, the tendency has been to use the national name, as in the Albanian Orthodox Church, the Bulgarian Orthodox Church, and so on.

As a *group,* the Orthodox Churches are now generally known as the Eastern Orthodox Church. All Eastern Orthodox bodies are in full communion with each other; they hold the same beliefs and observe the same rituals.

In two ways: (1) by the apostles of Jesus Christ; and (2) by missionaries of these first churches. The four original Patriarchates of the Church are in Constantinople (Istanbul), in Alexandria, in Antioch, and in Jerusalem. These churches were established by the apostles Andrew, Mark, Paul, and Peter and James, respectively. The Church of Cyprus, established by the apostles Paul and Barnabas, is also considered an original church.

To the second class belong the national churches of Albania, Bulgaria, Finland, Greece, Poland, Rumania, Russia, and others.

DOES THE EASTERN ORTHODOX CHURCH AS A WHOLE HAVE ONE HEAD?

No, not in the sense that the Pope is the head of the Roman Catholic Church. Each Orthodox Church is independently administered by a Council of Bishops, called a synod.

The Patriarch of Constantinople, oldest of the Patriarchates, is known as "the first among equals," and is generally regarded as the spiritual leader of world Orthodoxy. At present, His Holiness Athenagoras I, Archbishop of Constantinople, New Rome and Ecumenical Patriarch holds this position. (From 1931 to 1948 he served as Greek Orthodox Archbishop of the Americas.)

When the Papacy was first founded, the Pope was in effect another patriarch.

WAS THE EASTERN ORTHODOX CHURCH EVER THE SAME AS THE ROMAN CATHOLIC CHURCH?

Yes, for over 1,000 years. In 1054 A.D. the united Church of Christ finally divided into Eastern and Western segments. This break, known as the great schism, had been building up for centuries; it contained both political and ecclesiastical roots. Politically, the Eastern emperors had for centuries supported the Patriarchs, while the emperors of Rome gave support to the Popes. Gradually, ecclesiastical differences also arose as the Patriarchs of the East exercised a growing independence that denied the authority of the Pope. The Western Church of Rome became known as Roman Catholic. The Church of Constantinople, the site of ancient Byzantium, has since been called the Greek or Eastern Orthodox Church.

The Eastern Church has always maintained that it was the Roman Catholic Church which drew apart from the original Christian Church. The Eastern Orthodox Church considers itself the continuation of the original and true Church of Christ. The Roman Catholic Church, on the other hand, considers that the Eastern Church separated from it. (Catholicism considers Orthodoxy as "separated," not "heretical.")

WHAT ARE THE MAIN DOCTRINES OF THE EASTERN ORTHODOX CHURCH?

Orthodoxy believes that God is one in substance and a Trinity in persons. Orthodoxy worships one God in the Trinity and the Trinity in unity, neither confusing the persons nor dividing the substance.

Orthodoxy holds the creation to be the work of the blessed Trinity and believes the world is neither self-created nor has it existed from eternity; it is the product of the wisdom, the power and the will of one God in Trinity. God the Father is the prime cause of the creation, God the Son perfected the creation, and God the Holy Ghost gives it life.

The Orthodox believe that our Lord Jesus Christ, while truly God, begotten of the same substance as the Father and consubstantial with Him, is also truly a man in every respect except sin. The denial of His humanity would constitute a denial of His incarnation and of our salvation

WHAT IS THE BASIC CREED OF THE ORTHODOX CHURCH?

The official creed accepted by Orthodoxy, formulated and adopted by the First Ecumenical Council of Nicaea (325 A.D.) and the Second Ecumenical Council of Constantinople (381 A.D.), is generally known as the Nicaean Creed. It reads as follows:

I believe in one God, the Father Almighty, maker of heaven and earth and of all things visible and invisible; and in one Lord Jesus Christ, the only begotten Son of God, begotten of His Father before all ages: light of light, very God of very God, begotten, not made, consubstantial with the Father, by Whom all things were made, Who for all men and for our salvation came down from heaven, and was incarnate by the Holy Ghost of the Virgin Mary, and was made man; and was crucified also for us under Pontius Pilate. He suffered and was buried; and the third day He arose again according to the Scriptures, and ascended into heaven, and sitteth on the right hand of the Father. And He shall come again with glory to judge both the quick and the dead, whose kingdom shall have no end.

And I believe in the Holy Ghost, the Lord and giver of life, who proceedeth from the Father, who with the Father and Son together is worshiped and glorified, and who spoke by the prophets.

I believe in one, holy, catholic and apostolic church; I acknowledge one baptism for the remission of sins. I look for the resurrection of the dead, and for the life of the ages to come.

WHAT ARE THE SACRAMENTS OR "MYSTERIA" RECOGNIZED BY THE ORTHODOX CHURCH?

Orthodoxy recognizes seven sacraments: baptism, chrismation, holy eucharist (or communion), confession, ordination, marriage and holy unction. All but ordination and marriage are obligatory. Chrismation is the anointment of the baptized with holy oils. It symbolizes a confirmation in the faith. In the Orthodox Church, chrismation is administered immediately following the traditional baptism of infants, children, or, in rare cases, adults.

ARE ROMAN CATHOLICISM AND EASTERN ORTHODOXY MORE ALIKE THAN DIFFERENT IN THEIR BELIEFS?

Yes. Actually, the basic tenets of both bear the sanction of the same seven ecumenical councils, the last of which took place in 787 A.D., when the Eastern and Western branches of Christianity were still united.

WHAT, THEN, ARE THE MAIN DIFFERENCES TODAY BETWEEN THE EASTERN ORTHODOX CHURCH AND THE ROMAN CATHOLIC CHURCH?

There are differences of administration, of doctrine and of practice. Most important in the first category is the refusal of the Eastern Orthodox Church to accept the concentration of the church in one person— a person, moreover, considered infallible, as Roman Catholics consider the Pope. The Orthodox Church considers as infallible only the Church as a whole.

In doctrine, the Eastern Orthodox Church differs from Roman Catholicism in the following:

(1.) The Roman Catholic Church holds that the holy spirit proceeds "and from the Son" (a doctrine known as the "filioque" clause), as well as from the Father. Eastern Orthodoxy believes that the holy spirit proceeds only "from the Father."

(2.) Roman Catholicism affirms the existence of a purgatory, in addition to a heaven and a hell. Eastern Orthodoxy does not accept the idea of a purgatory, though it does believe in an intermediate state between heaven and hell where souls experience a foretaste of the bliss or the punishment that will eventually be theirs.

(3.) The Roman Catholic Church believes in the Immaculate Conception of the Virgin, a doctrine which Eastern Orthodoxy does not accept. The Orthodoxy hold that only Christ was conceived and born without original sin, that the Virgin Mary was cleansed of it on Annunciation Day.

(4.) The Roman Catholic dogma that the body of the Virgin Mary "was taken up into heaven" (declared by Pope Pius XII) is not subscribed to by Eastern Orthodoxy, which does not believe in such a physical assumption.

(5.) Orthodoxy does not recognize the saints canonized by the Catholic Church after the Schism of 1054, unless these saints have also been proclaimed by Eastern Orthodox synods.

In ritual and practices, the following differences exist between the Eastern Orthodox and the Roman Catholic churches:

(1.) The Eastern Orthodox Church does not subscribe to the custom, traditionally practiced by the popes, of granting indulgences on the grounds that the head of the church has authority to transfer to others the surplus good works of Christ, the Blessed Virgin and the saints.

(2.) Roman Catholicism does not grant divorce. Eastern Orthodoxy issues ecclesiastical divorces under certain circumstances.

(3.) In the Roman Catholic Church, Holy Communion is not given until the age of 12. In the Eastern Orthodox Church, the Holy Eucharist may be partaken after birth.

(4.) In the Roman Catholic Church, chrismation (the anointment with holy oil) is practiced from the ages of 7 to 11. The Eastern Orthodox Church gives chrismation at the baptismal ceremony, usually of infants.

(5.) Celibacy is obligatory for Roman Catholic deacons, priests and bishops (though there are certain exceptions). Orthodoxy requires celibacy among bishops only.

(6.) Roman Catholics celebrate the sacrament of baptism by pouring water on the head of the baptized person. In the Orthodox Church, the baptismal rite is performed by a triple immersion into water.

(7.) The Roman Catholic Church uses unleavened bread in Holy Communion. The Holy Eucharist of the Eastern Orthodox Church is given with a leavened bread, as occurred in the Last Supper.

(8.) The Roman Catholic Church serves the holy bread and the holy wine, symbolizing the body and blood of Christ, to the clergy only. In the Eastern Orthodox Church, both clergy and laity partake of both.

(9.) A Roman Catholic priest may receive permission to celebrate several Masses on the same day and on the same altar. An Eastern Orthodox priest may celebrate only one liturgy (which is the equivalent, in Orthodoxy, of a Mass) on one day.

WHAT LANGUAGE IS USED IN ORTHODOX CHURCH SERVICES?

Originally, the language of the Orthodox liturgy was the Greek of the gospels, a form closer to modern than to classical Greek. Later,

early church fathers made translations of the gospels for ethnic Orthodox groups. Today, each Eastern body uses the national language in
the services and rites of the church. In the United States, there is a growing tendency to substitute English translations for the various ethnic
languages.

DO EASTERN ORTHODOX MAKE THE SIGN OF THE CROSS DIFFERENTLY FROM ROMAN CATHOLICS?

Roman Catholics make the sign of the cross with open palm from
left to right. Eastern Orthodox communicants cross themselves from
right to left with the thumb, forefinger and middle finger closed
together (to represent the Holy Trinity).

HOW IS THE DIVINE LITURGY PERFORMED?

The Divine Liturgy is performed so as to rise to a climax. The main
rituals are:

(1.) The Little Entrance, which includes the litany of peace, the
secret prayer, the apostle reading and the sermon of the preacher.
The Little Entrance is climaxed by the priest, accompanied by choir
boys, descending the altar steps from the sanctuary, holding the Bible
and chanting the gospel of the day.

(2.) The Great Entrance, which begins with the supplication within
the sanctuary and the censing of the holy icons and the faithful. The
priest with his choir boys comes out of the altar, holding in each hand
a square veil, the "aer," which symbolizes the holy gifts offered to God,
and in honor of which a prayer is then recited.

(3.) The "Anaphora," which is the offering of the special prayer
to the Almighty. The Nicaean Creed is recited, as are other hymns
and prayers.

(4.) The Communion, which includes a prayer for worthiness to
receive the Holy Eucharist. With heads inclined, the congregation
recites the Lord's Prayer, followed by the chant "holy things to the
holy." The priest, who now has come forth alone from the altar bearing the communion chalice, then says to those who are about to receive
communion, "With fear of God, with faith and with love, draw near."
After the communicants have received the Holy Eucharist, the priest
intones the benediction: "We have seen the light."

(5.) The Dismissal, in which is chanted the thanksgiving "Arise . . .

let us give due thanks." The Divine Liturgy ends with the prayer, "Be the Lord's name blessed," addressed to the icon of Christ at the gate of the altar, and with the final benediction by the celebrant. The Divine Liturgy is traditionally preceded by the morning prayer, during which the priest comes forth from the altar with his altar boys, holding the gold-encased Bible used in Orthodox churches. Anyone in the congregation may come forth to kiss the Bible. When a bishop, archbishop or patriarch officiates at a Divine Liturgy, he is usually assisted by several priests, and at the end of the service ascends the episcopal throne to address the congregation.

DO THE ORTHODOX STAND THROUGHOUT THE SERVICE?

Until very recent times, Eastern churches contained no seats or pews; the worshipers remained standing throughout the long service (two or more hours). Now, in America, the communicants may sit throughout most of the liturgy, but stand or kneel at the more sacred moments. In the Old World, the men occupy the right portion of the church, the women the left, and all stand throughout the service.

IS THERE MORE THAN ONE ORTHODOX DIVINE LITURGY?

There are five Orthodox liturgies: the one named after Saint James of Jerusalem, performed on October 23; the one of Saint Mark, celebrated on April 25, in Alexandria; Saint Basil's, which is used on Christmas and Epiphany eves, on the first five Sundays of Easter Lent, on Holy Thursday, Holy Saturday, and January 1; the fourth, and most widely used, is that of Saint Chrysostom, traditionally celebrated every Sunday and on saints' days; the fifth is the liturgy of the presanctified gifts, the oldest and most mystical, which is celebrated every Wednesday and Friday of Easter Lent, and on Holy Monday, Tuesday and Wednesday of Easter Week.

WHEN SHOULD THE ORTHODOX RECEIVE HOLY COMMUNION?

Each communicant may decide for himself when he is worthy. Communion may be received every Sunday, and on every day that the liturgy is celebrated.

Custom holds that every member of the church should have communion at least four times a year, after proper fasting and adequate spiritual preparation: on Christmas, Easter, the Commemoration of the Apostles on June 30, and the Assumption of the Virgin Mary on August 15.

DOES CONFESSION PRECEDE COMMUNION IN THE ORTHODOX CHURCH?

Strictly speaking, yes. Confession (together with repentance) is a sacrament, through which the sinful man is cleansed, and by which the regeneration of the human soul is achieved. Most Orthodox priests, however, will not refuse communion to those who have not confessed— if the communicant himself feels that his conscience allows him to be worthy of the Holy Eucharist. But confession at least once a year is considered a prerequisite to communion in most Orthodox churches.

HOW DOES ORTHODOX CONFESSION DIFFER FROM ROMAN CATHOLIC?

The practice of confession in Orthodoxy is more personal. The communicant is encouraged to choose a confessor-priest who knows him personally, even intimately, and who is acquainted with, and sympathetic to, his problems. The confessional is held in the open, not in a confessional booth, usually facing the altar of the church. If the communicant wishes more privacy for his confession, he may ask the priest to receive him in private.

HOW DO THE ORTHODOX REGARD THE VIRGIN MARY?

The Orthodox honor her most of all the saints, but do not consider her a deity. They venerate her especially for her supreme grace and the call she received from God. Though not exempt from original sin, from which she was cleansed at the time of the Annunciation, it is believed that by the Grace of God she committed no actual sin.

DO THE ORTHODOX VENERATE ICONS AND RELICS?

Yes. Veneration of sacred icons and relics is a part of the Orthodox tradition. But in accordance with the decree of the Seventh Ecumenical

Council of Nicaea, in 787 A.D., this veneration is directed not to the images, as such, but to the holy persons whom they represent. The Orthodox, therefore, venerate flat, two-dimensional icons; they do not pray to three-dimensional statues, as do other religious groups, because these representations may be too realistic and may become in themselves idols of veneration.

WHAT ARE THE ORDERS OF SERVICE IN THE EASTERN ORTHODOX CHURCH?

There are three orders of service: deacon, priest and bishop. Those holding the higher ranks—metropolitans, archbishops and patriarchs—are, in effect, bishops.

A metropolitan is the head of an ecclesiastical district; an archbishop is the head of a church; a patriarch is the head of a see, which may also be a separate church. Metropolitans, archbishops and patriarchs are elected by a holy synod of a church and assume office by enthronement.

ARE THERE MONKS AND NUNS IN THE EASTERN CHURCH?

Yes. Monasteries and convents are widespread within the old Eastern Churches, but are few in America (and wherever Orthodoxy has spread in modern times) mainly because priests are urgently needed for the active ministry.

Orthodox monasticism has three main divisions: (1) the robe wearers (*rasofori*), who are on trial, can leave at any time, and can even marry, if they are not already ordained; (2) the small-gowned (*mikroschema*), who are ordained; and (3) the large-gowned (*megaloschema*), who can enter the final step of monkhood only after thirty years of pious service.

Orthodox nuns are also divided into ordained and lay groups, the latter active in philanthropy and charitable deeds.

WHAT VESTMENTS DO ORTHODOX PRIESTS WEAR?

In the old countries, Orthodox clergymen wear a full-length, cassock-like robe, black or deep blue in color, which is known as the "rasso." In the United States and in modern cities, priests often adopt the usual clerical garb and collar for street wear. Metropolitans, archbishops and patriarchs never use modern dress.

The traditional headgear of the Orthodox clergy is the "kalimafki," a cylindrical-like hat, about 6-inches high, with a protruding flat top. Over this those of episcopal rank, as well as celibate archimandrite priests, wear a black veil, attached to the "kalimafki," which falls backward over the shoulders.

When officiating at liturgical services, hierarchs wear a golden miter, often glittering with jewels. They also wear the "engolpion," a relic- arium with representations of the saints, suspended from a gold chain. In the celebration of the liturgy, Orthodox priests and bishops wear multi-colored vestments, embroidered in gold and silver.

ARE ALL ORTHODOX PRIESTS BEARDED?

Until very modern times, all Orthodox priests wore beards, to emulate Christ and the fathers of the chruch. This tradition still persists in old Orthodox centers. But in America, most priests are cleanshaven. However, hierarchs of the church, as well as monastics, remain bearded.

ARE ORTHODOX PRIESTS ALLOWED TO MARRY?

An Orthodox clergyman is permitted to marry *before* ordination into priesthood. Married clergymen may not become bishops. Unmarried priests may attain the rank of archimandrite, a high order of priesthood which observes life-long celibacy. Bishops are usually chosen from the archimandrites.

DO THE ORTHODOX CHURCHES ALLOW MIXED MARRIAGES?

Marriages within the faith are preferred and encouraged, but mixed marriages are permitted—if the non-Orthodox has been baptized in the name of the Holy Trinity (even in another Christian denomi- nation), and if he or she agrees to baptize the children of the marriage in the Orthodox church.

An Orthodox who marries outside the church is denied partici- pation in the sacraments, and is not allowed to be a sponsor at an Ortho- dox wedding or baptism.

DO THE ORTHODOX CHURCHES PERMIT DIVORCE?

Though Orthodox churches believe in the essential indissolubility of marriage, divorce is permitted as a last resort, in certain cases, and after all attempts for reconciliation by the clergy have failed.

Typical are the canons of the Patriarchate of Constantinople, which allows divorce only for the following reasons: adultery, fornication or immoral acts; treacherous actions and threats against life by either of the spouses; abortion without the consent of the husband; impotence, existing prior to marriage and continuing for two years; abandonment of a wife or husband for more than two years; apostasy and the falling into heresy; or incurable insanity, lasting four years after marriage.

Remarriage of the innocent party is permitted, though not more than three marriages are allowed. In addition to the civil divorce of the land, a church separation, granted by an ecclesiastical court of an archdiocese, is required.

WHAT IS THE VIEW OF ORTHODOXY ON BIRTH CONTROL?

Though birth control is not mentioned in the binding seven ecumenical councils, it has been repeatedly disapproved of by Orthodox synodical and patriarchal pronouncements and encyclicals.

MAY ORTHODOX PRIESTS PARTICIPATE IN INTERRELIGIOUS SERVICES?

Orthodox priests cannot take part in interreligious services without violating church doctrine.

DOES THE ORTHODOX CHURCH HAVE MISSIONARY ACTIVITIES?

Eastern Orthodoxy was, from its beginnings, a missionary church. Its highest level of missionary activity was reached in the ninth century, when the Christian faith was brought to the Slavic and other ethnic groups in Central and Northern Europe.

When Constantinople came under Ottoman rule in 1453, Greek Orthodoxy was faced with the question of survival. It could no longer send out missions. The Russian Church, however, continued missionary activities in Japan, Korea and the Far East. Recently, the Greek Orthodox Church has initiated missionary activities in Africa and Asia.

Orthodoxy does not approve of the practice of proselytizing other Christian denominations. But genuine converts are accepted and welcomed.

HOW ARE THE ORTHODOX SAINTS CANONIZED?

An Orthodox saint is canonized by the holy synod of a patriarchate, or an autonomous church, *after he or she has been accepted as such by the people*. It is the Orthodox faithful who, in fact, make the saints of their churches; the ruling ecclesiastical bodies later verify the sainthood by official decree.

WHY DO EASTERN ORTHODOX CHURCHES CELEBRATE CHRISTMAS AND SAINTS' DAYS ON DATES DIFFERENT FROM THOSE IN THE WEST?

Because they retain the Julian calendar, instead of the newer Gregorian calendar used by the Western churches. (The Gregorian calendar has been adopted by some of the Eastern churches.) The holidays of the Julian calendar occur 13 days later than those of the Gregorian calendar: thus, Christmas is celebrated on January 7, and New Year on January 14.

IS THAT WHY THE ORTHODOX EASTER IS CELEBRATED ON A DIFFERENT DATE FROM THE WESTERN EASTER?

Differences concerning the date of Easter arose between the East and the West as early as the second century. The date of the Orthodox Easter was finally fixed by the Council of Nicaea in 325 A.D., which decreed that Easter should be celebrated on the Sunday immediately following the first full moon after the vernal equinox (the first day of spring), but always after the Hebrew Passover. This maintains consistency with the Biblical sequence of events. The Easter of the Western churches is not necessarily preceded by the Hebrew Passover.

Once every few years, Eastern and Western Easters coincide, though not in a fixed pattern. When they do not fall on the same date, the Eastern always follows the Western. The dates of the two Easters through the year 1970 are as follows:

	EASTERN	WESTERN
1963	April 14	April 14
1964	May 3	March 29
1965	April 25	April 18
1966	April 10	April 10
1967	April 30	March 26
1968	April 21	April 14
1969	April 13	April 6
1970	April 26	March 29

IS THERE A DISTINCTIVE ARCHITECTURAL FORM FOR AN ORTHODOX CHURCH?

Yes. Orthodox churches follow the form of the cross, with a dome over the center. The interior of an Orthodox church is divided into three main parts: the sanctuary, or altar; the main church; and the narthex, or entrance. The sanctuary should be at the eastern end of the church building. The altar, "the holy of holies," is divided from the main church, which is occupied by the congregation, by a screen, called the "iconostasion," where icons (two-dimensional paintings) are placed, often with metal adornments, of Jesus Christ, the Virgin Mary, Saint John the Baptist, and other saints and martyrs.

The sanctuary is reached by three entrances, the central one of which is known as the royal or holy gate (when the eucharist is celebrated, the holy gifts are brought forth through it). Though unordained men may go into the sanctuary, they are not permitted to enter it through the holy gate. No women, except girls less than six years of age, are permitted to enter the altar, which closes by two wooden leaves or panels, representing the entrance into heaven. These are closed off, at solemn moments during the Divine Liturgy, by a curtain of silken material.

The openings to the left and right of the congregation are called the northern door and the southern door. On these doors are painted the archangels Michael and Gabriel, the guardians of paradise.

Over the holy gate is placed a painting of the Last Supper, to symbolize the preparation of the Holy Eucharist on the holy table. The holy table is covered, first, with a cloth of fine linen, symbolizing the swaddling clothes that wrapped Jesus after His birth, and the winding sheet that enveloped the body of Jesus in the tomb. Over this cloth, a rich material is spread, to reflect the glory of the king of heavens. Under and in the holy table, relics of saints are placed to honor the holy fathers and martyrs. A light, signifying the eternity of the faith, always burns above the holy table.

ARE THERE EASTERN CHURCHES WHICH ARE NOT ORTHODOX CHURCHES?

Strictly speaking, yes. Autonomous churches, among the oldest of Christianity, which differ from Orthodoxy only in minor respects, are known as the ancient oriental churches. The more important are the Armenian, the Coptic and Ethiopian of Africa, the Church of Malabar in South India, and certain Syrian groups. Their communicants are called "monophysites" (from Greek words meaning "a single nature") since they reject the dual nature of Christ, which Orthodoxy accepts, and believe that He was divine at all times, rather than mortal on earth. The ancient oriental churches are not bound by all the seven ecumenical councils. Some of them recognize only the first and the second.

These Eastern churches, however, are not Roman Catholic Churches. They should not be confused with other churches of the East that do owe allegiance to the Vatican, such as the Greek Catholic Church (also known as the Byzantine Rite or the Uniate Church).

DOES THE ORTHODOX CHURCH PARTICIPATE IN THE ECUMENICAL MOVEMENT?

"Ecumenical," from the Greek word *oikoumene,* means "for all the world." In this movement, a hope and plan for the eventual union for all Christian Churches, Orthodoxy has long played a leading part. Dr. Francis House, Associate Secretary of the World Council of Churches, has written as follows:

The Ecumenical Patriarchate of Constantinople has behind it many centuries of concern . . . for unity among Christians. A thousand years ago the patriarchs were already distinguished for their concern for unity and their missionary zeal. In spite of the excommunication of the Patriarch by the Pope in 1054, and of the terrible injuries caused to the relations between Eastern Orthodox and Western Christians by the sack of Constantinople by the Crusaders in 1204, the Ecumenical Patriarchs made many friendly contacts with Western Christians, expecially after the Reformation. . .

During the last hundred years these contacts became increasingly frequent.

In 1920, the church of the Patriarchate of Constantinople issued a call "to the churches of Christ everywhere" to create a union of the different denominations. The detailed proposals correspond closely to the World Council of Churches, established in 1948, which includes Eastern Orthodox churches. The present Ecumenical Patriarch, a great champion of the unity of the Christian Churches, has a permanent representative at the Geneva headquarters of the World Council of Churches.

HOW MANY GREEK AND EASTERN ORTHODOX CHURCHES ARE THERE IN AMERICA?

Over twenty Orthodox groups are represented in America. Most of them are under old-country ecclesiastical jurisdictions, although some are now independent of foreign ties. Their communicants total about 4,000,000. The Greek Orthodox Church in North and South America, the largest of the American bodies, has almost 1,500,000 members.

There are three leading Russian branches, totaling over 800,000. (By far the largest of these is the Russian Orthodox Greek Catholic Church of America, which was independently established here after the Russian Revolution, with about 750,000 worshipers.)

Other Orthodox bodies include the Serbian (200,000), Ukrainian (130,000), Carpatho-Russian (100,000), Syrian (80,000), Rumanian (50,000), and smaller branches of national extractions including the Bulgarian, Estonian, Latvian, Lithuanian and others.

Who Are Jehovah's Witnesses?

MILTON G. HENSCHEL

Milton G. Henschel is a director of the Watch Tower
Bible and Tract Society, the governing body of Jehovah's Witnesses. A third-generation Witness, he was
born in Pomona, New Jersey, in 1920, and began
house-to-house preaching at the age of eight. By the
time he was fourteen, he was devoting himself entirely
to the work of the ministry.

Mr. Henschel is an ordained minister of Jehovah's
Witnesses and has traveled to eighty countries in his
official duties as executive aide to the president of the
Watch Tower Bible and Tract Society.

WHAT IS THE BASIC CREED PROFESSED BY JEHOVAH'S WITNESSES?

The Witnesses have no creed. They follow the Bible all the way, not halfway. They feel the Bible is entirely consistent—both the Hebrew and Greek Scriptures—and practical for our day.

WHERE DID THE NAME COME FROM?

The name Jehovah's Witnesses is found in the Bible in Isaiah 43:12: "Ye are my witnesses, saith Jehovah, and I am God." A history of Jehovah's Witnesses and their service to God takes us back 6,000 years. Abel and other men of faith before Christ are called "witnesses" in Hebrews 11 and 12:1. Christ is "the faithful and true witness" in Revelation 3:14. He designated others to continue the testimony, saying, "Ye shall be witnesses unto me . . . unto the uttermost part of the earth" —Acts 1:8.

Jehovah's Witnesses today are merely the last of a long line of servants of God. They are not an incorporated body. They use the nonprofit Watch Tower Bible and Tract Society, which was incorporated in Pennsylvania by Charles Taze Russell and associated Christians in 1884, as the governing body.

WHAT ARE THE TEACHINGS OF JEHOVAH'S WITNESSES?

That Jehovah is the only true God. His supremacy has been challenged by Satan, who caused the rebellion in Eden and who puts the integrity of all men to the test. God's primary purpose is the vindication of this supremacy. In carrying out this purpose, God sent Jesus to earth to provide the ransom sacrifice and to lay the foundation for God's new system of things.

Jehovah will not tolerate wickedness on earth forever. The beginning of the end for Satan came when Christ took power in heaven as King. This happened in 1914. Christ's first act was casting Satan out of heaven, and this was followed by great troubles on earth. This will be climaxed in God's battle, Armageddon: the complete destruction of the Devil and his system of things, his world. This is the vindication of Jehovah's name and the beginning of the 1,000-year reign of Christ. Then all that breathe will praise Jehovah.

Christ is now in his second presence. He will always remain invisible to humans, but his presence is proved by world events since 1914, which fulfill all the predictions of Matthew 24.

Now the Christian's duty is to keep integrity to Jehovah, to announce the King's reign, and to help neighbors find the way to godly service and everlasting life.

DO JEHOVAH'S WITNESSES BELIEVE IN THE VIRGIN BIRTH?

Jesus was born miraculously, a virgin birth in fulfillment of the prophecy of Isaiah 7:14. He died a ransom to relieve man from sin inherited from the first parents in the Garden of Eden. As I Corinthians 15 shows, Christ died a human body but was resurrected as a mighty spirit creature.

DO WITNESSES BELIEVE IN THE HOLY TRINITY?

Jehovah's Witnesses believe that Jehovah God and Christ Jesus are two distinct persons and are not combined with a so-called "Holy Ghost" in one godhead called a Trinity.

DO WITNESSES SALUTE THE FLAG?

Saluting a flag, of any nation, is regarded by Jehovah's Witnesses as unchristian image worship. Any national flag is a symbol of sovereign power, regarded by people as sacred.

Jehovah's Witnesses cannot conscientiously participate in an act that ascribes salvation to the national emblem and to the nation for which it stands, for, in the Ten Commandments, it says: "Thou shalt not make unto thee any graven image, or any likeness of any thing that is in heaven above, or that is in the earth beneath, or that is in the water under the earth: thou shalt not bow down thyself to them, nor serve them." Jehovah's Witnesses do not wish to incur the wrath of God by acts of worship contrary to his commands. They do not oppose anyone's desire or right to salute the flag. Each must decide for himself what he will do. That is true freedom of worship. The Supreme Court of the United States has so declared in a case involving Jehovah's Witnesses: Its decision was that there is no requirement of the conscientious to salute the flag of the United States.

DO THE WITNESSES DENY GOVERNMENT AUTHORITY?

No. Without governments, anarchy and chaos would reign. Earthly governments have the right to make laws to regulate morals, protect persons and property, and maintain public order. Jehovah's Witnesses obey all such laws, *if* they are in accord with God's laws. When there is direct conflict between God's law and that of a government, they obey the supreme law of God as set forth in the Bible.

WHY DO THE WITNESSES CLAIM SERVICE EXEMPTION?

Because they have conscientious objections, based on the commandments of God, against taking part in the *world's* wars. Wars between nations today are not the same as Israel's wars in ancient times. Israel was Jehovah's theocratic nation, and the Israelites were fighters in God's wars. No political nation today can properly claim that status.

Though not pacifists, Jehovah's Witnesses fight only when God commands them to do so. Since the days of ancient Israel, God has not commanded men to fight in wars between nations. That is why Christians of the first century refused to serve in the imperial armies of Rome. Besides, ministers of religion are exempted from military service by law in many countries. Because the vocation of each Jehovah's Witness is the ministry, all Witnesses claim exemption under such laws.

They do not oppose the desire of any person to serve in the armed forces of any nation. Nor do they oppose the efforts of any nation to raise an army by conscripting its manpower. They merely keep their own neutrality, refusing to break their allegiance to their God and Savior. Their position is that of neutral ambassadors for Christ the King.

Having a good conscience toward God does not make a person a weakling or a coward. Fear of death does not cause the Witnesses to take this position; in some lands, they are executed by firing squads because of it. It takes more courage to stand up for unpopular principles than it does to go along with the majority.

WHAT DO THE WITNESSES BELIEVE ABOUT HELL?

Hell is the grave; it is *not* a place of fiery, eternal torment. Hell is a place of rest, in hope of resurrection, not a place of torture from which one can never escape. Peter said Jesus was in hell after his death. Death and hell will both be destroyed at the end of the thousand-year rule of Christ. Purgatory is not mentioned once in the Bible. It is an invention of men. There is no "intermediate" state of the dead. Such ideas are found in the ancient pagan religions, not in the Bible.

WHAT DO WITNESSES BELIEVE ABOUT HEAVEN?

Heaven is the habitation of spirit creatures; it is the place of God's throne. The reward of spiritual life with Christ Jesus in heaven for men on earth is limited to those who inherit the Kingdom of God. In Revelation 7:4, the number of these is given as exactly 144,000.

WHAT WILL BECOME OF THE BILLIONS OF PEOPLE WHO HAVE LIVED ON THE EARTH?

After mentioning the 144,000 who will go to heaven, Revelation 7 tells of "a great multitude, which no man could number, of all nations," standing before the throne. These are destined to live forever on the earth.

The apostle Peter said: "We, according to his promise, look for new heavens and a new earth." This means the removal of the wicked and oppresive system under Satan and the ushering in of the righteous rule of Christ.

Then the earth will be made a paradise. "There shall be no more death, neither sorrow, nor crying, neither shall there be any more pain"—Revelation 21:4. Jehovah will provide all things needed by the human family, and animals now ferocious will be at peace with man—Isaiah 65. There will be no more national boundaries, no political divisions and no war—Micah 4. It is to such a world that those in the graves will be resurrected.

DO THE WITNESSES BELIEVE IN BAPTISM?

Yes. Baptism is a symbol of dedication to the will of Jehovah. We consider baptism to be complete submersion, not just sprinkling. The baptism that started with Jesus is not meant for cleansing from sin, because Jesus was no sinner—Hebrews 7. Matthew 28 shows that the baptized ones must first be taught. This, with Jesus's baptism at the age of thirty, shows that baptism is not for infants but for persons of responsible age who have the ability to learn.

CAN ANY WITNESS BE AN ORDAINED MINISTER?

Yes, for true ordination comes from God. Jehovah, through Christ, ordains his witnesses to serve as ministers—John 15:16. Jesus chose fishermen, tax collectors, and other untrained men, as well as the learned Paul. Similar men may become ordained ministers today. Jehovah's Witnesses are, indeed, a society or body of ministers.

The public ceremony of water immersion identifies one as a minister of God. It marks him as a person who has dedicated his entire life to the service of Jehovah; it implies acceptance of the obligations which the ministry imposes. Jesus set the example by his baptism in the River Jordan, after which he devoted his life to the ministry. We believe that titles like "Reverend" and "Father" are not properly applied to ministers but belong to God alone—Matthew 23:9. Clerical garb is never used.

ARE BOYS AND GIRLS ALLOWED TO PREACH?

Yes. Youths are not only permitted to preach, but they are invited to do so—just as the boys Samuel, Jeremiah and Timothy did. Jesus was only twelve when he was about his "Father's business," discussing the Scriptures.

ARE MINISTERS AND WORKERS PAID?

Ministers at our national headquarters in Brooklyn, New York, and in the field are voluntary workers. All officers of the Watch Tower Bible and Tract Society and others at headquarters receive $14 allowance per month for personal needs. They are given free room and board. As a means of support, most of the Witnesses do secular work.

HOW ARE JEHOVAH'S WITNESSES GOVERNED?

The governing body consists of seven ministers serving as a board of directors. They are elected by the 402 members of the Watch Tower Bible and Tract Society, who reside in 29 countries. The board chooses one director as president. The present president is N. H. Knorr of Brooklyn.

WHAT IS THE ATTITUDE TOWARD DIVORCE?

Divorces may be obtained only on the ground of marital unfaithfulness. Adultery is a violation of God's law. If a Witness obtains a divorce on other grounds and remarries, he must be expelled from the congregation.

WHAT IS THE ATTITUDE TOWARD BIRTH CONTROL?

The purpose of marriage is the rearing of children. Jehovah's Witnesses regard birth control as an entirely personal matter.

WHY DO THEY REFUSE BLOOD TRANSFUSIONS?

Leviticus 17:10 says: "Whatsoever man . . . eateth any manner of blood; I will . . . cut him off from among his people." And Acts 15:20: "Abstain from . . . things strangled, and from blood." This is explicit.

Jehovah's Witnesses see no difference between being fed blood through the mouth or nose or intravenously. In emergencies, blood substitutes may be used. The Witnesses would risk "temporary" death rather than accept a blood transfusion and incur God's disapproval.

We do not condemn medical practice; there are many physicians and dentists among Jehovah's Witnesses.

Some defend transfusions because they save lives, and refer to Jesus as the greatest example of giving a blood transfusion. This is shallow reasoning: Christ Jesus's blood was not drained off and preserved. What little of his blood was literally shed, fell to the ground. None of his blood was used to put into the veins of someone else.

WHY DO WITNESSES ENTER PEOPLE'S HOMES TO TRY TO CONVERT THEM?

Jehovah's Witnesses preach at the homes of the people because Christ Jesus did and they are to take him as their example and follow in his footsteps. Paul said that he taught "publicly and from house to house."

We believe we have the most urgent message of all time and should follow the example in the Bible and take it to people's homes.

WHY DO WITNESSES DISTRIBUTE LITERATURE ON STREET CORNERS?

Many people cannot be reached at their residences. Jehovah's Witnesses believe they must preach to people around the world before this generation passes away, and they use all possible ways of doing it. Preaching in the streets is one way. The apostle Paul preached in the market places. Jesus taught on the streets of the people. Hence this method has its foundation in the Bible.

WHY ARE WITNESSES PERSECUTED?

The Bible says, "All that will live godly in Christ Jesus shall suffer persecution"—2 Timothy 3:12. Jehovah's Witnesses believe their work is of God. They know their real persecutor is the Devil. They have been arrested, beaten, and jailed in many countries, including all communist countries, where they are banned.

DO JEHOVAH'S WITNESSES BELIEVE THEIRS IS THE ONLY TRUE FAITH?

Certainly. If they thought someone else had the true faith, they would preach that. There is only "one faith," said Paul.

Jehovah's Witnesses do not believe that there is more than one way to gain salvation, or that the majority of people will meet the strict requirements of true faith. Jesus showed that only a minority would be right: "Narrow is the way which leadeth unto life, and few there be that find it."

What Is a Jew?

MORRIS N. KERTZER

Morris N. Kertzer, rabbi of the Larchmont Temple, Larchmont, New York, is a former president of the National Association of Jewish Chaplains in the Armed Forces. In World War II, he received the Bronze Star Medal for "meritorious achievement" as chaplain on the Anzio beachhead. He was formerly director of inter-religious activities for the American Jewish Committee and has lectured throughout the United States on religious education and interfaith cooperation.

Dr. Kertzer was born in 1910 in the "bush country" of Northern Ontario, Canada, where his father was a pioneer. A graduate of the University of Toronto, he was ordained at the Jewish Theological Seminary and pursued graduate studies at three American universities: Columbia, Illinois and Michigan. He spent seven years as associate professor in the School of Religion at the University of Iowa, and has traveled widely in Europe, Asia and Africa.

From 1946 to 1949, Dr. Kertzer was associate rabbi of the Park Avenue Synagogue in New York. He has served as chairman of the Social Action Commission of the Synagogue Council of America and is presently Chairman of the Church-State Commission of the Central Conference of American Rabbis and a member of the executive committee of the New York Board of Rabbis.

Dr. Kertzer is the author of three books: *With an "H" on my Dog Tag*, based on his experiences as a chaplain during World War II; *A Faith to Live By*, a booklet designed for men in the army; and *What Is a Jew?*, an authoritative exposure of Judaism which expands the following article.

WHAT IS A JEW?

It is difficult to find a single definition. A Jew is one who accepts the faith of Judaism. That is the *religious* definition. A Jew is one who, without formal religious affiliation, regards the teachings of Judaism— its ethics, its folkways, its literature—as his own. That is the *cultural* definition of a Jew. A Jew is one who considers himself a Jew or is so regarded by his community. That is the "*practical*" definition of a Jew. Professor Mordecai Kaplan calls Judaism "a civilization." Jews share a common history, common prayer, a vast literature and, above all, a common moral and spiritual purpose. Judaism is really a way of life.

WHAT ARE THE PRINCIPAL TENETS OF JUDAISM?

Judaism holds that man can most genuinely worship God by imitating those qualities that are godly: As God is merciful, so must we be compassionate; as God is just, so must we deal justly with our neighbor; as God is slow to anger, so must we be tolerant.

Some 1,800 years ago, one of our sages taught: "He who is beloved of his fellow men is beloved of God." To worship God is to love the works of His hands.

The Jewish prayer book speaks of three basic principles of faith:

(1.) *The love of learning.* As long ago as the first century, Jews had a system of compulsory education. The education of the poor and the fatherless was a responsibility of the Jewish community, as well as of the family. And the ancient rabbis knew something about the psychology of learning. On the first day of school, youngsters were fed honey cakes shaped in the letters of the alphabet so that they would associate learning with sweetness.

(2.) *The worship of God.* From their earliest childhood, Jews are taught that He is to be worshiped out of love, not out of fear.

(3.) *Good deeds*—deeds that stem from the heart. There is no Hebrew word for "charity" because, to the devout Jew, there is no such thing as "charity." According to the ancient rabbis: "We are *required* to feed the poor of the gentiles as well as our Jewish brethren. . . ." No one is exempt from obligations to his fellow men. The Talmud informs us that "even one whom the community supports must give to the poor." It is interesting to note that, in Jewish tradition, kindness to animals is the purest form of goodness because it is done without any hope of reward.

DO JEWS BELIEVE IN HEAVEN AND HELL?

Jews believe in the immortality of the soul—an immortality whose nature is known only to God—but they no longer accept the literal idea of heaven and hell. There was a time when heaven and hell were accepted in Jewish theology but, even then, rarely as physical entities. A soul tormented with remorse for misdeeds was "in hell"; a soul delighting in a life well lived was "in heaven." The twelfth-century philosopher Maimonides opposed the idea of rewards and punishments for behavior; the reward for virtuous living, he said, is simply the good life itself. (Maimonides makes this point in his *later* writings. He gives a more literal interpretation of the hereafter in his "Thirteen Principles," written at the age of twenty. Thus, Judaism can be said to have two concepts of the hereafter—one sophisticated and philosophical, the other relatively simple.)

DO JEWS BELIEVE THAT JUDAISM IS THE ONLY TRUE RELIGION?

Jews do not presume to judge the honest worshiper of any faith. Our prayer book tells us:

"The righteous of *all* nations are worthy of immortality." We Jews know that there are many mountain tops—and all of them reach for the stars.

DO CHRISTIANITY AND JUDAISM AGREE ON ANYTHING? ON WHAT POINTS DO THEY DIFFER?

Christians and Jews share the same rich heritage of the Old Testament, with its timeless truths and its unchanging values. They share their belief in the fatherhood of one God—all-knowing, all-powerful, ever-merciful, the God of Abraham, Isaac and Jacob. They share their faith in the sanctity of the Ten Commandments, the wisdom of the prophets, and the brotherhood of man. Central to both faiths is the firm belief in the spirit of man; in the pursuit of peace and the hatred of war; in the democratic ideal as a guide to the political and social order; and, above all, in the imperishable nature of man's soul. These are the points of agreement—the broad common ground of Judaism and Christianity that makes up the Judeo-Christian heritage.

The chief areas of disagreement between the two religions are these: Jews do not accept the divinity of Jesus as the "only begotten Son" of God. Jews recognize Jesus as a child of God in the sense that we are all God's children. The ancient rabbis taught us that God's greatest gift is the knowledge that we are made in His image. Jews also cannot accept the principle of incarnation—God becoming flesh. It is a cardinal tenet of our faith that God is purely spiritual; He admits of no human attributes. Nor can Judaism accept the principle of vicarious atonement—the idea of salvation *through* Christ. It is our belief that every man is responsible for his own salvation. We believe that no one can serve as an intermediary between man and God, even in a symbolic sense. We approach God—each man after his own fashion—without a mediator.

Judaism does not accept the doctrine of original sin. We do not interpret the story of Adam and Eve as reflecting man's fall from grace. Nor do we consider our bodies and their appetites as sinful. We look upon them as natural functions of life itself, for God created them.

DO JEWS TRY TO CONVERT GENTILES?

No. Modern Judiasm is not a proselytizing creed. There has been no active missionary effort in Jewish religious life for many centuries. Jews have always welcomed converts who embraced Judaism out of true conviction. Our tradition makes no distinction between Jews born in or out of the faith. Conversion to Judaism is not uncommon today. I have participated in the conversion of a number of Protestants and Catholics to the Jewish faith.

DOES JUDAISM OPPOSE INTERMARRIAGE?

Practically all religions are opposed to marriage outside their faith. Religious Jews oppose intermarriage for the same reasons. When husband and wife disagree on an issue as basic as their religious creed, the prospect for a lasting and harmonious relationship may be harmed.

ARE JEWS FORBIDDEN TO READ THE NEW TESTAMENT?

No. Jews cannot conceive of being "forbidden" to read anything. There has certainly never been a ban against reading the New Testament or any other Christian writings. I have even seen pious Jews poring over the contents of missionary literature; and many Jewish scholars know the Gospels as intimately as the Old Testament which is the basis of our creed.

ARE THERE VARIOUS CREEDS AND SECTS AMONG JEWS?

American Judaism contains three religious groupings: the Orthodox, the Conservative, and the Reform (sometimes called the Liberal).

The *Orthodox* Jew regards his faith as the main stream of a tradition that has been unaltered for the past three thousand years. He accepts the Bible as the revealed Will of God. He does not change with each new "wind of doctrine"; he says that his way of life yields neither to expediency nor to comfort. Orthodox Jews observe the Sabbath strictly (no work, no travel, no writing, no business dealings, no carrying of money). They observe every detail of the dietary laws. They maintain separate pews for women in the synagogue. They use only Hebrew in prayer and ceremonial services.

Conservative Jews follow the pattern of traditional Judaism, by and large, but regard Judaism as an evolving and ever-growing religion. They feel that change should be the result of natural growth and in consonance with the spirit of Jewish law. They regard Reform Judaism as too sharp a break with the past. The Conservative Jew follows the dietary laws, with only minor relaxations. He observes the Sabbath, high holidays, and festivals in traditional ways. But he has borrowed many of the forms of Reform Judaism—such as the late-Friday-evening service and the use of English in prayers.

Reform Jews differ sharply from the Orthodox on the matter of Revelation. A Reform Jew accepts as binding only the *moral* laws of the Bible and those ceremonies that "elevate and sanctify our lives." He does not follow customs he believes "not adapted to the views and habits of modern civilization." Reform Jews feel that faith must be rational and capable of withstanding the careful scrutiny of reason and science. The worship of Reform Judaism departs from traditional forms. There is complete equality of the sexes in the temple. Prayer is largely in English (or the vernacular). There is greater flexibility in the choice of prayers. Instrumental music is permitted in the temple. The prayer shawl (*tallith*) is not worn by the male worshipers.

EXACTLY WHAT IS A RABBI AND WHAT DOES HE DO?

Literally, rabbi means "teacher." The authority of a rabbi is based not on his position but upon his learning. He has no special privileges. He is in no sense an intermediary between man and God. In Orthodox Jewish practice, the rabbi *rarely* leads in the services: it is the cantor who conducts worship. And any well-informed layman may rise to the pulpit to lead the congregation in prayer. There is no religious hierarchy in the Jewish faith. The influence of an individual rabbi is determined solely by his ability to keep the respect of laymen and colleagues as an interpreter of Jewish law. The modern rabbi, like the minister, is responsible for religious education, for worship in the synagogue, for ceremonials surrounding birth, confirmation, marriage, and death, and for pastoral guidance.

IS IT TRUE THAT IN JUDAISM THE HOME IS MORE IMPORTANT THAN THE SYNAGOGUE?

Yes. Many times in history, Jews have been forbidden to worship publicly: synagogues and temples have been closed by law. Yet Jewish religious life has continued intact. The center of Judaism resides in the family and the home. Jews regard the home as a fitting place of worship—just as they regard marriage as a three-way partnership between husband, wife, and God. Our religion is essentially a family religion. The mother, lighting the Sabbath candles; the father, blessing his children at the table; the many happy rituals that surround holidays, the scroll (*mezuzah*) on the doorpost which signifies that God is in the home—each of these is an integral part of Jewish life.

The Catholic weekly *America* has said that "the disproportionately small number of Jewish children requiring public care is a tribute to Jewish family life." Juvenile delinquency is rare among Jews and alcoholism almost unheard of. Though divorce is permitted by the laws of the Talmud, the divorce rate is far below community average. (Divorce is permitted when love and harmony have ceased to exist between a man and a woman, and their marriage has become empty and meaningless.)

DO ALL JEWS WEAR HATS WHEN THEY PRAY?

No. *Orthodox* Jews wear a hat or skullcap at all times—not only during prayer. *Conservative* Jews cover the head only during acts of worship. *Reform* Jews generally pray without hats. In ancient times, Jews covered their heads during worship by lifting their prayer shawls over their heads in order to cover their eyes. This removed all distraction from prayer and made it possible to attain the greatest concentration during worship. The hat or skullcap is the symbolic descendant of the prayer-shawl covering.

WHAT ARE THE "KOSHER" LAWS?

The Old Testament (Leviticus) sets down certain definite dietary restrictions: (1) It is forbidden to eat the meat of certain animals (such as the pig and horse) and certain seafoods (shrimp, lobster, crab and oyster). (2) Meats must be slaughtered according to ritual and must meet specific health standards. (3) Meat products and dairy products may not be eaten together. (The Bible says that meat must not be boiled in milk. This was a pre-Biblical, pagan custom.)

Maimonides, a distinguished physician as well as a philosopher, said that "kosher" food restrictions were health measures—particularly in the case of pork, which deteriorates rapidly in warm climates. He also saw important moral values in applying restraint to eating habits, for if we practice discrimination in satisfying our appetite, we may be more self-controlled with the other temptations of life. Many of the laws concerning kosher food deal with the *method* of slaughtering the animal: it must be done without pain to the beast, with the greatest possible speed, and by a God-fearing man. Incidentally, Jews are forbidden to hunt.

Jews who follow the dietary laws do not feel a sense of deprivation. They regard kosher practices as a symbol of their heritage, a daily lesson in self-discipline, and a constant reminder that human beings must feel pity for all living things. How many Jews obey the dietary laws today? No one can answer authoritatively. A safe guess is that less than 20 per cent of the Jews in America conform strictly to the laws governing kosher food.

WHAT IS THE TALMUD?

The Talmud consists of sixty-three books of legal, ethical and historical writings of the ancient rabbis. It was edited five centuries after the birth of Jesus. It is a compendium of law and lore. It is the legal code which forms the basis of Jewish religious law and it is the textbook used in the training of rabbis. Interlaced with the legal discussions of the scholars are thousands of wonderful parables, biographical sketches, historical notes, humorous anecdotes and epigrams—a storehouse of wisdom which is as real today as it was many centuries ago. Many of the moral maxims of the Talmud have become household phrases: "Give every man the benefit of the doubt." "An ignorant man cannot be a pious one." "Don't look at the flask but at what it contains." "Words without deeds are like a tree without roots—a puff of wind, and it collapses." "Why are we born into the world with clenched fists and leave it with outstretched fingers? . . . To remind us that we take nothing with us."

WHAT IS THE TORAH?

The word "Torah" is used in two ways. Broadly, "Torah" means a way of life. It is synonymous with learning, wisdom, love of God. Without this, life has neither meaning nor value. More narrowly, the Torah is the beautiful, handprinted scroll of the Five Books of Moses (the Bible from Genesis to Deuteronomy) which is housed in the Ark of the synagogue. A portion of the Torah is read aloud every Sabbath during worship. The worshiper stands when the Torah is taken out of the Ark. A pious Jew kisses the Torah by placing his prayer shawl on the parchment (so his fingers will not touch the scroll), then lifting the fringes of the shawl to his lips. The Torah is the most sacred *object* in Jewish worship. Throughout history, men have bled and died to save the revered scroll from desecration.

WHAT IS YOM KIPPUR?

Yom Kippur means "Day of Atonement," the last of the Ten Days of Penitence. It is marked by twenty-four hours of prayer and fasting, during which the worshiper (and the congregation collectively) re-counts the catalogue of human transgressions—pride, greed, jealousy, vanity, lust, and so on. Throughout this day runs the prayer: "Father, *we* have sinned before Thee." Judaism stresses that prayer is not the sole avenue to God's grace. Equally important in God's eyes are deeds of love and compassion. A story is told of Rabbi Israel Salanter, who failed to appear for worship one Yom Kippur eve. His congregation was frantic, for it was inconceivable that their beloved rabbi would be absent on this holiest night. After a long search, they found him in the barn of a Christian neighbor. On his way to the synagogue, the rabbi had found his neighbor's calf, lost and tangled in the brush. He had freed the calf tenderly and brought it back to its stall. The rabbi's prayer was his act of mercy.

WHAT IS ROSH HASHANAH?

Rosh Hashanah means New Year. It ushers in the Ten Days of Penitence during which mankind "passes in judgment before the heavenly throne." It is the season when Jews also sit in judgment on themselves —by comparing their aspirations to their conduct during the year which has just ended. The Rosh Hashanah of 1962 marked the Jewish year 5724. Among the Rosh Hashanah prayers is one which asks the Lord to hasten the day when "all men shall come to serve Thee"— when mankind will be joined in universal brotherhood under the Fatherhood of God.

IS AN AMERICAN JEW'S FIRST LOYALTY TO ISRAEL OR AMERICA?

The only loyalty of an American Jew is to the United States of America—without any ifs, ands or buts. To the Jew, the state of Israel is the ancestral home of his forefathers, the birthplace of his faith and his Bible. It is the haven for over a million Jews—after the agonies and nightmares and murders of the past twenty years. Surely, it is not surprising that Israel has great and special meaning for Jews all over the world. Nor is it surprising that the courage and the pioneering of the people of Israel have won the respect of men of every religious faith. But spiritual bonds and emotional ties are quite different from political loyalty. Many Americans retain strong attachments to the land of their fathers. But their political loyalty—whether they be Irish or German or Italian; Catholic, Protestant or Jew—is and will always be to America alone.

What Is a Lutheran?

G. ELSON RUFF

G. Elson Ruff has been editor of *The Lutheran* for seventeen years, and is president of the Associated Church Press, an organization consisting of 125 Protestant church periodicals. His syndicated feature column, "Church in the News," has several times received the Associated Church Press Award as the most distinguished reporting on religious news in an American denominational paper.

Dr. Ruff was born in Dunkirk, New York, in 1904. He received an A.M. degree from the University of Pennsylvania. He also studied at Thiel College, which later awarded him an honorary Litt. D., and the Philadelphia Lutheran Theological Seminary. He was ordained to the ministry of the Evangelical Lutheran Church in 1926 and served for fourteen years as a Lutheran pastor in Pennsylvania.

Dr. Ruff's thoughtful and scholarly book, *The Dilemma of Church and State,* was published in 1954.

HOW DID LUTHERANISM ORIGINATE?

On October 31, 1517, there was only one Protestant—Martin Luther.*
A few years later, there were millions. The violent explosion known
as the Reformation split the church of the sixteenth century into a
number of segments, of which the Lutheran Church is one.

Luther had been a Roman Catholic priest who loved the Church
and had no intention of separating from it. But he ventured to protest
in 1517 against the Church's sales of certificates, called indulgences,
which were said to reduce the time a soul must stay in purgatory.
Luther had learned from Scripture that full forgiveness of sin is promised
through faith in the merciful God revealed in Christ. This central idea
led Luther to criticize many Roman Catholic teachings and practices.
Soon the break was beyond repair.

WHAT ARE THE BASIC TENETS OF THE LUTHERAN CREED?

Lutherans don't claim any doctrines different from the common Christian faith described in the New Testament and first summarized in the
Apostles' Creed. We are created by God, but we employ the freedom
given us by God to disobey our Creator. The result is continual tragedy
in human life. But God does not abandon us in our tragedy. He shares
it with us.

In Christ, He reveals Himself as the Savior God, suffering punishment and death so we may share with Him in the resurrection from
death. Through faith in Christ, a new life begins in us. It is nourished
by God's gifts through His Word and sacraments. The Word is recorded in the Bible, but the Word itself is a living, active thing through
which the Holy Spirit stirs us to growth in understanding and obedience to God's will.

WHAT DISTINGUISHES LUTHERANS FROM OTHER PROTESTANT GROUPS?

You don't hear Lutherans say, "It doesn't matter what you believe
just so you live right." Lutherans think that a way of living is a by-
product of a way of believing. Since Lutheranism developed from

---

*"Protestant," as a term describing the followers of Luther, was not actually used until
1529, when it was applied to the princes at the Diet of Spires, who protested against the
edict decreed by the majority. Of course, there were many before Luther who protested
against abuses in the church in the Middle Ages; but Lutherans were the first to be called
"Protestants."

Luther's intense experience of salvation through faith, it has been marked by concern for faith as the essential part of religion. So Lutherans, more than most of the other Protestants, emphasize doctrine. They insist on unusually thorough education of their pastors and require young people to engage in a long period of study of the Lutheran Catechism before being admitted to full church membership.

Lutherans do not stress prohibitions or blue laws. They think of the Christian life as a grateful response to a loving Father rather than as obedience to a stern monarch. Such life should achieve a high ethical level without emphasis on rules and regulations. In this, Lutheranism is sharply different from some other forms of Protestantism.

Since Luther had been an ardent Roman Catholic before his excommunication, he was less drastic than some later reformers in abandoning Catholic forms of worhsip. These are retained among Lutherans in a simplified form, and in the language of the people instead of in Latin. Lutherans observe the festivals and seasons of the historic church year. In their churches, they have the altar, cross, candles, vestments, and other equipment of worship which most other Protestants discarded as "too Catholic." Lutherans believe that these forms of liturgy are not required, but are valuable because of their beauty and because, through them, we share in the experiences of the family of Christian worshipers of all the ages. Lutheran music is world-famous, especially the compositions of Johann Sebastian Bach.

DO LUTHERANS WORSHIP MARTIN LUTHER?

Luther had faults. He was of a violent temperament and sometimes scalded his opponents with intemperate abuse. When driven into a corner, in the turbulent events of his career, he made several unfortunate compromises which nobody defends today. Luther asked his followers not to call themselves "Lutherans." The name was given to them by their opponents as a mark of contempt. They called themselves "Evangelicals"—believers in the gospel. Yet Lutherans deeply respect Martin Luther as one of the greatest teachers and liberators of the church. His ideas still stimulate fresh thinking. Every year, Lutheran scholars write many books exploring his thoughts. But nobody worships him.

DO LUTHERANS WORSHIP ANY SAINTS?

Every Christian is a saint. In the Apostles' Creed, the church is called "the communion of saints." A saint is not a perfect person but one who, by God's grace, is progressing toward holiness. Every Christian is also a sinner until the day he dies, even such great Christians as Peter and Paul. Lutherans worship God alone. They do not pray to the Virgin Mary or to anyone but God.

WHAT IS THE LUTHERAN CONCEPT OF SIN?

Sin is the word describing the situation of all people as disobedient to God. Sin is not specific wrongdoing (this is the *result* of sin), but the basic condition of our personality. It is our nature to try to make ourselves the center of our lives. Sin means trying to pretend that we are God. It is refusal to accept the restriction on our freedom which is the inescapable consequence of the fact that we are created beings and that the only reason for our existence is doing the will of our Creator. This is portrayed in the old story of Adam and Eve in the garden, who were not satisfied to accept the one limitation placed on them—that they must not eat the fruit of a certain tree.

HOW DO LUTHERANS BELIEVE MORTALS ARE SAVED?

We can no more escape by our own efforts from our condition as sinners than we could swim to shore if we fell off a ship in mid-Atlantic. Our only hope is to be rescued. Salvation is a *gift* from God. The only thing we can do about it is to want it. Even this desire comes from God.

In other words, when we recognize our fatal human weakness, and are thoroughly dissatisfied with it, we are prepared to let God come to us with His gift of faith. This was Luther's situation during his long "dark night of the soul," when, as a monk, he was trying to do all the things that were supposed to result in salvation. He discovered, when he got through trying to save himself, that the merciful and loving God was waiting to save him through faith in Christ. If people could be saved by obeying laws or fulfilling ritual requirements, they would be saving themselves. Lutherans believe that only God can save us.

HOW DO LUTHERAN SACRAMENTS DIFFER FROM ROMAN CATHOLIC SACRAMENTS?

Luther came to the conviction that the complete sacrifice for man's sin had already been made in our Lord's crucifixion. So the Roman teaching of the Mass as a sacrifice no longer had meaning for Luther.

The Lord's Supper, in Lutheran teaching, is an encounter of the believer with the living Lord, Who is truly present in the Holy Communion to forgive sins and renew the spiritual life of believers. But no physical change takes place in the bread and wine of the Communion.

This teaching was perhaps the most radical part of the Reformation. It attacked the whole Roman Catholic idea of the church as a treasury of merit stored up through saying masses, and of the priesthood as divinely ordained to celebrate the sacrifice of the Mass. In the "priesthood of all believers," of which Luther often spoke, each Christian directly encounters God and receives His saving grace.

Lutherans believe that, in baptism, a person is born into the Kingdom of God and becomes an heir of salvation. It is the beginning of the life of faith in which each day our human nature "should be drowned through daily repentance; and that day after day a new self should arise to live with God in righteousness and purity forever." (*The Small Catechism*, by Martin Luther.)

The remaining five of the seven sacraments of the Roman Catholic Church were discarded by Luther, and by all Protestants since his day, as not true sacraments because they were not established by Christ. Confirmation, marriage, and ordination of the clergy are rites of the church to which no unique promise of divine grace is attached. Penance is not necessary because God promises complete forgiveness to all who ask for it in faith. There is no guilt "left over" which penance can erase or for which one must make amends in purgatory. Anointing of the sick with oil, with prayers for their recovery, is good Christian therapy, but not a Scriptural requirement.

DO LUTHERANS BELIEVE IN THE HOLY TRINITY?

They do, along with orthodox Christians of all ages. God the Father is our Creator. God the Son is our Redeemer. God the Holy Ghost is the Sanctifier and Nourisher of our souls. Yet there is one God in three personalities. It is not possible to make any essential Christian teaching—such as how God could be a man, how the dead can live eternally, how one God can be three personalities—conform to mathematical formulae or submit to scientific proof. Such things are beyond the range of human reasoning and are matters of faith.

ARE THERE ANY SPECIAL RITUALS IN LUTHERAN WORSHIP?

There is no requirement that Lutheran congregations should all worship in the same way. There is wide variation between the ritual of a cathedral of the Church of Sweden, for instance, and of a small country parish in Saskatchewan. The service of confirmation of youth (usually at age fourteen) on Palm Sunday or Pentecost is a rite which has a distinctive form in Lutheran churches. Also preceding each celebration of the Lord's Supper, there is a service of public confession which is characteristically Lutheran. Private confession is practiced by Lutherans in some places but is not required. In the Lord's Supper, the communicants kneel at the altar rail and receive both bread and wine.

DO LUTHERANS BELIEVE IN HEAVEN AND HELL?

The goal of the Christian life is the perfect existence which will finally be ours when we can be completely obedient to our Creator. Lutherans do not believe this Kingdom of God will come through gradual improvement of human nature. Fulfillment of God's purposes lies beyond the limits of our present life. Those who live and die in faith in Christ will live with Him eternally, freed from the limitations of time and space. Predictions about this eternal life must necessarily be in some sort of picture language, for it is beyond the range of finite minds. Naïve descriptions of heaven and hell, which were common in old times, are obviously inadequate. But victory over death is the certain destiny of God's people.

WHAT IS THE ATTITUDE OF THE LUTHERAN CHURCH TO THE POPE? TO THE ROMAN CATHOLIC CHURCH? TO ROMAN CATHOLICS?

We are more moderate in speaking of the Pope than Luther was. For one thing, the Papacy has been drastically reformed since Luther's time. However, Lutherans absolutely reject any teaching that God has delegated supreme authority over the souls of His people to any man.

There is only one church, we believe, but it is not any visible institution, such as the Roman Catholic Church or the Lutheran Church. It consists of all the congregations of believers "among whom the gospel is preached in its purity and the holy sacraments are administered according to the gospel." (*Augsburg Confession,* Article 7.)

As for our personal attitude toward Roman Catholics, we should love them as Christian brothers, however much we disagree in our understanding of the gospel. The Pope and bishops of the Roman Catholic Church often make profound statements of Christian truth and peace. Lutherans know that among Roman Catholics are many of the finest Christians on earth.

WHAT IS THE LUTHERAN POSITION ON DIVORCE?

God intends marriage to be lifelong. He established the family as the training school in which His children may learn to love and serve one another. But human sinfulness crops up in the marriage relation just as everywhere else. Some marriages become so badly eroded by infidelity and selfishness that to declare them no longer existing is less evil than to try to keep them going. Following the New Testament, Lutherans agree that adultery and desertion may be grounds for divorce. Christians should not legislate general principles to apply to all cases. Every case must be considered individually.

In recent years within Lutheran churches, there has been considerable re-study of the problem of divorce. The main emphasis ought to be positive, on the education of people in the Christian principle of lifelong fidelity, rather than on means of dissolving the marriage relation.

DO LUTHERANS BELIEVE IN BIRTH CONTROL?

There have not been many statements by Lutheran churches on this question, but there is no general objection to the well-known fact that countless Lutherans practice birth control. The United Lutheran Church in America in 1956 adopted a statement which included these sentences:

Husband and wife are called to exercise the power of procreation responsibly before God. This implies planning their parenthood in accordance with their ability to provide for their children and faithfully nurture them in fulness of Christian faith and life. The health and welfare of the mother-wife should be a major concern in such decisions. Irresponsible conception of children up to the limit of biological capacity and selfish limitation of the number of children are equally detrimental. Choice as to means of conception control should be made upon professional medical advice.

On this and other ethical questions, the Lutheran Church has little tendency to legislate. The church is not a law-making society but an agency through which the Holy Spirit shapes and directs Christian lives in their growth toward holiness.

HOW IS THE LUTHERAN CHURCH GOVERNED?

There is no pattern which prevails in all countries, because Lutherans believe that church government is a practical concern without doctrinal significance. Lutheran churches in Europe have bishops, but none of the Lutheran churches in America follow this example. Church conventions, which elect presidents and other officials, are the main instruments of authority in the American churches.

The foundation of this authority is in the congregations themselves, because in them the free people of God exercise their right to hear the gospel and receive the sacraments. They cannot be held in obedience to an earthly hierarchy. Each Lutheran congregation owns its church building or other property and is self-governing in all of its local affairs. Men are called to the office of the ministry by God through the congregations, and if they cease to perform the functions of their office they cease to be ministers.

DOES THE LUTHERAN CHURCH PERMIT ITS PASTORS TO MARRY?

Luther taught that enforced celibacy of the priesthood was a mistake. Eight years after the beginning of the Reformation, he himself married a nun who had left her convent as a result of Luther's teaching. (The date is important because enemies of Luther often assert that "he left the church to get married.")

IS LUTHERANISM INTERNATIONAL?

Lutheranism includes almost the entire population of Denmark, Finland, Iceland, Norway and Sweden, a majority of the Germans, Latvians, Estonians, and minorities in most other European countries. Mission work has resulted in Lutheran churches in South America, Africa, Asia and Australia.

Lutherans constitute almost half of the Protestants of the world. It is impossible to give the total accurately. Of the 5,000,000 Lutherans who were in Russia in 1918, no one knows how many there are now.

The same is true in all Iron Curtain countries. Perhaps 70 million would be a reasonable guess at the present world total.

Lutheran membership in the United States at the end of 1960 was 8,188,289. An additional four or five million persons give "Lutheran" as their church preference when they fill out questionnaires.

DO LUTHERANS BELIEVE IN SEPARATION OF CHURCH AND STATE?

In America, they emphatically do. Luther taught that church and state are both ordained by God and that each has separate, clear-cut functions. Church-state separation is a logical application of the Lutheran principle of resistance to the attempts of human authorities to rule men's souls.

In the Scandinavian countries and Finland, the Lutheran Church is the state church, under nominal control of Parliament (as is the Anglican Church in England).

There has usually been some connection between the Lutheran Church and the government in other European countries, due to the historical development of the churches. Yet, in Norway under the wartime Quisling government, the Lutheran Church rebelled against the authority of the state. All bishops and most pastors refused to obey its orders. In Germany also, some pastors were strong leaders in the opposition to Hitler. They quoted Luther who wrote, "If your worldly master is wrong, and you know for certain he is wrong, then fear God more than man and do not serve him." At present, Lutheran churchmen in the Russian zone of Germany are struggling against Communist tyranny.

Lutherans in the United States have been unanimous in opposing the appointment of an ambassador to the Vatican because they believe it is contrary to a basic American principle to send a diplomatic representative to the headquarters of a church. They have expressed practically unanimous opposition to governmental support for church-directed schools and other institutions.

DO LUTHERANS BELIEVE THEIRS IS THE ONLY TRUE RELIGION?

Yes, but they don't believe they are the only ones who have it. There are true Christian believers in a vast majority of the churches, perhaps in all. Lutherans are among the leaders in interchurch assemblies, such as the World Council of Churches, because they are eager for better understanding and cooperation among Christians everywhere.

What Is a Methodist?

RALPH W. SOCKMAN

Ralph W. Sockman has been selected in various non-denominational surveys as "one of the greatest religious leaders in America today." He retired in 1961, after forty-four years as minister of Christ Church, Methodist (formerly Madison Avenue Methodist Episcopal Church), in New York City—a record for pulpit tenure in a single Methodist parish. Dr. Sockman is known as the "Dean of Religious Broadcasters" because of his thirty-four seasons as minister of the Sunday morning "National Radio Pulpit," the oldest Protestant broadcast in America. He also writes a nationally syndicated column entitled "Lift for Living."

Born in 1889 in Mt. Vernon, Ohio, Dr. Sockman studied at Ohio Wesleyan University and received an M.A. in 1913 from Columbia University. He was graduated from Union Theological Seminary in 1916 and received his Ph.D. from Columbia University.

Dr. Sockman has been awarded twenty-one honorary degrees from prominent institutions, including Duke University, Northwestern University, New York University and Oberlin College. He has delivered the Lyman Beecher lectures at Yale and has served as visiting professor of Homiletics at Yale Divinity School. He has been a member of the Harvard University Board of Preachers and is presently the Chaplain of New York University.

In 1949, Dr. Sockman was elected Director, for his lifetime, of the Hall of Fame for Great Americans. He is president of the Council on Religion and International Affairs (Church Peace Union), and was president of the Board of World Peace of the Methodist Church from 1928 to 1960. He is a member of the Central Committee of the World Council of Churches and has been twice president of the Protestant Council of the City of New York.

Dr. Sockman's radio ministry has been honored by the Television, Radio and Film Commission of the Methodist Church with an annual $3500 award, the Ralph W. Sockman Graduate Fellowship in Communications Study, for training in communications for religious work.

In addition to many magazine articles, Dr. Sockman is the author of twenty books, including *The Higher Happiness, The Whole Armor of God, How To Believe, The Paradoxes of Jesus,* and the most recent, *The Meaning of Suffering.*

WHAT IS A METHODIST?

The Methodist Church is "a unique blend of New Testament Christianity, the Protestant Reformation and the influence of John Wesley." Wesley himself was fond of saying: "A Methodist is one who has the love of God shed abroad in his heart by the Holy Ghost given unto him, one who loves the Lord his God with all his heart, with all his soul, with all his mind, and with all his strength."

Methodism began in England as a movement within the existing Protestant Church, and not as a new sect.

HOW DO METHODISTS REGARD THE BIBLE?

They regard it as the "Holy Scriptures." Methodists look upon the Bible as a library of inspired books containing the progressive revelation of God. They recognize the various types of literature in the Bible —law, poetry, prophecy, allegory, gospels, epistles.

Realizing that the Scriptures have been translated from their original tongues, the Methodists make allowance for differences of interpretation. They believe in the "open Bible" and encourage the individual to read it for himself, leaving him free to make his own interpretation under the guidance of the Holy Spirit.

Methodists believe that "the Holy Scriptures contain all things necessary to salvation; so that whatsoever is not read therein, nor may be proved thereby, is not to be required of any man, that it should be believed as an article of faith, or be thought necessary to salvation." [From the Methodist Articles of Religion.]

HOW DID THE METHODIST CHURCH BEGIN?

The Methodist Church was born in the Church of England through the work of John Wesley. Educated at Oxford and ordained to the Anglican priesthood, the young Wesley sought in vain for religious satisfaction by the strict observance of religious rules and the ordinances of the church. The turning point in his life came at a prayer meeting in London on May 24, 1738. There he learned what Saint Paul had discovered—that it is not by rules and our own efforts at self-perfection that man may enter upon life and peace, but only by faith in God's mercy.

When Wesley went forth to preach his new, heart-warming experience, the people who had been unreached by the church flocked to hear him. Multitudes came asking Wesley to teach and direct them. He gathered these people into societies "in order to pray together, to receive the word of exhortation, and to watch over one another in love, that they might help each other to work out their own salvation."

He appointed leaders, assigned them to various fields of labor, and supervised their work. The movement spread rapidly over England, then to Ireland and America. Wesley's intention was not to form a new sect but only to organize societies within the Church of England. The preachers were not ordained, and the members were supposed to receive the sacraments in the Anglican Church. But the Bishop of London, to whose diocese Wesley belonged, would not ordain ministers to serve the Methodist societies. Nor would he consecrate their meeting places. If Wesley's work was to expand, he had to take the irregular steps of ordination and consecration.

Furthermore, Wesley was confronted with the care of his followers in America, where the Anglican clergy had nearly all returned to England as Tories during the War of the Revolution. The 15,000 American Methodists at the close of the Revolutionary War clamored for clerical leadership. Wesley responded to their demand by asking the Bishop of London to ordain some ministers for America. Failing in his request, Wesley himself ordained two men to "preside over the flock in America."

Under their leadership, the Methodist Episcopal Church in America was organized at Baltimore on December 24, 1784.

WHERE DID THE NAME METHODIST COME FROM?

It arose from the methodical habits of the "Holy Club" which John and Charles Wesley founded at Oxford University. The members arranged a daily schedule of duties, setting hours for visiting the sick and those in prison, conducting schools among the poor, and observing the religious offices of the church. They prayed aloud three times each day and stopped for silent prayer every hour.

These strict rules of conduct aroused the ridicule of the student body. "Methodists" was almost the mildest epithet hurled at the Holy Club. The name clung to the followers of Wesley because he continued to stress rules of conduct and religious observance.

WHAT IS THE METHODIST ATTITUDE TOWARD THE TRINITY?

Methodists do not pretend to understand fully the meaning of the Trinity. Who does? Even ·Saint Augustine, after writing the classic exposition of the doctrine of the Trinity, confessed that it still remained a mystery. If God could be fully explained, he would cease to be God.

The doctrine of the Trinity is the expression of the three aspects in *our experience* of God. We conceive of God as the Creator, the First Cause of all things—as God the Father. We think of God revealed historically in the personality of Christ—as God the Son. We feel him as a pervading, continuing presence and power in our lives—as God the Holy Spirit.

The doctrine of the Trinity is also our formula for understanding the personality of God. God is Love, but whom did He love before He created man and the universe? Love must have an object. The object of God's love in the pre-Creation period was Christ the Son, co-eternal with the Father. And the divine activity linking God the Father with the object of his love, God the Son, was and eternally is God the Holy Spirit.

HOW DO METHODISTS REGARD THE VIRGIN BIRTH?

The original Methodist Articles of Religion declare that Christ the Son "took man's nature in the womb of the blessed Virgin." The great majority of Methodists continue to hold this belief. Some would distinguish the biological aspects of the Virgin Birth from its theological implications. Some believe that the deity of Christ does not rest on the uniqueness of his physical birth but on the inexplicable quality and power of his life and work.

Hence, some Methodists do not feel it necessary to believe that Jesus Christ was born without a human father in order to assert that he is the Only Begotten Son of the Heavenly Father. The Methodist Church does not disown this latter group as long as they believe in the Deity of Christ.

DO METHODISTS PRAY TO SAINTS?

No. They believe God is directly accessible to each of his children. Since God is Love, no intermediary is needed to intercede for his children. Methodists, like other Protestants, believe in the "individual priesthood of all believers."

DO METHODISTS BELIEVE IN HEAVEN AND HELL?

Methodists believe in divine judgment after death. Goodness will be rewarded and evil punished.

The concepts of heaven and hell vary widely, according to the educational and religious background of the believers. Some have very concrete ideas of golden streets in heaven and fiery furnaces in hell. But the majority of Methodists are emancipated from the prescientific view of a physical heaven "up there" and a physical hell "down there." They trust the promise of Christ: "I go to prepare a place for you." Heaven is the realm of mind and spirit where the redeemed keep company with God and His Risen Son, Jesus Christ. Hell is the state where such fellowship is absent.

DO METHODISTS BELIEVE IN PURGATORY?

No. Methodists find no scriptural warrant for the Roman Catholic belief in purgatory. They do not presume to peer behind the veil of death or departmentalize the processes of divine judgment. Many Methodists believe that God's punishments are redemptive rather than punitive. They trust the justice and love of God to care for the departed.

WHAT SACRAMENTS DO METHODISTS RECOGNIZE?

Methodists hold only two sacraments as ordained of God: baptism and the Lord's Supper. Baptism is not only a sign of profession but also of regeneration, or a new birth. The Supper of the Lord is the sacrament of our redemption by Christ's death and a sign of the love which Christians ought to have among themselves.

Methodists maintain the general Protestant position of only two sacraments because, according to the Gospel record, only two had the direct touch of Jesus. This does not mean that the Methodists have a weakened conception of other rites, such as marriage and confirmation. These are held in high reverence, but Methodists still limit the word "sacrament" to the two ordinances which Christ Himself performed.

DO METHODISTS BAPTIZE INFANTS?

Yes. We believe "all men are heirs of life eternal and subjects of the saving grace of the Holy Spirit." Christ himself said, "Suffer the little children to come unto me, and forbid them not, for of such is the Kingdom of God."

While an infant is not aware of the meaning of the sacrament, the parents are—and are thereby committed to the Christian nurture of the child. The church assumes responsibility for her baptized children and awaits the time when they will be mature enough to appreciate and assume for themselves the vows made at baptism.

DO METHODISTS ACCEPT ROMAN CATHOLIC BAPTISM AS VALID?

Yes. Methodists believe that the sacrament of baptism is a sign of God's grace and man's regeneration. Methodists and Roman Catholics believe in the same God.

DO METHODISTS BELIEVE IN THE "REAL PRESENCE" OF CHRIST IN THE SACRAMENT OF THE LORD'S SUPPER?

Yes, but not in the sense that Roman Catholics regard the "real presence." In the Mass, Roman Catholics are taught that the bread becomes the Body of Christ and the wine becomes the Blood of Christ, so that Christ is present in body and soul.

Methodists accept Christ's own words that "God is a spirit: and they that worship him must worship him in spirit and in truth." Hence, they believe that the body of Christ is given, taken, and eaten in the sacrament only in "a heavenly and spiritual manner." And faith is the means whereby the body of Christ is received and eaten in the Lord's Supper.

DO METHODIST MINISTERS HEAR CONFESSIONS?

Methodist churches have no "confessionals" as do Roman Catholic churches. Methodist ministers perform a great deal of counseling. Persons often come to confess their sins as well as their troubles. But the pastor does not presume to give "penance" or to pronounce words of absolution. Methodists believe that each individual can go directly to God, trusting the New Testament promise: "If we confess our sins, He is faithful and just to forgive us our sins. . . ."

WHAT DO METHODISTS MEAN BY SALVATION?

Salvation means not only security in heaven after death, but a present experience of God's grace and power. When men truly and earnestly repent of their sins, God forgives the guilt of past transgressions. Also, he imparts the power which fortifies men against future sins.

God calls men to that holiness of life which, as Wesley insisted, is "social holiness," the love and service of their fellow men. Man cannot attain this holiness merely by obeying laws and doing good works. Man's salvation comes by faith and through the grace of God. God sent Christ to reveal his love to men. When men behold how Christ died for them, their hearts are moved and their lives are transformed. They confess Christ as their Savior. He is the power of God unto salvation.

DO METHODISTS HAVE TO ACCEPT A CREED?

They are not required to sign any formal creed. Those joining the church are asked to answer affirmatively two questions:

"Do you confess Jesus Christ as your Savior and Lord and pledge your allegiance to His Kingdom?"

"Do you receive and profess the Christian faith as contained in the New Testament of Our Lord, Jesus Christ?"

Wesley, the founder, once declared: "I believe the merciful God regards the lives and tempers of men more than their ideas." One of his basic principles was, "Think and let think." With its emphasis on life rather than creed, Methodism has been relatively free from heresy trials.

ARE METHODISTS STRICTER THAN OTHERS IN MATTERS OF PERSONAL CONDUCT, ESPECIALLY AS TO AMUSEMENTS?

Methodists today are about as broad and liberal in their codes of behavior as are other leading Protestants. Methodists traditionally have fought against intemperance, gambling and licentious indulgence. John Wesley formulated a list of general rules for the members of his societies because he believed they needed concrete standards as well as ideals.

For many years, the church had a provision forbidding diversions such as card-playing and dancing. This provision was changed nearly thirty years ago to read, "not taking such diversions as cannot be used in the name of the Lord Jesus."

WHAT IS THE METHODIST POSITION ON BIRTH CONTROL?

The General Conference of the Methodist Church has stated: "Parenthood is a Christian privilege and responsibility; and the highest ideals of the Christian family can be achieved when children are wanted, anticipated and welcomed into the home. We believe that planned parenthood practiced in Christian conscience fulfills rather than violates the will of God."

The justifying motive must be unselfish. The children we bring into the world have a right to a wholesome home life. Toward that end, the spacing of children, the health of parents and adequate economic support are factors to be considered. The Discipline recommends courses of instruction for young married couples on "life adjustments and personality problems."

WHAT IS THE METHODIST POSITION ON DIVORCE?

Methodists deplore the prevalence of divorce and seek to preserve the marriage bond by every means humanly possible. However, they recognize that situations do arise where the sanctity of individual personality requires the severance of a marital relationship. They hold that those who have been wronged have the right to a second chance.

No Methodist minister should solemnize the marriage of a divorced person whose wife or husband is living and unmarried: but this rule shall not apply (1) to the innocent person, when it is clearly established by competent testimony that the true cause for divorce was adultery or other vicious conditions which, through cruelty or physical peril, invalidated the marriage vow; nor (2) to divorced persons who seek to be reunited in marriage.

WHAT DISTINGUISHES METHODISTS FROM OTHER PROTESTANT DENOMINATIONS?

It is difficult to say, because modern practices and the growing spirit of church unity tend to draw the leading Protestant denominations ever closer together. The Methodist Church retains, in general, the theology of the Anglican Church from which it sprang. Some Methodist parishes preserve much of the Protestant Episcopal liturgy. On the other hand, in some Methodist churches, the services of worship are very informal. Within the 40,000 American Methodist churches, there is probably as wide variation in types of thought and worship as there is between Methodists, Presbyterians, Congregationalists and others.

Of course, Methodists do have some differences from the other branches of the Protestant Church. For instance, the Protestant Episcopal Church believes that divine grace is imparted through apostolic succession. Methodists do not hold to this doctrine. Hence, a Methodist minister cannot administer the sacraments in an Episcopal church. And the confirmation of members in the Methodist Church is an office not limited to bishops, as in the Protestant Episcopal Church, but can be given by all ordained ministers.

Also, the Methodist Church differs from the Baptist and some others in the matter of baptism. Not only do Methodists believe in infant baptism, which the Baptists do not, but also they baptize usually by sprinkling rather than by immersion. Other differences might be cited if space permitted consideration of the various denominations.

The two most marked Methodist emphases are the inner experience of religion and the social applications of conscience. John Wesley stressed "the witness of the spirit," "an inward impression on the soul whereby the spirit of God immediately and directly witnesses to my spirit that I am a child of God . . . that all my sins are blotted out and I am reconciled to God." Holding this emphasis, Methodism has made much of conversion, revivals and testimonies of religious experience.

The Methodist social conscience has kept the church in the forefront of reform movements, such as the improvement of labor conditions, the inculcation of temperance, and the abolition of war. In the number of missions, hospitals and colleges, Methodism leads in Protestantism.

The Methodist Church also emphasizes the democratic principle in its organization and government. Laymen are increasingly given leadership in the church councils.

HOW IS THE METHODIST CHURCH GOVERNED?

Since British Methodism differs in its organization from that of the American church, we shall speak only of the United States and the main body of Methodists here.

Organized at about the time the United States Constitution was adopted, the Methodist Church parallels rather uniquely the pattern of American government. The executive branch of the Church consists of a Council of Bishops, whose members are elected by jurisdictional conferences composed of ministers and laymen. A bishop presides over a geographical "Area" (comprised of one or more Annual Conferences); there are forty-four Areas in the United States and sixteen in mission fields abroad. The bishops appoint the ministers of individual parishes.

The legislative power of the Methodist Church is vested in a General Conference, which meets every four years and is composed of both clergy and laymen—in equal numbers. The delegates to the General Conference are democratically elected by annual conferences and on a proportional basis.

The supreme judicial power of the Church rests in a Judicial Council, whose members and qualifications are determined by the General Conference of the Church.

HOW MANY METHODISTS ARE THERE?

The 1961 figures give 10,046,262 members of the Methodist Church in the United States, not including 1,663,367 preparatory members.

There are also three main Negro Methodist bodies: the African Methodist Episcopal Church (1,166,301 members in 1951); the African Methodist Episcopal Zion Church (770,000 in 1959); and the Christian Methodist Episcopal Church (392,167 in 1951).

The great majority of Methodists have as a goal an integrated church. Some of the steps by which that will be reached have already been taken, others are being considered. Progress is being made, but many problems remain to be solved.

Methodists throughout the world number approximately 15,500,000 in full membership (those who have passed through a course of training as preparatory members and who have been formally received into the church), and claim a total constituency of 25,000,000 as adherents (those who support or attend the church, or the husband or wife of a member, unless such a person is otherwise affiliated).

What Is a Mormon?

RICHARD L. EVANS

Richard L. Evans is a member of the Council of Twelve of the Church of Jesus Christ of Latter-day Saints, and since 1930 has written and narrated the famed CBS broadcast of "Music and the Spoken Word," with the Salt Lake Mormon Tabernacle Choir and Organ from Temple Square.

Mr. Evans was born in Salt Lake City in 1906. Following three years of church and editorial work in Europe, he received B.A., M.A. (and later LL.D.) degrees from the University of Utah. He is a member of the Board of Regents of the University of Utah, and of the Board of Trustees of Brigham Young University, and is director of Temple Square, Salt Lake City. He is married, and the father of four sons, and travels and lectures extensively.

For some years Mr. Evans wrote a widely circulated newspaper column for King Features Syndicate. He has written ten books, including *Unto the Hills, This Day—and Always, The Spoken Word* and *The Everlasting Things*. His writings have appeared in *Look, Reader's Digest* and many other periodicals.

NOTE TO THE READER: This article presents the doctrines and practices of the Church of Jesus Christ of Latter-day Saints, Salt Lake City, Utah, the largest Mormon body in the world (1,823,661 members in 1961).

The position of other Latter Day Saints bodies should be noted: The Reorganized Church of Jesus Christ of Latter Day Saints, with headquarters in Independence, Missouri (178,514 members in 1962), claims to be the legal successor of the church founded by Joseph Smith; it refers to an Ohio court decision (1880) to substantiate this claim. In 1860, some sixteen years after Joseph Smith's martyrdom, the son of the founder became president of the Reorganized Church, which denied the leadership of Brigham Young and has always condemned polygamy.

The Church of Christ, Temple Lot, with headquarters in Independence, Missouri (3,000 members in 1956), and several groups with memberships under 2,500 (Cutlerites, Bickertonites, Strangites), hold different views on questions concerning succession to the presidency of the Church, the use of temples, and certain matters of organization and procedure.

WHAT IS A MORMON?

Strictly speaking, there is no such thing as a Mormon, and there is no Mormon Church. Mormon is merely a nickname for a member of the Church of Jesus Christ of Latter-day Saints.

ARE MORMONS CHRISTIANS?

Unequivocally yes—both as to the name of the Church and in unqualified acceptance and worship of Jesus the Christ.

ARE MORMONS PROTESTANTS?

No. Joseph Smith (*see below*) never belonged to any other church. He claimed no authority by succession from any other church or sect. He inferred no authority from the Bible. He and his associates testified that they received their authority by direct divine bestowal.

WHEN AND HOW WAS THE CHURCH OF JESUS CHRIST OF LATTER-DAY SAINTS FOUNDED?

The Latter-day Saint believes that the Gospel of Jesus Christ was proclaimed in the heavens before the world was; that it was on earth anciently, and known to Adam and others; but that mankind has repeatedly departed from it (as in the days of Noah); and that it has had to be "restored" in various "dispensations" (as through Abraham, Moses, and others). He believes that the last such "restoration" occurred in the early nineteenth century, beginning "the dispensation of the fullness of times" (Ephesians 1:10).

In 1820, near Palmyra, in western New York, in a period of religious unrest and "revival," Joseph Smith (then in his fifteenth year) related how (prompted by an impression from reading James 1:5) he retired one morning to a grove near the family farm to petition the Lord in prayer. What he saw and experienced is recorded in a widely published pamphlet (*Joseph Smith's Testimony*), including the appearance of "two Personages, whose brightness and glory defy all description. . . One of them spake unto me . . . and said, pointing to the other—'This is my Beloved Son. Hear Him!' " (*See also* Matthew 3:17 and 17:5.) The declarations that followed indicated the need for a "restoration" of the Gospel of Jesus Christ (which many among the religious "reformers" had long recognized).

As a legal entity, the "restored Church" was organized at Fayette, Seneca County, New York, April 6, 1830. Membership quickly increased, and so did opposition. The main body first moved to Ohio, then to Missouri, then to Illinois. After Joseph Smith was martyred by an armed mob at Carthage, Illinois, in 1844, the Latter-day Saints moved westward under the leadership of the senior member of the Twelve Apostles, Brigham Young, into the valley of the Great Salt Lake (1847), into "a land that nobody wanted."

In each move they made, they left behind them homes and prosperous farms and other possessions—including Nauvoo (population 20,000), which they had built from a swampland on the Mississippi and which was then (1846) the largest city in Illinois.

In the two following decades, some 80,000 Mormon pioneers traversed the thousand miles of plains and Rocky Mountains, from the Missouri River to the Great Basin. Some rode in wagons; some pushed all their possessions in handcarts; some walked—and more than 6,000 died along the way.

It was no passing persuasion that enabled them to do what they did or that induced them, time after time, to leave what they left.

HOW DO THE MORMONS LOOK UPON JOSEPH SMITH?

They look upon him as one who was commissioned of God to effect a "restoration" of the Gospel of Jesus Christ and to open a new Gospel "dispensation." They look upon him as a prophet of God, in the same literal sense as they look upon other prophets of the Old and New Testaments (and they so accept Joseph Smith's successors; from Brigham Young and including the present president of the Church, David O. McKay).

Joseph Smith was born in Sharon, Vermont, in 1805. His progenitors were early New England settlers, the first arriving in 1638. His forebears fought with the Colonial forces.

DO MORMONS BELIEVE IN THE HOLY TRINITY?

Yes. The Latter-day Saint accepts the Godhead as three literal, distinct personalities: God the Father; His Son, Jesus the Christ (who is one with the Father in purpose and in thought, but separate from Him in physical fact); and the Holy Ghost, a Personage of spirit (Acts 7:55, etc.). Here, the Mormon points to literal scriptural language. He believes in a loving, understanding Father who made his children "in His own image" (Genesis 1:27), and Jesus His Son is said to be in "the express image of his person" (Hebrews 1:3).

WHAT DO THE MORMONS BELIEVE ABOUT JESUS CHRIST?

They believe Him to be the Son of God, "the only begotten of the Father" in the flesh. They believe in His atoning sacrifice and literal resurrection. They accept Him as the Savior and Redeemer of mankind. They look to Him as the "one mediator between God and men" (I Timothy 2:5), and pray to the Father in His name. They believe that He will come again and reign on earth (Acts 1:9-11).

DO MORMONS BELIEVE IN THE VIRGIN BIRTH?

Yes. The Latter-day Saint accepts the miraculous conception of Jesus the Christ.

WHAT DO MORMONS BELIEVE ABOUT THE BIBLE?

The Bible is basic to Mormon belief. The King James version is officially used, and is believed "to be the word of God as far as it is translated correctly" (8th Article of Faith).

WHAT IS THE BOOK OF MORMON?

The Book of Mormon is not the "Mormon Bible," as is sometimes supposed. It is one of the complementary works that the Mormon accepts as scripture. The Mormon does not believe that the revelations of God were confined to ancient Israel. He does not believe that a loving Father would restrict his communication to one part of His family, to one time of history, or to one land. He believes "all that God has revealed, all that He does now reveal, and . . . that He will yet reveal many great and important things pertaining to the Kingdom of God" (9th Article of Faith).

The Book of Mormon is part of a record, both sacred and secular, of prophets and peoples who (with supplementary groups) were among the ancestors of the American Indians. It covers principally the peoples of the period from about 600 B.C. to 421 A.D. These peoples were of Asiatic origin, of the House of Israel, and left Jerusalem during the reign of King Zedekiah, eventually to cross the sea to the Western world, where they built great cities and civilizations. Ultimately, they all but destroyed themselves in warring with one another.

They brought with them certain records of the Old Testament. In addition, their historians, statesmen, and prophets kept records of important events of their own civilization, some of which were engraved on gold plates. It was from such plates "preserved by the gift and power of God" that Joseph Smith translated the Book of Mormon (first published in 1830).

The book takes its title from a man whose name was Mormon, who was one of the later prophets of the thousand-year period, and who was not greatly different from the prophets of Old and New Testament times, except that he lived in the Western Hemisphere among some of the Savior's "other sheep" (John 10:16). The Book of Mormon witnesses that Jesus the Christ visited the inhabitants of this hemisphere after His ascension.

WHAT DOES THE MORMON BELIEVE ABOUT MAN'S IMMORTALITY?

Energy, matter and "intelligence" exist eternally and are indestructible. And man himself has existed from the premortal past and will continue, with his individual identity, into the endless eternal future.

At an appointed time, after the change called death, man will emerge as a resurrected being with a deathless union of spirit and body, literally following the promise and pattern set by the Savior.

WHO WILL BE "SAVED"?

The Latter-day Saint believes in universal "salvation"—"For as in Adam all die, even so in Christ shall all be made alive. *But every man in his own order . . .*" (I Corinthians 15:22-23.)

The Savior referred to "many mansions" (John 14:2). Paul speaks of the man "caught up to the third heaven" (II Corinthians 12:2), and further observed (I Corinthians 15:40, 41, 42) that there are different "degrees of glory." While "salvation" is universal, "exaltation" (with the highest eternal opportunities) must be earned by obedience to laws, ordinances and commandments of the Kingdom.

DO MORMONS BELIEVE IN HEAVEN AND HELL?

The "heaven" the Mormon looks to and lives for is a real place of eternal progress, with endless association with loved ones, with families and friends. For those who are willfully indifferent to their opportunities on earth, the knowledge that they have fallen short of their highest possible happiness will be part of the penalty of the "hell" of hereafter.

WHY DO THE MORMONS EMPHASIZE EDUCATION?

This can best be answered by quoting three significant sentences:

"The glory of God is intelligence, or . . . light and truth" (Doctrine and Covenants 93:36).

"It is impossible for a man to be saved in ignorance" (*ibid.* 131:6).

"Whatever principle of intelligence we attain unto in this life, it will rise with us in the resurrection" (*ibid.* 130:18).

Brigham Young said: "Our religion is simply the truth. It is all said in this one expression—it embraces all truth, wherever found in all the works of God and man. . . ."

Since the Latter-day Saint believes that the "intelligence" each man attains will remain forever with him, his search for knowledge, for truth, for light is not only a permissible privilege but also an inescapable obligation.

DO MORMONS PRACTICE POLYGAMY?

No. For any Church member, the penalty for plural marriage today is excommunication.

Polygamy or plural marriage was at one time practiced by a small part of the Mormon people. Federal laws prohibiting this practice were passed, but were questioned by the Church as an unconstitutional infringement of religious liberty. In 1890, after the constitutionality of these laws had been reaffirmed by the Supreme Court of the United States, Wilford Woodruff, then president of the Church, issued a manifesto which, upon acceptance by the Church, proscribed the further practice of polygamy.

Polygamy was practiced at certain periods in Biblical times, righteously and with divine sanction. And those who entered into polygamy in the nineteenth century did so with a conviction that it was also for them so sanctioned. They honored their wives and families.

The practice of polygamy was revoked by the same authority by which it had been sanctioned.

WHAT IS THE MORMON CONCEPT OF MARRIAGE?

The Mormon believes that there can be no heaven for him without his family, and if he fully conforms to the teachings of his Church, he enters into a marriage covenant that lasts not only until "death do us part" but continues "for time and eternity." "Neither is the man without the woman, neither the woman without the man, in the Lord" (I Corinthians 11:11).

Such marriages are performed in Mormon temples. Marriages performed outside of temples, by civil ceremony alone, are not believed to be binding beyond death unless they are later solemnized for "eternity."

Marriages with non-Mormons are contrary to counsel, and are not solemnized in the temples.

DO MORMONS PERMIT DIVORCE?

Divorce is deplored and discouraged. "Temple divorces" (as distinguished from civil divorces) may be granted only by the president of the Church, for serious cause, including infidelity.

DO MORMONS BELIEVE IN BAPTISM? CONFIRMATION? HOLY COMMUNION?

As to baptism—yes—by immersion, and by those having authority, according to the pattern set by the Savior, who was baptized by John *in the River Jordan.* The Mormon believes that the symbolism of being "buried with Him in baptism" (Colossians 2:12) is not found in any other form but by immersion.

The Latter-day Saint does not believe in baptizing infants, but only those who have become "accountable" for their actions, at the age of eight years and over. He believes "that men will be punished for their own sins, and not for Adam's transgression" (2nd Article of Faith). Infants are innocent and will not be held accountable here or in heaven for the actions or errors of others, "for of such is the Kingdom of God" (Mark 10:14).

A simple confirmation immediately follows baptism, "by the laying on of hands for the gift of the Holy Ghost."

As to communion: The sacrament of the Lord's Supper is administered in a simple manner. Bread and water are blessed and partaken of by all the congregation "in remembrance" of the Savior, and as a witness that "they are willing to keep His commandments."

WHAT ARE MORMON TEMPLES USED FOR?

All men are welcome to worship in Mormon chapels and meeting places throughout the world. But Mormon temples (of which there are twelve in use today) are not places of public worship. Temples are used for solemnizing marriages, and for other sacred ordinances.

God (who is a God of law and order) has set certain requirements for citizenship in the highest "Kingdom" of the hereafter. But obviously all men have not known the laws and commandments and requirements of the "Kingdom." Yet the Mormon believes that a just God will give to all those who have ever lived an adequate opportunity to hear and accept the gospel and its required earthly ordinances. In the words of Peter: "For this cause was the gospel preached also to them that are dead . . ." (I Peter 4:6). Thus these essential ordinances—including baptism—are "vicariously" performed in the temples for those who have died without adequate opportunity to receive them for themselves. Ancient knowledge of this principle and practice is suggested by Paul: ". . . if the dead rise not at all? Why are they then baptized for the dead?" (I Corinthians 15:29).

The principle of doing for others what they cannot do for themselves is not new. The Savior performed a "vicarious" service for all of us (I Peter 3:18).

WHAT IS THE MORMON ATTITUDE ON BIRTH CONTROL?

The Church has always advocated the rearing of large families, and birth control, as commonly understood, is contrary to its teachings.

DO THE MORMONS HAVE MINISTERS?

Among the Latter-day Saints, there is no "professional" clergy. The Church offers opportunity for participation and responsibility for everyone. Any worthy man may be called to be a bishop or to fill any other priesthood office for an unspecified time, and without financial compensation. For his livelihood, he would usually continue his lay profession or occupation.

A boy or girl of eight or ten may occupy a pulpit for a short talk. Boys beginning at the age of twelve are ordained to an office in the priesthood. There are organizations within the Church that provide for study, for service, and for the cultural and recreational activities of every man, woman and child of all ages. All are expected to participate and to perform some service.

The Mormon is proud of his "practical" religion which takes into account the "wholeness" of man and teaches that "men are that they might have joy" (Book of Mormon, II Nephi 2:25), and touches upon the needs and activities of every day, as well as the hereafter.

DO MORMONS BELIEVE THERE IS CONFLICT BETWEEN SCIENCE AND RELIGION?

To the Latter-day Saint, truth is an eternal whole, and if there are seeming discrepancies between science and religion, it is simply because men do not know enough. And where there is doubt and controversy, the Mormon feels that he can afford to wait for final answers—for truth and intelligence and life are everlasting.

HOW MANY MORMONS ARE THERE?

The Church of Jesus Christ of Latter-day Saints (with headquarters in Salt Lake City, Utah) numbers 1,823,661 (1961) with some 5,000 congregations throughout the world. There are also some schismatic groups with historical and doctrinal differences. The Reorganized Church of Jesus Christ of Latter Day Saints, Independence, Missouri, numbers 178,514 (1962).

DO THE MORMONS PROSELYTE OTHER PEOPLE?

Yes. Missionaries have gone out since the 1830's in an earnest endeavor to carry the message of the "Restoration" "to every nation, and kindred, and tongue, and people" (Revelation 14:6).

This work is done principally by young men about twenty years of age (supplemented by young women and older people also), taken from all walks of life. During their missionary service, they are ordained ministers. They pay their own expenses (assisted by families or friends) and give usually two or more years of their time.

HOW IS THE CHURCH GOVERNED?

The 6th Article of Faith affirms that the offices and organization of the Church of Jesus Christ should follow the plan and pattern set by the Savior: "We believe in the same organization that existed in the Primitive Church, *viz.*, apostles, prophets, pastors, teachers, evangelists, etc.," including high priests, seventies, elders, bishops, priests, and deacons, as named in the New Testament.

The Church has a strong central organization, with a First Presidency of three presiding high priests ("after the order of Melchisedec"— Hebrews 5:10), followed in order by the Council of the Twelve Apostles (with assistants); a patriarch; the First Council of the Seventy; also a Presiding Bishopric who preside over the Aaronic Priesthood.

Geographically, the Church is divided into "stakes" and "wards" (somewhat resembling the diocese and parishes), and "missions."

HOW IS THE CHURCH FINANCED?

Principally by tithing—the scriptural tenth (Malachi 3:8-11).

Work, thrift and industry are taught as the best cure for want. Acceptance of government "dole" or any "unearned" public aid is discouraged. Through the voluntary spare-time labors of men of many occupations and professions, a church welfare program provides means to rehabilitate those in need, and to see that no one goes without the necessities of life.

WHAT IS THE MORMON ATTITUDE ON LIQUOR AND TOBACCO?

A code of health and conduct given in 1833 and known as the "Word of Wisdom" disapproves the use of tobacco, alcoholic beverages and "hot drinks" (specifically tea and coffee). The spirit of the "Word of Wisdom" requires abstinence from all injurious substances and suggests that man should enjoy all the wholesome things of the earth "with prudence and thanksgiving" (Doctrine and Covenants, 89).

WHAT IS THE MORMON PHILOSOPHY OF FREEDOM?

When Joseph Smith was asked how he governed his people, he replied: ". . . teach them correct principles, and let them govern themselves."

The Mormon loves freedom as he loves life. He believes that there is no principle more basic to the Gospel of Jesus Christ than the God-given free agency of every man. He believes that a war in heaven was fought for freedom; that the right of choice is essential to the soul's salvation; and that anyone who seeks to enslave men in any sense is essentially in league with Satan himself.

Further, as to freedom, he cites these Articles of Faith:

We claim the privilege of worshiping almighty God according to the dictates of our own conscience, and allow all men the same privilege, let them worship how, where, or what they may.

We believe in being honest, true, chaste, benevolent, virtuous, and in doing good to all men. . . . If there is anything virtuous, lovely or of good report or praiseworthy, we seek after these things.

With these convictions, the Mormon stands willing to leave all things and all men in the hands of a just Judge and loving Father.

What Is a Presbyterian?

JOHN S. BONNELL

John Sutherland Bonnell is minister emeritus of the Fifth Avenue Presbyterian Church. In January 1962 he resigned as senior minister, after more than twenty-six years of service. He is presently lecturing and conducting preaching missions throughout the nation.

In addition to his New York pastorate, Mr. Bonnell has lectured for twenty years at the Theological Seminary, Princeton. He has also been honored by invitations to conduct ten nationally known lectureships, such as the Sprunt Lectures at Union Theological Seminary, Richmond, Virginia, and the Chancellor's Lectures, at Queen's University, Kingston, Ontario.

Mr. Bonnell was born on Prince Edward Island, Canada, in 1893. He received his B.A. degree from Dalhousie University, Halifax, N.S., and his B.D. degree from Pine Hill Divinity Hall in the same city. He was ordained in 1922 and served as minister of Saint Andrew's Presbyterian Church, Saint John, N.B., and Westminster United Church, Winnipeg, Manitoba. In 1927 he undertook post-graduate studies in London, England, and in New York City, and has since received six honorary doctorates.

Mr. Bonnell served in World War I with the Canadian Artillery in France as a senior sergeant. He was twice wounded. In World War II, he lectured extensively in military camps on psychology and religion and counseled with chaplains and military personnel.

Mr. Bonnell has traveled widely in Europe and the Soviet Union studying the religious situation in a dozen countries. For his wartime mission to Britain in 1941, he was awarded the King's Medal for Service in the Cause of Freedom.

For twenty-three years, while minister of the Fifth Avenue Presbyterian Church, Mr. Bonnell conducted coast-to-coast radio programs, among which was the well-known "National Vespers."

He is the author of ten books including *Pastoral Psychiatry, Psychology for Pastor and People, I Believe in Immortality*, and his most recent work, *Certainties for Uncertain Times*.

WHAT IS A PRESBYTERIAN?

A Presbyterian is a Protestant who belongs to a particular form of church government. The word Presbyterian refers not to a special system of doctrine or worship, but to a representative form of church government. In Greek, *presybteros* means "elder." The Presbyterian Church is governed by elders: teaching elders, who are ordained ministers or pastors, and ruling elders elected from the ranks of the Church.

In each congregation these elders, with a minister at their head as Moderator, form the Session with supreme authority in all spiritual matters in the local church. There are two additional boards in each congregation: the deacons have responsibility for distributing charity and in some congregations other duties have been allocated to them, and the trustees hold the property for the congregation and are entrusted with its upkeep. They are also charged with responsibility for the finances of the church. In some Presbyterian churches the responsibilities of the Board of Trustees are performed by the Board of Deacons.

WHAT IS THE BASIS OF THE PRESBYTERIAN CREED?

In 1643 the Parliament of England appointed 151 laymen, clergymen, and church scholars to draw up a system of Reformation doctrine and government. They labored for six years, holding 1,163 sessions, and produced among other important theological works the Westminster Confession of Faith, which is recognized as the creed of English-speaking Presbyterians. Most Presbyterians accept also the creeds of the early undivided Christian Church—the Nicene and the Apostles' Creeds.

WHAT DO PRESBYTERIANS BELIEVE ABOUT THE BIBLE?

Presbyterians believe the Scriptures of the Old and New Testaments to be the Word of God and "the only infallible rule of faith and practice," and that they are the source of those truths by which men live. They believe in the "inspiration" of the Scriptures: that God spoke through men whose minds and hearts He had touched. They therefore emphasize inspired men, not inspired words.

Most Presbyterians have rejected the view of inspiration, held by pre-Christian pagan writers, that the personalities of inspired men were "possessed" or entranced by a spirit so that they became "pens of God" or wrote down what Deity had dictated. Rather they believe that God employed the personalities of chosen men in making His Divine revelation. Presbyterians do not equate tradition with the Bible. Tradition plays a decidedly inferior role in Presbyterian thinking.

DO PRESBYTERIANS BELIEVE IN HEAVEN AND HELL?

Yes. The Bible and human experience teach that we are living in a moral universe where sin carries its own appropriate penalty and righteousness its own reward, including the vision of God. The New Testament emphasizes the dread nature of the punishment which sin inevitably incurs, the severest of which is separation from God.

It is understandable that men should think of the spiritual world in material terms: heaven as streets of gold and gates of pearl. Similarly, hell has been pictured in such material imagery as fire and brimstone. While these are symbols, it must not be forgotten that they represent a spiritual reality.

All thoughtful Christians will, however, reject as immoral and unchristian the teaching once proclaimed that the bliss of the redeemed will be heightened by watching the sufferings of the damned.

Heaven and hell are not only places; they are also states of mind and character. They have their commencement in the here and now. An utterly selfish, godless man could find no happiness in the Christian heaven because he carries hell in his heart.

WHAT SACRAMENTS ARE OBSERVED?

Only two: Holy Communion (the Lord's Supper) and baptism. With the vast majority of Protestants, Presbyterians believe that Jesus instituted only these two sacraments.

DO PRESBYTERIANS BELIEVE THAT CHRIST IS PHYSICALLY PRESENT IN THE SACRAMENT OF HOLY COMMUNION?

No. Presbyterians believe that Christ is *spiritually* present in the Lord's Supper. Presbyterians do not believe that Christ is offered up in the sacrament to the Father, or that any real sacrifice is made. The sacrament is a *commemoration* of the sacrifice of Christ once offered for all men.

The Westminster Confession of Faith expresses the doctrine in this way: "Worthy receivers outwardly partaking of the visible elements of this sacrament do then inwardly by faith, really and indeed, yet not carnally and corporally, but spiritually receive and feed upon Christ crucified, and all the benefits of His death, the body and blood of Christ . . . really but spiritually present to the faith of believers. . . ."

DO PRESBYTERIANS BELIEVE THAT BAPTISM IS NECESSARY TO SALVATION?

No. They accept this rite, ordinarily performed by sprinkling water on the person, as a holy sign or seal of the Covenant of Grace—an outward symbol of inward regeneration. While baptism is urgently recommended in the Presbyterian Church, and while its omission is regarded as a grave fault, it is not held to be necessary for salvation. The Confession of Faith declares: "Grace and salvation are not so inseparably annexed unto it that no person can be regenerated or saved without it."

DO PRESBYTERIANS BAPTIZE CHILDREN?

Yes—to signify that they, too, are received as members of the Church and are in union with Christ. When these children have reached the age of discretion, they will assume the obligation taken on their behalf by their parents. Presbyterians do not believe that children, dying without baptism, are excluded from the bliss of heaven or the vision of God.

DO PRESBYTERIANS BELIEVE THAT JESUS CHRIST IS THE SON OF GOD?

Yes. This belief is central in Presbyterian doctrine, which teaches that Jesus Christ, the Eternal Son of God, for us and for our salvation became man. Therefore, He is true God and true man: at once the Revealer of God and the Savior of men.

DO PRESBYTERIANS BELIEVE IN THE TRINITY?

Yes. The Trinity is frequently invoked in worship, at every baptism, and in the benediction at the close of each service. When God is spoken of as three Persons—Father, Son and Holy Spirit—Presbyterians do not think of Him as three individuals. That is tritheism. One God reveals Himself in three manifestations.

The word "Persons" used of the Godhead is employed in the same sense as "persona." It signifies a character or a representation. Various analogies have been employed by theologians to explain this doctrine but most Presbyterians accept it by faith.

DO PRESBYTERIANS ACCEPT THE VIRGIN BIRTH?

Yes. A majority of Presbyterians, among whom this author is included, undoubtedly believe that the entrance of Jesus into our world was by a miraculous birth as related by Saint Matthew and Saint Luke. This doctrine is set forth in the Apostles' Creed, the Westminster Confession of Faith, and in the Doctrinal Statement of the Basis of Union of Presbyterian Churches. All Presbyterians believe in the Incarnation—that God was made flesh and came to man in Jesus Christ.

Some find a symbolic rather than a physical meaning in the accounts of the birth of Jesus. They base their views on the contention that the physical details of His birth were not taught by Paul or Jesus Himself.

Presbyterians honor and revere Mary as the Mother of our Lord. But they reject the traditions which have grown up through the centuries concerning her. These have resulted in such dogmas as the Immaculate Conception and the Assumption which, Presbyterians hold, have no foundation in the Scriptures.

DO PRESBYTERIANS EMPLOY THE CONFESSIONAL?

Not in the same sense as Roman Catholics or High Church Episcopalians. Believing in "the priesthood of all believers," Presbyterians make their confession directly to God—without a human intermediary.

The great increase of spiritual counseling has taught Presbyterians that confession is sometimes more searching and thorough-going when it is made to God in the presence of a pastor. Such confession is voluntary, never compulsory; and the confession is made to God, not the pastor.

WHAT DO PRESBYTERIANS BELIEVE ABOUT SALVATION?

They believe that salvation is not earned by good works but is the gift of God. Good works are the *fruits* of salvation, evidence that we are growing in grace and in the knowledge of Christ.

Presbyterians believe that salvation is found only through a complete commitment and surrender to God as He is revealed in Christ. God pardons our sins and accepts us, not for any merit of our own, but because of our faith in the perfect obedience of Christ and His sacrificial death. Forgiveness, grace, and salvation are obtained through a direct personal relationship to God—without the mediation of ministers or priests. Presbyterians accept the New Testament witness: "For there is one God, and one mediator between God and men, the man Christ Jesus."

DO PRESBYTERIANS BELIEVE IN THE RESURRECTION?

Yes. With a few exceptions, Presbyterians do not interpret the phrase in the Apostles' Creed, "the resurrection of the body," as meaning the *physical* body. Saint Paul writes: "Flesh and blood cannot inherit the kingdom of God; neither doth corruption inherit corruption." They understand "the resurrection of the body" as a reference to the *spiritual* body of the resurrection. Paul writes: "It is sown a natural body, it is to a spiritual world.

Presbyterians believe in the Resurrection of Jesus Christ. Our Lord's sinless body did not see corruption. It was transformed into a spiritual body. Saint John in his Gospel suggests that the resurrected body of Jesus for evidential purposes retained certain physical properties.

According to the New Testament and especially Saint Paul, man's body, unlike that of Jesus, will experience corruption. But the body of believers will be transformed into a spiritual body which will be the body of the resurrection. Paul writes: "It is sown a natural body, it is raised a spiritual body. There is a natural body, and there is a spiritual body" (I Corinthians 15:44).

DO PRESBYTERIANS EMPLOY SYMBOLISM IN WORSHIP?

Yes. There was a time when Presbyterian churches were largely devoid of religious symbols and noted for their austere appearance. This was due to the desire of Scottish reformers to avoid everything that might suggest the veneration of religious objects and relics. Such practices were regarded as idolatrous.

The descendants of these reformers, however, came to see that a legitimate use may be made of symbolism in worship and that holiness and beauty are not contradictory, that there is indeed a "beauty of holiness." This change of emphasis brought a return to Gothic architecture, the construction of chancels, the use of organs and choirs, and the employment of candelabra and the cross.

When a cross is used as a religious symbol in Presbyterian churches, it is the cross of the Resurrection—the empty cross—symbolizing the risen, victorious Christ. The crucifix is never employed.

CAN PRESBYTERIANS ALTER THEIR CONFESSION OF FAITH?

Yes. Presbyterians, believing the promise that God's Holy Spirit will lead us constantly into larger truth, have never adopted a slavish attitude toward the Westminster Confession of Faith. While ministers, ruling elders and deacons at their ordination are required to "sincerely receive and adopt the Confession of Faith as containing the system of doctrine taught in the Holy Scriptures," the Presbyterian Church, both in Scotland and America, has constantly maintained its right to say in what sense the declarations of this Confession are to be understood.

The Presbyterian Church of the United States, the United Presbyterian Church of North America, and the Presbyterian Church in the United States of America have all from time to time amended the Confession of Faith or adopted Declaratory Statements as "permissible and legitimate interpretations" of the doctrines set forth in this Confession.

DO PRESBYTERIANS BELIEVE IN PREDESTINATION?

Presbyterians believe that God alone determines man's salvation. Salvation is not a human achievement. The wording of the Westminster Confession leads some to believe that predestination deprived man of all freedom of choice—that his fate was "sealed" at birth. But the Declaratory Statement adopted by the Presbyterian Church in the United States in 1903 states: "Men are fully responsible for their treatment of God's gracious offer (of salvation) and . . . no man is hindered from accepting it and . . . no man is condemned except on the ground of his sin."

DO PRESBYTERIANS PERMIT DIVORCED PERSONS TO REMARRY?

Yes, but with important safeguards. No Presbyterian minister may remarry persons who have been divorced less than twelve months. Divorce is permitted to the innocent party on Scriptural grounds (adultery) and such innocent party may remarry. It is also permitted in case of "such willful desertion as can in no way be remedied by the Church or civil magistrate." In other circumstances if the Presbyterian minister is in doubt as to what ought to be done to avoid injustice, he can consult his Presbytery's Committee on Divorce.

Presbyterian churches are seeking to curb this widespread evil by a more careful examination of persons presenting themselves for marriage and by organizing groups of young people in "Preparation for Marriage" classes.

DOES THE PRESBYTERIAN CHURCH FORBID BIRTH CONTROL?

The Presbyterian Church does not legislate for its people on personal moral issues. Nothing in the Church's teaching, however, can be construed as forbidding an intelligent, conservative and unselfish employment of birth control. The commandment of God to our first parents, "Be fruitful and multiply," was given at a time when the world was underpopulated. Presbyterians do not believe this precept is relevant today when overpopulation in many areas produces hunger and famine.

WHO WAS THE FOUNDER OF PRESBYTERIANISM?

John Calvin, who broke with the Church of Rome at the age of twenty-four, did more than any other man to set forth the principles upon which modern Presbyterianism is built. But it is questionable whether the term "founder" is appropriate. Calvin summoned Christians to return to a form of government which was prevalent in the first century A.D. John Knox, during his exile from Britain, lived in Geneva where he studied Calvin's teaching. Knox was the most powerful single force in establishing Presbyterianism in Scotland, where it is the dominant creed.

DO PRESBYTERIANS BELIEVE THAT THEIRS IS THE ONLY FORM OF CHURCH GOVERNMENT AUTHORIZED BY THE NEW TESTAMENT?

No. While they find ample evidence in the Gospels and the Epistles of their type of government, Presbyterians believe that church polity varied from place to place and time to time.

Presbyterians, in agreement with many able New Testament scholars, believe that no Christian church today can claim exclusive possession of a system of church government authorized by Christ.

After the second century A.D., the bishop came to be the chief official of the Church, supplanting the authority of the elders. This new development gave rise to an autocratic form of church government which in the Middle Ages became corrupt, making inevitable the Protestant Reformation.

WHAT IS THE PRESBYTERIAN ATTITUDE TOWARD EDUCATION?

From the time of John Calvin, the denomination has always stressed the importance of education for the laity as well as the ministry.

In Scotland, from John Knox to this day, the public schoolhouse has stood beside the kirk. On the mantelpiece of many a crofter's tiny home in the highlands of Scotland, where Presbyterianism is deeply rooted, may be seen the pictures of a son or daughter in academic robes. The fact that the Presbyterian Church has always put the Bible into the hands of its people, printed in their mother tongue, has been a powerful incentive to public education and has raised the standard of literacy in Scotland.

HOW IS THE PRESBYTERIAN CHURCH GOVERNED?

The Presbyterian system of church government is itself a representative democracy. The people govern the Church through elected representatives. The layman has a prominent role in the Presbyterian Church. All property is vested in laymen—not in ministers or bishops. In the larger courts of the Church, the vote of every minister is balanced by the vote of a layman. Laymen are eligible for the highest office (moderator) in each court.

WHAT ARE THE COURTS OF THE PRESBYTERIAN CHURCH?

There are four: the Session, with which we have already dealt; the Presbytery; the Synod; the General Assembly. Each has its own function. The Presbytery, made up of ministers and elders, has oversight of all congregations within its prescribed area. The Synod is composed of ministers and representative elders from congregations within a specified number of Presbyteries. The General Assembly is the court of final appeal. It is representative of the whole Church and is attended by delegates—ministers and elders—from all the Presbyteries. An equal number of elders and ministers are appointed as delegates to the three highest courts of Presbyterianism.

HOW MANY PRESBYTERIANS ARE THERE THROUGHOUT THE WORLD?

Only an approximate answer can be given to this question. There is general agreement, however, that Presbyterians—in the broadest sense —number more than twenty million, constituting one of the largest and most influential Protestant groups in the world. We know that Presbyterian churches are found even behind the Iron Curtain. There are, for instance, more than two million Presbyterians in communist Hungary, six hundred thousand in Rumania, and between one-third and one-half million in Czechoslovakia. In the United States there are over four million communicant members of Presbyterian churches. The Presbyterian form of church government is strong in the Netherlands, and by far the greater part of the population of Scotland is affiliated with the Presbyterian Church.

WHAT ROLE DID PRESBYTERIANS PLAY IN THE ESTABLISHMENT OF AMERICAN DEMOCRACY?

So great was the participation of Presbyterians in the Revolutionary War that it was described in the British House of Commons as this "Presbyterian rebellion." An historian writing in the *Encyclopaedia Britannica* says: "The Presbyterians exerted a great influence in the construction of the Constitution of the United States, and the government of the Church was assimilated in no slight degree to the civil government of the country."

Presbyterians are proud of the fact that the Reverend John Witherspoon was the only clergyman who signed the Declaration of Independence. At least thirteen other signers of this historic document can be identified as Presbyterians.

Having suffered greatly from persecution in the Old World, Presbyterians had an immense fear of political and religious oppression in the New. The words of John Knox to Mary, Queen of Scots, the Roman Catholic sovereign of Scotland, were frequently quoted during the war in America: "If princes exceed their bounds, Madam, they may be resisted and even deposed."

What Is a Protestant?

HENRY P. VAN DUSEN

Henry P. Van Dusen, president of the faculty of Union Theological Seminary and Auburn Theological Seminary, is one of the most distinguished churchmen in America. He is a member of the board of trustees of the Rockefeller Foundation, the General Education Board, the Fund for the Republic, and Princeton University. He is president of the United Board for Christian Higher Education in Asia, chairman of the Board of Founders of Nanking Theological Seminary, and chairman of the Interdenominational Theological Center in Atlanta, Georgia.

Mr. Van Dusen was born in Philadelphia in 1897. He is a graduate of Princeton University, Union Theological Seminary, and Edinburgh University, Scotland, from which he received his Ph.D. He has taught at Union Theological Seminary for over thirty-five years and has been awarded fourteen honorary degrees.

Mr. Van Dusen has played a major role in the development of the World Council of Churches from its inception in 1939, and served from 1954 to 1961 as chairman of the Joint Committee of the World Council of Churches and the International Missionary Council. Since 1958, he has been a member of the Commission on Ecumenical Mission and Relations of the United Presbyterian Church. He has been a delegate to many national and international conferences on religion, has been active in the Young Men's Christian Association for thirty-five years, and is a member of the Board of Governors of the Council for Clinical Training of Theological Students.

He is the author of fourteen books and has edited seven more. Among his better-known works are *In Quest of Life's Meaning, Reality and Religion* and *God in Education.* Mr. Van Dusen's latest publication is *One Great Ground of Hope: Christian Missions and Christian Unity.*

WHAT IS PROTESTANTISM?

Protestantism is the branch of Christianity which sprang up in the sixteenth century in the attempt to recover original, authentic Christian faith and life by purging the Church of the West in that day of its worst perversions, abuses and excesses.

WHAT ARE PROTESTANTS "PROTESTING" AGAINST?

They are not protesting *against* anything.

The word "Protestant" comes from the Latin, and means "to profess," "to bear witness," "to declare openly," "to proclaim." Its primary meaning is positive and affirmative. Only secondarily does it mean to "protest" against wrong beliefs, false claims and unworthy practices.

Much the same misunderstanding attaches to the word "confession," the name which early Protestants gave to their creedal statements. It does not mean "admit" or "acknowledge" guilt; it means "a solemn declaration or affirmation of religious belief."

Thus, a Protestant is one who affirms or proclaims his faith.

ARE THERE ANY BELIEFS HELD BY ALL PROTESTANTS?

Yes. All Protestants agree in affirming the following:

Faith in Jesus Christ as Lord and Savior.

The Bible as the primary source of what is true and right.

The loving concern of God for every human being.

Direct and constant fellowship between God and each believer.

God's forgiveness in response to each person's penitence and faith.

The Church as the community of followers of Christ.

The responsibility of every Christian for his faith and life (the "priesthood of all believers").

The duty to discover and do God's will in his daily work (the "divine significance of every 'calling' ").

The obligation to seek to advance the Kingdom of God in the world.

Eternal life with God in the "communion of saints."

WHAT ARE THE DIFFERENCES BETWEEN PROTESTANTISM AND ROMAN CATHOLICISM?

There are many. Most of them focus in two areas—the authority claimed by the Roman Catholic hierarchy and the dominant trends within the Roman Catholic Church.

The Church of Rome claims that it is the only true Christian Church and that all others, Eastern Orthodox as well as Protestant, are schismatics or heretics or both. Neither Protestants nor Orthodox can accept that claim.

No less serious as an obstacle to Protestant–Roman Catholic collaboration are the dominant trends within Romanism, especially the increasing reliance upon miracles and the elaboration of the cult of the Virgin Mary.

DOES THE NAME "PROTESTANT" COVER ALL NON-ROMAN CATHOLIC CHRISTIANS?

No. There are *three* main branches of Christianity: Roman Catholicism, Protestantism, and Eastern Orthodoxy. Eastern Orthodoxy includes some twenty independent ("autocephalous," each-with-its-own-head) Churches, each of which draws its members mostly from one nation (the Churches of Greece, Russia, Serbia, Rumania, Bulgaria, etc.). They are all closely related through a common tradition and liturgy.

The first major division within Christendom came not between Roman Catholicism and Protestantism, but between the Eastern and Western Catholic Churches in the eleventh century. The separation of Protestants from Western Catholicism came five centuries later.

In the earlier Christian centuries, a number of groups separated from the main body of Christendom (the Coptic, Syrian, Armenian, and others) and have continued as independent Christian bodies to this day.

In the last century, a number of new and independent groups—"Adventist," "Pentecostal," "Holiness," "Churches of God," "Churches of Christ," etc.—have sprung up. They are mostly offshoots from Protestantism but are no longer within the main stream of Protestantism. They are multiplying rapidly all over the world. They call themselves "Evangelicals." They are sometimes referred to as a "Third Force"—in contrast to both Protestantism and Catholicism, whether Roman or Eastern.

ARE PROTESTANTS "FREE" TO BELIEVE "ANYTHING"?

Each individual Christian, as a person endowed by God with freedom, must of course believe what he honestly thinks to be true. But every Church, whether Roman Catholic or Eastern Orthodox or Protestant, has its own standard of belief which its members are expected to affirm.

WHAT IS THE FINAL AUTHORITY FOR PROTESTANTS—THE BIBLE, THE CHURCH, CONSCIENCE?

Each Protestant is responsible to God for his own belief and life.

In seeking to discover and do God's will, he turns to the Bible as the principal source of both light and strength, and finds help in the Church as the community of the faithful followers of Christ.

WHAT DO PROTESTANTS MEAN BY SALVATION?

Salvation is trust in Jesus Christ to free the Christian from error and sin, to assure him of God's forgiveness of his past mistakes and misdeeds, and thus to restore him to full and free fellowship with God within the community of the Church.

WHAT DO PROTESTANTS BELIEVE ABOUT HEAVEN AND HELL?

Protestants believe that eternal life in fellowship with God is "heaven," and that permanent separation from God is "hell."

It is doubtful whether many educated Protestants today believe in "heaven" and "hell" as literal physical places; rather, they indicate the spiritual state of the soul, especially in relation to God, after death.

DO PROTESTANTS BELIEVE IN ORIGINAL SIN?

Most Protestants recognize that there is a powerful bent toward willfulness and wrongdoing in every person. Some hold that this tendency is an inheritance from the ancestry of the race. Others are reluctant to call it "original sin" because of what they consider mistaken associations with the term.

HOW DO PROTESTANTS REGARD THE HOLY TRINITY?

All Protestants affirm that God makes Himself known in three ways: as the "Father Almighty, Maker of heaven and earth"; as Jesus Christ, His Son; and as the Holy Spirit, "the Lord and Giver of Life," the "Comforter."

HOW DO PROTESTANTS REGARD THE BIBLE?

Protestants revere the Bible as the inspired record of God's disclosure of Himself to man and the major guide for the Christian's faith and life.

HOW DO PROTESTANTS VIEW DIVORCE?

All Protestants recognize divorce as a lamentable failure of marriage— as God has intended it and as those joined in marriage have pledged themselves to maintain it. Beyond that, Protestants differ as to when and under what circumstances divorce is justified.

HOW DO PROTESTANTS VIEW BIRTH CONTROL?

Virtually all Protestants believe that sexual union is a divine provision, not only for the propagation of children but also for the deepening and sanctifying of the spiritual union of husband and wife. An increasing number of Protestants favor an intelligent and consecrated use of means to assure the number and spacing of children which will best further the divine intention for the family ("planned parenthood").

WHY ARE SO MANY PROTESTANTS BEING CONVERTED TO ROMAN CATHOLICISM?

They aren't. A recent nation-wide survey indicates that in the previous ten years, *about four times as many former Catholics had become Protestants as ex-Protestants had become Roman Catholics.*

The minister of one of the largest parishes in the East reports that about *one-fifth* of nearly 5,000 persons accepted into the membership of his church, during his twenty-five-year pastorate, have been from Catholic backgrounds. In a metropolitan diocese of the Protestant Episcopal Church, out of a total of 1,891 persons received into membership in 1952, 132 or 7 per cent were of previous Roman Catholic affiliation. In a relatively small Protestant church in a suburban area on the West Coast, among 200 new members added in the past two years, 75 were former Roman Catholics.

WHAT DO PROTESTANTS BELIEVE ABOUT THE "SEPARATION OF CHURCH AND STATE"?

All Protestants accept the fundamental American principle, embedded in our Constitution, that no particular religion or church should be "established" or given preferred privileges.

Beyond that, there is wide divergence of view among Protestants as to the most desirable relation between church and state today. Some favor the erection of an absolute "wall of separation." Others hold that the authentic American tradition recognizes that we are a religious people, that all religious groups should be equally respected as important bulwarks of national life, and that the state should continue, as in the past, to support religion—for example, by granting tax exemption to churches and church contributions, and by providing chaplains for Congress, the Armed Forces, and other government institutions.

WHAT DO PROTESTANTS MEAN BY "RELIGIOUS TOLERANCE"?

"Religious tolerance" recognizes the right and duty of every citizen to worship God, or to refrain from such worship, as his conscience dictates.

IS PROTESTANTISM AS STRONG A SHIELD AGAINST COMMUNISM AS CATHOLICISM IS?

The best answer lies in the facts. They are impressive facts.

The countries in which communism or its twin tyranny, fascism, are the gravest threat today are, almost without exception, countries in which Protestantism has *not* been the preponderant form of Christianity —Russia and her satellites, Italy, France, Spain, Portugal, and many Latin American nations.

Even more striking is this fact: there is not a single instance where a country in which Protestantism has been the formative influence— Scandinavia, Holland, Switzerland, Great Britain, the United States— has fallen victim to communism or is seriously threatened by communism.

WHY ARE THERE SO MANY DIFFERENT PROTESTANT CHURCHES?

For three reasons:

(1) Protestantism sprang up at the Reformation, not as a single movement, but as a number of independent attempts to reform the Church of that day. There were then, and are today, four main types of Protestantism: first, Lutheran; second, Calvinist or "Reformed"; third, Anglican or Episcopalian; and a fourth type, variously called

"independent" or "radical" or "free church" Protestantism. All branches of this fourth type stress each person's direct approach to God, the church as an intimate fellowship of believers, the responsibility of the laity, and the church's independence of the state. Among the Communions of this type are the Baptists, Congregationalists, Disciples of Christ, Evangelicals, Friends, Methodists, and many other groups. This type of Protestantism has become the predominant form in the United States and is rapidly becoming so throughout the world.

(2) The large number of different Protestant Communions in the United States is the result of the fact that immigrants from many European countries brought their own traditions with them and reproduced here the churches of their homelands. A good illustration was the division within American Lutheranism into German, Slovak, Norwegian, Danish, Swedish and Finnish Lutheran churches.

(3) In almost every instance, the birth of a new Protestant Communion was due to a discovery or rediscovery of some genuine and valuable Christian insight or experience which had been neglected or lost.

The major branches of Protestantism, therefore, represent not so much opposed or competing interpretations of Christianity, as complementary emphases upon different Christian truths. The number of Protestant denominations is less an evidence of the pettiness of Protestants than it is a testimony to the greatness and manifoldness of God's disclosure of Himself to men.

WHY DON'T PROTESTANTS BEGIN TO GET TOGETHER?

They have and are doing so more and more every day.

Sir Ernest Barker of Cambridge University wrote several years ago, "Our century has its sad features. But there is one feature in its history which is not sad. That is the gathering tide of Christian union." That "tide" began to flow a century and a half ago. It has been running with steadily accelerating pace straight through the present century. It is flowing more powerfully at this moment than at any previous time in Christian history.

WHAT PROGRESS IS BEING MADE IN CHURCH UNION?

In thousands of American communities, competing local congregations have been united. Where formerly two or five separate Protestant churches struggled to maintain a precarious existence, today there is a single vigorous Church of Christ.

More significant, and much more difficult, have been the unions of great national church bodies—that is, entire denominations. In the past century, over a hundred "church unions" have taken place between different denominations in various areas of the world. Some have reunited branches of a single Communion, such as the unification of the three major branches of American Methodism to form The Methodist Church. Many have united churches of different denominational families. In 1925, the Presbyterian, Methodist, and Congregational Churches in Canada joined to form the United Church of Canada.

The most far-reaching church unions have occurred in the Orient. In South India, the Anglican, Congregational, Methodist, and Presbyterian-Reformed groups united in 1947 to constitute the Church of South India. In Japan, the Church of Christ embraces more than a score of previously separate bodies, and now includes about 50 per cent of all Christians in Japan. In different parts of the world, Baptists, Congregationalists, Christians, Episcopalians, Methodists, Presbyterians —all the major Protestant denominations except the Lutherans—have participated in mergers.

WHAT IS THE "ECUMENICAL MOVEMENT"?

"Ecumenical" means "embracing the whole world."

The Ecumenical Movement includes every aspect of the effort for larger Christian fellowship and cooperation throughout the world. It has a double objective: (1) to extend Christianity to all the peoples of the earth, and (2) to unite the many Christian Churches in fellowship and cooperative action.

Christian missions and *Christian unity* are the two closely interrelated phases of Ecumenical Christianity.

WHAT IS THE WORLD COUNCIL OF CHURCHES?

It is "a fellowship of churches which confess the Lord Jesus Christ as God and Savior according to the Scriptures and therefore seek to fulfill together their common calling to the glory of the one God, Father, Son, and Holy Spirit." Projected in 1938, it maintained a difficult yet vigorous existence as a body "in process of formation" all through the strains of World War II. The World Council of Churches increased its membership year by year, holding its member-churches on both sides of every battlefront in constant communication. It was formally instituted at Amsterdam in 1948, held its Second Assembly in Evanston, Illinois, in 1954, and its Third Assembly in New Delhi, India, in 1961.

The World Council is *not* an exclusively Protestant organization. Its membership is drawn from Eastern Orthodoxy as well as Protestantism. At present, it includes 198 member churches (denominations) in over 50 countries on every continent. These include almost all the major Protestant Communions (exceptions: Southern Baptists and Missouri Synod Lutherans in the United States, three Dutch Reformed Churches in South Africa, the Churches in China) and an increasing number of representatives of Eastern Orthodoxy. In total memberships, the World Council accounts for about one-third of all the Christians in the world.

ARE ROMAN CATHOLICS AND PROTESTANTS DRAWING CLOSER TOGETHER?

When this book was first published seven years ago, the answer to this question was "No." Today, the answer is emphatically "Yes."

In the past few years, an historic change has taken place in the official attitude of Roman Catholic leaders toward Protestants and Orthodox. This has been warmly welcomed and reciprocated by leading Protestants. The example of the leadership has encouraged a very considerable multiplication of friendly contacts and conversations at lower levels. Indeed, one of the most striking and heartening features of Christendom today is the growth of what is often called a "Catholic-Protestant Dialogue." This does not imply any fundamental change in the official claims of the Roman Catholic Church, with respect to other Christian Churches, but it does reflect a radical alteration in the personal relations of spokesmen and laymen of the major branches of Christendom.

WHAT IS THE ATTITUDE OF THE ROMAN CATHOLIC CHURCH TOWARD MOVEMENTS FOR CHRISTIAN UNITY?

In the early years of the Christian unity development, the Vatican maintained benevolent interest. The Pope was invited to participate. In explaining the necessity for a negative reply, he expressed sympathetic good wishes. At the early Christian unity conferences, numbers of Roman Catholics were welcomed as observers; local Catholic bishops entertained the delegates and authorized prayers for the outcome of the conferences.

But as the Ecumenical Movement grew in extent and strength, the attitude of the Vatican appeared to cool and stiffen. At the First Assembly of the World Council of Churches at Amsterdam in 1948, visitors' seats were reserved for Catholics, and a considerable number of individual Catholics applied; but a short time before the Assembly opened, an edict from the Vatican forbade the attendance of any Catholic.

Then, with the accession of the present Pope, John XXIII, a re-reversal of policy has taken place. The Pope has welcomed various representatives of other Churches in private conversations. The Catholic Church has manifested a greatly quickened and much more sympathetic interest in the Ecumenical Movement. Catholic scholars have published several excellent studies of the World Council of Churches. Perhaps most significant, the Vatican appointed five official "Observers" to attend the World Council Assembly at New Delhi, and Protestant and Orthodox Observers will attend the "Ecumenical Council" which Pope John XXIII summoned in the autumn of 1962. It would be unwise to exaggerate the possibilities of these developments for ultimate Roman Catholic-Protestant union, but they do indicate a new and promising era of Catholic-Protestant *rapprochement*.

WHAT ARE THE POSSIBILITIES OF ULTIMATE ROMAN CATHOLIC-PROTESTANT UNION?

None whatever, so long as the Vatican holds to its claim of exclusive and absolute authority and insists that other Christian churches acknowledge that claim.

WHAT IS THE MOST PROMISING PATHWAY TO CHRISTIAN UNITY?

It is not through the acceptance by all other churches of the exclusive claims of any one of them. Rather, it is through each church recognizing that its understanding of Christian truth, while important, is partial and needs to be completed by joining with those of other Christians to constitute a larger whole. This "principle of comprehension" is accepted by the official spokesmen of almost all non-Roman Christian bodies. At one of the earliest great modern church conferences on Christian unity, at Lausanne in 1927, this principle was unanimously set forth in words which have been reaffirmed repeatedly since:

We therefore recognize that these several elements must all . . .

have an appropriate place in the order of life of a reunited Church, and that each separate Communion, recalling the abundant blessing vouchsafed to its ministry in the past, should gladly bring to the common life of the united Church its own spiritual treasures.

This statement is the accepted signpost to Christian unity among Protestants.

What Is a Quaker?

RICHMOND P. MILLER

Richmond P. Miller has been secretary of the Central
Philadelphia Monthly Meeting, and of the Philadelphia
Yearly Meeting of the Religious Society of Friends,
since 1939. He is a vice-president of the Historical
Society of Pennsylvania and a former president of the
Friends Social Union. An active officer of the Greater
Philadelphia Council of Churches, he also serves on
the boards of the National Council of Churches and the
World Council of Churches.

Mr. Miller was born in Reading, Pennsylvania, in
1902 and studied at Swarthmore College, Harvard
College and Woodbrooke Graduate School in England. He has been a member of the faculty of Swarthmore College, and was Director of Religious Interests
at the George School. He is a Fellow of the National
Council on Religion in Higher Education and a member of many Quaker boards and committees, including
the American Friends Service Committee and the
Friends Committee on National Legislation.

As secretary of the Friends William Penn Committee,
Mr. Miller has visited Friends centers abroad. In 1952,
he was a leader of the Friends World Conference at
Oxford, which commemorated the 300th anniversary
of the founding of the Quaker movement.

His writings have appeared in numerous magazines,
newspapers and anthologies, and he was the editor of
The Quaker Persuasion. He writes *The Messenger* magazine for the Philadelphia Yearly Meeting of Friends.

NOTE TO THE READER: American Quakerism split into two groups in 1827-28 be-
cause of differences concerning evangelical and "mystical" emphases. The more
"evangelical" group became the Five Years Meeting; the more "liberal" group
became the Friends General Conference.

The major difference between the branches of Quakerism probably lies in the
services of worship. This article describes the distinctive practices followed in the
so-called liberal group, in many conservative meetings, and in numerous inde-
pendent meetings. These practices are fairly characteristic of Friends meetings
throughout the world.

But it should be noted that some Quaker groups use "the pastoral system," in
which an employed pastor conducts services which resemble those of most Protes-
tant churches (except for the Lord's Supper and the celebration of baptism). There
is acknowledgment among Friends of their diversities, but all branches of Quakerism
meet and work amicably—in the American Friends Service Committee, the Friends
World Committee for Consultation, and world conferences.

WHAT DOES A QUAKER BELIEVE?

A Quaker is a member of the Religious Society of Friends, a world-wide fellowship of those who believe that there is "that of God in every man." Quakers hold that the worship of God is the primary purpose of the religious life. For non-Friends, this is accomplished by receiving sacraments, performing rituals, listening to sermons, reading from the Scriptures, singing sacred music. For Friends, group worship is a fellow-ship of the spirit—based on silent communion without any program, yet resulting in vocal prayer, "witness," testimony or exhortation. Quakers believe that God speaks to all men and women through the still, small inner voice. This was true not only in the past. God speaks also in the present; his revelation is continuing. That is the Quaker contribution to religious experience.

WHAT DOES "QUAKER" MEAN?

"Quaker" was the nickname given to the followers of George Fox in seventeenth-century England when, at a magistrate's trial in Derby, they trembled at the word of God. Early Quakers called themselves "Children of the Light" and "Friends in the Truth." They might have been styled "Seekers," for they were searching for religious truth. Quakers arose as a group in the century after Martin Luther and carried the Protestant Reformation to its logical conclusion.

DO THEY CONSIDER THEMSELVES PROTESTANTS?

Quakers consider themselves a "third way" of Christians, emphasizing fundamentals differently from Roman Catholics and Protestants. Roman Catholics emphasize Church authority, the hierarchy and an absolute creed. Protestant denominations emphasize one or another interpretation of religion as found in the Holy Bible. But the Society of Friends puts its mark on religion as a fellowship of the Spirit, a movement which can and does grow, develop, and change because it has within it the inward power of expansion. To Friends, all those who do the will of the Father are brethren of Jesus in the Spirit.

WHAT ARE THE BASIC TENETS OF QUAKER FAITH?

The faith of a Friend is simple and rests on absolute sincerity. Quakers believe that God can be approached and experienced by the individual directly—without any intermediary priest or preacher. God is experienced through the "Inward Light," which is the spirit of "Christ Within." From this contact, God's will is determined, direction is given for all human affairs, and the power to live the abundant life is shared. This is a universal grace. "The Quakers, of all Christian bodies, have remained nearest to the teaching and example of Christ," wrote the Anglican prelate Dean William Ralph Inge. Many Friends are embarrassed when such praise is poured upon them. After all, they are human followers of the "Way of Christ," and know they are fallible and weak in performance. But Friends know what kind of Christians they *ought* to be.

DO THE QUAKERS HAVE A CREED?

No, not a written or spoken formal creed. They do have deep and strong beliefs. The Society never requires of its members the acceptance of any formula of belief. Friends hold that the basis of religious fellowship is an inward, personal experience. The essentials of Quaker unity are the love of God and the love of man, conceived and practiced in the spirit of Jesus Christ. George Macaulay Trevelyan put it this way·

The finer essence of George Fox's queer teaching was surely this —that Christian qualities matter much more than Christian dogmas. No church or sect had ever made that its living rule before. To maintain the Christian quality in the world of business and domestic life, and to maintain it without hypocrisy, was the great achievement of these extraordinary people.

WHAT IS THE "INWARD LIGHT"?

The "Inward Light" is not conscience. It is what Quakers call "that of God" in every man. It instructs and transforms the conscience as the true guide of life. Most often it is termed the "Inner Light" or the "Light Within." It exists in all men and women. It resembles the doctrine of the Holy Spirit. But to Quakers, it is known directly, without any mediation by any prophet or priest. For Friends, it is the source of all reality in religion, leading immediately to the experience of God.

DO THE FRIENDS HAVE AN ORDAINED CLERGY?

From the beginning, Friends have believed that everyone has the potentiality to become a minister. Among Friends, there is no division between clergy and laity. The vocation of every Friend is to be a lay minister and to practice the free ministry of all laymen. (That includes women.) Overseers, and sometimes elders, are appointed to serve each meeting on suggestions by a nominating committee.

Individual Friends are given the "oversight" of the religious meetings for worship, for marriage, and for memorial services at the time of death. All meetings have a recorder who is responsible for the careful keeping of all vital statistics. Overseers look after the pastoral care of the membership. When a minister is found to be gifted in the ministry, then he (or she) is recommended in some meetings to be recorded (as it were, in the ministry), and a record kept of these names.

HOW DO QUAKERS WORSHIP?

The "Meeting for Worship" is a form of church service that has no fixed, pre-arranged character. It is held without ritual or an ordained minister, and with no outward sacraments or formalized program. It takes place in a meeting house without a steeple, stained-glass windows, altar, reredos or organ.

Friends gather at the appointed time "on the basis of silence." Out of their silent waiting may flow spiritual messages, vocal prayer, Bible reading, or ministry—from anyone who feels called to participate. After about an hour of worship, the meeting is broken by everyone shaking hands with the neighbor who sits beside him, following the lead of those Friends who have been appointed to have oversight of the meeting, and who sit on the benches facing the meeting.

It should be emphasized that the form of Quaker worship and ministry is not prescribed or uniform. In some parts of the United States, Meetings for Worship differ from the description given above. Where Quaker meetings follow a programmed system, they are called "Pastoral Meetings."

WHAT IS MEANT BY THE QUAKER "WITNESS"?

An essential part of the Quaker tradition is that all members bear individual and group witness to their principles by the simplicity, integrity, uprightness, and directness they exhibit in personal life and in their dealing with all peoples. The outward expression of Quaker beliefs is found in group testimonies against war, for penal reform, against capital punishment; in opposition to slavery and all forms of discrimination and segregation; in efforts for better intercultural relations, a more Christian economic and social order, intelligent treatment of the mentally ill, equality for women, and in opposition to the use of alcohol and gambling.

WHAT IS THE "MEETING FOR BUSINESS"?

The affairs connected with organization are discussed at a "Meeting for Business," at another time than on First-day (Sunday) morning. Pure democracy is practiced in all decisions, which are recorded in minutes written by the clerk of the meeting. There is no vote. The clerk takes down "the sense of the meeting" after full discussion has reached agreement. The local meeting is the Monthly Meeting; groups in a particular district form a Quarterly Meeting; the Yearly Meeting is the inclusive body for all meetings in a region. In the United States and Canada, there are 25 Yearly Meetings and four regional conferences that meet annually, comprising over 1,000 Monthly Meetings.

HOW DO QUAKERS TRY TO CONVERT OTHERS TO THEIR FAITH?

Friends are always alert to discover those who are in unity with them and nurture them until they are accorded full membership—following a written request of the applicant to become a member.

New members are called "convinced." Those whose parents are Friends acquire membership by right of birth and are called "birthright" members.

HOW DID THE QUAKER MOVEMENT BEGIN?

A schoolboy once wrote: "The Quakers are a peculiar people invented by Oliver Cromwell. They are a quiet people, do not fight, and never answer back. My father is a Quaker. My mother is not!" This is amusing but not true.

Quakerism sprang up in England's Lake District during the turbulent seventeenth century. It spread quickly after 1652. There were several sects which protested against the religious hierarchy, the domination of the church by the state, excessive formalism in religious doctrine, and elaborate rituals in religious ceremonies. Friends suffered imprisonment, mob violence, loss of property, and severe persecution. (In Massachusetts, they were banished or put to death.) Yet all this only fired them into a remarkable band of "publishers of Truth." It was a heroic period similar to the days of early Christian persecution by the Romans.

The great American philosopher William James wrote:

The Quaker religion which George Fox founded is something which it is impossible to overpraise. In a day of shams, it was a religion of veracity rooted in spiritual inwardness, and a return to something more like the original gospel truth than men had ever known in England. So far as our Christian sects today are evolving, they are simply reverting in essence to the position which Fox and the early Quakers so long ago assumed.

Among Friends who have won a high place in American life are William Penn, Herbert Hoover, John Woolman, Lucretia Mott, John Greenleaf Whittier, Senator Paul H. Douglas and Vice-President Richard M. Nixon.

WHAT IS MEANT BY THE "PLAIN" LANGUAGE?

A characteristic of early Friends which has persisted through three centuries is the "plain" language—which means refusing to use "you," the plural form, in addressing one person. (This differentiated plain people from those of noble status in the seventeenth century.) Quakers went back to Biblical Christianity and used "thee" and "thou." Friends also replaced the customary names of the months and days of the week because of their pagan origins. Even today, they use "First-day" for Sunday or "Fourth-day" for Wednesday, "First month" for January or "Third month" for March. Use of the plain language is now generally confined to conversations among members of the Society of Friends and in intimate family life.

WHAT IS THE "PLAIN" DRESS?

The early Friends refused to doff their hats, as a sign either of honor or respect, except in prayer to God. For both of these customs, they suffered bitter ridicule and persecution. When William Penn, whose father was an admiral, a general, and a courtier, first visited the court after his conversion to Quakerism, he advanced to meet King Charles II with his conscience dictating that he keep his hat upon his head. The King, with a smile, removed his own hat. Whereupon Penn asked with surprise, "Friend Charles, wherefore dost thou uncover thyself?" "Friend Penn," King Charles replied, "it is the custom of this place for only one man to wear a hat at a time."

"Hat honor" no longer prevails; Friends today follow custom in tipping their hats. But there are still some Friends who wear hats into meeting and take them off only when they rise to pray in the presence of the Lord. In like manner, Quaker simplicity in dress and color (gray for the women and black for the men) has largely disappeared—because of the disappearance of the trimmings and foppery which separated the plain people of God from "the world's people" in the seventeenth century. Some women Friends still wear plain dresses and sugar-scoop bonnets, while their men use plain gray suits, without lapels or useless buttons, no neckties and broad-brimmed plain hats.

WHY DO QUAKERS OBJECT TO SWEARING IN COURTS?

Instead of swearing to the truth, Quakers affirm that they are telling the truth. The Quaker stand against judicial oaths has caused them great trouble throughout their history. The objection to swearing an oath was once the one way to catch Quakers and persecute them legally. Objection to swearing is in conformity with Biblical injunctions to "Swear not at all" and "Above all things my brethren, swear not."

Besides, swearing to the truth implies a double standard of truth: If one tells the truth *only* when under oath, then obviously a man's word is not good unless he is under oath. Quakers believe in telling the truth at all times. Today, laws permit affirmations in court, instead of the conventional oath.

HOW DO QUAKERS GET MARRIED?

Friends practice a simple wedding ceremony without music or ritual, held in connection with a Meeting for Worship. The bride and the groom "marry each other" in the presence of God. Their families and their friends are witnesses. Permission is obtained from the meeting to secure "oversight" of the marriage, called "passing meeting." In Pennsylvania and other states, a special marriage-license form certifies to a legal marriage. This form is signed by witnesses, rather than an ordained minister or official.

After the legal license has been obtained, the couple go to the meeting house on the appointed wedding day. The bride and groom repeat their vows to each other. The certificate of marriage is read publicly. The certificate is signed by all who witnessed the marriage. The whole ceremony is in the form of a Meeting for Worship. Prayer may be offered, poetry recited, or a message given suitable to the occasion. Silent waiting bathes all those present. After the meeting, there is a reception for the newly married couple.

DO QUAKERS PERMIT DIVORCE?

Divorce is contrary to the "Discipline of Friends." Marriages are promises to love, cherish, and obey until death. Since divorce is legal, however, there *are* divorces within the Society—but not nearly as frequently as would be expected statistically.

Quakers have committees on family relationships and offer marriage counsel to deal constructively with family problems and prevent family breakdown. Marriage study, education, advice, and Friendly interest apply to the entire membership—not only to those in marital difficulties.

WHAT IS THE QUAKER POSITION ON BIRTH CONTROL?

This is a matter for the individual conscience. Friends, like other Christians, have always regarded marriage as a continuing religious sacrament, not merely a civil contract. Education for marriage and parenthood has long been a concern of Quakers, particularly as part of their stand for the equality of women and the religious basis of all family relationships.

WHAT DO QUAKERS BELIEVE ABOUT SIN?

For over 300 years, the Quakers have pointed to the inherent goodness in men and women, instead of emphasizing the inheritance of sin from the fall of Adam and Eve as recorded in the Bible. In this, Friends oppose the views of both Catholics and the majority of Protestants. Roman Catholics hold that it is the high calling of the Church, through its sacraments, to save its members from sin. The majority of Protestants regard sin as the fundamental fact of man's life on earth and hold that the will of God is discovered through faith, not reason.

Quakers believe that while sin is a fact in life, it is best described as existing in a universe like a checkerboard of black (sin) and white (goodness) squares. But the black squares are imposed on the basic white squares, not the reverse. There is an "ocean of light over the ocean of darkness," George Fox said. To Friends, the term "original sin" overemphasizes the power of evil. Even when he is fallen, man still belongs to God, who continues to appeal to the goodness within him.

WHAT THEN IS THE SOLUTION TO EVIL IN THE WORLD?

The Quakers believe that evil is destroyed by "concern." Everywhere Quakers "have a concern"—to eliminate war, to make for righteousness in economic and political life, to treat all humans as equals on the basis of freedom, to stimulate education, to bear witness to the testimonies of integrity, simplicity, sincerity in every walk of life.

One of the first committees established by the Society was called the "Meeting for Sufferings." One of the prayers most often used by Quakers (written by John Wilhelm Rowntree) is this:

Thou, O Christ, convince us by Thy spirit; thrill us with Thy divine passion; drown our selfishness in Thy invading love; lay on us the burden of the world's sufferings; drive us forth with the apostolic fervor of the early church. So only can our message be delivered. Speak to the children of Israel that they go forward.

WHAT IS THE ATTITUDE OF FRIENDS TOWARD JESUS?

Quakers have a common belief in the revelation of God in Christ. There is a variety of points of view among Friends, but there is a universal witness (a common faith) that God expressed His love historically in Jesus of Nazareth, and eternally through the Spirit of Christ. To many Friends, these are two experiences of the same reality—the historical Jesus and the risen Christ within.

DO QUAKERS BELIEVE JESUS WAS DIVINE?

This is a difficult question to answer categorically for all Friends. Friends refer to the "Seed," the "Light of Christ," the "Inner Guide," the "Inner Light" as the external creative power of God, expressed supremely and uniquely in the supreme gift of God to man—Jesus Christ.

DO QUAKERS BELIEVE IN THE VIRGIN BIRTH?

The question of the Virgin Birth does not seem as important a problem for Quakers as the meaning and teaching of Christ's life on earth and His continuing power to reveal Himself at all times and to all seekers.

DO QUAKERS BELIEVE IN THE SACRAMENTS?

For Friends, there is no necessity for any ritual to establish relationship between man and God. Friends believe in all the sacraments but only in their inward and spiritual revelation of the Divine presence. All life is sacramental. At all times, and to all men and women, God is available to those who reverently wait upon Him.

DO FRIENDS BAPTIZE?

No. They do believe in the baptism of the Spirit but practice no form of baptism. At birth, the infant's name is recorded on the official books of the meeting to which his parents belong.

WHAT ABOUT HEAVEN, HELL, AND PURGATORY?

Quakers consider these matters for individual interpretation. *The Book of Discipline, Faith and Practice* does not deal with these theological issues.

Friends do believe in life after this life and usually refer to the funeral service of a deceased member as a "Memorial Meeting for Worship."

WHAT ABOUT THE TRINITY?

Again, there is wide freedom for personal opinion. It must be remembered that Quakerism is based on a religious way of life rather than accepted dogmas. The Quaker faith is a religion of experience. Whatever is known experimentally about God, the Holy Spirit, the Christ Within, becomes the True Guide. Friends tend to believe in the immanence of God rather than His transcendence.

WHAT ABOUT THE BIBLE?

Friends have always believed that the truth is found in the Bible, rather than holding that what has been written is true *because* it is in the Bible. Quakers have always been students of the Bible, placing strong emphasis on its value and use. A Quaker scholar was a member of the committee that issued the American Standard Version of the Bible, and another Quaker, a New Testament scholar, served on the group that translated the new Revised Standard Version of the Bible, published in 1952. Another Friend was a member of the Joint Committee on the New Translation of the Bible that resulted in The New English Bible publication of The New Testament in 1962.

ARE ALL QUAKERS PACIFISTS?

No. Some Quakers have given up their pacifism and gone to war. But Quakers as a group hold that non-violent forms of peacemaking are the only ways to solve international strife. William Penn maintained that it was "not fighting but suffering" to which Friends were called. The witness for peace is one of the most universal of all Quaker testimonies.

Quakers have always been among the conscientious objectors to war. When Oliver Cromwell asked George Fox to fight with him in 1650, Fox wrote in his *Journal:* "I told him I knew from whence all wars arose and that I lived in the virtue of that life and power that took away the occasion of all wars."

During World War I, the right of conscientious objectors was not recognized and many Friends went to jail. Selective Service legislation today establishes the right of conscientious objectors to be assigned to civilian service of national importance, in lieu of military service.

DO THE QUAKERS HAVE ANY SUBSTITUTE FOR A CREED?

Yes—the "Queries." Originally, the Queries were a set of questions designed to encourage the faithfulness of the members in their religious life. It is the practice to answer one of the Queries in meeting each month and to report on all twelve at the annual Yearly Meeting.

Typical Queries are: Do your meetings give evidence that Friends come to them with hearts and minds prepared for worship? Are love and unity maintained among you? Do you manifest a forgiving spirit and a care for the reputation of others?

What are you doing as individuals or as a meeting: To aid those in need of material help? To insure equal opportunities in social and economic life for those who suffer discrimination because of race, creed or social class? To understand and remove the causes of war? To develop the conditions and institutions of peace? To assure freedom of speech and of religion, and equal educational opportunities for all?

Do you frequently and reverently read the Bible and other religious literature? Are you punctual in keeping promises, just in the payment of debts, and honorable in all your dealings? In all your relations with others, do you treat them as brothers and equals?

HOW IS QUAKER INFLUENCE FELT?

Service is the Quaker word which represents for many Friends what missionary activity does for the churches. It grows out of spiritual conviction. In social service, foreign relief, reconciliation and mediation—both at home and abroad—Quakers carry on an enormous amount of activities around the globe. The American Friends Service Committee and Friends Service Council, London, won the Nobel Peace Award for 1947 and Friends enjoy consultative status in the United Nations. The eight-pointed star of the American Friends Service Committee is known all over Europe and in Israel, India, China, Japan, Korea and Africa.

HOW LARGE IS THE QUAKER MOVEMENT?

There are 195,664 members of the Society of Friends all over the world, according to the latest count from the Friends World Committee for

Consultation offices (located at Woodbrooke, Selly Oak, Birmingham, 29, England).

There are 123,411 Friends in the United States, including Alaska and Hawaii, with an additional 822 in Canada and Mexico, and 5,871 in Central and South America.

The membership in Great Britain and Ireland totals 23,226.

There are 52 Yearly Meetings in the world-wide movement, which is now found on every continent.

WHAT MESSAGE DO FRIENDS OFFER THE WORLD TODAY?

In 1952, the Friends commemorated their 300th anniversary as a religious movement with a World Conference at Oxford, England. There, they dedicated themselves anew to God's will and purpose and to the "Way of Jesus Christ." At the conclusion of ten days of conference, 900 Quakers from 22 countries issued this message to persons everywhere:

The Christian faith, which we believe is the hope of our troubled world, is a revolutionary faith. It is rooted in inward experience, but, wherever it is genuine, it leads to radical changes in the ways in which men live and act. We rejoice in the movements, appearing in many parts of the world at once, which are inspired by the desire for social justice, equal rights for all races and the dignity of the individual person. These changes can neither be achieved nor prevented by war. War leads to a vicious circle of hatred, oppression, subversive movements, false propaganda, rearmament and new wars. An armaments race cannot bring peace, freedom or security. We call upon peoples everywhere to break this vicious circle, to behave as nations with the same decency as they would behave as men and brothers, to substitute the institutions of peace for the institutions of war.

Let us join together throughout the world to grow more food, to heal and prevent disease, to conserve and develop the resources of the good earth to the glory of God and the comfort of man's distress. These are among the tasks to which in humility for our share in the world's shame, and in faith in the power of love, we call our own Society and all men and nations everywhere.

What Is a Seventh-day Adventist?

ARTHUR S. MAXWELL

Arthur S. Maxwell has been editor of *Signs of the Times*, leading evangelistic journal of the Seventh-day Adventists, for over twenty-five years. He is the author of more than ninety books, some of which (stories for children) have been translated into twenty-three languages.

Mr. Maxwell was born in London in 1896. He attended Stanborough College in England, was manager of the Stanborough Press from 1925 to 1932, and served as editor of *Present Truth* from 1920 to 1936.

Four of his children are ordained ministers in the Seventh-day Adventist Church.

Among Mr. Maxwell's writings are *This Mighty Hour, Our Wonderful Bible, Great Prophecies for our Time, Your Bible and You, Courage for the Crisis* and *The Bible Story*.

WHAT IS A SEVENTH-DAY ADVENTIST?

A Seventh-day Adventist is one who, having accepted Christ as his personal Savior, walks in humble obedience to the will of God as revealed in the Holy Scriptures. A Bible-loving Christian, he seeks to pattern his life according to the teachings of this book, while looking for the imminent return of his Lord. He lives under a sense of destiny, believing it his duty to warn mankind that the end of the world is at hand.

ARE SEVENTH-DAY ADVENTISTS PROTESTANTS?

Yes. Like the reformers of the sixteenth century, Seventh-day Adventists believe that every individual may have immediate access to God by prayer—without the intervention of any priest, saint or other ecclesiastical functionary.

They believe that their Church constitutes the nucleus of a twentieth-century Reformation, a world-wide revival of New Testament Christianity.

HOW DO SEVENTH-DAY ADVENTISTS DIFFER FROM OTHER PROTESTANTS?

Most noticeably in their observance of Saturday, not Sunday, as the Sabbath. But they also differ from many (but not all) Protestants in their teaching concerning the nature of man, the state of the dead, and the manner of Christ's second coming.

Seventh-day Adventists claim that they are not inventors of new doctrines but recoverers of old truths—truths long eclipsed by the infiltration of pagan traditions and superstitions into the Christian Church.

WHY DO SEVENTH-DAY ADVENTISTS OBSERVE SATURDAY AS THE SABBATH?

Because God, in the beginning, set apart the seventh day of creation week as a perpetual memorial of His creative power. Saturday is the seventh day of the week. Sunday is the *first* day of the week.

In Exodus 20:8-11, it is written, "Remember the Sabbath day, to keep it holy. Six days shalt thou labor, and do all thy work: but the seventh day is the Sabbath of the Lord thy God: in it thou shalt not do any work, thou, nor thy son, nor thy daughter, thy manservant, nor thy maidservant, nor thy cattle, nor the stranger that is within thy gates: for in six days the Lord made heaven and earth, the sea, and all that in them is, and rested the seventh day: wherefore the Lord blessed the Sabbath day, and hallowed it."

It is distinctly stated of Christ that it was His "custom" to attend the synagogue on "the Sabbath day" (Luke 4:16). And after His crucifixion, His closest disciples were so loyal to His teaching and example they would not even embalm His body on the holy seventh day. Instead, "they . . . rested the Sabbath day, according to the commandment" (Luke 23:56).

As Seventh-day Adventists have never been able to find a single text in the Bible suggesting that Christ authorized a change of the Sabbath from the seventh day of the week to the first, they say, "What else can a true Christian do but follow the clear teaching of the Word?"

HOW DO SEVENTH-DAY ADVENTISTS KNOW SATURDAY IS THE SEVENTH DAY?

By the calendar. Every calendar shows Saturday as the seventh day of the week. Two unquestionable pieces of evidence confirm this: First, the fact that Orthodox Jews, from time immemorial, have observed the seventh-day Sabbath on Saturday; and, second, millions of Christians, for many centuries, have observed Sunday because Christ *rose* on the first day of the week.

DO SEVENTH-DAY ADVENTISTS ACCEPT THE BIBLE LITERALLY?

Yes. They believe that the original authors were inspired by God. As the apostle Peter said, "Holy men of God spake as they were moved by the Holy Ghost."

Seventh-day Adventists, of course, know that there have been many translations of the Bible, but hold that the original intent of the inspired authors has come down unimpaired through the centuries. Because words change in meaning with the passage of time, occasional revisions of translations are desirable, but through them all the original message is clearly discernible and "the word of the Lord endureth forever."

WHAT DO SEVENTH-DAY ADVENTISTS TEACH ABOUT THE BEGINNING OF THE WORLD?

They believe God created the world by divine fiat, in six literal days. They believe that the record of creation in the first chapter of Genesis is not fable but fact. They consider that if the omnipotent Creator could make billions of suns (which the astronomers claim to have seen circling through the immensities of space), it was no great problem for Him to call this one planet into existence.

The evidence to which geologists and paleontologists point to support their theory that the earth is millions of years old is regarded by Seventh-day Adventists as substantiating the Bible story of the Flood. That global catastrophe, they hold, affords a completely satisfactory explanation of all the fossils, buried coal beds, and oil-bearing strata.

Supporting this view are such Seventh-day Adventist scientists as Professor George McCready Price and Dr. Frank Marsh.

HOW DID THE SEVENTH-DAY ADVENTIST MOVEMENT START?

It grew out of the world-wide discussion in the early decades of the nineteenth century concerning the second advent of Christ. At that time, many godly scholars, in many countries and of many denominations, simultaneously came to the conclusion, from their study of Bible prophecy, that the coming of Christ was near. Between 1820 and 1830, more than 300 clergymen of the Church of England, and twice that number of Nonconformists, were advocating this belief.

In America, a similar advent movement began, supported by 200 leading clergymen—including Presbyterians, Baptists, Congregationalists, Episcopalians, and Methodists. Led by William Miller, a farmer, they stirred America with the message that Christ would come in 1844. When He failed to come, the movement melted away. One of the smaller groups decided to restudy the prophecies and search for clearer light. In doing so, they caught the vision of a world to be *warned* before Christ could come again. Penniless but full of faith, this group set out to accomplish the task. Accepting the Sabbath truth from the Seventh-day Baptists, they became the nucleus of the Seventh-day Adventist movement, which now claims over a million around the globe.

DO SEVENTH-DAY ADVENTISTS BELIEVE IN THE TRINITY?

They do. Reverently they worship Father, Son and Holy Spirit, "three Persons in one God." And they do so because they believe this to be the teaching of the Bible concerning God in His relation to this world and the human race.

DO SEVENTH-DAY ADVENTISTS BELIEVE IN THE VIRGIN BIRTH?

Most definitely. They hold that it is one of the vital truths of the Christian faith, foretold in the Old Testament and confirmed in the New.

DO ADVENTISTS BELIEVE IN BAPTISM?

Yes. Heeding Christ's teaching that "he that believeth and is baptized shall be saved" (Mark 16:16), they require all who would enter the Church to be baptized by immersion, the method followed by the Church of New Testament times.

DO ADVENTISTS TEACH THAT PEOPLE MUST OBEY THE TEN COMMANDMENTS IN ORDER TO BE SAVED?

No. Salvation is by grace alone. There is only one way of salvation. That is faith in the atoning death of Jesus Christ.

No one can "work his way" into the kingdom of God. No degree of obedience, no works of penance, no amount of money entitles anyone to any divine favor. Nevertheless, "faith without works is dead."

Keeping the commandments is the result, the evidence, of salvation. It is a matter of love, not legal duty. "If ye love me," said Jesus, "keep my commandments" (John 14:15).

WHAT DO ADVENTISTS BELIEVE ABOUT CHRIST'S RETURN?

The word "Adventist" indicates their special concern for this phase of Christian teaching. From their study of the Bible, they have become convinced not only that Christ is coming but that He is coming soon. They believe He will come personally, exactly as He went away (Acts 1:11).

Christ's second coming will climax a sequence of stupendous events —political and religious—which will involve the entire population of the globe and mark the end of the world, or age, as we know it today. In that day, when "the Lord Himself shall descend from heaven with a shout, with the voice of the Archangel and with the trump of God," the graves of all God's children will be opened, the "dead in Christ" shall rise, and all true Christians alive at that moment will be "caught up together with them in the clouds, to meet the Lord in the air" (I Thessalonians 4:16-17).

The effect of Christ's coming upon unbelievers is described, Seventh-day Adventists believe, in Revelation 6, where they are pictured as fleeing from His presence, only to be destroyed by "the brightness of his coming" (II Thessalonians 2:8).

DO SEVENTH-DAY ADVENTISTS BELIEVE IN A MILLENNIUM?

Yes. They believe that the followers of Christ who are raised, or translated, at His second coming will live and reign "with Christ a thousand years" (Revelation 20:4). However, they believe this reign will take place in heaven, not on earth, which will remain a desolated, depopulated wilderness throughout this period.

At the close of the millennium, the earth will again become a scene of great activity, with the resurrection of the wicked, the return of the righteous from heaven, the setting up of the New Jerusalem on earth and the execution of final judgment upon the unrepentant (Revelation 20).

After that, Seventh-day Adventists believe, the earth will be purified by fire and re-created at the command of Christ into the eternal home of His redeemed. "The eyes of the blind shall be opened, and the ears of the deaf shall be unstopped" (Isaiah 35:5). "And there shall be no more death, neither sorrow nor crying, neither shall there be any more pain" (Revelation 21:4). Then all sorrows will be over, and all man's brightest hopes will be realized. This will be "heaven on earth" at last, not only for Seventh-day Adventists but for all who love the Lord Jesus Christ in sincerity.

WHAT MAKES ADVENTISTS THINK CHRIST IS COMING SOON?

The signs of the times. Notably, certain developments among the nations and in the social, economic, and religious life of the masses— including the invention of the hydrogen bomb. As never before, a great fear grips the nations—fear of war, fear of inflation, fear of atomic annihilation. And this fear is driving men, in their search for security, to combine into massive confederacies, as foreshadowed in Bible prophecies.

This tragic situation, Seventh-day Adventists believe, was predicted by Christ Himself when, enumerating the signs of His second coming, He said, "There shall be . . . upon the earth distress of nations, with perplexity; . . . men's hearts failing them for fear, and for looking after those things which are coming on the earth: for the powers of heaven shall be shaken. And then shall they see the Son of Man coming in a cloud with power and great glory" (Luke 21:25-27).

Seventh-day Adventists believe another striking sign is the amazing multiplication of inventions that have changed man's whole way of life. This unprecedented increase of knowledge, with multitudes running to and fro, was prophesied to occur in the "time of the end" (Daniel 12:4).

Still another sign is the moral collapse so evident in social and political life today. Everybody admits that the moral underpinnings of Western civilization are giving way. And while there is still much outward show of religion, there is little inward piety or spiritual power. This too, Seventh-day Adventists believe, was forecast by the apostle Paul to happen in "the last days" (II Timothy 3).

DO SEVENTH-DAY ADVENTISTS SET A TIME FOR CHRIST TO COME?

No. Nor have they ever done so. They accept Christ's statement, "Of that day and hour knoweth no man, no, not the angels of heaven, but my Father only" (Matthew 24:36). However, they give special force to His declaration, "When ye shall see these things come to pass, know that it is nigh, even at the doors" (Mark 13:29).

WHAT IS THE ADVENTIST POSITION REGARDING DIVORCE?

Briefly, it is the Biblical position, enunciated by Jesus Christ when He said, "Whosoever shall put away his wife, except it be for fornication, and shall marry another, committeth adultery: and whoso marrieth her which is put away doth commit adultery" (Matthew 19:9). Seventh-day Adventists believe that this counsel is very clear and that members who knowingly depart from it should not continue in the fellowship of the Church.

WHAT IS THE ATTITUDE OF ADVENTISTS TOWARD DRINKING AND SMOKING?

No Seventh-day Adventist drinks alcoholic beverages or smokes tobacco. They accept at face value Paul's statement that man's body is the "temple of the Holy Spirit." Believing this, they refrain from all harmful indulgencies which might weaken their efficiency and the sincerity of their witness, as workers for God. They are also motivated by a regard for the example that true Christians should set before others who do not acknowledge Christ, and in particular, before children and youth.

HOW MANY SEVENTH-DAY ADVENTISTS ARE THERE?

In December, 1960, the total number of baptized members in North America was 332,364; the world total was 1,245,125. In addition, many thousands who have accepted the teachings of the Church are awaiting baptism.

DO SEVENTH-DAY ADVENTISTS HAVE MISSIONARIES?

Yes—all over the world. The foreign mission budget for 1960 was $16,729,066. Throughout the world, they employ 48,890 full-time workers—18,362 in direct evangelistic service and 30,528 in publishing, medical and educational institutions. They issue publications in 228 languages.

Seventh-day Adventists carry on a large health and ·medical work alongside their evangelistic activities. They have a chain of sanitariums, hospitals and clinics in all the principal countries of the world. Patients treated annually total some 3,000,000.

ARE ADVENTISTS INTERESTED IN WELFARE WORK?

Very much. Most churches have a Dorcas Society, which is active in caring for the local needy and in projects of wider significance. At strategically located welfare centers, at home and overseas, Seventh-day Adventists stockpile quantities of clothing and bedding which are kept ready for instant shipment to disaster areas.

An unusual phase of Seventh-day Adventists' welfare work is their interest in prisoners in state penitentiaries. Wherever arrangements can be made, they visit inmates, conduct religious services, distribute literature, and generally spread the hope of the Gospel.

DO ADVENTISTS BELIEVE IN RELIGIOUS LIBERTY?

They certainly do. As champions of religious liberty, they fought— and helped to defeat—the calendar reformers before the League of

Nations in 1931 and later. They are opposed to all religious legislation such as "blue" laws. They are ardent supporters of the principle of separation of church and state. They publish the quarterly *Liberty* magazine, devoted exclusively to the preservation and extension of religious liberty.

DO ADVENTISTS BELIEVE IN LIFE AFTER DEATH?

Yes. But they hold that life comes only from Christ, the source of life. No one, they assert, can have eternal life apart from Christ. Man by himself is mortal, subject to death. Only Christ can make him immortal. And immortality, says the Bible, will not be conferred until the resurrection at the second coming of Christ in glory.

Seventh-day Adventists hold that the ancient supposition that people go to heaven or hell immediately upon death is an infiltration of pagan mythology into Christian theology. Bible teaching on this subject, they claim, is as clear as day—that the dead are asleep until the glorious return of Jesus Christ as King of Kings and Lord of Lords. Then, but not till then, will final rewards and punishments be meted out.

What Is a Unitarian?

KARL M. CHWOROWSKY

Karl M. Chworowsky is minister emeritus of the First Unitarian Church of Fairfield County in Westport, Connecticut. He is a member of the United World Federalists, the Unitarian Fellowship for Social Justice, the American Christian Palestine Committee, the American Civil Liberties Union, and the American Humanist Association.

Mr. Chworowsky was born in Riga, Russia, in 1887. His father was a Lutheran minister who came to the United States to take over a church in South Dakota, and who spent forty-five years in the ministry in various places in the Middle West.

Mr. Chworowsky attended Wartburg College and Wartburg Theological Seminary, an orthodox Lutheran institution in the Iowa District. He pursued graduate studies at the University of Wisconsin. He engaged in Lutheran religious activities for many years, serving as minister in the Evangelical Synod (now part of the Evangelical and Reformed Church) in Oconto, Wisconsin, from 1918 to 1921. He taught and acted as pastor at the College of the Evangelical Synod in Elmhurst, Illinois, where he became known for his work and interest in interfaith and interracial groups.

Mr. Chworowsky joined the Unitarian Church in 1935. He served the Unitarian Church in Newburgh, New York, in 1936, and for twelve years was minister of the Unitarian Church of Flatbush in Brooklyn. He has written many articles, sermons, and reviews which have been reprinted in journals throughout the world.

NOTE TO THE READER: Since 1961, Unitarians in North America have been part of a new and larger organization—the Unitarian Universalist Association, a consolidation of the American Unitarian Association and Universalist Church of America.

The first yearbook of the Unitarian Universalist Association listed 651 active churches and 358 Fellowships (smaller lay groups usually not served by full-time ministers). The total constituency includes over 200,000 adults. There are 77,500 children enrolled in Sunday schools.

Universalists, though rising from a somewhat different history, are, like the Unitarians, decidedly individualistic in their religion, which is based "on a free and disciplined search for truth, love to God and love to Man."*

WHAT IS A UNITARIAN?

In general, a Unitarian is a religious person whose ethic derives primarily from that of Jesus, whose belief is in one God, not in the Trinity, and whose faith affirms the principles of freedom, reason and the dignity of man.

Unitarians believe that the church should be universal in its appeal, and should welcome all men and women, of every race, color and creed, who wish to share the quest for the good life, and to serve their fellow-man.

Membership in the Unitarian Church depends not upon the acceptance of a dogmatic creed, but simply upon the honest desire in a person's heart, "to do justly, to love kindness, and to walk humbly with thy God." The only thing that can destroy such membership is, in the words of the beloved Unitarian Minister William Ellery Channing, "the death of goodness in his own breast."

ARE UNITARIANS CHRISTIANS?

If to be a Christian is to profess and sincerely seek to practice the religion of Jesus, so simply and beautifully given in the Sermon on the Mount, then Unitarians are Christians. But because Unitarians do not acknowledge Jesus as their "Lord and Savior," they are often thought of as being non-Christian and, in fact, are not eligible for membership in the National Council of the Churches of Christ in the U.S.A.

Unitarians hold that the orthodox Christian world has forgotten and forsaken the real, human Jesus of the Gospels, and has substituted

*From "Purposes and Objectives" in the new Constitution of the Unitarian Universalist Association.

a "Christ" of dogmatism, metaphysics and pagan philosophy. Many Unitarians today prefer to be called "liberal Christians," or simply "religious Liberals." The seeming intolerance and prejudice of many Christians make it difficult, at times, for Unitarians to rejoice in the name of "Christian."

Unitarians worship as earnestly and reverently as those of any other faith or church. They worship differently because they believe that every individual has the right to approach ultimate values in his own way, that truth may be found in the teachings of the great prophets of humanity in every age and tradition, and that a religious community has the duty of creating such patterns of worship as best serve its needs.

DO UNITARIANS BELIEVE IN GOD?

Unitarians follow no formal or central creed. Their ministers and members are not required to pass any test of faith. Freedom of belief among Unitarians is broad enough to include agnosticism, humanism, even atheism, on the one hand, and, on the other, a belief in God which can be manifested in a wide range of definitions—from that of a "personal God" to an "Ultimate Reality." Many Unitarians find the word "God" a stumbling block to communication about the supreme matters of the spirit. They choose to avoid an excessive use of all words that stand in the way of, instead of encouraging, profound understanding.

HOW DID THE NAME "UNITARIAN" ARISE?

It can be said that the roots of Unitarianism go back to the early years of the Christian Church, when those who disagreed with the developing "Christology" were active under such names as Ebionites, Samosatenians, Arians and Photinians. These dissenters formed small movements of protest against what they considered to be a caricature of the simple monotheism of Jesus and his first Jewish followers.

However, the first significant Unitarian movement began in Europe very early in the period of the Protestant Reformation. The name "Unitarians" was first used in the sixteenth century to describe certain Protestants who dissented from the dogma of the Trinity. Francis David, Faustus Socinus, and Michael Servetus, who was burned at the stake in John Calvin's Geneva in 1553 for his "Unitarian heresy" (contained in his book *On the Errors of the Trinity*), were among the pioneers of modern Unitarianism. In 1568, King John Sigismund, the Unitarian ruler of Transylvania (now part of Hungary), issued the first great edict for religious freedom in his land. By 1600 there were 425 Unitarian churches in that country.

HOW DID UNITARIANISM DEVELOP IN AMERICA?

Along with the Universalists, the Unitarians trace their history in the United States back to revolutionary days. The first Universalist church was established in 1779 by John Murray in Gloucester, Massachusetts. In 1794, Joseph Priestley, the discoverer of oxygen, came to America as a religious refugee from England and began preaching Unitarianism in Pennsylvania. In 1805, Harvard College called a Unitarian, Henry Ware, to be Hollis Professor of Divinity. This brought to a head a bitter debate between the liberals and the conservatives in the Congregational churches, and precipitated a number of schisms in New England.

Many churches proceeded to become Unitarian. William Ellery Channing, Ralph Waldo Emerson and Theodore Parker were among the most influential scholars in the development of early Unitarian thought. The American Unitarian Association was founded in 1825.

The Unitarian church declined in the early 1900s, but during the post-war years, under the vigorous leadership of Frederick May Eliot, who died in 1958, the Unitarian movement has doubled in size.

WHAT DO UNITARIANS BELIEVE ABOUT THE BIBLE?

The Scriptures occupy a position of high esteem and affection among Unitarians. This immortal book of religious inspiration, with its prose, poetry and drama, is used in Unitarian churches. Divinity students in their preparation for the Unitarian ministry undergo a thorough training in the Bible.

DO UNITARIANS BELIEVE THE BIBLE IS DIVINELY INSPIRED, AS "THE WORD OF GOD," AND INFALLIBLE?

No. The doctrine of revelation, of the absolute and indisputable authority of the Bible, is alien to our faith and teaching.

Unitarians hold the Bible very dear, but they reserve the prerogative of critical appreciation, which is intimately related to freedom of thought and intellectual honesty. These lines from James Russell Lowell express the Unitarian attitude:

Slowly the Bible of the race is writ,
　And not on paper leaves or leaves of stone;
Each age, each kindred, adds a verse to it,
　Texts of despair or hope, of joy or moan.

Unitarians believe that every revelation of truth, every unfolding of beauty, every voice of wisdom that human experience discovers in its slow progress toward clearer understanding, freedom and the Good Life, should be revered.

WHAT DO UNITARIANS BELIEVE ABOUT JESUS?

Unitarians love the person and message of the great Galilean. They consider him one of the rarest of personalities that have walked among men. Jesus is one of the greatest religious teachers, and Unitarians endorse his prophetic preaching, his moral teaching and his spiritual insight. But Unitarians have refused to "make a God" of one who was so utterly human in all his words and deeds, and who once even protested against being called "good."

DO UNITARIANS DENY THE DIVINITY OF CHRIST?

Unitarians do not believe that Jesus is either the Messiah of Jewish hope or the Savior of Christian belief. They do not believe he is "God incarnate" or "the Second Person in the Trinity," or the final arbiter at the end of time who "shall come to judge the quick and the dead."

On the authority of reason and common sense, and on the basis of modern research in the Bible, Unitarians look upon Jesus as a great moral and spiritual teacher.

DO UNITARIANS DENY THE VIRGIN BIRTH?

Unitarians repudiate the dogma or doctrine of the Virgin Birth.

WHAT DO UNITARIANS TEACH ABOUT SIN?

Unitarians recognize the evil in our world and man's responsibility for it. They do not agree with the Christian doctrine that holds that the disobedience of Adam (original sin) has so completely incapacitated man for anything good that only God's "grace," operating through a church and its rites and sacraments, can save him.

Most orthodox Christian churches teach that because of the total depravity of man, God sent His only-begotten Son into the world to die, in order that "whosoever believeth in Him may have everlasting life." Such doctrine Unitarians find unbelievable and un-Biblical. It is certainly inconsistent with the nature of God or the dignity of man, whom the Eternal One created "in his own image" to love with "an everlasting love."

Unitarians believe that man has innate capacities for both good and evil. His natural tendency for good can grow through proper environment, effective education and spiritual awareness. Man, in striving for the good life, can achieve the stature of "the man of God."

DO UNITARIANS BELIEVE IN "SALVATION"?

Unitarians believe in "salvation by character." They hold that enlightened religion can "save" us by inspiring and helping us to build a society in which moral values and spiritual insight are the motivating forces, a society in which modern scientific knowledge will be shared among all people. Thus can we find "salvation" and the road that leads to peace, justice and brotherhood.

While man needs all the inspiration that noble example and good education can give him, there is practical wisdom in the saying "God helps those who help themselves." Man at his best is the certain proof that salvation lies within him. If man is to be saved, his God-given mental capacity and his potential for good will save him here, and hereafter.

DO UNITARIANS BAPTIZE?

While many Unitarians do practice baptism of infants and, more rarely, of adults, they prefer to look upon baptism as a symbolic act of dedication and naming. It is not considered a conveyor of "forgiveness of sin" or of God's "special grace" toward sinners.

Unitarians find it hard to discuss with restraint the teaching in some churches that baptism washes away the stain of "original sin." They are horrified by the idea of "infant damnation," which consigns unbaptized infants to perdition. You can become a Unitarian without being baptized, and you can remain a good Unitarian without baptism.

DO UNITARIANS OBSERVE HOLY COMMUNION?

Where communion is observed in Unitarian churches it is a symbolic rite of remembrance and fellowship. It is intended to remind the participants of the Last Supper. For Unitarians, this is a ceremony in which the sharing of bread and wine, in solemn fellowship of reverent memory and devotion, brings back the inspiring image of him whose life was devoted to the establishment of peace and good will on earth. We do not believe that any supernatural power or "grace" resides in this sacrament, or that its observance automatically conveys any special spiritual gift, such as the forgiveness of sin. Communion remains for Unitarians a ceremony through which "the still, small voice" of faith and hope and love speaks to us.

DO UNITARIANS BELIEVE IN HEAVEN AND HELL?

If by heaven you mean an abode of eternal light, where the "saved and redeemed" enjoy everlasting bliss, and if by hell you mean the devil's eternal darkness, where the wicked suffer unending torment and punishment—then Unitarians emphatically repudiate such beliefs.

Unitarians believe that evil defeats itself and that virtue is the reward of those who obey the laws of man and God. The idea that a God of Love and Mercy would want to consign a human being, because of wrong-doing during a relatively brief spell of mortal existence, to eternal damnation, or that God will reward the mortal doers of good with everlasting happiness, appears to most Unitarians as absurd— entirely inconsistent with any moral concept of Deity.

As regards our notion of heaven, these lines by Edwin Markham may indicate what many Unitarians believe:

We men of Earth have here the stuff
Of Paradise—we have enough!
We need no other stones to build
The Temple of the Unfulfilled— ...
Here on the paths of every-day—
Here on the common human way
Is all the stuff the gods would take
To build a Heaven, to mold and make
New Edens. Ours the stuff sublime
To build Eternity in time.

Unitarians think of hell as man's failure to be and live up to his best. Hell is injustice, violence, tyranny, hatred, war, and everything that fits these Satanic categories. Let us fight these evil forces here and now to help create that Paradise of which the poets speak.

DO UNITARIANS BELIEVE IN IMMORTALITY?

Unitarian attitudes toward immortality vary widely. Some Unitarians hold views which closely approach traditional Judaism and Christianity; others admit to being humble agnostics as regards "life after death" or "life everlasting." Religious Liberals sometimes hold conceptions of immortality that are sympathetic to such Eastern religions as Hinduism and Buddhism. Socrates' noble sentiments about immortality, in the *Phaedo,* have captured the imagination of many who find them emotionally satisfying.

Unitarians believe that life goes on, and that its tomorrow will be determined not by the arbitrary judgment of a tyrannical God, but by our actions here and now, according to God's eternal way.

MAY A UNITARIAN BELIEVE WHAT HE PLEASES?

While Unitarians believe in freedom of conscience and freedom of choice in religion, they do not follow every wind of doctrine, or accept uncritically whatever they read or hear.

To believe, in the Unitarian sense, is to arrive at conviction through mental discipline and labor of the spirit and the heart. Dr. Charles Eliot, the late Unitarian president of Harvard University, called Unitarianism "a cheerful religion." It is cheerful because it encourages the individual's victory over ignorance, superstition, fear and uncertainty.

DO UNITARIANS BELIEVE IN PRAYER?

Of course they do. Some Unitarians prefer to call prayer "meditation" or "aspiration." But in their prayers and meditations, Unitarians do not pray "in the name of the Father and the Son and the Holy Ghost," nor do they commonly end their prayers in the name of Jesus. An observer will find that Unitarians fully appreciate the mood of heart and mind that finds expression in prayer.

WHAT IS THE UNITARIAN POSITION ON DIVORCE?

Unitarians recognize no specifically theological doctrine as regards divorce. This question is referred to the individual's conscience, intelligence and common sense. The church is always ready to offer counsel and advice, in keeping with its ethical and spiritual ideals.

WHAT IS THE UNITARIAN POSITION ON BIRTH CONTROL?

Most Unitarians are strong advocates of birth control in a world that is threatened with a population explosion.

HOW IS THE UNITARIAN CHURCH ORGANIZED?

In Unitarian Church organization, "congregational polity" prevails. Each local church enjoys full self-determination in all matters and jealously guards its interests as an autonomous body. This continues to be true for the Unitarian Universalist Association.

DO UNITARIAN SERVICES DIFFER FROM THOSE IN OTHER CHURCHES?

Some forms of Unitarian worship resemble services in other Protestant churches. In one city, a Unitarian church may have the atmosphere of a Lutheran or Episcopalian or Congregationalist service. In another, worship is characterized by the utmost simplicity. Each church is free to develop a service of worship that best serves its people, and Unitarian ministers through long tradition are accorded the right of a free pulpit.

Unitarians employ many variations of the great human-divine theme of *religion* as expressed in meditation, music and poetry.

DO UNITARIANS TRY TO MAKE CONVERTS?

No. Unitarians do not proselytize; they do not send out missionaries. They do, quietly and effectively, let people know who they are and what they stand for. "He that hath an ear, let him hear what the Spirit saith."

HOW DOES ONE BECOME A UNITARIAN?

Not by baptism or confirmation, nor by the required acceptance of dogmatic creeds. To become a Unitarian you should (1) feel within your own heart and mind the love of freedom of thought and conscience; (2) recognize the demand of the voice of reason, challenging you to examine the truths you would incorporate into the texture of your personal faith; (3) affirm and promote the dignity of man; (4) remain receptive to new knowledge; and (5) uphold the ideals of democracy.

It is your own mind and heart that will make you a Unitarian, not what somebody else thinks or says or does. You will enter into fellowship with other men and women who seek to worship and celebrate the highest values in life through truth, beauty and goodness.

WHAT ROLE HAVE UNITARIANS PLAYED IN AMERICAN HISTORY?

Many Unitarian names are in "The Hall of Fame" of New York University. Here, among the immortal leaders of our republic, you will find Thomas Jefferson, John and John Quincy Adams, George Bancroft, William Cullen Bryant, William Ellery Channing, Ralph Waldo Emerson, Oliver Wendell Holmes, Henry W. Longfellow, James Russell Lowell, Horace Mann and Francis Parkman.

Present-day Unitarians are proud of the distinguished humanitarian work of the Unitarian Service Committee as a practical application of one of their principles, "Helping others to help themselves."

Whether you think of public schools or the abolition of slavery, of equal rights, of peace, of the just demands of labor, of the rights of minority groups, of penology or public health—in all these movements to make America truly "the land of the free," men and women of the Unitarian Universalist Church have given and are giving of their best efforts, their noblest devotion and their creative imagination.

What Is an Agnostic?

BERTRAND RUSSELL

Bertrand Russell, winner of the Nobel Prize in literature, is one of the most original, incisive and significant minds of the twentieth century. Through more
than forty books, Mr. Russell has made lasting contributions to many fields:
philosophy, mathematics, logic, political thought, theories of education and
social problems. His Nobel Prize citation called him one who has "constantly
figured as a defender of humanity and freedom of thought."

Bertrand Arthur William Russell was born in 1872 at Ravenscroft, England,
in a family which has played an important role in English history since the sixteenth century. (His grandfather was twice Prime Minister.) He became the
third Earl Russell in 1931, when his older brother died, but does not choose to
be addressed as Lord Russell.

Bertrand Russell's first intellectual loves were mathematics (he studied Euclid
when he was eleven) and philosophy. He received an M.A. from Trinity College,
Cambridge, and won international attention with *The Principles of Mathematics*
(1903), in which he explored the relationship between mathematics, logic and
symbols. With Alfred North Whitehead, he wrote the monumental three-volume
Principia Mathematica.

Russell has been active in political affairs for three decades. He was a member
of the Fabian Society, an early advocate of women's suffrage, and once decided
to stand for Parliament. (He was turned down by the Liberal party because he
was an avowed freethinker.) A pacifist and conscientious objector, he spent
four months in an English prison during World War I —and used the time to
write his admirable *Introduction to Mathematical Philosophy.*

Mr. Russell has traveled widely and made many lecture tours throughout the
United States. He has taught at Harvard University, the University of Chicago,
the National University in Peking (China), the University of California at Los
Angeles, and the College of the City of New York —where, it will be remembered,
a storm of public protest revolved around him as "an enemy of religion and
morality."

In recent years, Bertrand Russell has devoted his prodigious energy to the
campaign for disarmament and against nuclear testing. He is leader and spokesman for the Committee of 100, a militant group within the Campaign for Nuclear
Disarmament in England which reinforces its arguments with a policy of civil
disobedience.

During 1961, the year of his ninetieth birthday, Russell served a week in prison
—in the same jail where he had been imprisoned in World War I —for refusing
to call off a massive sit-down protest against the British government's nuclear
weapons policy.

The insight, power, and originality of Russell's mind are suggested by a few
of the writings for which he is famed: *The Principles of Mathematics, Our Knowledge of the External World, The Problems of China, Education and the Social Order,
Mysticism and Logic, Marriage and Morals, The Conquest of Happiness, The Scientific Outlook, The ABC of Relativity, A Free Man's Worship, Human Knowledge: Its
Scope and Limits, A History of Western Philosophy, Common Sense and Nuclear
Warfare, Why I Am Not a Christian* and *Unpopular Essays.*

Among the many honors Mr. Russell has received are the Order of Merit, the
Nicholas Murray Butler Medal of Columbia University, the Sylvester Medal of

the Royal Society and the de Morgan Medal of the London Mathematical Society.

Mr. Russell's literary style, celebrated for clarity and precision, has earned him a high place among the masters of English prose. When Russell was awarded the Nobel Prize in 1950, the Swedish Academy cited him as "one of our times' most brilliant spokesmen of rationality and humanity, and a fearless champion of free speech and free thought in the West."

ARE AGNOSTICS ATHEISTS?

No. An atheist, like a Christian, holds that we *can* know whether or not there is a God. The Christian holds that we can know there is a God; the atheist, that we can know there is not. The agnostic suspends judgment, saying that there are not sufficient grounds either for affirmation or for denial. At the same time, an agnostic may hold that the existence of God, though not impossible, is very improbable; he may even hold it so improbable that it is not worth considering in practice. In that case, he is not far removed from atheism. His attitude may be that which a careful philosopher would have toward the gods of ancient Greece. If I were asked to *prove* that Zeus and Poseidon and Hera and the rest of the Olympians do not exist, I should be at a loss to find conclusive arguments. An agnostic may think the Christian God as improbable as the Olympians; in that case, he is, for practical purposes, at one with the atheists.

SINCE YOU DENY "GOD'S LAW," WHAT AUTHORITY DO YOU ACCEPT AS A GUIDE TO CONDUCT?

An agnostic does not accept any "authority" in the sense in which religious people do. He holds that a man should think out questions of conduct for himself. Of course, he will seek to profit by the wisdom of others, but he will have to select for himself the people he is to consider wise, and he will not regard even what they say as unquestionable. He will observe that what passes as "God's law" varies from time to time. The Bible says both that a woman must not marry her deceased husband's brother, and that, in certain circumstances, she must do so. If you have the misfortune to be a childless widow with an unmarried brother-in-law, it is logically impossible for you to avoid disobeying "God's law."

HOW DO YOU KNOW WHAT IS GOOD AND WHAT IS EVIL? WHAT DOES AN AGNOSTIC CONSIDER A SIN?

The agnostic is not quite so certain as some Christians are as to what is good and what is evil. He does not hold, as most Christians in the past held, that people who disagree with the government on abstruse points of theology ought to suffer a painful death. He is against persecution, and rather chary of moral condemnation.

As for "sin," he thinks it not a useful notion. He admits, of course, that some kinds of conduct are desirable and some undesirable, but he holds that the punishment of undesirable kinds is only to be commended when it is deterrent or reformatory, not when it is inflicted because it is thought a good thing on its own account that the wicked should suffer. It was this belief in vindictive punishment that made men accept hell. This is part of the harm done by the notion of "sin."

DOES AN AGNOSTIC DO WHATEVER HE PLEASES?

In one sense, no; in another sense, everyone does whatever he pleases. Suppose, for example, you hate someone so much that you would like to murder him. Why do you not do so? You may reply: "Because religion tells me that murder is a sin." But as a statistical fact, agnostics are not more prone to murder than other people, in fact, rather less so. They have the same motives for abstaining from murder as other people have. Far and away the most powerful of these motives is the fear of punishment. In lawless conditions, such as a gold rush, all sorts of people will commit crimes, although in ordinary circumstances they would have been law-abiding. There is not only actual legal punishment; there is the discomfort of dreading discovery, and the loneliness of knowing that, to avoid being hated, you must wear a mask even with your closest intimates. And there is also what may be called "conscience": If you ever contemplated a murder, you would dread the horrible memory of your victim's last moments or lifeless corpse. All this, it is true, depends upon your living in a law-abiding community, but there are abundant secular reasons for creating and preserving such a community.

I said that there is another sense in which every man does as he pleases. No one but a fool indulges every impulse, but what holds a desire in check is always some other desire. A man's anti-social wishes may be restrained by a wish to please God, but they may also be restrained by a wish to please his friends, or to win the respect of his community, or to be able to contemplate himself without disgust. But if he has no such wishes, the mere abstract precepts of morality will not keep him straight.

HOW DOES AN AGNOSTIC REGARD THE BIBLE?

An agnostic regards the Bible exactly as enlightened clerics regard it. He does not think that it is divinely inspired; he thinks its early history legendary, and no more exactly true than that in Homer; he thinks its moral teaching sometimes good, but sometimes very bad. For example: Samuel ordered Saul, in a war, to kill not only every man, woman, and child of the enemy, but also all the sheep and cattle. Saul, however, let the sheep and cattle live, and for this we are told to condemn him. I have never been able to admire Elisha for cursing the children who laughed at him, or to believe (what the Bible asserts) that a benevolent Deity would send two she-bears to kill the children.

HOW DOES AN AGNOSTIC REGARD JESUS, THE VIRGIN BIRTH AND THE HOLY TRINITY?

Since an agnostic does not believe in God, he cannot think that Jesus was God. Most agnostics admire the life and moral teachings of Jesus as told in the Gospels, but not necessarily more than those of certain other men. Some would place him on a level with Buddha, some with Socrates and some with Abraham Lincoln. Nor do they think that what He said is not open to question, since they do not accept any authority as absolute.

They regard the Virgin Birth as a doctrine taken over from pagan mythology, where such births were not uncommon. (Zoroaster was said to have been born of a virgin; Ishtar, the Babylonian goddess, is called the Holy Virgin.) They cannot give credence to it, or to the doctrine of the Trinity, since neither is possible without belief in God.

CAN AN AGNOSTIC BE A CHRISTIAN?

The word "Christian" has had various different meanings at different times. Throughout most of the centuries since the time of Christ, it has meant a person who believed in God and immortality and held that Christ was God. But Unitarians call themselves Christians, although they do not believe in the divinity of Christ, and many people nowadays use the word God in a much less precise sense than that which it used to bear. Many people who say they believe in God no longer mean a person, or a trinity of persons, but only a vague tendency or power or purpose immanent in evolution. Others, going still further, mean by "Christianity" merely a system of ethics which, since they are ignorant of history, they imagine to be characteristic of Christians only.

When, in a recent book, I said that what the world needs is "love, Christian love, or compassion," many people thought this showed some change in my views, although, in fact, I might have said the same thing at any time. If you mean by a "Christian" a man who loves his neighbor, who has wide sympathy with suffering, and who ardently desires a world freed from the cruelties and abominations which at present disfigure it, then, certainly, you will be justified in calling me a Christian. And, in this sense, I think you will find more "Christians" among agnostics than among the orthodox. But, for my part, I cannot accept such a definition. Apart from other objections to it, it seems rude to Jews, Buddhists, Mohammedans and other non-Christians, who, so far as history shows, have been at least as apt as Christians to practice the virtues which some modern Christians arrogantly claim as distinctive of their own religion.

I think also that all who called themselves Christians in an earlier time, and a great majority of those who do so at the present day, would consider that belief in God and immortality is essential to a Christian. On these grounds, I should not call myself a Christian, and I should say that an agnostic cannot be a Christian. But, if the word "Christianity" comes to be generally used to mean merely a kind of morality, then it will certainly be possible for an agnostic to be a Christian.

DOES AN AGNOSTIC DENY THAT MAN HAS A SOUL?

This question has no precise meaning unless we are given a definition of the word "soul." I suppose what is meant is, roughly, something nonmaterial which persists throughout a person's life and even, for those who believe in immortality, throughout all future time. If this is what is meant, an agnostic is not likely to believe that man has a soul. But I must hasten to add that this does not mean that an agnostic must be a materialist. Many agnostics (including myself) are quite as doubtful of the body as they are of the soul, but this is a long story taking one into difficult metaphysics. Mind and matter alike, I should say, are only convenient symbols in discourse, not actually existing things.

DOES AN AGNOSTIC BELIEVE IN A HEREAFTER, IN HEAVEN OR HELL?

The question whether people survive death is one as to which evidence is possible. Psychical research and spiritualism are thought by many to supply such evidence. An agnostic, as such, does not take a view about survival unless he thinks that there is evidence one way or the other. For my part, I do not think there is any good reason to believe that we survive death, but I am open to conviction if adequate evidence should appear.

Heaven and hell are a different matter. Belief in hell is bound up with the belief that the vindictive punishment of sin is a good thing, quite independently of any reformative or deterrent effect that it may have. Hardly any agnostic believes this. As for heaven, there might conceivably someday be evidence of its existence through spiritualism, but most agnostics do not think that there is such evidence, and therefore do not believe in heaven.

ARE YOU NEVER AFRAID OF GOD'S JUDGMENT IN DENYING HIM?

Most certainly not. I also deny Zeus and Jupiter and Odin and Brahma, but this causes me no qualms. I observe that a very large portion of the human race does not believe in God and suffers no visible punishment in consequence. And if there were a God, I think it very unlikely that He would have such an uneasy vanity as to be offended by those who doubt His existence.

HOW DO AGNOSTICS EXPLAIN THE BEAUTY AND HARMONY OF NATURE?

I do not understand where this "beauty" and "harmony" are supposed to be found. Throughout the animal kingdom, animals ruthlessly prey upon each other. Most of them are either cruelly killed by other animals or slowly die of hunger. For my part, I am unable to see any very great beauty or harmony in the tapeworm. Let it not be said that this creature is sent as a punishment for our sins, for it is more prevalent among animals than among humans. I suppose the questioner is thinking of such things as the beauty of the starry heavens. But one should remember that stars every now and again explode and reduce everything in their neighborhood to a vague mist. Beauty, in any case, is subjective and exists only in the eye of the beholder.

HOW DO AGNOSTICS EXPLAIN MIRACLES AND OTHER REVELATIONS OF GOD'S OMNIPOTENCE?

Agnostics do not think that there is any evidence of "miracles" in the sense of happenings contrary to natural law. We know that faith healing occurs and is in no sense miraculous. At Lourdes, certain diseases can be cured and others cannot. Those that can be cured at Lourdes can probably be cured by any doctor in whom the patient has faith. As for the records of other miracles, such as Joshua commanding the sun to stand still, the agnostic dismisses them as legends and points to the fact that all religions are plentifully supplied with such legends. There is just as much miraculous evidence for the Greek gods in Homer as for the Christian God in the Bible.

THERE HAVE BEEN BASE AND CRUEL PASSIONS, WHICH RELIGION OPPOSES. IF YOU ABANDON RELIGIOUS PRINCIPLES, COULD MANKIND EXIST?

The existence of base and cruel passions is undeniable, but I find no evidence in history that religion has opposed these passions. On the contrary, it has sanctified them, and enabled people to indulge them without remorse. Cruel persecutions have been commoner in Christendom than anywhere else. What appears to justify persecution is dogmatic belief. Kindliness and tolerance only prevail in proportion as dogmatic belief decays. In our day, a new dogmatic religion, namely, communism, has arisen. To this, as to other systems of dogma, the agnostic is opposed. The persecuting character of present-day communism is exactly like the persecuting character of Christianity in earlier centuries. In so far as Christianity has become less persecuting, this is mainly due to the work of freethinkers who have made dogmatists rather less dogmatic. If they were as dogmatic now as in former times, they would still think it right to burn heretics at the stake. The spirit of tolerance which some modern Christians regard as essentially Christian is, in fact, a product of the temper which allows doubt and is suspicious of absolute certainties. I think that anybody who surveys past history in an impartial manner will be driven to the conclusion that religion has caused more suffering than it has prevented.

WHAT IS THE MEANING OF LIFE TO THE AGNOSTIC?

I feel inclined to answer by another question: What is the meaning of "the meaning of life"? I suppose what is intended is some general purpose. I do not think that life in general has any purpose. It just happened. But individual human beings have purposes, and there is nothing in agnosticism to cause them to abandon these purposes. They cannot, of course, be certain of achieving the results at which they aim; but you would think ill of a soldier who refused to fight unless victory was certain. The person who needs religion to bolster up his own purposes is a timorous person, and I cannot think as well of him as of the man who takes his chances, while admitting that defeat is not impossible.

DOES NOT THE DENIAL OF RELIGION MEAN THE DENIAL OF MARRIAGE AND CHASTITY?

Here again, one must reply by another question: Does the man who asks this question believe that marriage and chastity contribute to earthly happiness here below, or does he think that, while they cause misery here below, they are to be advocated as means of getting to heaven? The man who takes the latter view will no doubt expect agnosticism to lead to a decay of what he calls virtue, but he will have to admit that what he calls virtue is not what ministers to the happiness of the human race while on earth. If, on the other hand, he takes the former view, namely, that there are terrestrial arguments in favor of marriage and chastity, he must also hold that these arguments are such as should appeal to an agnostic. Agnostics, as such, have no distinctive views about sexual morality. But most of them would admit that there are valid arguments against the unbridled indulgence of sexual desires. They would derive these arguments, however, from terrestrial sources and not from supposed divine commands.

IS NOT FAITH IN REASON ALONE A DANGEROUS CREED? IS NOT REASON IMPERFECT AND INADEQUATE WITHOUT SPIRITUAL AND MORAL LAW?

No sensible man, however agnostic, has "faith in reason alone." Reason is concerned with matters of fact, some observed, some inferred. The question whether there is a future life and the question whether there is a God concern matters of fact, and the agnostic will hold that they should be investigated in the same way as the question, "Will there be an eclipse of the moon tomorrow?" But matters of fact alone are not sufficient to determine action, since they do not tell us what ends we ought to pursue. In the realm of ends, we need something other than reason. The agnostic will find his ends in his own heart and not in an external command. Let us take an illustration: Suppose you wish to travel by train from New York to Chicago; you will use reason to discover when the trains run, and a person who thought that there was some faculty of insight or intuition enabling him to dispense with the timetable would be thought rather silly. But no timetable will tell him that it is wise to travel to Chicago. No doubt, in deciding that it is wise, he will have to take account of further matters of fact; but behind all the matters of fact, there will be the ends that he thinks fitting to pursue, and these, for an agnostic as for other men, belong to a realm which is not that of reason, though it should be in no degree contrary to it. The realm I mean is that of emotion and feeling and desire.

DO YOU REGARD ALL RELIGIONS AS FORMS OF SUPERSTITION OR DOGMA?
WHICH OF THE EXISTING RELIGIONS DO YOU MOST RESPECT, AND WHY?

All the great organized religions that have dominated large populations have involved a greater or less amount of dogma, but "religion"
is a word of which the meaning is not very definite. Confucianism, for
instance, might be called a religion, although it involves no dogma.
And in some forms of liberal Christianity, the element of dogma is
reduced to a minimum.

Of the great religions of history, I prefer Buddhism, especially in its
earliest forms, because it has had the smallest element of persecution.

COMMUNISM, LIKE AGNOSTICISM, OPPOSES RELIGION.
ARE AGNOSTICS COMMUNISTS?

Communism does not oppose religion. It merely opposes the Christian
religion, just as Mohammedanism does. Communism, at least in the
form advocated by the Soviet government and the Communist party,
is a new system of dogma of a peculiarly virulent and persecuting sort.
Every genuine agnostic must therefore be opposed to it.

DO AGNOSTICS THINK THAT SCIENCE AND RELIGION
ARE IMPOSSIBLE TO RECONCILE?

The answer turns upon what is meant by "religion." If it means merely
a system of ethics, it can be reconciled with science. If it means a system
of dogma, regarded as unquestionably true, it is incompatible with the
scientific spirit, which refuses to accept matters of fact without evidence,
and also holds that complete certainty is hardly ever attainable.

WHAT KIND OF EVIDENCE COULD CONVINCE YOU THAT GOD EXISTS?

I think that if I heard a voice from the sky predicting all that was going
to happen to me during the next twenty-four hours, including events
that would have seemed highly improbable, and if all these events
then proceeded to happen, I might perhaps be convinced at least of
the existence of some superhuman intelligence. I can imagine other
evidence of the same sort which might convince me, but so far as I
know, no such evidence exists.

Can a Scientist Believe in God?

WARREN WEAVER

Warren Weaver, scientist, mathematician and educator, was vice-president for the natural and medical sciences of the Rockefeller Foundation until 1959; since then he has been vice-president of the Alfred P. Sloan Foundation.

He was born in Reedsburg, Wisconsin, in 1894 and received his Ph.D. at the University of Wisconsin, where he was chairman of the Mathematics Department. He has been awarded an honorary LL.D. from his alma mater, and a Doctor of Science degree from the University of Sao Paulo, Brazil.

Mr. Weaver has had a distinguished career in government service. During World War II, he was chief of the Applied Mathematics Panel of the National Research Defense Committee of the Office of Scientific Research and Development. He has served as a member of the War Department's Research Advisory Panel and was chairman of the Naval Research Advisory Committee. He is a member of the Board of Scientific Consultants of the Sloan-Kettering Institute for Cancer Research. He has been chairman of the board of the American Association for the Advancement of Science, and is currently vice-president of the board of trustees of the Academy of Religion and Mental Health, and chairman of the board of the Salk Institute for Biological Studies.

Mr. Weaver has received the U.S. Medal for Merit, is an officer of the Legion of Honor, and was awarded the King's Medal for Service in the Cause of Freedom. He has edited the compilation entitled *The Scientists Speak,* and is co-author of *The Electromagnetic Field* (with Max Mason), *Elementary Mathematical Analysis,* and *The Mathematical Theory of Communication* (with Claude Shannon).

WHAT IS SCIENCE?

It is the activity whereby man gains understanding and control of nature. It is practiced professionally and intensely by a few, but practiced to some degree by every person. It proceeds by observing and experimenting, by constructing theories and testing them; by discarding the theories that do not check with the facts, and by improving good theories into better ones. It is never perfect, never absolute, never final; but it is useful and it improves.

Not every scientist would accept this definition. Almost every scientist would want to change it a little, and a few would change it a lot. But, by and large, a scientist is ready to define science. He doesn't feel the need (as he would in trying to define religion) to qualify his statement by saying, "This is *my* kind of science—this is what science means to me."

WHAT IS RELIGION?

Religion is a highly personal affair. I can only tell you what *I* mean by the word.

Religion, to me, has two main aspects. It is, first and foremost, a guide to conduct. Second, it is the theory of the moral meaning of our existence.

Do not be surprised that this definition of religion involves a practical aspect, which touches every act of every day, and a more "intellectual" aspect, which comes into play relatively seldom. This double answer is to be expected from a scientist, as we shall see. And scientists are precisely the kind of people who should not be surprised if these two aspects are not "consistent" with each other.

Science tries to answer the question "How?" How do cells act in the body? How do you design an airplane that will fly faster than sound? How is a molecule of insulin constructed?

Religion, by contrast, tries to answer the question "Why?" Why was man created? Why ought I tell the truth? Why must there be sorrow or pain or death?

Science attempts to analyze how things and people and animals behave; it has no concern as to whether this behavior is good or bad, is purposeful or not. But religion is precisely the quest for such answers: whether an act is right or wrong, good or bad, and why.

I realize that when theologians define religion they emphasize more abstract considerations. They would probably say that "religion is the service and adoration of God" or "a system of faith and worship"; or that religion is primarily "an apprehension, awareness, or conviction of the existence of a supreme being . . . controlling man's destiny and nature's."

HOW DO YOU DEFINE GOD?

Some regard God in very human terms, as a father who is kind but nevertheless subject to spells of wrath. Others assign to God a lot of other human qualities (love, anger, sympathy, knowledge, etc.) but expand these qualities beyond human possibilities (limitless love, infinite wisdom, total knowledge, etc.). Still others take a mystical attitude toward the concept of God: God is a spirit, and it is not useful or possible to describe God in any other way.

I am sure that each of these ideas has well served different persons at different times. But my own concept of God is rather different.

The difficulty I find with the three conceptions of God just summarized is not that they are vague; not that they depend upon faith rather than reason; not that they may even involve contradiction. I think that vagueness is sometimes not only inevitable but even desirable; that faith, in certain realms of experience, is more powerful than logic. And scientists accept such contradictions more readily than most people think.

My difficulty with the views of God sketched above is simply that though they bring comfort on the emotional plane, they do not seem to bring satisfaction on the intellectual plane. When I take any such idea of God and try to work with it mentally, try to clarify it or think it through, I find myself getting confused or embarrassed, using words with which I am not fundamentally content, words which cover up difficulties rather than explain them. It therefore gratifies me to use additional ways of thinking about God—ways which seem to me intellectually satisfying, and consistent with the thinking I try to do along other lines—scientific or not. Indeed, it is these additional ways which very directly relate to scientific thinking and scientific theories. Let me illustrate this.

When I am troubled or afraid, when I am deeply concerned for those I love, when I listen to the hymns which go back to the loveliest memories of my childhood, then God is to me an emotional and comforting God—a protecting Father.

When I am trying to work out a problem of right and wrong, then God is a clear and unambiguous Voice, an unfailing source of moral standard. I do not in the least understand how these things happen; but I know perfectly well, if I listen to this Voice, what is the right thing to do. I have many times been uncertain which course of action would best serve a certain practical purpose; but I cannot think of a single instance in my life when, asking what was the really *right* thing to do, the answer was not forthcoming.

These two statements cover my everyday relation with God. I do not find it helpful—or necessary—to try to analyze these statements in logical terms. They state facts of *experience*. You can no more convince me that there is no such God than you can convince me that a table or a rock is not solid—in each case the evidence is simple, direct and uniform.

As a scientist who is familiar with the detailed explanations of the atomic structure of, say, the table and the rock, it does not surprise me, nor disturb me, that these everyday concepts of God do not offer me detailed logical explanation. God on an intellectual plane (corresponding to the theoretical plane of the physicist) is something else.

That "something else," just as a scientist would expect, is very abstract: on the intellectual level, God is, to me, the name behind a consistent set of phenomena, all of which are recognizable in terms of moral purpose and which deal with the control of man's destiny. I shall explain this in greater detail in a moment.

CAN A SCIENTIST BELIEVE IN GOD?

Some persons think that scientists simply can't believe in God. But I think scientists have unique advantages here—for scientists are precisely the persons who believe in the unseeable, the essentially undefinable.

No scientist has ever seen an electron. No scientist soberly thinks that anyone ever could. In fact, "electron" is simply the name for a set of things that happen under certain circumstances. Yet nothing is more "real" to a scientist than an electron. Chairs and tables and rocks—these are in fact not very "real" to a scientist, if he is thinking deeply. A table, viewed with the precise tools of the atomic physicist, is a shadowy, swirling set of electric charges, these electric charges themselves being very vague and elusive. So viewed, the table completely loses its large-scale illusion of solidity.

In fact, the modern scientist has two sets of ideas about the world, which he carries in his head simultaneously. He uses the simpler set of ideas when it works, and he falls back on the more fundamental set when necessary. The simpler set of ideas deals with large-scale objects —you, me, tables, chairs, rocks, mountains. For these large-scale objects, the scientist has a workaday set of ideas about solidity, location, reality, etc. In these everyday terms, a rock is solid and real because it hurts your toe when you kick it. You know how to measure where a star is and how it is moving. These ideas are extremely useful. If a scientist got up some morning without these workaday ideas, he couldn't even succeed in getting his shoes on. Indeed, he would never figure out how to get out of bed.

But the scientist also knows that all these large-scale ideas simply *do not stand up under close examination*. When he forces his thinking down to basic levels, a wholly new and strangely abstract set of ideas comes into play. Solids are not really solid. "Real objects" are not even composed, as physicists thought a half-century ago, of submicroscopic atoms like billiard balls.

Consider the electron, for example. For a while physicists thought it was a particle. (You mustn't really ask what "particle" means, any more than you should ask just what it means when you say God has certain human characteristics.) Then physicists realized that electrons are wave motions. (Wave motions of *what*? Well, it isn't useful to ask this question, either.) Today, physicists think of electrons as being both (or either) particles or waves.

Further, you can't pin down this electron-object, whatever it is. If you ask the electron more and more insistently "Where *are* you?" you end up with less and less information about where it is going. Or, if you demand to know more and more accurately "Where are you *going*?" you end up with less and less information about where it *is*. I am not being facetious. Modern physics simply cannot tell both where a particle is and where it is going; it can answer one or the other, but not both.

Or suppose you carry out careful measurements and consult the best theories of physics to determine what an electron is going to do next. Well, it turns out that you can only say what it is *likely* to do next. Science can predict with great definiteness on large-scale, everyday sort of phenomena; but this definiteness fades away and vanishes as you proceed down the scale of size, to individual events. If a scientist is studying just two electrons, it turns out to be completely hopeless for him even to try to keep track of which is which.

All this may seem funny or ridiculous to you. But you had better not jump to unwise conclusions. Science may move on to more advanced views of the ultimate nature of things; but there is not the slightest promise that the "improved" view can be any less abstract.

Most scientists, I think, have had to come to an entirely new concept of what "explaining," "understanding," or "defining" really mean. And this holds for science no less than religion.

To "explain" something used to mean that you described a strange situation in terms of more familiar situations; you "understand" the thing which was "explained" with more familiar ideas. But if you have any mental curiosity, you are bound to say "How about the more familiar ideas? Explain *them!*" And then you run into a real dead end. For any "explanation," however useful and however comforting, finally comes to rest on the *unfamiliar*—because when you get to the bottom step of an explaining process there simply are no terms which you can use to become "familiar" with the bottom step.

Let's take stock of where we are. I am trying to explain whether or not a scientist can believe in God. To do this, I am trying to explain the way scientists think. And we find that a scientist is, by his training, specially prepared to think about things in two ways: the everyday way, and a second way which is a deep, logical, restless, and detailed way. In this second way of thinking, the scientist is forced to live with very abstract ideas. He has come to feel their value and their inevitability. He has developed skepticism concerning easy answers or the "obvious" nature of events. He is the last to expect that an "ultimate explanation" is going to involve familiar ideas. He is convinced, moreover, that reality is not simply denseness or visibility, hardness or solidity. To the scientist, the real is simply what is *universally experienced*.

Does this sound abstract and difficult? Of course it does: The scientist knows that when he is pushed back to a point at which his thinking should begin, he is forced to deal with difficult abstractions. A scientist is just the one who should not say that an abstract concept of God results in an "unreal" God. For the scientist knows that the everyday reality of the table and the rock is an illusion, and that reality is in fact a very subtle, evasive, and somewhat abstract business.

A scientist does not accept ideas just because they are abstract or unreal. He raises a very basic question: "Does this definition *work* successfully?" "Electron" is only the name behind a set of phenomena, but essentially all physicists agree as to what these electron-phenomena are; and there is a high degree of agreement on the rules which govern electron-phenomena. If there is this kind of consistency, then a definition "works"—and the scientist finds it acceptable and satisfying.

Man has not attained the same universal agreement, or consistent explanations, for what can be called God-phenomena. Yet I accept the idea of God for three reasons: First, in the total history of man there has been a most impressive amount of general agreement about the existence (if not the details) of "God." This agreement is not so logically precise as the agreements about electrons; but far, far more people believe and have believed in God than believe or have ever believed in electrons.

Second, I know I cannot think through the realm of religious experience as satisfactorily as I can think through certain smaller and less important problems. The nuclear physicist today only has incomplete and contradictory theories. But the theories work pretty well, and represent the best knowledge we have on a very important subject.

Third, I accept two sets of ideas of God—the everyday concept of an emotional and intuitive God, and the intellectual concept of an abstract God—for the very solid reason that I find both of them personally satisfying. It does not at all worry me that these are two rather different sets of ideas: if an electron can be two wholly inconsistent things, it is a little narrow to expect so much less of God.

CAN A SCIENTIST BELIEVE THE BIBLE?

I think that God has revealed Himself to many at many times and in many places. I think, indeed, that he keeps continuously revealing Himself to man today. Every new discovery of science is a further "revelation" of the order which God has built into His universe.

I believe that the Bible is the purest revelation we have of the nature and goodness of God. It seems to me natural, indeed inevitable, that the human record of divine truth should exhibit a little human frailty along with much divine truth. It seems to me quite unnecessary to be disturbed over minor eccentricities in the record.

There are, of course, sincere and earnest persons who find it necessary to place a literal interpretation on every word in the Bible, and who accept every statement as divinely revealed truth. This attitude seems to me to lead to both spiritual and intellectual poverty.

The reports of miraculous happenings in Biblical times seem to me more reasonably understandable as poetic exaggeration, as ancient interpretations of events which we would not consider miraculous today, or as concessions (on the part of Christian writers) to the problem of competing with the magical claims of other religions.

CAN A SCIENTIST BELIEVE IN MIRACLES?

Put a kettle of water on the stove. What happens? Does the water get hot and boil, or does it freeze? The nineteenth-century scientist would have considered it ridiculous to ask this question. But scientists today, aware of the peculiarities of modern physical theories, would say, "In the overwhelming proportion of the cases, the water will get hot and boil. But in one of a vast number of trials, it is to be expected that the water will *freeze* rather than boil."

Modern science recognizes the exceedingly rare possibility of happenings—like water freezing on a hot stove, or like a brick spontaneously moving upward several feet—which so contradict the usual order of events that they can be called "miracles." No one can logically hold that science rules out "miracles" as impossible.

If my religious faith required miracles, my scientific knowledge would not necessarily deny them. But my religious faith does not at all rest on the validity of ancient miracles. To me, God gains in dignity and power through manifestations of His reason and order, not through exhibitions of caprice.

CAN A SCIENTIST BELIEVE IN "LIFE AFTER DEATH"?

Scientists are very heavily (but not exclusively, as some claim) influenced by evidence: If there is good evidence for a statement, they accept or believe the statement; if there is good evidence *against,* they reject. If it seems impossible to produce any evidence—either for or against a statement—then scientists tend to consider such statements as unprofitable matters of inquiry.

So far as I am concerned, "life after death" is a matter in which I can neither believe nor disbelieve. To date, at least, I have been too much interested in this life to feel any urge to indulge in pure speculation about another.

Sixty-six Million Americans Do Not Belong to Any Church:

What Do They Believe?

JEROME NATHANSON

Jerome Nathanson is chairman of the Fraternity of Leaders of the American Ethical Union, a member of the Board of Leaders of the New York Society for Ethical Culture, and a member of the board of directors of the International Humanist and Ethical Union. From 1945 to 1961, he served on the board of trustees of the National Child Labor Committee. He is Chairman of the New York Committee to Abolish Capital Punishment and a member of the Clergymen's Advisory Committee of Planned Parenthood.

Mr. Nathanson was born in Chicago in 1908. He was graduated from Cornell University and worked on the Yonkers *Herald* for several years. He received an M.A. at Columbia University in 1931 and joined the staff of the New York Society for Ethical Culture in 1937. He was chairman of the National Committee on Federal Aid to Public Education from 1949 to 1952, and served as chairman of the Conference on the Scientific Spirit and the Democratic Faith from 1944 to 1947. He is a member of Phi Beta Kappa, the American Association of Arbitrators and the American Philosophical Association.

Mr. Nathanson is the author of *John Dewey: The Reconstruction of the Democratic Life,* and *Forerunners of Freedom.* A contributor to various journals, he has also edited two books: *Science for Democracy* and *The Authoritarian Attempt to Capture Education.*

If anyone were to ask you how many Americans belong to a church or temple or synagogue, you would probably say, "Almost all." But the facts are startling. Actually, 66,000,000 Americans—36.4 per cent of the population—are not even *claimed* as church members. This figure is all the more remarkable if we remember that some denominations count as members not simply those who go to church but anyone who was baptized or who ever belonged to the group and subsequently left.

Why are so many Americans members of no church? Has religion failed them?

There is no simple answer. Many of those who do not belong to any church have taken the hard rather than the easy road, for they have withstood great pressure in order to stay out of groups it is so easy to join, and for which high approval from neighbors and community is given.

We all know that many people join a church out of habit, or out of respect for their parents, or for family tradition. Some do so in order to wear the badge of respectability, or get a testimonial to good character. Businessmen and professional men often prize the "contacts" they make in a church or a temple; their careers are helped if they conform to the community's values. Some parents want their children to have a religious education, even though they themselves feel no strong need for a formal faith. Other parents want their children to "belong," to do what others in the group do, to associate with the "right" people, to make a good marriage with a decent and moral spouse. In addition, in these terrible days of anxiety and fear—with war and annihilation hanging over our heads—millions upon millions, not knowing where to turn or whom to trust, attend religious services which promise inner peace, salvation and life eternal. It is small wonder that ours is a day of a great religious revival.

The great majority of churchgoers are undoubtedly sincere and devout; they believe in God, in morality, in the specific articles of their church's creed. But in the light of the variety of motives which lead people into church membership, we can see how many and how varied are the pressures which are brought to bear on those who do not join any church. Why, then, do so many millions stay away from our churches and the solace they offer, the hope they proffer? Is it because they are "bad" people? Surely not.

Many stay away from a church because of the denominational rivalries and bickering. Some dislike formal, elaborate rituals. And some (though they do not know it) follow the example of the noblest man our land has produced, Abraham Lincoln, who made this startling and little-known statement of his faith when he declared that he had never united himself to any church because he found difficulty in giving his assent, without mental reservations, to the long complicated statements of Christian doctrine which characterize their articles of belief and confessions of faith. "When any church will inscribe over its altar as its sole qualifications for membership the Savior's condensed statement of the substance of both the law and the gospel, 'Thou shalt love the Lord thy God with all thy heart, and with all thy soul, and with all thy strength, and with all thy mind; and thy neighbor as thyself'—that church will I join with all my heart and all my soul."*

Now the Americans who do not go to church are not without faith; nor is it true that life has neither meaning nor purpose for them. As Tennyson says:

> There lives more faith in honest doubt,
> Believe me, than in half the creeds.

For some have a faith that resists conformity, that impels a man to face the problems of life and death and God and the hereafter for himself, that considers creeds or rituals an unnecessary part of true religious affirmation. Such a faith means a code of honor and decency and— above all—humane relations with other human beings. In one sense, the faith that finds belief and conduct enough—without church affiliation—is a logical development of the Protestant tradition. For deep in Protestantism is the powerful idea that there need be no intermediary between a man and God—no preacher or priest or rabbi, no liturgy, no ceremonials, no public demonstration of faith. Many of the 66,000,000 Americans who do not belong to any church would probably agree with John Lovejoy Elliott, who declared: "I have known many good men who believed in God. I have known many good men who did not believe in God. But I have never known a human being who was good who did not believe in man."

We must realize that the overwhelming majority of our 66,000,000 are not *anti*-religious. To be sure, some of them profess atheism openly —but they are a very small fraction of the total. And some are agnostics—those who say they simply do not *know* whether there is or is not a God, or a heaven and hell, or a life hereafter. They hold that to go to church without real conviction and unquestioning faith is hypocritical, a profanation of the religious idea. They may even quote Holy Scripture to support their stand: "Lord, I believe; help thou mine unbelief" (Saint Mark, 9:24). And some follow the ringing words of

*Deming, Henry Champion, *Eulogy of Abraham Lincoln*. (Hartford: A. N. Clark, 1865).

Thomas Jefferson: "Fix reason firmly in her seat, and call to her tribunal every fact, every opinion. Question with boldness even the existence of a God; because, if there be one, he must more approve of the homage of reason, than that of blindfolded fear. . . . Your own reason is the only oracle given you by heaven, and you are answerable, not for the rightness, but uprightness of the decision."

For, strange though it may seem, most of the millions who do not go to church *are* religious. Many have a profound faith in God; they simply do not believe that any existing organized religion is a satisfactory expression of God's will. They cannot overlook the many differing conceptions of God—from Christianity to Buddhism and the other great religions of the East. The monotheism of Jews is not the same as the Trinitarian conception of Christians. The Protestant conception of man's relation to God is so different from the Catholic that it was one of Luther's chief reasons for revolting from Rome. Baptist conceptions of faith and worship differ as much from Episcopalian as Lutherans differ from Mormons.

For there are surely many conceptions of God: Matthew Arnold thought of God as the Power-not-ourselves which makes for good; William James believed in a limited but growing God, who needs our help in making the good more prevalent; Henri Bergson spoke of the creative force which expresses itself in the evolutionary process. Some scientists speak of a "cosmic consciousness" which gives meaning to existence. Some philosophers believe in an absolute moral law, embedded in the very structure of the universe. But how many of these conceptions are organized into a formal church with a rigid ritual and set ideas about sin or salvation?

We should remember that many people hold fast to a faith about which, intellectually, they are a little uneasy. Two six-year-olds were recently engaged in an earnest discussion of death. "When my mother dies," said the first, "she will go to heaven, and when I die I'll see her there."

"I don't think so," the other remarked.

"Oh, yes, I will. When I die an angel will come down to me. And when the angel brushes my cheek with its wing, then I'll go to heaven and see my mother."

"Do you *really* think that?" the second boy asked.

"Well, I don't really *think* it," came the rejoinder, "but I believe it."

Do the 66,000,000 Americans who refuse to "believe" in this way have anything in common—except the fact that they do not go to church? Yes. They share an important attitude—the idea that it is possible to be "religious," moral, decent, without joining a group and worshiping *en masse*. They believe the individual can get as close to the idea of God as any cleric or institution can bring him. They hold the high faith that men are responsible for what they do with their lives, how they think and live. They do not feel the need for "official" forgiveness or rituals or catechisms to make them men of virtue. They try to lead a life which is honorable, productive, satisfying, right, good —for *them*. (It may or may not be right or good for someone else.) A good life, to their minds, does not depend upon church attendance. They believe, as did some of the greatest men the human race has produced, that personal morality is not dependent on organized religion.

Is it bad for our country that so many Americans hold this independent attitude? The Founding Fathers did not think so: they created the First Amendment to the Constitution for the specific purpose of letting each man have the right to his own form of worship—or his own independence from religious groups.

The very richness and creativity of American life rests on the fact that people can and do think different thoughts, hold different beliefs, live in different ways. James Madison, "the Father of the Constitution," went so far as to say: "The best and only security for religious liberty in any society is a multiplicity of sects. Where there is such a variety of sects, there cannot be a majority of any one sect to oppress and persecute the rest."

Democracy means that people respect the rights of others, including *the right to be different*. Only dictatorships want everybody to think, feel, and act the same.

Are "bad" lives—immorality, crimes, anti-social conduct—greater among those who do not go to church than among church members? Not at all. Two social scientists, May and Hartshorne, in their *Studies in Deceit,* found a surprisingly high percentage of "dishonesty" among Sunday school graduates. The research of Negley K. Teeters and other sociologists has demonstrated that criminals are not found more often among non-churchgoers. The majority of Americans are identified with one church or another. The majority of criminals are identified with a church. It would be absurd to conclude that churches are responsible for delinquency and crime. But it is equally false to conclude that the failure to attend church is responsible. The facts do not support this.

Some people feel guilty because they do not belong to a church. Is there any reason for this? Of course there is. As children, they were taught to hold certain beliefs; but as they grew up they found that they no longer believed these things. This did not happen because they *wanted* to disbelieve or because they were "bad" people. It happened because their experiences and development and intelligence led them to question or doubt their earlier beliefs. Often they long for the sense of security they got from their childhood faith. Often they would *like* to believe again what they once accepted. But they cannot honestly do so, and they feel uneasy about "betraying" the good people who taught them what a good life means.

Yet they have done nothing wrong. On the contrary, they refuse to give lip service to what they do not really believe. They have the courage to stand up for their own faith. They honor their own convictions and try to maintain their own integrity. Just so did the Hebrew prophets speak to the people of Israel. Just so did Socrates defy the Athenians in his search for truth. Just so did Jesus assail all those who would sacrifice the spirit of love for the letter of the law.

No, the nonconformist need not feel guilty. He is following some of the greatest visions of the human spirit—to seek dignity without dogma.

Now when moral and religious questions are discussed in our country, we refer to the position of Catholics, Protestants and Jews. That takes care of "the religious groups." The 66,000,000 Americans who are not members of a church or temple or synagogue are dismissed as of little importance. They live as individuals and are not united into any one group; *no one* speaks for them.

We must remember that when the "three faiths" have expressed themselves, we have *not* canvassed all sides of religious and moral questions. The real concern with living a good life represents the ground for unity between those who go to church and those who do not. This unity will not be achieved through discussions of theory or theology. It will be achieved through common *action* in behalf of common goals. Despite differences about the meaning of religion, all of us have a common stake in improving the health and education of our people, in developing the fullest talents of our children and youth, in lessening discrimination, in advancing welfare and security, in forwarding democracy, in striving for world peace and world unity.

Beyond this, there is an ancient vision which can be revived for our common benefit. For however each of us may make his peace with the universe, our faith in *man* expresses the vision of the human-ness, the humaneness, the humanity of man. It is the vision which speaks in the following prayer:

May I be no man's enemy, and may I be the friend of that which is eternal and abides. . . . May I never devise evil against any man; if any devise evil against me, may I escape . . . without the need of hurting him. May I love, seek, and attain only that which is good. May I wish for all men's happiness and envy none. . . . When I have done or said what is wrong, may I never wait for the rebuke of others, but always rebuke myself until I make amends. . . . May I win no victory that harms either me or my opponent. . . . May I reconcile friends who are wroth with one another. May I, to the extent of my power, give all needful help . . . to all who are in want. May I never fail a friend in danger. . . . May I respect myself. . . . May I always keep tame that which rages within me. . . . May I never discuss who is wicked and what wicked things he has done, but know good men and follow in their footsteps.

No, this is not the prayer of a Catholic priest, a Protestant minister, a Jewish rabbi, a Quaker teacher. These words are those of Eusebius, a "pagan" who lived some two thousand years ago.* In these words is the voice of man's best hope on earth.

---

*Quoted by Gilbert Murray, *Five Stages of Greek Religion*. London, G. Watts and Co., 1946, pp. 197–198.

part two

Facts, Figures and Opinions on Religion in the United States

Church Membership and Religious Preference
Clergy, Church Organization and Recent Church Mergers
Religion and Education
Religion in American History
Religion in Contemporary American Life:
    Sociological Data and Polls

Church Membership and Religious Preference

Church Membership Statistics

1. APPRAISAL OF CHURCH MEMBERSHIP STATISTICS

1a. What Does a Leading Authority Think About Church Statistics?

Excerpted from "Confessions of a Church Statistician," by Benson Y. Landis, *National Council Outlook,* National Council of Churches of Christ in the U.S.A., February, 1957, vol. 7, no. 2, p. 3.

FOR almost forty years I have compiled and studied church statistics on an interdenominational basis. During that time I have been interested in noting the various responses to the publication of my elementary summaries and compilations. They may be grouped under these heads:

(1) Most people who have published comments have, in my opinion, overestimated the value or significance of these products of simple arithmetic and an ordinary adding machine.

(2) Some will have nothing to do with them because they are church statistics. In this group are eminent social scientists.

(3) Others, possibly a small group, have sought to make careful use of church statistics, have tried to understand the nature of the sources, and have engaged in inquiry concerning their meaning.

Since the federal Census of Religious Bodies, 1926, there have been no compilations for U. S. A. by uniform methods, gathered at one time, with the relatively full cooperation of the local churches. The federal census of 1936 was marred because of the non-cooperation of about 20 per cent of the local churches. That of 1946 was begun and never completed. In 1956 the executive branch of a government with leaders vocal on religion did not bother to request an appropriation from Congress.

Many religious bodies make annual reports of the figures that they obtain from their local churches. But it is not even known how many of the 268 religious bodies gather such information annually. Perhaps half of them do.

Thus much of the quality of the reporting is dependent on what the local churches have by way of records and on the willingness of pastors or lay people to make careful accountings. Many of the published figures come from local church records that are apparently not carefully kept, either by clergymen or lay people.

What about those that do not make annual collections of reports from local churches? Some gather figures at irregular intervals, and others simply make crude estimates of their constituencies.

Just as local churches vary in the care of their reporting, so the various religious bodies vary in their conceptions of membership and of the formality with which people are related to their churches. There has never been a compilation of definitions of church membership. In some Protestant denominations it is only by custom, and not by formal action, that many persons are taken into full membership at age 13.

Also, a number of Protestant bodies do count all baptized children, including infants; it is not correct to say that Protestants, of course, only count persons aged 13 years and over. In 1945, I estimated carefully and found 5,000,000 Protestant church members officially reported under age 13.

Roman Catholics include all baptized persons. Jewish congregations include all Jews in communities having congregations. The Eastern Orthodox include all persons in the cultural or nationality or racial group served. The relation of many Negro families to their churches is a very informal one, and it is difficult for these churches to keep records.

The great migrations have brought problems for the churches, one of which may be a higher proportion of non-resident and inactive members than in former years. We may also be getting to a place where duplication of membership is more than negligible.

There are careful observers who think that it is in the suburbs that much of the current church activity, including building, is taking place. There are many "inner cities" and rural communities whose churches do not seem to be gaining membership, and are thus not participating in the overall gains whereby officially reported church membership has been increasing more rapidly than population.

There should come a day when church statistics generally are presented to consumers more carefully than other statistics. At present that day is far from dawning. In simple justice to consumers, there should be intensive cooperation toward that end.

1b. *Statistics Not Standardized*

Excerpted from "Trends in Church Membership in the United States," by Benson Y. Landis, *Annals of the American Academy of Political and Social Science,* November, 1960, vol. 332, pp. 3-4, 6-8.

CAN comparisons be made between the latest information and earlier statistics? What can be said about trends? Between 1890 and 1958 there were thirty compilations of church membership. Five of these were made by the Bureau of the Census according to standardized methods. The other compilations were made by the *Christian Herald,* a periodical published in New York, and by the Federal Council of Churches and the National Council of Churches. The National Council has compiled the latest information annually since 1951. The difficulty is that the private compilations were not made by uniform methods. Because of the lack of uniformity and the irregularity with which figures are reported, there currently are no national statistics compiled by standardized methods. Thus no direct comparisons between religious bodies can be made on a national basis.

The federal religious censuses were made by means of standard forms mailed to the pastors and clerks of local congregations. The figures were summarized by denominations and were distributed by states, counties and cities. The *Census of Religious Bodies* for 1926 is generally regarded as the most adequate book on church statistics ever published in the United States. The 1936 statistics were much less satisfactory. The Bureau of the Census stated that the census for that year was "incomplete." It seems that about 20 per cent of the local churches did not report to the Bureau even after a series of requests. The number of local churches recorded by the census was about 20 per cent lower than the number reported that year to the *Christian Herald,* which had collected figures in various previous years. The 1946 *Census of Religious Bodies* was begun but never completed owing to the refusal of Congress to make an appropriation sufficient for the project. In 1956 no recommendation was made to Congress by the administration concerning the matter, and no member of Congress appears to have been sufficiently interested to raise a question about it, and no official of a religious body appeared before a congressional committee to request an appropriation for the purpose. Officials of religious bodies have occasionally made representations to the Bureau of the Census regarding the value of these projects.

As the censuses between 1906 and 1926 indicate, there has been a tendency on the part of some religious bodies to report on a more inclusive basis in the later as compared with the earlier years. Thus some of the alleged gains reflect in part changes in the method of reporting. It would appear, however, that there have been no major changes in the basis of reporting since the year 1926.

Two additional sources on religious affiliation should be noted: a church distribution study and a survey of a sample of the civilian population conducted by the Bureau of the Census. Data from 114 religious bodies for the year 1952 were published in a series of eighty bulletins entitled "Churches and Church Membership in the United States" by the National Council of Churches. These bulletins revealed a total membership of 74,125,462 persons in 182,856 local churches in the 114 religious bodies cooperating. Roman Catholic and Jewish figures were included along with figures for many large Protestant denominations. The large Negro Protestant bodies as well as many others, totaling 137 in number, were not studied because the figures were not obtainable for states, counties and cities on a comparable basis. This study brought out significant differences between the metropolitan and the non-metropolitan areas. Fifty-seven per cent of the people of the nation lived in metropolitan areas, according to the 1950 Census of Population. In these areas were found 46 per cent of the Protestants included in the study and 75 per cent of the Roman Catholics and all but a small percentage of the Jews. Forty-three per cent of the people lived in non-metropolitan areas. These included 54 per cent of the Protestants studied and 25 per cent of the Roman Catholic membership. On a regional basis, comparing denominational strength with population distribution, the Protestants were strongest in the South and weakest in the Northeast; the Catholics were strongest in the Northeast and weakest in the South.

For several decades there has been an interest in the inclusion of a question on religion in the decennial Census of Population. In 1956, the Bureau of the Census began a consultation among many agencies concerning the inclusion of the question "What is your religion?" in the forthcoming population census of 1960. The question was tried in a few localities, and in March 1957 a sample of persons over 14 years of age in 35,000 households in all parts of the nation were questioned. Officials of the Bureau of the Census indicated that if the question were used in 1960 it would probably be asked only of a sample of 20 per cent of the households enumerated.

Considerable discussion of the proposal ensued in church circles and elsewhere during 1957. Roman Catholic officials and press were, with one exception, in favor of the proposal; Jewish press and agencies, again with one exception, were opposed; Protestant officials and press were apparently sharply divided.* Religious liberty—the freedom of the individual in relation to the power of the government—was the overriding consideration among those opposed. A journal edited by Roman Catholic laymen, *The Commonweal,* New York, regarded the inclusion of the question as an invasion of privacy. *The Commonweal* seems to have been the lone Catholic dissenting voice.

Information Service of the National Council of Churches, vol. 37, no. 6.

Asking the question was favored by those who felt that there was some value in learning the religious leanings of the people by localities, states and regions. It was opposed by some persons with experience in population surveys as of little value for research purposes because the replies would indicate both preference and affiliation with no distinction between them.

After careful study of the discussion, the Director of the Bureau of the Census issued a statement on December 12, 1957, to the effect that the Bureau would not ask a question on religion in the census of 1960. It was recognized at the time that a considerable number of persons would be reluctant to answer and the refusal to answer would be legally punishable. The value of statistics based on the question was not considered great enough to justify overriding such an attitude. Cost factors were also a consideration. In the statement it was also said that the decision did not preclude inclusion of the question in some later census or the publication of information obtained in voluntary surveys.

On February 2, 1958, the results of a voluntary inquiry appeared under the title *Religion Reported by the Civilian Population of the United States; March 1957.* Two out of every three persons 14 years of age and over reported themselves as Protestants and 1 out of every 4 as Roman Catholic. More women than men were reported for the major religious groups. 96 per cent of the respondents reported a religion; 3 per cent stated that they had no religion; and 1 per cent made no report on religion. It was found that the more rural the community, the higher the proportion of Protestants; the more urban the community the higher the percentage of Roman Catholics. About 100,000 persons were included in the sample. Figures were stated to be not comparable with the reports of the religious bodies, because the latter included only formal affiliation, while the survey of the population asked simply about religion.

1c. Nature and Limitations of the Data*

Quoted from "An Approach to the Religious Geography of the United States: Patterns of Church Membership in 1952," by Wilbur Zelinsky, *Annals of the Association of American Geographers,* June, 1961, vol. 51, no. 2, pp. 141-42.

BEGINNING with the Seventh Census in 1850, information on churches was compiled in connection with each of the decennial enumerations until 1890, although the 1880 material never reached the publication stage. In 1906, the

* There is no single comprehensive bibliography of the statistical data and general literature on religion in the United States, but the best general guides are Benson Y. Landis, "A Guide to the Literature on Statistics of Religious Affiliation with References to Related Social Studies," *Journal of the American Statistical Association,* vol. 54 (1959), pp. 335-57, and Dorothy Good, "Questions on Religion in the United States Census," *Population Index,* vol. 25 (1959), pp. 3-16.

Bureau inaugurated a special Census of Religious Bodies which was continued at ten-year intervals until 1936.*

It is generally believed that the 1926 Census was the most complete and successful in the series. The 1850, 1860 and 1870 enumerations resulted in the publication of information on the number and seating capacity of church edifices, as well as a variety of facts about finances, educational, missionary and other activities of the denominations, but not statistics on membership. The earliest figures on number of members (for each denomination, on a county basis) appeared in the reports of the 1890 Census; and this material was published for all the subsequent Censuses of Religious Bodies.

In every instance, the Census canvass involved the procurement of information from the local congregation, at first by direct interrogation by an enumerator and later by means of mailed inquiries. No effort was ever made to ascertain the church affiliation or preference of individuals by including a religious query in the regular census schedule. A single attempt to do so on a sample basis in 1957 proved to be abortive.†

The constitutional doctrine of the separation of church and state had come to be interpreted in many quarters as even prohibiting the collection by a government agency of any information concerning churches, much less any facts regarding the religious status of individuals. It was apparently a growing sensitivity on this issue that led to a marked deterioration in the response to the 1936 canvass and the failure to publish the partial results of the 1946 Census of Religious Bodies or even to initiate one in 1956. With

Valuable bibliographical material on immigrant religious communities can be found in Stanley J. Tracy, ed., *A Report on World Population Migrations, as Related to the United States of America* (Washington, 1956).

*The basic tabulations appear in the following publications:

Seventh Census of the United States: 1850, Table 14 "Church Property, etc.," 1853.

Eighth Census of the United States: 1860. Statistics of the United States (Including Mortality, Property, etc.) in 1860, 1866.

Ninth Census of the United States: 1870, vol. 1, Tables 40, 41, 42, 1872.

Eleventh Census of the United States: 1890, vol. 9, Report on Statistics of Churches in the United States, 1894.

Religious Bodies: 1906. Part I, Summary, Part 2, Separate Denominations, 2 vols., 1910.

Religious Bodies: 1916. Part I, Summary, Part 2, Separate Denominations, 2 vols., 1919.

Religious Bodies: 1926. vol. 1, Summary, vol. 2, Separate Denominations, 2 vols., 1929–1930.

Religious Bodies: 1936. vol 1, Summary, vol. 2, Statistics, History, Doctrine, Organization, and Work, 2 vols. in 3, 1941.

†Only a portion of the material that had been collected and analyzed had appeared ("Religion Reported by the Civilian Population of the United States; March 1957," *Current Population Reports,* Series P-20, Population Characteristics no. 79, Washington, February 2, 1958) before the Bureau decided to suspend further publication.

the withering away of the decennial Census of Religious Bodies and the failure despite a concerted campaign to have a question on religious preference included in the 1960 enumeration schedule, it is highly unlikely that any additional religious statistics will be issued by the Bureau of the Census until 1970, if then.

Critics of the various Census efforts to tally church membership have unanimously appraised them as seriously defective in terms of completeness, reliability and comparability. These shortcomings stem from the highly variable responses of the thousands of local church officials involved and the many different criteria of church membership used by the various denominations. An additional factor, for which the Census officials are completely blameless, is the frequency with which religious bodies in the United States splinter, merge, change their names, simply vanish, and otherwise make it difficult to keep track of their identity from one enumeration to another.

2. NATIONAL CHURCH MEMBERSHIP STATISTICS

2a. Membership Figures for All Reporting Churches in the U.S.

From the 1962 *Yearbook of American Churches,* Benson Y. Landis, ed., National Council of Churches of Christ in the U.S.A., New York, 1961, pp. 249–54.

Editor's Note: Alternative names of denominations have been added and cross-referenced, and totals for denominations have been added.

Mainly for the Calendar Year 1960 or a Fiscal Year Ending in 1960

Name of Religious Body	Year	No. of Churches Reported	Inclusive Church Membership
Adventist Bodies:			**355,290**
Advent Christian Church	1960	435	30,966
Church of God (Abrahamic Faith)	1960	110	5,505
Life and Advent Union	1960	3	370
Primitive Advent Christian Church	1960	12	597
Seventh-day Adventists	1960	3,032	317,852
African Orthodox Church	1957	24	**6,000**
Amana Church Society	1960	7	**761**
American Evangelical Christian Churches	1960	40	**Not available**
American Rescue Workers	1960	35	**2,350**
Apostolic Overcoming Holy Church of God	1956	300	**75,000**
Armenian Church, Diocese of Amer., Diocese of Calif.	1960	51	**125,000**
Assemblies of God	1960	8,233	**508,602**
Associated Gospel Churches	No report		
Baha'i Faith	No statistics available		
Baptist Bodies:			**21,148,862**
American Baptist Association	1960	3,091	648,000
American Baptist Convention	1959	6,262	1,543,198
Baptist General Conference	1960	536	72,056
Bethel Baptist Assembly, Inc.	1960	27	6,925
Christian Unity Baptist Association	1959	12	643
Conservative Baptist Association of America	1960	1,350	300,000
Duck River (and Kindred) Associations of Baptists	1959	28	3,139
Evangelical Baptist Church, Inc., Gen. Conf.	1952	31	2,200
Free Will Baptists	1960	2,232	191,448
General Association of Regular Baptist Churches	1960	934	136,292
General Baptists	1960	792	58,530
General Six-Principle Baptists	1959	2	58
Independent Baptist Church of America	1960	2	30
National Baptist Convention of America	1956	11,398	2,668,799
National Baptist Convention, U.S.A., Inc.	1958	26,000	5,000,000
National Baptist Evangelical Life and Soul Saving Assembly of U.S.A.	1951	264	57,674
National Primitive Baptist Convention of the U.S.A.	1957	1,100	80,983
North American Baptist Association	1959	1,980	330,265
North American Baptist General Conference	1960	300	50,646
Primitive Baptists	1950	1,000	72,000
Regular Baptists	1936	266	17,186
Separate Baptists in Christ	1960	85	7,358
Seventh Day Baptist General Conference	1960	61	5,849
Seventh Day Baptists (German, 1728)	1951	3	150
Southern Baptist Convention	1960	32,251	9,731,591
Two-Seed-In-The Spirit Predestinarian Baptists	1945	16	201
United Baptists	1955	586	63,641
United Free Will Baptist Church	1958	836('52)	100,000
Bible Protestant Church	1960	49	**2,480**
Bible Way Churches of Our Lord Jesus Christ World Wide, Inc.	1960	125	25,000

Name of Religious Body	Year	No. of Churches Reported	Inclusive Church Membership
Brethren (German Baptists):			**248,249**
Brethren Church (Ashland, Ohio)	1959	114	18,207
Brethren Church (Progressive)	1960	175	25,355
Church of the Brethren	1960	1,074	199,947
Church of God (New Dunkards)	1958	8	667
Old German Baptist Brethren	1960	56	4,073
Brethren, Plymouth	**1960**	**665**	**33,250**
Brethren (River):			**7,870**
Brethren in Christ	1959	151	6,698
Old Order, or Yorker, River Brethren	1936	7	291
United Zion Church	1959	21	881
Buddhist Churches of America	**1960**	**53**	**20,000('59)**
Catholic Apostolic Church	**1936**	**7**	**2,577**
Catholic, Roman (see Roman Catholic)			
Christadelphians	**1957**	**500**	**15,000**
Christian and Missionary Alliance	**1960**	**1,016**	**59,657**
Christian Catholic Church	**1959**	**4**	**7,000**
Christian Church of North America, Italian	**1960**	**130**	**17,000**
Christian Churches (Disciples of Christ), International Convention	**1960**	**8,001**	**1,801,821**
Christian Nation Church	**1960**	**20**	**250**
Christian Scientists (see Church of Christ, Scientist)			
Christian Union	**1959**	**122**	**7,300**
Christ's Sanctified Holy Church	**1957**	**30**	**600**
Church of Christ (Holiness), U.S.A.	**1959**	**146**	**7,621**
Church of Christ, Scientist	**No statistics furnished**		
Church of Eternal Life	**1940**	**2**	**113**
Church of God and Saints of Christ	**1959**	**217**	**38,127**
Church of God in Christ	**1960**	**3,800**	**392,635**
Church of the Gospel	**1960**	**3**	**39**
Church of Illumination	**1945**	**7**	**5,000**
Church of the Nazarene	**1960**	**4,458**	**307,629**
Church of Our Lord Jesus Christ of the Apostolic Faith, Inc.	**1954**	**155**	**45,000**
Church of Revelation, The	**1960**	**7**	**1,360**
Churches of Christ	**1960**	**18,680**	**2,163,493**
Churches of Christ in Christian Union	**1960**	**200**	**5,799**
Churches of God:			**473,276**
Church of God (Anderson, Ind.)	1960	2,278	142,796
Church of God (Cleveland, Tenn.)	1960	3,280	170,261
Church of God (Greenville, S. C.)	1959	5	100
Church of God (Seventh Day)	1960	7	2,000
Church of God, Inc., The (Original)	1959	50	7,000
Church of God, The	1959	1,901	74,209
Church of God (Seventh Day), Denver, Colo., The	1960	123	3,900
Church of God by Faith, The	1960	101	2,380
Church of God of Prophecy, The	1960	1,262	33,240
Churches of God in N. A. (General Eldership)	1960	376	37,390
Churches of God, Holiness	**1957**	**42**	**25,600**
Churches of the Living God:			**34,925**
Church of the Living God (Motto: Christian Workers for Fellowship)	1960	256	32,575
House of God, Which is the Church of the Living God, the Pillar and the Ground of the Truth, Inc.	1956	107	2,350
Churches of the New Jerusalem:			**5,875**
General Church of the New Jerusalem	1960	12	1,805
General Convention of the New Jerusalem in the U.S.A.	1960	56	4,070
Congregational Christian Churches	**1960**	**5,401**	**1,427,863**
Congregational Holiness Church	**1959**	**147**	**4,664**
Disciples of Christ (see Christian Churches)			
Divine Science Church and College, Inc.	**No report**		

Name of Religious Body	Year	No. of Churches Reported	Inclusive Church Membership
Eastern Orthodox Churches:			2,698,663
Albanian Orthodox Archdiocese in America	1960	14	16,000
American Carpatho-Russian Orthodox Greek Catholic Church	1960	64	100,000
American Catholic Church (Syro-Antiochean)	1958	40	4,563
American Holy Orthodox Catholic Apostolic Eastern Church, The	1959	27	3,500
American Orthodox Church, The	No report		
Apostolic Episcopal Church	1947	46	7,086
Assyrian Orthodox Church	1951	4	3,300
Bulgarian Eastern Orthodox Church	1960	22	86,000
Church of the East and of the Assyrians	1952	10	3,200
Eastern Orthodox Catholic Church in America	1960	2	46
Greek Archdiocese of North and South America	1960	382	1,200,000
Holy Orthodox Church in America (Eastern Catholic and Apostolic)	1960	3	218
Holy Ukrainian Autocephalic Orthodox Church in Exile	1960	10	4,500
Rumanian Orthodox Episcopate of America	1960	52	50,000
Russian Orthodox Catholic Church, Archdiocese of the Aleutian Islands and North America, The	No statistics available		
Russian Orthodox Church Outside Russia, The	1955	81	55,000('51)
Russian Orthodox Greek Catholic Church of America, The	1957	352	755,000
Serbian Eastern Orthodox Church	1960	71	125,000
Syrian Antiochian Orthodox Church	1960	81	110,000
Syrian Orthodox Church of Antioch	1960	29	50,000
Ukrainian Orthodox Church of America	1959	37	40,250
Ukrainian Orthodox Church of U.S.A.	1960	96	85,000
Ethical Culture Movement	**1960**	**28**	**6,700**
Evangelical and Reformed Church	**1960**	**2,726**	**813,271**
Evangelical Congregational Church	**1960**	**164**	**29,938**
Evangelical Covenant Church of America	**1960**	**510**	**60,090**
Evangelical Free Church of America	**1960**	**468**	**31,543**
Evangelical United Brethren Church	**1960**	**4,298**	**748,216**
Evangelistic Associations:			58,139
Apostolic Christian Church (Nazarean)	1960	38	2,024
Apostolic Christian Church of America	1960	65	8,400
Christian Congregation, The	1960	178	31,280
Church of Daniel's Band	1951	4	200
Church of God (Apostolic)	1954	22	600
Church of God as Organized by Christ	1938	14	2,192
Metropolitan Church Association	1958	15	443
Missionary Bands of the World, Inc.	Merged, 1958, with Wesleyan Methodist Church		
Missionary Church Association	1960	120	7,900
Pillar of Fire	1948	61	5,100
Federated Churches	**1936**	**508**	**88,411**
Fire-Baptized Holiness Church	**1958**	**53**	**988**
Fire-Baptized Holiness Church (Wesleyan)	**1957**	**53**	**1,007**
Free Christian Zion Church of Christ	**1957**	**728**	**18,989**
Friends:			126,199
Central Yearly Meeting of Friends	1960	11	506
Five Years Meeting of Friends	1960	528	71,552
Ohio Yearly Meeting of Friends Church (Independent)	1959	89	6,569
Oregon Yearly Meeting of Friends Church	1960	64	5,537
Pacific Yearly Meeting of Friends	1960	25	1,077
Philadelphia Yearly Meeting of the Religious Society of Friends	Statistics included in statistics for Religious Society of Friends (General Conference)		
Religious Society of Friends (Conservative)	1960	10	860
Religious Society of Friends (General Conference)	1959	291	31,530
Religious Society of Friends (Kansas Yearly Meeting)	1960	90	8,568

Greek Orthodox (see **Eastern Orthodox Churches**)

Name of Religious Body	Year	No. of Churches Reported	Inclusive Church Membership
Holiness Church of God, Inc.	1960	26	674
House of David	No statistics available		
Independent Churches	1936	384	40,276
Independent Fundamental Churches of America	1960	754	90,040
Independent Negro Churches	1936	50	12,337
International Church of the Foursquare Gospel	1960	721	82,624
Jehovah's Witnesses	1960	4,170	250,000
Jewish Congregations	1960	4,079('54)	5,367,000
Kodesh Church of Immanuel	1936	9	562
Latter-day Saints:			1,647,546
Church of Christ, Temple Lot	1956	12	3,000
Church of Jesus Christ (Bickertonites)	1960	46	2,346
Church of Jesus Christ (Cutlerites)	1957	1	22
Church of Jesus Christ of Latter-day Saints	1960	3,491	1,486,887
Reorganized Church of Jesus Christ of Latter Day Saints	1960	848	155,291
Liberal Catholic Church	1956	8	4,000
Lithuanian National Catholic Church	1960	4	3,950
Lutherans:			8,080,867
Evangelical Lutheran Synodical Conference of North America:			
Evangelical Lutheran Synod	1959	77	14,302
Lutheran Church—Missouri Synod	1960	5,215	2,391,195
Negro Missions of the Synodical Conference	1960	54	8,531
Synod of Evangelical Lutheran Churches (formerly Slovak Evangelical Lutheran Church)	1960	54	19,192
Wisconsin Evangelical Lutheran Synod (formerly Evangelical Lutheran Joint Synod of Wisconsin and Other States)	1960	829	235,073
National Lutheran Council Constituents:			
American Evangelical Lutheran Church	1960	80	24,201
American Lutheran Church, The	1960	4,625	2,242,259
Augustana Evangelical Lutheran Church	1960	1,207	608,289
Evangelical Lutheran Church, The	Merged, 1961, see The American Lutheran Church		
Finnish Evangelical Lutheran Church (Suomi Synod)	1960	153	35,529
Lutheran Free Church	1960	340	87,250
United Evangelical Lutheran Church	Merged, 1961, see The American Lutheran Church		
United Lutheran Church in America, The	1960	4,308	2,385,224
Other Lutheran Churches:			
Church of the Lutheran Brethren of America	1959	51	5,889
Evangelical Lutheran Church in America (Eielson Synod)	1957	44	4,220
Finnish Apostolic Lutheran Church of America	1957	60	6,567('53)
National Evangelical Lutheran Church	1960	55	10,146
Protestant Conference (Lutheran)	1960	8	3,000('58)
Mennonite Bodies:			160,230
Beachy Amish Mennonite Churches	1960	27	2,542
Church of God in Christ (Mennonite)	1960	36	5,000
Conference of the Evangelical Mennonite Church	1960	22	2,349
Conservative Mennonite Conference	Statistics included with Mennonite Church		
Evangelical Mennonite Brethren	1959	26	2,536
General Conference, Mennonite Church	1959	208	35,531
Hutterian Brethren	1959	20	2,250
Krimmer Mennonite Brethren Conference	1959	21	1,578
Mennonite Brethren Church of N.A.	1959	72	11,582
Mennonite Church	1960	869	73,125
Old Order Amish Mennonite Church	1960	251	17,284
Old Order (Wisler) Mennonite Church	1960	31	4,606
Reformed Mennonite Church	1958	17	615
Unaffiliated Conservative and Amish Mennonite Churches	1960	21	1,232
Methodist Bodies:			12,424,623
African Methodist Episcopal Church	1951	5,878	1,166,301

Name of Religious Body	Year	No. of Churches Reported	Inclusive Church Membership
African Methodist Episcopal Zion Church	1959	4,083	770,000
African Union First Colored Methodist Protestant Church, Inc.	1953	33	5,000
Christian Methodist Episcopal Church	1951	2,469	392,167
Congregational Methodist Church	1957	223	14,274
Congregational Methodist Church of U.S.A.	1954	100	7,500
Cumberland Methodist Church	1954	4	65
Evangelical Methodist Church	1959	112	6,200
Free Methodist Church of N.A.	1960	1,193	55,338
Fundamental Methodist Church, Inc.	1960	12	643
Holiness Methodist Church	1960	26	800
Independent A.M.E. Denomination	1940	12	1,000
Lumber River Annual Conference of the Holiness Methodist Church	1959	7	360
Methodist Church, The	1960	38,882	9,893,094
New Congregational Methodist Church	1958	11	518
Primitive Methodist Church, U.S.A.	1960	91	12,360
Reformed Methodist Union Episcopal Church	1954	33	11,000
Reformed Zion Union Apostolic Church	1956	52	12,000
Southern Methodist Church	1959	48	4,608
Union American Methodist Episcopal Church	1957	256	27,560
United Wesleyan Methodist Church of America	No statistics furnished		
Wesleyan Methodist Church of America	1960	1,063	43,835
Moravian Bodies:			67,519
Moravian Church in America (Unitas Fratrum)	1960	157	61,368
Unity of the Brethren	1960	32	6,151
Mormons (see **Latter-day Saints**)			
Muslims	No report		
National David Spiritual Temple of Christ Church Union (Inc.), U.S.A.	**1960**	**66**	**40,710**
New Apostolic Church of N.A., Inc.	**1960**	**157**	**14,204**
Old Catholic Churches:			182,408
American Catholic Church, Archdiocese of N.Y.	1947	20	8,435
North American Catholic Church	1959	52	71,521
North American Old Roman Catholic Church	1960	64	84,565
Old Catholic Archdiocese of Americas & Europe	1960	24	7,100
Old Catholic Church in America	1958	22	6,000
Old Catholic Episcopal Synod Free Catholic Church	1960	35	2,570
Reformed Catholic Church (Utrecht Confession), Province of North America, The	1957	20	2,217
Open Bible Standard Churches, Inc.	**1960**	**278**	**26,000**
Pentecostal Assemblies:			409,927
Calvary Pentecostal Church, Inc.	1960	22	8,000
Emmanuel Holiness Church	1955	56	1,200
International Pentecostal Assemblies	1960	92	15,000
Pentecostal Assemblies of the World, Inc.	1960	550	45,000
Pentecostal Church of Christ	1960	42	1,191
Pentecostal Church of God of America, Inc.	1958	900	103,500
Pentecostal Evangelical Church of God, National & International	1960	4	213
Pentecostal Fire-Baptized Holiness Church	1960	41	573
Pentecostal Free-Will Baptist Church, Inc.	1960	127	7,000
Pentecostal Holiness Church, Inc.	1960	1,239	53,250
United Pentecostal Church, Inc.	1960	1,900	175,000
Pilgrim Holiness Church	**1960**	**1,018**	**32,709**
Polish National Catholic Church of America	**1960**	**162**	**282,411**
Presbyterian Bodies:			4,333,249
Associate Presbyterian Church of N.A.	1960	6	650
Associate Reformed Presbyterian Church (General Synod)	1960	147	27,397
Bible Presbyterian Church, Inc.	1959	69	5,956
Cumberland Presbyterian Church	1960	975	88,452

Name of Religious Body	Year	No. of Churches Reported	Inclusive Church Membership
Cumberland Presbyterian Church in U.S. and Africa (formerly Colored Cumberland Presb. Church)	1944	121	30,000 ('49)
Orthodox Presbyterian Church	1960	90	10,647
Presbyterian Church in the U.S.	1960	3,995	902,849
Reformed Presbyterian Church in N.A. (General Synod)	1960	18	2,073
Reformed Presbyterian Church of N.A. (Old School)	1959	72	6,214
United Presbyterian Church in the U.S.A., The	1960	9,383	3,259,011
Protestant Episcopal Church	**1959**	**7,657**	**3,444,265**
Quakers (see **Friends**)			
Reformed Bodies:			**484,952**
Christian Reformed Church	1960	549	242,593
Hungarian Reformed Church in America	1959	40	11,110
Netherlands Reformed Congregations	1960	14	2,500
Protestant Reformed Churches of America	1960	21	2,822
Reformed Church in America	1960	867	225,927
Reformed Episcopal Church	**1960**	**70**	**7,577**
Roman Catholic Church	**1960**	**23,393**	**42,104,900**
Russian Orthodox (see **Eastern Orthodox Churches**)			
Salvation Army	**1960**	**1,255**	**254,141**
Schwenkfelder Church, The	**1960**	**5**	**2,500**
Social Brethren	**1960**	**28**	**1,581**
Spiritualists:			**175,257**
International General Assembly of Spiritualists	1956	209	164,072
National Spiritual Alliance of the U.S.A.	1960	34	3,185
National Spiritualist Association of Churches	1960	225	8,000
Triumph the Church and Kingdom of God in Christ	**1960**	**670**	**66,740**
Unitarian Churches	**1960**	**392**	**101,205**
Unitarian Universalist (see **Unitarian Churches** and **Universalist Church of America**)			
United Brethren Bodies:			**21,663**
United Brethren in Christ	1960	328	21,133
United Christian Church	1959	14	530
United Church of Christ (see **Congregational Christian Churches** and **Evangelical and Reformed Church**)			
United Holy Church of America, Inc.	**1960**	**470**	**28,980**
United Missionary Church	**1960**	**204**	**10,566**
United Seventh Day Brethren	**1960**	**4**	**70**
Universalist Church of America	**1959**	**387**	**70,542**
Vedanta Society	**1960**	**11**	**1,000**
Volunteers of America	**1960**	**204**	**28,320**
Totals: (259 bodies reporting membership)		**318,697**	**114,449,217**

2b. Constituency of the National Council of Churches of Christ in the U.S.A.

From the 1962 *Yearbook of American Churches,* Benson Y. Landis, ed., National Council of Churches of Christ in the U.S.A., New York, 1961, pp. 270-71.

Editor's Note: This table does not include all of the churches which make up the above denominations. For example, less than half of the Baptist and Lutheran churches are constituents of the National Council of Churches of Christ in the U.S.A.

Constituent Body	Year	Number of Churches	Inclusive Membership	Pastors With Charges
Armenian Church, Diocese of America, of California	**1960**	**51**	**125,000**	**43**
Baptist:				
American Baptist Convention	1959	6,262	1,543,198	5,271
National Baptist Convention of America	1956	11,398	2,668,799	7,598
National Baptist Convention, U.S.A., Inc.	1958	26,000	5,000,000	26,000
Seventh Day Baptist, General Conference	1960	61	5,849	41
Brethren, Church of the	**1960**	**1,074**	**199,947**	**885**
Christian Churches (Disciples of Christ), International Convention	**1960**	**8,001**	**1,801,821**	**4,244**
Eastern Orthodox:				
Greek Archdiocese of North and South America	1960	382	1,200,000	417
Rumanian Orthodox Episcopate of America	1960	52	50,000	34
Russian Orthodox Greek Catholic Church of North America	1957	352	755,000	349
Serbian Eastern Orthodox Church	1960	71	125,000	65
Syrian Antiochian Orthodox Church	1960	81	110,000	110
Syrian Orthodox Church of Antioch	1960	29	50,000	6
Ukrainian Orthodox Church of America	1959	37	40,250	43
Evangelical United Brethren Church	**1960**	**4,298**	**748,216**	**3,046**
Friends:				
Five Years Meeting of Friends	1960	528	71,552	375
Philadelphia Yearly Meeting of the Religious Society of Friends	1960	117	17,679	None
Lutheran:				
American Evangelical Lutheran Church	1960	80	24,201	58
Augustana Evangelical Lutheran Church	1960	1,207	608,289	964
United Lutheran Church in America	1960	4,308	2,385,224	3,437
Methodist:				
African Methodist Episcopal Church	1951	5,878	1,166,301	5,878
African Methodist Episcopal Zion Church	1959	4,083	770,000	2,400
Christian Methodist Episcopal Church	1951	2,469	392,167	1,820
The Methodist Church	1960	38,882	9,893,094	24,543
Moravian:				
Moravian Church in America	1960	157	61,368	132
Unity of the Brethren	1960	32	6,151	10
Polish National Catholic Church in America	**1960**	**162**	**282,411**	**151**
Presbyterian:				
Presbyterian Church in the U.S.	1960	3,995	902,849	2,625
The United Presbyterian Church in the U.S.A.	1960	9,383	3,259,011	7,407
Protestant Episcopal Church	**1959**	**7,657**	**3,444,265**	**4,963**
Reformed:				
Hungarian Reformed Church in America	1959	40	11,110	26
Reformed Church in America	1960	867	225,927	781
United Church of Christ:				
Evangelical and Reformed Church	1960	2,726	813,271	1,919
General Council of the Congregational Christian Churches	1960	5,401	1,427,863	3,571
TOTAL (34 bodies)		**146,121**	**40,185,813**	**109,212**

(The "communicant" membership of the Council was reported as 37,426,982 in 1959.)

2c. Church Membership and Population Trends

From the 1962 *Yearbook of American Churches,* Benson Y. Landis, ed., National Council of Churches of Christ in the U.S.A., New York, 1961, pp. 275–76, Tables 2–4.

Inclusive Membership of Religious Bodies

The number of church members of all faiths increased from 54,576,346 in 1926 to 86,830,490 in 1950, and 114,449,217 in 1960.

During the same period the estimated population of the United States increased from 117,136,000 in 1926 to 180,004,000 in 1960, including Hawaii and Alaska in 1960.

The figures for 1950 and 1960 appearing below include estimates of the number of persons in the armed forces serving overseas, since the church members among those in the armed services are undoubtedly included on the rolls of their home churches.

Total Number of Members—All Religious Bodies

1926	1940	1950	1960
54,576,346	64,501,594	86,830,490	114,449,217

Estimated Population of the United States

1926	1940	1950	1960
117,399,000	131,669,000	151,132,000	180,004,000

Sources: U. S. Bureau of the Census; figures for 1950 and 1960 include an estimate of the numbers in the armed forces overseas (Alaska and Hawaii included in 1960). The 1960 figure is for April 1, 1960, as published by the Bureau of the Census in its Series P-25, No. 225, published March 17, 1961. It includes the 1960 population count plus the number of persons in armed forces abroad.

Members Per Church

Since 1926, the average membership per local church (parish, congregation) of all religious bodies has been increasing. In 1926 the figure was 235; by 1950, it was 304; and by 1960, 359.

Comparing 1926 and 1959, the increase was about 52 per cent.

Average Number of Members Per Church—All Religious Bodies

1926	1936	1940	1945	1950	1960
235	262	265	249	304	359

Sources: *Census of Religious Bodies,* U.S. Bureau of the Census, for 1926 and 1936; *Yearbook of American Churches,* for succeeding years.

2d. Comparison of Protestant and Catholic Membership Figures

From the 1962 *Yearbook of American Churches,* Benson Y. Landis, ed., National
Council of Churches of Christ in the U.S.A., New York, 1961, pp. 277–78, Tables
7–10.

Protestant and Roman Catholic Comparisons

No precise comparison is possible between Protestant and Roman Catholic
figures. Most Protestant churches enumerate as members persons who
have attained full membership, usually at age 13. Roman Catholics regard
all baptized persons, including children, as members.

Since 1926, the total membership of Protestant churches increased from
31,511,701 to 51,079,578 in 1950, and 63,668,835 in 1960.

Protestants were 27 per cent of the total population of Continental
United States in 1926; 33.8 per cent in 1950; and 35.4 per cent in 1960.

The membership of the Roman Catholic Church increased from
18,605,003 persons in 1926 to 28,634,878 in 1950 and 42,104,900 in 1960.
Roman Catholics were 23.6 per cent of total population in 1960.

	1926	1940	1950	1955	1960
Membership of All Protestant Bodies	31,511,701	37,814,606	51,079,578	58,448,567	63,668,835
Protestants as Percentage of Total Population	27.0%	28.7%	33.8%	35.5%	35.4%
Membership of The Roman Catholic Church	18,605,003	21,284,455	28,634,878	33,396,647	42,104,900
Roman Catholics as Percentage of Total Population	16.0%	16.1%	18.9%	20.3%	23.6%

2e. Catholics and Non-Catholics as Percentages of Total Church Membership: 1952

From "An Approach to the Religious Geography of the United States" by Wilbur Zelinsky, *Annals of the Association of American Geographers,* June, 1961, vol. 51, no. 2, p. 168.

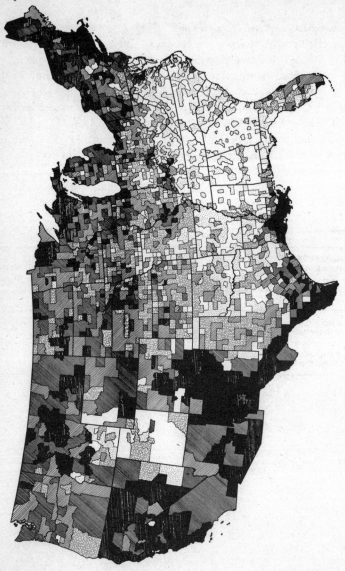

Editor's Note: The darkest areas are more than 50 per cent Catholic. The lightest areas contain almost 99.5 per cent non-Catholics. This map is based on the Churches and Church Membership study of the National Council of Churches of Christ in the U.S.A.

2f. Growth of Denominations: 1906-1956

From "Religious Trends in the United States," by Richard C. Wolf, *Christianity Today,* April 27, 1959, vol. 3, no. 15, p. 4.

Denomination	1906	1956		Percentage of Growth
Eastern Orthodox	129,606	2,396,906	1.	1754.7%
Churches of Christ	159,649	1,700,000	2.	964.8%
Latter-day Saints	256,647	1,372,640	3.	430.9%
Lutheran	2,112,494	7,286,589	4.	244.4%
Baptist	5,662,234	19,165,780	5.	238.4%
Protestant Episcopal	886,942	2,759,994	6.	210.9%
Roman Catholic	12,079,142	33,574,017	7.	177.9%
Presbyterian	1,830,555	3,858,709	8.	110.7%
Methodist	5,749,838	11,775,731	9.	104.8%
Disciples of Christ	982,701	1,897,736	10.	93.1%
Congregational	845,301	1,342,045	11.	58.7%

3. CHURCH MEMBERSHIP STATISTICS BY STATES AND REGIONS

3a. Editor's Note on Church Membership Statistics by States

STATISTICS FOR CATHOLICS for the 114 dioceses in the United States are issued yearly in the *Official Catholic Directory* published by P. J. Kenedy and Sons, New York. State figures can be compiled from the diocesan data but not with complete accuracy, for in several cases diocesan boundaries cross state lines.* The *Official Catholic Directory* provides statistical information about many subjects, including Roman Catholic Church membership, clergy, educational, health and welfare institutions, and vital statistics on baptisms, marriages and deaths.

STATISTICS FOR JEWS are given in the annual *American Jewish Year Book,* published jointly by the American Jewish Committee, New York, and the Jewish Publication Society of America, Philadelphia. This book contains yearly estimates, derived from a variety of community surveys, of the Jewish population by communities and states.

STATISTICS FOR PROTESTANTS are not available annually on a state by state basis. Although many Protestant churches publish annual reports or year books, Protestant religious bodies as a group do not follow standardized methods of collecting and reporting data on church membership. Definitions of membership vary greatly, and subdivisions of national figures are more frequently made by ecclesiastical units (diocese, synod, conference, congregation, etc.) than by states.

IN 1952 a major study entitled *Churches and Church Membership; An Enumeration and Analysis by Counties, States and Regions* was undertaken

* *See* p. 238, Church Membership by States: Catholic and Jewish Population for 1960, column 2, for states with a dagger (†). One or more dioceses in these states cross state lines.

by the Bureau of Research and Survey of the National Council of Churches of Christ in the U.S.A. The results were reported in a series of 80 bulletins published between 1956 and 1958.

This study is a compilation of statistics submitted by the national headquarters of the religious bodies listed in the 1953 *Yearbook of American Churches.* Of the 251 bodies invited, both Protestant and non–Protestant, 114 groups (with 74,125,462 members in 182,856 churches) participated.

Most of the 137 religious bodies *not* included in the study were relatively small groups; but there were several important omissions: approximately 9,500,000 members of independent Negro churches (a large proportion of all Negro church members in the United States); the Eastern Orthodox, Old Catholic and Polish National Catholic Churches, with an estimated 2,720,739 members; the Churches of Christ, with an estimated 1,500,000 members; and the Church of Christ Scientist (which does not report its membership as a matter of principle), whose membership was last estimated to be 268,915 in the 1936 Census of Religious Bodies.

Although the data on which the study *Churches and Church Membership; An Enumeration by Counties, States and Regions* is based were collected in the early 1950s, the study is the most recent source available for Protestant statistics by states.

3b. Catholic and Jewish Populations: 1960*

Data from:

1962 *World Almanac,* New York *World–Telegram and The Sun,* New York, p. 255.
General Summary of Statistics, supplement to *Official Catholic Directory,* New York, P. J. Kenedy and Sons, 1961.
American Jewish Year Book, Morris Fine and Milton Himmelfarb, eds., American Jewish Committee, New York, and Jewish Publication Society of America, Philadelphia, vol. 62, Table 2, pp. 62-63.

State	Population (Census 1960)	Reported Catholic Population (1960)	Estimated Jewish Population (1960)
Alabama	3,266,740	111,924†	10,000
Alaska	226,167	35,500	300
Arizona	1,302,161	304,691	14,800
Arkansas	1,786,272	45,385	3,400
California	15,717,204	3,418,940	530,300
Colorado	1,753,947	327,505	21,300
Connecticut	2,535,234	1,159,757	101,300
Delaware	446,292	97,437†	8,500
District of Columbia	763,956	301,322	40,300
Florida	4,951,560	495,071	112,100
Georgia	3,943,116	60,973	24,800
Hawaii	632,772	200,000	700
Idaho	667,191	42,636	500
Illinois	10,081,158	2,961,452	297,300

State	(Official Census) (1960)	Reported Catholic Population (1960)	Estimated Jewish Population (1960)
Indiana	4,662,498	632,802	24,700
Iowa	2,757,537	446,474	9,100
Kansas	2,178,611	281,776	3,200
Kentucky	3,038,156	294,126	11,000
Louisiana	3,257,022	1,113,575	16,100
Maine	969,265	259,190	8,100
Maryland	3,100,689	431,606	118,100
Massachusetts	5,148,578	2,615,065	226,100
Michigan	7,823,194	1,969,586	102,700
Minnesota	3,413,864	889,916	34,900
Mississippi	2,178,141	64,868	4,000
Missouri	4,319,813	717,438	80,900
Montana	674,767	153,800	600
Nebraska	1,411,330	250,618	9,000
Nevada	285,278	50,002	2,400
New Hampshire	606,921	222,467	5,200
New Jersey	6,066,782	2,408,817	326,300
New Mexico	951,023	359,159†	2,700
New York	16,782,304	5,877,739	2,533,900
North Carolina	4,556,155	41,969	10,300
North Dakota	632,446	159,838	1,400
Ohio	9,706,397	2,043,269	162,200
Oklahoma	2,328,284	99,232	6,400
Oregon	1,768,687	208,088	8,800
Pennsylvania	11,319,366	3,524,535	454,600
Rhode Island	859,488	518,717	24,700
South Carolina	2,382,594	33,819	7,100
South Dakota	680,514	128,170	900
Tennessee	3,567,089	77,077	16,800
Texas	9,597,677	1,883,696†	60,900
Utah	890,627	42,075	1,500
Vermont	389,881	124,180	2,500
Virginia	3,966,949	205,081†	31,200
Washington	2,853,214	351,536	13,200
West Virginia	1,860,421	111,224†	5,200
Wisconsin	3,951,777	1,301,474	38,400
Wyoming	330,066	48,500	800
Military Ordinate		2,000,000	
Eastern Rite Totals		600,802	
Totals	179,323,175	42,104,899	5,531,500

*See Editor's Note page 237 for explanation of omission of Protestant figures from this table.
†Dioceses which do not precisely conform to state lines.

3c. Church Membership as Per Cent of Total Population by States: 1952

From *Churches and Church Membership in the United States; An Enumeration and Analysis by Counties, States and Regions,* published by the Bureau of Research and Survey, National Council of Churches of Christ in the U.S.A., New York, 1956–58, Series A, no. 3, Tables 5 and 6.

Editor's Note: The following table, which we have prepared by combining and condensing two tables from the Churches and Church Membership *study, relates Jewish, Roman Catholic, Protestant and All Faiths (i.e., total) church membership figures as reported in 1952 to the total population (1950 Census).*

In making the original tables, two steps were taken in order to make the figures more reliable for comparisons. First, Negro population figures were subtracted from total population figures because no church membership data from the major Negro denominations, to which most Negro church members belonged, were included in the study. Second, the Protestant figures were modified in order to allow for differences in reporting statistics between Protestant denominations which count membership from infant baptism and those which count from confirmation.

State	Jewish	Roman Catholic	Protestant	All Faiths
		Membership as Per Cent of Total Population (Less Negroes)		
			Protestant Membership (Adjusted)	
Alabama	0.4	2.5	61.2	64.1
Arizona	1.4	25.5	23.0	49.9
Arkansas	0.2	1.9	49.5	51.6
California	4.2	23.1	18.4	45.7
Colorado	1.3	17.0	29.3	47.6
Connecticut	4.6	38.3	22.7	65.6
Delaware	2.4	12.4	45.5	60.2
District of Columbia	11.5	20.9	48.1	80.6
Florida	3.5	7.1	45.3	56.0
Georgia	0.7	1.3	68.9	70.9
Idaho	*	5.3	43.1	47.5
Illinois	4.5	29.0	29.5	63.0
Indiana	0.6	12.4	41.1	54.1
Iowa	0.4	14.4	46.9	61.7
Kansas	0.1	11.4	46.4	57.8
Kentucky	0.4	9.4	49.6	59.3
Louisiana	0.8	47.7	40.4	88.8
Maine	0.8	25.1	19.3	45.2
Maryland	4.1	22.9	35.8	62.7
Massachusetts	4.4	49.2	17.6	71.2
Michigan	1.4	23.7	24.1	49.2
Minnesota	1.3	23.3	40.5	65.1
Mississippi	0.2	4.5	73.9	78.6
Missouri	2.0	16.3	43.3	61.6
Montana	0.1	24.3	26.0	49.3
Nebraska	0.6	15.8	44.3	60.7
Nevada	0.8	17.7	21.7	40.2
New Hampshire	0.6	35.7	20.9	57.2
New Jersey	5.1	39.4	20.6	65.1
New Mexico	0.2	44.7	26.4	71.3
New York	18.4	31.8	16.4	66.6
North Carolina	0.2	1.0	67.2	68.4
North Dakota	0.2	21.6	44.5	66.3
Ohio	2.0	20.5	33.1	55.6
Oklahoma	0.2	3.8	53.3	57.3
Oregon	0.5	7.4	24.4	32.2
Pennsylvania	3.6	29.1	35.8	68.5
Rhode Island	3.0	39.9	16.3	79.3
South Carolina	0.3	1.7	80.8	82.8
South Dakota	0.1	17.1	46.2	63.4
Tennessee	0.5	1.6	59.1	61.2
Texas	0.8	21.1	50.2	72.1
Utah	0.2	4.4	69.7	74.3
Vermont	0.4	30.3	27.7	58.4
Virginia	0.8	3.6	57.0	61.5
Washington	0.5	11.4	22.7	34.6
West Virginia	0.3	5.3	37.4	43.0
Wisconsin	1.1	29.8	36.5	67.4
Wyoming	0.2	16.8	31.0	48.0
United States	**3.8%**	**21.9%**	**35.5%**	**61.1%**

*less than 0.1

3d. Distribution of Church Members by Regions: 1952

These maps are based on percentages given in *Churches and Church Membership in the United States; An Enumeration and Analysis by Counties, States and Regions,* published by the Bureau of Research and Survey, National Council of Churches of Christ in the U.S.A., New York, 1958, Series E, no. 1.

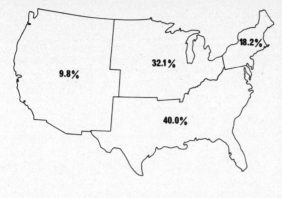

Per cent of total reported PROTESTANT church members who reside in Northeastern, North Central, Southern and Western regions of United States

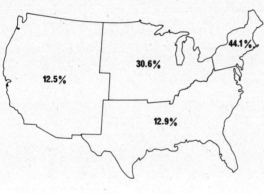

Per cent of total reported ROMAN CATHOLIC church members who reside in Northeastern, North Central, Southern and Western regions of United States

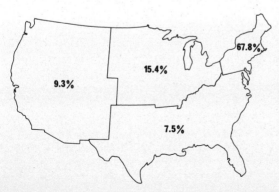

Per cent of total reported JEWISH population who reside in Northeastern, North Central, Southern and Western regions of United States.

From *Churches and Church Membership in the United States; An Enumeration and Analysis by Counties, States and Regions,* published by the Bureau of Research and Survey, National Council of the Churches of Christ in the U.S.A., New York, 1956-1958, Series E, no. 1, Table 140.

	North-eastern	North Central	South	West
% OF U.S. POPULATION IN REGION	26.2	29.5	31.3	13.0
% OF CHURCH MEMBERS IN REGION				
All faiths	32.0	30.3	26.9	10.8
Roman Catholic	44.1	30.6	12.9	12.5
Jewish	67.8	15.4	7.5	9.3
All Protestants	18.2	32.1	40.0	9.8
American Baptist	34.8	37.9	10.0	17.4
Southern Baptist	0.0	6.8	91.0	2.1
Congregational Christian	42.8	37.8	7.2	12.2
Evangelical & Reformed	36.0	53.2	9.7	1.1
Disciples of Christ	3.4	49.4	35.9	11.4
Evangelical United Brethren	29.0	55.9	11.1	4.0
Latter-day Saints	0.3	0.4	2.1	97.3
American Lutheran	5.0	73.5	13.9	7.6
Evangelical Lutheran	1.6	86.7	0.5	11.2
Missouri Synod Lutheran	9.7	73.0	7.8	9.5
United Lutheran	55.0	27.4	14.4	3.3
Methodist	16.0	30.7	47.2	6.2
Presbyterian U.S.	0.0	3.0	96.9	0.1
Presbyterian U.S.A.	35.8	39.6	10.2	14.5
Protestant Episcopal	44.3	18.9	25.0	11.9

Religious Preference

1. HOW DO AMERICANS IDENTIFY THEMSELVES?

Most figures on church affiliation are based on membership reports from church organizations. There is, however, another and quite different question which is asked by researchers more and more frequently: *How do Americans identify themselves* with respect to religion, regardless of whether they belong to any church?

Several recent studies *(see below)* of scientifically selected samples of the total population of the United States show how people classify themselves when they are asked "What is your religion?" or "What is your religious preference?" The very large majority of Americans (96 per cent) readily identify themselves as Catholics, Jews or Protestants. A small number (3 per cent) reply that they have no religion, while about 1 per cent give no answer. The percentages of Protestants and Catholics vary slightly, according to the proportion of individuals under the age of 21 included in a given survey.

The following table has been compiled from:

(1) U.S. Bureau of the Census, "Religion Reported by the Civilian Population of the U.S.: March 1957," *Current Population Reports,* February 2, 1958, Series P-20, no. 79.

(2) Ben Gaffin and Associates Survey for the *Catholic Digest,* January 1953, pp. 2-3.

(3) American Institute of Public Opinion (Gallup Poll), March 20, 1955.

(4) Survey Research Center, University of Michigan, studies reported in Bernard Lazerwitz, "A Comparison of Major United States Religious Groups," *Journal of the American Statistical Association,* September 1961, p. 569.

(5) National Opinion Research Center study reported in Donald J. Bogue, *The Population of the United States,* Glencoe, Illinois, Free Press, 1959, p. 698.

Comparison of Answers to Question,

"What is your religion?" or "What is your religious preference?"

Age of Respondents	(1) Census Bureau 1957 14 yrs. and over	(2) Gaffin 1953 18 yrs. and over	(3) AIPO (Gallup) 1955 21 yrs. and over	(4) Survey Research Center 1957-8 21 yrs. and over	(5) NORC 1953-5 "heads of house-holds"
Protestants	66.2%	68.0%	70.8%	71.8%	71.5%
Catholics	25.7%	23.0%	22.9%	21.8%	21.1%
Jews	3.2%	4.0%	3.1%	3.2%	3.0%
All Others	4.9%	5.0%	3.2%	3.2%	4.4%
Total	100.0%	100.0%	100.0%	100.0%	100.0%

2. U.S. BUREAU OF THE CENSUS VOLUNTARY SURVEY (1957)

From U.S. Bureau of the Census, "Religion Reported by the Civilian Population of the United States: March 1957," *Current Population Reports,* February 2, 1958, Series P-20, no. 79, p. 1, Figure 1, and p. 6, Tables 1 and 2.

Editor's Note: A survey of approximately 35,000 households in the United States was made by the Bureau of the Census in March 1957. The Bureau explained the survey as follows: "The answers to the question 'What is your religion?' were obtained on a voluntary basis. This survey was the first in which the Bureau asked a nationwide sample of persons a question on their religion, although the Bureau had obtained membership data from religious organizations in several Censuses of Religious Bodies.* The question did not relate to church membership, attendance at church services or gatherings, or religious belief. The results are not directly comparable with the reports on membership issued by religious organizations. In replying to the question as asked, many persons, in addition to those who maintain formal affiliation with a religious organization, associated themselves with such a group and reported its name."

Although further reports on the data obtained in the survey had been promised, only the bulletin cited above was released.

---

*See pp. 222, 224–26 for discussion of religious data collected by the U.S. Government.

In this report, the "civilian population" includes about 809,000 members of the armed forces living off post or with their families on post, but excludes all other members of the armed forces.

Religion Reported by Persons 14 Years Old and Over: Civilian Population, March 1957.

Religion	Total	Percent Distribution White Male	White Female	Non-white Male	Non-white Female
Protestant	**66.2**	**62.4**	**65.1**	**85.4**	**89.4**
Baptist	19.7	15.1	15.2	59.1	62.0
Lutheran	7.1	7.9	7.7	0.3	0.2
Methodist	14.0	13.1	14.1	17.0	17.5
Presbyterian	5.6	5.8	6.4	1.0	0.8
Other Protestant	19.8	20.5	21.7	8.0	8.9
Roman Catholic	**25.7**	**27.8**	**27.9**	**6.4**	**6.6**
Jewish	**3.2**	**3.6**	**3.6**	...	**0.1**
Other Religion	**1.3**	**1.3**	**1.2**	**1.5**	**1.5**
No Religion	**2.7**	**4.0**	**1.3**	**5.4**	**1.7**
Religion not Reported	**0.9**	**0.9**	**0.9**	**1.3**	**0.7**
Total, 14 years and over	**100.0%**	**100.0%**	**100.0%**	**100.0%**	**100.0%**

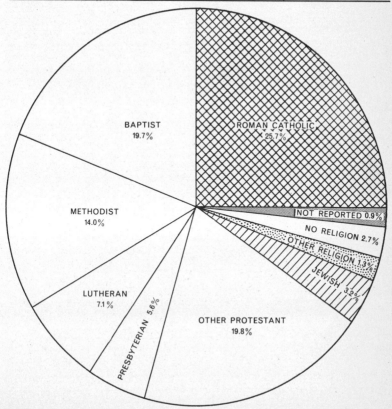

Region of Residence of Persons 14 Years Old and Over, by Religion Reported: Civilian Population, March 1957.
Section on Percent by Residence, provided data for the following maps.

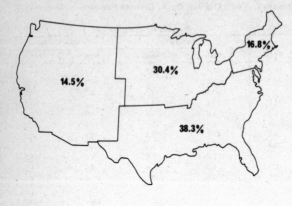

Where did people live who identified themselves as PROTESTANTS when asked by the Census Bureau in 1957?

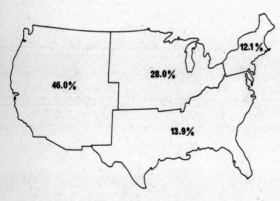

Where did people live who identified themselves as CATHOLICS when asked by the Census Bureau in 1957?

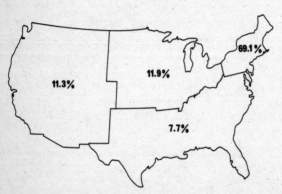

Where did people live who identified themselves as JEWS when asked by the Census Bureau in 1957?

Church Attendance

50,000,000 ADULTS WENT TO CHURCH DURING TYPICAL WEEK (1961)

Quoted from American Institute of Public Opinion (Gallup Poll), December 21, 1951.

ABOUT 50 million adults—or just under half of the adult population—went to church during a typical week in 1961.

Although this represents a slight increase in weekly church attendance over the previous year, it is due primarily to the overall growth of the adult population and not to an increase in the proportion who say they attended church during a typical week of the year.

For the last three years, in fact, church attendance in the U.S. has remained at a fairly constant level, after a "peak year" in 1958.

To arrive at an estimate of the average attendance figure, surveys of representative samples of the adult civilian population were made during selected weeks in March, June, October and December of 1961. The following question was put to the comparable samples of adults:

"Did you, yourself, happen to attend church in the last seven days?"

Attended Church in Typical Week

Year	1957	1958	1959	1960	1961
Per Cent	47	49	47	47	47
Total	48,500,000	50,500,000	49,000,000	49,500,000	50,000,000

(In the last five years, the adult civilian population has increased an estimated 3 million persons.)

Further analysis of this year's audit brings to light the following information about America's churchgoing:

(1) In 1961, as in previous years, women had a better church attendance record than men did: 50 per cent of women attended church during a typical week of the last year compared to 43 per cent of men.

(2) Residents of the Eastern and Midwestern states score highest in church attendance—49 per cent in both regions. In the South, 47 per cent attended during a typical week; in the Far West, the church attendance was 36 per cent.

(3) Catholics were more faithful in their churchgoing than Protestants were (71 per cent compared to 41 per cent). And Protestants attended more often than those of the Jewish faith (21 per cent).

(4) Fewer younger adults went to church during a typical week than was the case with older persons. The figures: adults 21-29 years of age—43 per cent; 30-49 years of age—47 per cent; 50 years and over—48 per cent.

(5) Persons with college training were more faithful than were those with less formal education: 52 per cent of college persons attended church in a typical week, compared to 47 per cent among those with high school educations and 44 per cent of persons with grade school educations.

PEOPLE IN U.S. ARE BETTER CHURCH ATTENDERS THAN DUTCH, GERMANS, BRITISH, NORWEGIANS

Quoted from American Institute of Public Opinion (Gallup Poll), December 23, 1961.

ON A typical Sunday of the last year, nearly half of the nation's adults could be found in church—an attendance record that matches or exceeds that of other countries surveyed by the Gallup Poll.

Churchgoing Abroad

In an international survey of religious beliefs and practices by European Gallup affiliates, only in Switzerland did church attendance during a given *month* compare with that of the U.S. In both countries, about six persons in ten attended religious services at some point during a one-month period.

By way of comparison, this was the attendance record in four other European nations:

Attended Church During Last Month

	West Germany	Holland	Great Britain	Norway
Per Cent Yes	54%	53%	42%	32%

A revealing facet in this international religious survey is the finding that small minorities in the U.S. and Switzerland (14 per cent and 13 per cent respectively) did not attend church at all during a year.

In Holland, Great Britain and Norway, however, almost four persons in ten did not go to a religious service once during the previous year.

Women More Faithful in All Countries

It is interesting to note that in each of the six countries surveyed, women had a better church attendance record than men did. The greatest discrepancy noted in this respect was in Germany where 61 per cent of the women attended church in the *month* measured against 46 per cent of the men.

In the U.S., the latest audit indicates that 50 per cent of women attended church during a typical *week* of the last year compared to 43 per cent of men.

Clergy, Church Organization and Recent Church Mergers

The American Clergy

1. CLERGY STATISTICS FOR MAJOR RELIGIOUS GROUPS

Condensed from 1962 *Yearbook of American Churches*, Benson Y. Landis, ed., National Council of Churches of Christ in the U.S.A., New York, 1961, pp. 262–68.

Denominations Reporting More Than 1,500 Ordained Persons	Number of Clergy	Denominations Reporting More Than 1,500 Ordained Persons	Number of Clergy
Adventist	3,031	International Church of the Foursquare Gospel	2,586
Assemblies of God	9,504	Jewish Congregations	3,965
Baptist	113,139	Latter-day Saints	11,919
Brethren	4,102	Lutheran	17,791
Christian Churches (Disciples of Christ)	7,582	Mennonite	3,924
Churches of God	8,771	Methodist	43,109
Church of God in Christ	4,900	Pentecostal	6,091
Church of the Nazarene	5,736	Presbyterian	17,088
Churches of Christ	8,366	Protestant Episcopal	8,708
Congregational Christian Churches	6,224	Reformed	1,880
Eastern Orthodox	1,748	Roman Catholic	54,945
Evangelical and Reformed Church	2,800	Salvation Army	3,854
Evangelical United Brethren Church	3,441	Triumph the Church and Kingdom of God in Christ	2,000

2.   CATHOLIC CLERGY: SUMMARY

From the General Summary of Statistics, supplement to *Official Catholic Directory*,
New York, P. J. Kenedy & Sons, 1961.

Hierarchy	Number in U.S.
Cardinals	5
Archbishops	30
Bishops	185
Total	**220**

Clergy	
Abbots	43
Priests, Diocesan*	33,141
Priests, Religious†	21,541
Total	**54,725**

Brothers and Sisters‡	
Brothers	10,928
Sisters	170,438
Total	**181,366**

Editor's Notes:

*Diocesan priests *are ordained ministers who function under the immediate supervision of the bishop of their diocese and are ordained for the work of the diocese.*

†Religious priests *are ordained members of orders and communities. They live under the supervision of the head of the religious community to which they belong. They are ordained to carry out the special work to which the community has been dedicated: education, care of the sick, contemplation, propagating the faith, and so on. In the U.S. (as of 1960) there are 90 religious orders of priests, 18 religious orders of brothers and 271 religious orders of women.*

‡Brothers and Sisters *are not considered part of the ordained clergy. Brothers, for instance, cannot conduct church services, lead the Mass, or administer sacraments.*

3.   HIERARCHY AND CLERGY OF THE CATHOLIC CHURCH BY STATES

From the General Summary of Statistics, supplement to *Official Catholic Directory*,
New York, P. J. Kenedy & Sons, 1961.

State	Cardinals	Archbishops	Bishops	Abbots	Diocesan Priests	Religious Priests
Alabama		1	1	1	197	204
Alaska			2		17	37
Arizona		1	1		117	123
Arkansas			2	1	125	62
California	(Los Angeles) 1	1	9	1	1,766	1,469
Colorado		1	3	1	241	223
Connecticut		1	3		842	354
Delaware			2		92	77
District of Columbia		1	1		285	767
Florida		1	1	2	201	141
Georgia			2	1	68	133
Hawaii			2		18	132
Idaho			1		72	16
Illinois	(Chicago) 1	2	8	3	2,329	2,154
Indiana		1	5	1	734	732
Iowa		1	4	1	966	146
Kansas		1	4	1	465	379
Kentucky		1	2	1	510	202
Louisiana		1	4	2	511	500
Maine			1		254	99
Maryland		1			294	434
Massachusetts	(Boston) 1		7	1	2,197	1,543
Michigan		1	7		1,413	624
Minnesota		1	6	1	1,063	393
Mississippi			2		89	100
Missouri	(St. Louis) 1		5	3	895	719

State	Cardinals	Arch-bishops	Bishops	Abbots	Diocesan Priests	Religious Priests
Montana			2		213	45
Nebraska		1	2		448	182
Nevada			1		53	12
New Hampshire			1	1	277	131
New Jersey		2	6	2	1,508	694
New Mexico		1	1		192	184
New York	(New York) 1		27	1	4,418	2,811
North Carolina			1	1	150	75
North Dakota			2	2	260	87
Ohio		2	9	1	1,910	1,019
Oklahoma			1	1	188	83
Oregon		1	1	3	213	271
Pennsylvania		2	10	2	3,029	1,435
Rhode Island			2		386	209
South Carolina			1	1	79	58
South Dakota			2	1	227	102
Tennessee			1		113	29
Texas		1	9	1	829	818
Utah			1	1	53	39
Vermont			1		174	67
Virginia			2	1	170	140
Washington		1	3	1	330	361
West Virginia		1			113	85
Wisconsin		1	6	2	1,554	759
Wyoming			1		59	6
Eastern Rite Totals			5		434	76
Grand Totals (1961)	**5**	**30**	**185**	**43**	**33,141**	**21,541**

4. WOMEN IN THE MINISTRY

Quoted from the 1962 *Yearbook of American Churches*, Benson Y. Landis, ed., National Council of the Churches of Christ in the U.S.A., New York, 1961, pp. 278-79.

ACCORDING to the Population Census of 1950, the Bureau of the Census has published figures reporting 6,777 women clergymen, or 4.1 per cent of the total number of clergymen, which was 168,419. The figures are for all religious bodies of all faiths, and there are no separate figures according to religious body.

A study of available *published* reports, appearing in *Information Service,* May 31, 1952 revealed 5,791 ordained or licensed women ministers, of whom 2,896 were pastors of local churches. Of the pastors reported about one-tenth were in communions affiliated with the National Council of Churches. A precise count could not be made, and the data were limited to the denominations publishing data. The figures could not be compared directly with any other compilation. It appeared that 63 religious bodies ordain women, while a total of 77 bodies ordain or license. Seven of these "give women special status of some sort." For a later discussion, "Women Ministers Today," see *Information Service,* National Council of Churches, March 6, 1954.

In 1956, the Presbyterian Church in the U.S.A. authorized the ordination of women, and the Methodist Church granted full clergy rights to women.

Quoted from *Occupational Outlook Handbook,* United States Department of Labor, Bureau of Labor Statistics, 1961, Bulletin no. 1300, p. 182.

LESS than 5 per cent of all ministers are women; however, about 80 denominations ordain women. In addition, in some denominations an increasing number of women who have not been ordained are serving as pastors' assistants.

Ordination of Women

Derived from *Summary of Facts about the Ordination of Women in the Member Churches of the World Council of Churches,* World Council of Churches, New York, 1958, mimeographed pamphlet, 33 pages.

THE FOLLOWING churches, members of the World Council of Churches, report ordination of women:

African Methodist Episcopal Church—in 1952, a woman was ordained and given a pastorate for the first time. Women may consecrate the communion elements.

African Methodist Episcopal Zion Church—in 1952, 25 women pastors of whom 15 were ordained or licensed.

American Baptist Convention—women have long been ordained and have full clergy rights.

Christian Churches (Disciples of Christ)—women have long been ordained as there has been full sex equality from time of founding of church.

Church of the Brethren—women ministers now serving as pastors, with privileges of ordained ministers, though not themselves ordained.

The Methodist Church—since 1956, women are on full and equal status with men in the Methodist ministry.

Presbyterian Church in the U.S.A.—in 1956, formal approval of full ministry with no restrictions for women.

The Religious Society of Friends—women "recognized" (corresponds to ordination) equally with men.

Salvation Army—all offices open to men and women alike.

Seventh Day Baptist General Conference—in 1952, had 1 woman pastor and 3 ordained women.

United Church of Christ—women ordained and have full-fledged clergy rights.

5. CLERGYMEN'S INCOME

5a. The Clergyman's Income

Quoted from *Occupational Outlook Handbook*, United States Department of Labor, Bureau of Labor Statistics, 1961, Bulletin no. 1300, p. 181.

THE AMOUNT of income clergymen receive depends, to a great extent, on the size and financial status of the congregation they serve and usually is highest in large cities or in prosperous suburban areas. Earnings of clergymen . . . usually rise with increased experience and responsibility. Most Protestant churches and a number of Jewish congregations provide their spiritual leaders with housing. Roman Catholic priests ordinarily live in the rectory of a parish church or are provided lodgings by the religious order to which they belong. Many clergymen receive allowances for transportation and other expenses necessary in their work. Clergymen often receive gifts or fees for officiating at special ceremonies such as weddings and funerals.

5b. Earnings of Protestant Ministers

Condensed from *The Church as Employer, Money Raiser, and Investor*, by F. Ernest Johnson and J. Emory Ackerman, New York, Harper & Brothers, 1959, Appendix, Table 3.

THE DATA presented in this table are based on responses to a questionnaire sent in 1956 to every tenth person on the pastoral lists of nine Protestant denominations.

Annual Cash Salaries of Full-Time Ministers by Denomination*

Denominations	Total	Average	Median†
The Methodist Church	792	$4,359	$4,072
Congregational Christian‡	142	$4,596	$4,277
Presbyterian in the U.S.A.‡	402	$4,841	$4,480
United Lutheran	156	$4,029	$3,757
American Baptist Convention	157	$4,230	$4,015
Church of the Brethren	40	$3,270	$3,167
Disciples of Christ	162	$4,541	$4,264
Evangelical and Reformed‡	97	$4,077	$3,863
Protestant Episcopal	224	$4,666	$4,206

*Does not include allowances, fees and perquisites which raise average from $4,436 to $5,827.
†One-half of ministers have larger salary and one-half smaller than the median.
‡It should be noted that the study antedated the union of the Congregational Christian and the Evangelical and Reformed, and of the Presbyterian in the U.S.A. and United Presbyterian denominations.

5c. Social Security Coverage of Ministers

Data from "Coverage of Ministers under Old-Age, Survivors and Disability Insurance," by Saul Waldman, *Social Security Bulletin,* April, 1961, published by the United States Department of Health, Education and Welfare, Social Security Administration, Washington, D.C., vol. 24, no. 4, pp. 20, 21, Table 4.

Editor's Note: A 1954 amendment to the Social Security Act made coverage available to ministers on an individual voluntary basis if they had an income of more than $400 per year. The United States Department of Health, Education and Welfare, Social Security Administration, has released figures estimating the number of clergymen eligible for coverage (an estimate based on figures in the 1959 Yearbook of American Churches), and reporting the number who actually applied for it (in 1957).

Social Security Coverage of Ministers, by Selected Denominations

Denomination (Those Reporting More Than 1,500 Ordained Persons)	Eligible for Coverage* (1959)	Electing Coverage† (1957)	
		Number	Per cent
Adventist	2,600	2,100	83%
Assemblies of God	7,400	5,100	70%
Baptist	59,000	23,200	40%
Brethren	2,200	1,200	56%
Christian Churches (Disciples of Christ)		not given in source	
Churches of God	7,900	1,700	21%
Church of God in Christ		not given in source	
Church of the Nazarene	3,800	3,500	93%
Churches of Christ	6,800	3,400	51%
Congregational Christian Churches‡	3,900	3,400	91%
Eastern Orthodox	1,600	1,100	71%
Evangelical and Reformed Church‡	2,300	2,200	96%
Evangelical United Brethren Church	2,800	2,200	80%
International Church of the Foursquare Gospel		not given in source	
Jewish Congregations	3,300	3,000	92%
Latter-day Saints		not given in source	
Lutheran	13,000	12,300	95%
Memmonite	2,400	600	23%
Methodist	33,700	17,100	51%
Pentecostal	3,700	600	15%
Presbyterian	10,500	9,400	90%
Protestant Episcopal	6,200	5,700	91%
Reformed		not given in source	
Roman Catholic	29,000	5,600	19%
Salvation Army	3,600	2,800	77%
Triumph the Church and Kingdom of God in Christ		not given in source	

*Includes ministers performing either full-time or part-time services in the ministry; estimates based on data from 1959 Yearbook of American Churches, adjusted to exclude inactive and retired ministers, those earning under $400 per year, and Catholic priests who have taken a vow of poverty.
†Excludes ministers whose denomination could not be identified.
‡The Congregational Christian Church and the Evangelical and Reformed Church have united to form the United Church of Christ.

Relatively many more white ministers than nonwhite ministers have elected coverage. Data for 1957 show that, out of a total of 177,000 white clergymen who were eligible to participate in the program, 130,000 or almost three-fourths have elected to be covered. Among the 23,000 nonwhite ministers, 4,500 or less than one-fifth have elected coverage.

Church Organization: Comparison of 16 American Denominations

Baptists. Baptists have no hierarchy, no centralized control of religious activity, no headquarters' "oversight" of churches or liturgies, practices or regulations. The local parish church is a law unto itself.

Christian Scientists. Christian Science has no ordained clergy or personal pastors. There is no personal preacher in a Christian Science service; texts are read aloud by a first and second reader. A Christian Science practitioner is one who prays for those who ask his prayers in their behalf. To be registered as a public practitioner, one must be approved by the Mother Church, the First Church of Christ, Scientist, in Boston, Massachusetts.

Congregationalists. Congregationalists have county and state associations of churches and a national association—the General Council; but these have no power over the internal life of any of the congregations. The freedom of the congregation is inviolable. No minister beloved by his people can be removed by external pressure. No church can be disbanded except by the wish of its people.

Disciples of Christ. The average Disciple church is administered by a pastor, an Official Board of Elders and Deacons, and perhaps representatives of the Christian Women's Fellowship. Elders look after the spiritual welfare of members; deacons manage incidental business. All matters of fundamental importance must ultimately be decided by the congregation as a whole.

Eastern Orthodox. There are three orders of service: deacon, priest and bishop. Those holding the higher ranks—metropolitans, archbishops and patriarchs—are, in effect, bishops. There are also orders of monks and nuns. A metropolitan is the head of an ecclesiastical district; an archbishop is the head of a church; a patriarch is the head of a see. Each member of the federation of Eastern Orthodox churches is independently administered by a council of bishops, called a synod, which elects its metropolitans, archbishops and patriarchs. The Patriarch of Constantinople, oldest of the Patriarchates, is known as "the first among equals," and is generally regarded as the spiritual leader of world Orthodoxy.

Episcopalians. There are three orders of ministry: bishops, priests and deacons. There are also many orders of monks and nuns. In the United States there are parishes with elected laymen to represent the congregation;

dioceses with the "convention" under which the bishop and his clergy carry on the Church's work; a general convention which meets every three years and represents the entire American Church. Neither bishops nor parish clergy have any autocratic rights; all must cooperate with the laity.

Jehovah's Witnesses. Jehovah's Witnesses are a society or body of ministers, for the public ceremony of water immersion identifies one as a minister of God. Boys and girls are invited to preach. Ministers at national headquarters and in the field are voluntary workers. The unincorporated body of Jehovah's Witnesses uses a number of corporations in its work, the principal one being Watch Tower Bible and Tract Society of Pennsylvania, members of which elect seven ministers as a Board of Directors; the board chooses one director as president. Clerical garb is never used.

Jews. There is no religious hierarchy in Judaism. The authority of the rabbi is based not on his position but upon his learning. In Orthodox practice, the rabbi rarely leads in services; the cantor conducts worship. Any well-informed layman may rise to the pulpit to lead the congregation in prayer. The modern rabbi is responsible for religious education, for worship in the synagogue, for ceremonials surrounding birth, confirmation, marriage, and death, and for pastoral guidance. Judaism is essentially a family religion; the home is often regarded as a fitting place of worship.

Lutherans. Church conventions, which elect presidents and other officials, are the main instruments of authority in the American churches. The foundation of this authority is in the congregations themselves. Each congregation owns its own church building or other property and is self-governing in all of its local affairs. Men are called to the office of the ministry by God through the congregations, and if they cease to perform the functions of their office they cease to be ministers.

Methodists. The Methodist Church in America parallels rather uniquely the pattern of American government. The executive branch consists of a Council of Bishops elected by jurisdictional Conferences composed of ministers and laymen. Each bishop presides over an Area. The bishops appoint the ministers of individual parishes. The legislative power is vested in a General Conference which meets every four years and is composed of both clergy and laymen in equal numbers. Delegates are democratically elected by an annual conference and on a proportional basis. The supreme judicial power rests in a Judicial Council whose members and qualifications are determined by the General Conference of the church.

Mormons. The Church has a strong central organization with a First Presidency of three presiding high priests followed in order by the Council of the Twelve Apostles (with assistants); a patriarch, the First Council of the Seventy; also a Presiding Bishopric who preside over the Aaronic Priesthood. Geographically, the Church is divided into "stakes" and "wards" (somewhat resembling the diocese and parishes), and "missions."

Presbyterians. The people govern the Church through elected representatives. The layman has a prominent role in the Presbyterian Church. All property is vested in laymen—not in ministers or bishops. Laymen are eligible for the highest office (moderator) in each court. The courts are the Session, made up of the elders and ministers who have supreme authority in the spiritual matters of the local church; the Presbytery, which has oversight of all congregations within its prescribed area; the Synod, composed of ministers and representative elders from congregations within a specified number of Presbyteries; and the General Assembly, which is the court of final appeal and representative of the whole church.

Quakers. Friends do not have an ordained clergy. They believe that everyone has the potentiality to become a minister. There is no division between clergy and laity because both ideas are eliminated. Elders and overseers are appointed to serve each meeting. Elders are given the "oversight" of the religious meetings for worship, for marriage, and for memorial services at time of death. Overseers look after the pastoral care of the membership. All meetings have a recorder who is responsible for the careful keeping of all vital statistics.

Roman Catholics. The Catholic Church describes itself as "the visible society founded by Jesus Christ and consisting of members throughout the world who are united by the same Faith, particularly the same Sacraments, and in spiritual matters accept the supreme authority of the Bishop of Rome (the Pope), the successor of Saint Peter." The Pope is assisted by the College of Cardinals. The Church is divided into bishoprics. Each Catholic lives under the jurisdiction of a bishop or archbishop, appointed by the Pope. Each bishopric is divided into parishes and each parish is directed by a pastor appointed by the bishop. Side by side with the parochial clergy are members of the religious orders (who may be priests, simple monks or nuns) who engage in a variety of activities under the ultimate direction of the hierarchy.

Seventh-day Adventists. Seventh-day Adventists have developed a global organization, comprising twelve divisions, directed by the General Conference. Each of these twelve divisions is made up of several union conferences, which in turn are made up of local conferences, each consisting of a group of churches. Lay members elect officers of their local churches and appoint delegates to local conferences for the election of their officers.

Unitarians. Unitarians practice a congregational form of government. Each local church enjoys full self-determination in all matters. Each church is free to develop a service of worship that best serves its people, and Unitarian ministers are accorded the right of a free pulpit.

Mergers and Proposed Mergers of
American Churches: 1955–1962

Chart based on data from *Britannica Book of the Year, 1955–1961, Encyclopedia Britannica* and news reports, 1962.

Merger Adopted	Name of Merged Church	Merger Proposed	Proposal Adopted
Congregational Christian Churches Evangelical and Reformed Church	United Church of Christ	1947	1957
Presbyterian Church in the U.S.A. United Presbyterian Church of North America	United Presbyterian Church in the U.S.A.	1955	1958
American Lutheran Church Evangelical Lutheran Church United Evangelical Lutheran Church	The American Lutheran Church	1954	1960
American Unitarian Association Universalist Church of America	Unitarian Universalist Association	1955	1961
American Evangelical Lutheran Church Augustana Evangelical Lutheran Church Finnish Evangelical Lutheran Church of America (Suomi Synod) United Lutheran Church in America	Lutheran Church in America	1955	1962

Merger Proposed	Name of Merged Church	Merger Proposed	
Christian Churches (Disciples of Christ) International Council of Community Churches United Church of Christ	(not announced)	1956	
Bible Presbyterian Church Christian Reformed Church Orthodox Presbyterian Church Reformed Presbyterian Church of America	(not announced)	1956 and 1959	
Church of the Brethren Evangelical United Brethren Church Methodist Church	(not announced)	1958	
Methodist Church Protestant Episcopal Church United Church of Christ United Presbyterian Church in the U.S.A.	(not announced)	1960	

Merger Proposed and Rejected		Merger Proposed	Proposal Rejected
United Presbyterian Church in the U.S.A. Presbyterian Church in the U.S. ("Southern")		1955	1955
Pilgrim Holiness Church Wesleyan Methodist Church of America		1958	1959

Religion and Education

Religious Instruction

Editor's Note: The figures for Catholic students in this section refer to elementary school pupils enrolled in public schools, for whom special religious instruction classes are held. Data on parochial school enrollment will be found in the next section, pp. 262 ff.

Catholic children who attend public elementary schools receive their religious instruction at various times, depending upon the customs, traditions and size of the local parish, and the laws of the state in which the diocese is located. If legally permissible, most Catholic children participate in the released-time program of their parish. Otherwise, they receive their instruction after school hours, or on Saturdays, or after Mass on Sunday. All Catholic public school children who are counted in official figures receive at least one hour of instruction per week.

1. DENOMINATIONS WITH ENROLLMENT OF 100,000 OR MORE

Quoted from the 1962 *Yearbook of American Churches,* Benson Y. Landis, ed., National Council of Churches of Christ in the U.S.A., New York, 1961, pp. 255-62.

Name of Religious Body	Total Enrollment*	Name of Religious Body	Total Enrollment*
Adventists	361,539	Independent Fundamental Churches of America	148,155
Assemblies of God	974,823	Jewish Congregations	262,662
Baptists	14,757,107	Latter-day Saints	1,497,364
Brethren	302,539	Lutherans	3,111,873
Christian Churches (Disciples of Christ)	1,108,835	Mennonites	182,484
Christian and Missionary Alliance	136,705	Methodists	8,126,780
Churches of God	783,625	Pentecostal Assemblies	423,218
Church of the Nazarene	671,174	Pilgrim Holiness Church	107,184
Congregational Christian Churches	747,546	Presbyterians	2,929,220
Eastern Orthodox Churches	112,505	Protestant Episcopal Church	979,637
Evangelical and Reformed Church	548,295	Reformed Churches	174,961
Evangelical United Brethren Church	732,827	Roman Catholic Church	2,558,483†

*Includes pupils, officers and teachers enrolled.

†Catholic children who attend public school. In addition, in 1960, 5,287,230 Catholic children were enrolled in parochial or private elementary and secondary Catholic schools.

2. *TRENDS IN SUNDAY OR SABBATH SCHOOL ENROLLMENT*

Quoted from the 1962 *Yearbook of American Churches,* Benson Y. Landis, ed.,
National Council of Churches of Christ in the U.S.A., New York, 1961, pp. 255
and 276-77.

THERE were 283,885 Sunday or Sabbath schools in all religious bodies
reported in 1960, with 3,637,982 teachers and officers, and a total enrollment of 43,231,018 persons.

A year earlier there was reported a total enrollment of 44,066,457. Thus
the decrease is 835,439, or 1.9 per cent. This decrease is in large part explained by a report from *The Official Catholic Directory* of 2,558,483 public
school children receiving religious instruction this year and 3,301,401 the
previous year.

The Protestant churches, which have generally emphasized the Sunday
school, reported 93.1 per cent of the total enrollment, and 91.1 per cent
a year earlier. The total Protestant enrollment in this compilation is
40,241,650, compared with 40,349,972 a year earlier.

Number of Sunday School Pupils, Ratio of Growth or Decline,
and Per Cent of Total Population from 1906 to 1959

Year	Protestant Pupils	Ratio	Non-Prot. Pupils	Ratio	Total Pupils	Ratio	Per Cent of Population
1906	13,152,205	100.0	1,533,792	100.0	14,685,997	100.0	17.2
1916	17,993,829	136.8	1,942,061	126.6	19,935,890	135.7	19.6
1926	19,741,339	150.0	1,297,187	84.5	21,038,526	143.2	17.9
1936	17,273,479	131.3	1,115,522	72.7	18,389,001	125.2	14.4
1945	21,426,453	162.9	3,183,355	207.5	24,609,808	167.6	17.6
1950	25,459,845	193.6	1,846,282	120.4	27,306,127	185.9	18.0
1955	33,607,212	255.5	2,706,633	176.5	36,313,845	247.3	22.0
1956	35,444,056	269.5	3,010,026	196.7	38,454,082	261.8	22.9
1957	35,778,377	272.0	3,108,830	202.7	38,887,207	264.8	22.7
1958	35,628,199	270.9	3,714,226	242.2	39,342,425	267.9	22.6
1959	36,429,269	277.0	3,533,787	230.4	39,963,056	272.1	22.6

Estimated Sunday School Enrollment by Age Levels:
Distribution of Protestant Sunday School Pupils,
Teachers, and Total Population by Age—1959

Age Groups	Protestant S.S. Pupils*	Protestant S.S. Teachers†	U.S. Population	% of Pop. in age-group who are Prot. S.S. Pupils	% of Pop. in age-group who are Prot. S.S. Teachers†
Cradle Roll Children (0-2)	2,732,000	—	11,827,000	23.1	—
Children (3-11)	12,969,000	—	33,554,000	38.7	—
Youth (12-23)	8,196,000	740,000	31,462,000	26.1	2.4
Adults (24-over)	12,532,000	2,961,000	100,261,000	12.5	3.0

*Based on 1959 statistics
from 43 Protestant and Eastern
Orthodox denominations.

7.5% of Pupils are on Cradle Roll (ages 0-2)
35.6% of Pupils are in Children's Division (ages 3-11)
22.5% of Pupils are in Youth Division (ages 12-23)
34.4% of Pupils are in Adult Division (ages 24 and older)

†Figures and percentages in these two columns are based on estimates that 20% of church school teachers and officers are youth and 80% are adult.

Source: Bureau of Research and Survey, National Council of Churches. Totals do not always correspond with those published in previous issues of the Yearbook of American Churches, because based on more recent reports from officers of religious bodies.

3. JEWISH EDUCATION STATISTICS

Editor's Note: In addition to Sunday and Sabbath school, Jewish children may receive religious instruction in Weekday Afternoon Hebrew Schools or in Yiddish Schools, also held after school.

Jewish All-Day Schools are like parochial schools in the sense that they combine religious and general, or secular, education.

In 1958, a study of Jewish education in the United States* reported that the Reform orientation predominated in the Sunday and-Sabbath schools, the Conservative in the Weekday Schools, and the Orthodox in the All-Day Schools. At that time, the combined enrollment in schools of all types was: Orthodox 21 per cent, Conservative 38.6 per cent, Reform 28 per cent, Yiddish 1.3 per cent and all other orientations 11 per cent. The following figures were provided by Dr. Uriah Engelman of the American Association for Jewish Education.

*Jewish Education in the United States, Summary by Alexander M. Dushkin and Uriah Z. Engelman, American Association for Jewish Education, New York, 1959.

Estimated Jewish School Enrollment, Spring 1962

Type of School	No. of Pupils
Sunday and Sabbath school	305,774
Weekday Afternoon Hebrew School	237,526
Yiddish School	5,126
All-Day School	48,897

Growth of Jewish School Enrollment, 1952-1962

Type of School	No. of Pupils 1962	No. of Pupils 1962	% Change
Sunday and Sabbath school	176,007	305,774	+ 73.3%
Weekday School (Hebrew and Yiddish, and All-Day)	160,077	291,549	+ 81.3%
Total	336,084	597,323	+ 77.7%

Secular Instruction

1. *ENROLLMENT IN ELEMENTARY AND HIGH SCHOOLS, PUBLIC AND NON-PUBLIC*

Adapted from *Health, Education and Welfare Trends,* 1962 edition, Department of Health, Education and Welfare, Washington, D.C., 1962, p. 42.*

TOTAL public and non–public school enrollment is estimated at 45.0 million for the 1961–62 school year. Of this total, 38.5 million are enrolled in public schools and 6.5 million are enrolled in non–public schools. Since the school year 1939–40 enrollments in non–public schools have increased from 9.4 to 15 per cent of total enrollment.

Public School Enrollment Compared with Total Enrollment (in numbers of students)

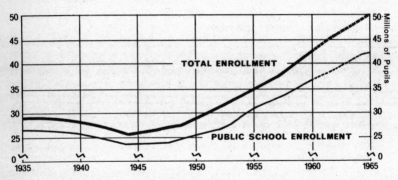

Non-public School Enrollment (as per cent of total school enrollment)

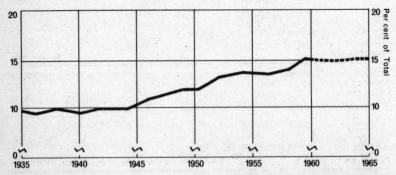

*Editor's Note: Dotted lines on charts indicate estimates of future enrollment. "Projected enrollments prepared in March 1962 are based upon Office of Education enrollment data and Bureau of Census unpublished projections of the population aged 5-19 by single years of age."

2. ELEMENTARY AND HIGH SCHOOLS AFFILIATED WITH CHURCHES

From "Church-Related Elementary and Secondary Schools in Continental United States," by Bertha Blair, *Information Service,* Bureau of Research and Survey, National Council of Churches of Christ in the U.S.A., New York, January 3, 1959, p. 4, Table 2.

Enrollment in Church-Related Elementary and Secondary Schools in the United States (1958)

Denominational Control	Enrollment by Type of School*		
	Kindergarten	Elementary [a]	Secondary [b]
10 Principal School Systems			
Roman Catholic	n.r.	3,400,000	690,000
Missouri Synod Lutheran	1,724	130,124	7,022
Seventh-day Adventist	—	42,069	13,380
Protestant Episcopal [c]	3,252	12,028	17,900
Joint Synod of Wisconsin	—	21,901	—
Christian Reformed [d]	—	31,874	6,664
National Association of Christian Schools	7	8,960	7,492
Mennonite (including Amish)	88	[e]	5,870
Friends	221	4,978	4,940
Jewish [f]	4,133	21,259	4,326
Other Denominations with Schools			
American Baptist Convention	—	—	968
American Lutheran Church	1,236	2,765	—
Augustana Lutheran Church	—	259	—
Council of Liberal Churches	—	—	126 [g]
Evangelical Lutheran Church	—	1,151 [h]	692 [i]
Evangelical Mission Covenant	—	—	944
Latter-day Saints	—	—	324
Los Angeles Baptist City Mission Society	—	2,949	—
Methodist Church, The	4,018 [j]	244	5,063
Moravian Church	—	—	574
National Evangelical Lutheran	21	38	—
New England Association of Christian Schools	91	218	173
Norwegian Synod Lutheran	—	379	—
Presbyterian U.S.	n.r.	1,130	970
Presbyterian U.S.A.	n.r.	—	—
Reformed Church in America	—	—	62
Slovak Evangelical Lutheran	—	147	—
Southern Baptist Convention	7,400 [k]	2,000	3,606
United Lutheran Church	—	625	—
Wesleyan Methodist Church	—	—	72

*Total reported Protestant enrollment: kindergartens 18,058; elementary 263,839; secondary 76,842.
[a] Includes schools with kindergartens but no schools with grades above grade 8.
[b] Includes all schools with one or more grades 9-12, including schools with elementary grades also. Does not include junior colleges or other institutions on college level that offer precollege level courses.
[c] Enrollment figures for this denomination were for 85 nursery-kindergartens, 112 elementary schools, and 84 secondary schools.
[d] The schools sponsored by this denomination comprise the National Union of Christian Schools.
[e] Included with figures for secondary schools.
[f] Does not include 550 for which level of instruction was not known.
[g] One school only reporting enrollment.
[h] Eight schools only reporting enrollment.
[i] Two schools only reporting enrollment.
[j] Includes 1,992 pupils in nursery schools.
[k] Includes an estimated 600 pupils in nursery grades.

3. *EXTENT OF DENOMINATIONAL INVOLVEMENT WITH CHURCH SCHOOLS*

Quoted from "Church-Related Elementary and Secondary Schools in Continental United States," by Bertha Blair, *Information Service,* Bureau of Research and Survey, National Council of Churches of Christ in the U.S.A., New York, January 3, 1959, p. 2.

THE UNITED STATES Office of Education estimates an enrollment of 34,717,000 pupils in the elementary and secondary grades of the nation's public schools in the school year 1958-59 and an enrollment of 5,695,000 pupils in the elementary and secondary grades of the non-public schools.[a] These figures represent an estimated actual increase of 2,558,000 in public school enrollment in the last two years and an estimated increase in enrollment of 562,000 in non-public schools in the same period. The relative increase in enrollment in non-public schools was greater, however, than in the public schools, 10.9 per cent as compared with 8.0 per cent.[a]

Schools under Roman Catholic auspices for many years have accounted for the major portion of the non-public school enrollment and they still do. But the proportion they represent at present appears to be slightly less than it has been for some time. In the school year 1957-58, schools under Roman Catholic auspices accounted for nearly 90 per cent of the non-public school enrollment according to Office of Education estimates, the other 10 per cent being accounted for by the schools maintained by other religious bodies and the schools under nonsectarian auspices.[b] Earlier reports showed that schools under Roman Catholic auspices accounted for 92 per cent of the total non-public school enrollment in elementary and secondary grades; 4 per cent was accounted for by schools under auspices of other religious bodies, and 4 per cent by schools under nonsectarian auspices.[c]

Office of Education figures for church schools other than those under the auspices of the Roman Catholic Church are estimates based partially on figures that were secured in the 1940-42 *Biennial Survey of Education,* so that they may not fully reflect the increases that have actually occurred in the meantime. However, our survey shows that only a relatively few of the some 250 religious bodies in the United States[d] maintain full-time week-day schools today, indeed only a relatively few of these with the largest memberships have such schools. So far as the survey has been able to determine, there actually are only eight religious bodies and one association other than the Roman Catholic Church that have well-established school systems of any size. Only three of these are among the seventeen religious bodies with memberships of a million or more—Lutheran Church-Missouri Synod, Protestant Episcopal Church, and the Jewish congregations. The five other denominations that have well-established school systems are the Seventh-day Adventists, Evangelical Lutheran Joint Synod of Wisconsin and other States, Mennonite Church (including Amish), Society of Friends, and Christian Reformed Church.[e] Some 150 schools maintained by local churches of a variety of denominations are affiliated with the National Association of Christian Churches. Some local churches appear to be establishing their own schools even though their national denominations are not promoting such a program.

As for actual statistics of enrollment, taking into consideration the known deficiencies of our figures, it would appear from our survey that enrollment in church schools other than those under Roman Catholic auspices is less than half a million.

a. *School Life,* Official Journal of the Office of Education, U.S. Department of Health, Education and Welfare, September, 1958.

b. *School Life,* October, 1957.

c. *Biennial Survey of Education in the U.S. 1940-42, vol. 2, chapter 9,* Statistics of Non-public Elementary and Secondary Schools, 1940-41; summarized in *The State and Non-public Schools,* Office of Education, U.S. Dept. of Health, Education and Welfare, Misc. no. 28, 1958, p. 2.

d. *Yearbook of American Churches for 1959,* Benson Y. Landis, ed., National Council of Churches.

e. The Christian Reformed Church has parent-controlled schools that comprise the National Union of Christian Schools.

4. ENROLLMENT IN CATHOLIC SCHOOLS, BY STATES, AS PERCENTAGE OF TOTAL (PUBLIC AND NON-PUBLIC) ENROLLMENT: 1960

From "The Constitutionality of the Inclusion of Church-Related Schools in Federal Aid to Education," Legal Department, National Catholic Welfare Conference, *Georgetown Law Journal,* Winter 1961, vol. 50, no. 2, pp. 443-44.

State	Total public and non-public school enrollment *	Number of students in Catholic schools†	Students in Catholic schools as % of total
Alabama	816,117	24,530	3.01%
Alaska	45,558	2,252	4.93
Arizona	333,887	22,746	6.81
Arkansas	433,325	10,150	2.34
California	3,698,762	313,784	8.48
Colorado	430,023	34,369	7.99
Connecticut	573,331	84,416	14.72
Delaware	102,604	18,544	18.04
District of Columbia	143,214	19,787	13.82
Florida	1,038,381	53,833	5.18
Georgia	949,864	16,659	1.75
Hawaii	161,841	15,590	9.63
Idaho	166,440	6,838	4.11
Illinois	2,274,666	484,506	21.30
Indiana	1,125,367	128,942	11.46
Iowa	672,855	86,473	12.85
Kansas	516,083	46,439	9.00

State	Total public and non-public school enrollment *	Number of students in Catholic schools†	Students in Catholic schools as % of total
Kentucky	707,746	81,402	11.50
Louisiana	847,164	121,058	14.29
Maine	234,597	27,104	11.55
Maryland	727,489	109,205	15.01
Massachusetts	1,072,240	234,414	21.90
Michigan	1,997,376	287,851	14.41
Minnesota	850,684	143,953	16.92
Mississippi	590,599	14,181	2.40
Missouri	984,156	145,237	14.76
Montana	166,480	18,332	11.01
Nebraska	334,763	47,060	14.06
Nevada	68,080	3,365	4.94
New Hampshire	137,758	28,899	20.98
New Jersey	1,370,894	287,717	20.99
New Mexico	248,217	22,967	9.25
New York	3,606,894	751,722	20.84
North Carolina	1,114,458	11,302	1.01
North Dakota	158,497	18,485	11.66
Ohio	2,349,326	362,249	15.42
Oklahoma	558,457	17,688	3.17
Oregon	420,672	29,165	6.93
Pennsylvania	2,569,738	562,861	21.90
Rhode Island	187,674	48,328	25.75
South Carolina	591,249	9,390	1.59
South Dakota	165,433	14,623	8.84
Tennessee	816,229	19,517	2.39
Texas	2,314,718	148,620	6.42
Utah	242,313	4,116	1.70
Vermont	90,402	14,101	15.60
Virginia	888,909	37,892	4.26
Washington	690,880	47,679	6.90
West Virginia	454,617	15,419	3.39
Wisconsin	975,455	227,686	23.34
Wyoming	83,094	3,784	4.55
	42,099,576	5,287,230	12.56%

*Column 1 is an estimate derived from the addition of three figures: (1) public school enrollment as given in Office of Education Circular no. 634, Fall 1960 Statistics on Enrollment, Teachers, and Schoolhousing in Full-Time Public Elementary and Secondary Day Schools, Table 3 (August 4, 1961); (2) Catholic elementary and secondary school enrollment as given in the General Summary of The Official Catholic Directory (1961); and (3) 10% of the Catholic enrollment as an estimate of the non-Catholic private elementary and secondary school enrollment. This 10% factor is based on the estimate in Biennial Survey of Education in the United States—1954-56: Statistics of State School Systems 1955-56, at 25-26 (1959).

†The totals given in Column 2 have been derived by adding the enrollments in four categories of the General Summary of The Official Catholic Directory (1961): High Schools, Diocesan and Parochial; High Schools, Private; Elementary Schools, Parochial and Institutional; Elementary Schools, Private.

5. ENROLLMENT IN CATHOLIC EDUCATIONAL INSTITUTIONS

From the General Summary of Statistics, *Official Catholic Directory*, New York, P.J. Kenedy and Sons, 1961.

Educational Institution	Number in U.S.	Number of students
Elementary schools, parochial and institutional	10,132	4,312,862
Elementary schools, private	462	89,548
High schools, diocesan and parochial	1,564	546,259
High schools, private	869	340,036
Catholic colleges and universities	267	321,999
Diocesan seminaries	96	13,834
Diocesan students in other seminaries		7,486
Seminaries, religious or scholasticates	441	20,551
Protective institutions	130	12,072
Total Enrollment*		**5,664,647**

KEY:

ELEMENTARY:

Parochial schools are schools supported by parish.

Private schools are those which charge tuition.

SECONDARY:

Diocesan high schools are schools supported by the diocese.

Parochial high schools are schools supported by the parish.

Private high schools are those which charge tuition.

SEMINARY:

Diocesan seminaries train for the priesthood of individual dioceses.

Religious seminaries train priests for religious and monastic orders.

Scholasticates are places where candidates for priesthood pursue their studies before entry into major seminaries.

*In the same year, 2,578,340 Catholic children attended public elementary schools, and 893,836 attended public high schools.

6. CATHOLIC PAROCHIAL SCHOOLS: DOCTRINE AND ORGANIZATION

Extracts quoted from "Some Effects of Parochial School Education in America," by Peter H. and Alice S. Rossi, *Daedalus,* Spring 1961, published by the American Academy of Arts and Sciences and the Wesleyan University Press, pp. 304-6.

THE DOCTRINAL basis of the Roman Catholic parochial schools stems from the Third Plenary Council of the American hierarchy held in Baltimore in 1884, and has been reiterated a number of times. The Council declared it morally binding on every Catholic to see to it that his children had proper religious training. The vehicle for such training was the parochial school, or, if such schools were not available, provision in some other fashion for such training. In order to provide for proper training, each parish was ordered to set up denominational schools within two years and to make provisions for the religious instruction of those children who could not be accommodated in parochial schools. In this pronouncement the hierarchy set the pattern of mass education under parochial jurisdiction.

The goal of a school in every parish, with every Catholic child in a parochial school, is still far from being fulfilled today.* Slightly more than half the parishes in the United States at present support parochial schools,

*Editor's Note: In 1959, 58 per cent of 16,753 parishes—or 9,614 parishes—had schools.

and about the same proportion of Catholics have attended them. It should be noted here that statistics on attendance in private schools are notoriously unreliable, and the proportions quoted here are subject to a large and unknown error.

With few exceptions, the Catholic elementary schools of today are financed and administered by individual parishes. The parish pastor undertaking to organize a school has full responsibility for raising the necessary capital, obtaining teaching personnel from one of the teaching orders, and providing operating funds. A diocese may often undertake to provide building funds to be repaid on easy terms. A diocesan superintendent of schools, whose powers are primarily administrative and advisory, provides some degree of uniformity in curriculum and standards. He may also have direct control over diocesan high schools; few parishes are large enough or rich enough to support the more expensive secondary education.

The Plenary Council of 1884 urged the establishment of free parochial schools. Today, however, most parochial schools charge tuition fees. Compared to those charged in secular private schools, these fees are nominal—estimated to be about $25 per year per pupil in the Chicago area—and are usually waived for pupils in need. The major part of school expenses is raised from voluntary contributions from the total congregation. Compared to that of public or secular private schools, the per capita cost of parochial schooling must be considerably less, since the salaries paid to the sisters and brothers are only nominal. In fact, mass denominational schooling is a tribute to the dedication of the members of the teaching orders.

The teaching personnel of the typical parochial school is provided to the parish by a religious community. The parish undertakes to furnish housing, subsistence, and a nominal salary. When it is not possible to obtain enough sisters from a religious community, lay persons may be employed to round out the full complement, a practice that has become more common recently during the postwar expansion of the parochial school system.

7. SOME SOCIOLOGICAL DATA ON CATHOLIC SCHOOL CHILDREN

Data from *Parochial School: A Sociological Study*, by Joseph H. Fichter, S. J., Notre Dame, Indiana, University of Notre Dame Press, 1958, pp. 106 and 222.

Editor's Note: A parochial school, St. Luke's in Chicago, Illinois, with an enrollment of 632 children, was selected as being representative of parochial schools throughout the nation. Curriculum, attendance, parent-school relationships, social development, comparisons with other schools, etc., were studied in great detail.

Table 1 shows the percentage of time in each week spent on various subjects by a typical eighth-grade pupil at St. Luke's.

Table 2 compares the religion of the friends of Catholic children who attend parochial school (St. Luke's) with the religion of friends of Catholic children who attend public school.

Table 1

Religion	10.0%	Music	6.7%
English	37.3%	Science and Health	5.3%
Arithmetic	15.0%	Art	4.0%
Social Studies	16.0%	Recess and miscellaneous	5.7%

Table 2

	Religion of three best friends				
	Three Catholic	Two Catholic	One Catholic	Three non-Catholic	No Information
Pupils from St. Luke's	49.6%	31.3%	11.4%	3.5%	4.2%
Catholic pupils in public school	1.7%	10.9%	42.8%	37.0%	7.6%

8. RELIGIOUS INFLUENCES IN AMERICAN PUBLIC SCHOOLS

From "The Extent of Religious Influence in American Public Schools," by R. B. Dierenfeld, *Religious Education*, May–June 1961, vol. 56, no. 3, pp. 173–79.

Editor's Note: This article reports the results of a questionnaire answered by 2,183 public school superintendents in all parts of the United States. The following questions and data have been selected from the more extensive material in the report.

8a. Religion and the Curriculum

Does your school system provide materials to classroom teachers to help in teaching about religion?

	U.S. as a Whole
YES	76.06%
NO	23.94%

Are there regular classes in the Bible in the schools of your system?

	U.S. as a Whole	West	Midwest	South	East
YES	4.51%	8.57%	4.14%	9.00%	1.32%
NO	95.48%	91.43%	95.86%	91.00%	98.68%

8b. Religion and Non-Curricular Activities*

Are Gideon Bibles distributed in your school system?

	U.S. as a Whole	**West**	**Midwest**	**South**	**East**
YES	**42.74%**	39.66%	50.35%	54.77%	26.24%
NO	**57.26%**	60.34%	49.65%	45.23%	73.76%

Are home-room devotional services held in the schools of your system?

	U.S. as a Whole	**West**	**Midwest**	**South**	**East**
YES	**33.16%** (all schools in the system)	2.41% (all)	6.40% (all)	60.53% (all)	68.33% (all)
	17.06% (some schools in the system)	6.21% (some)	19.55% (some)	28.16% (some)	11.83% (some)
NO	**49.76%**	91.38%	74.05%	11.32%	19.83%

Is there any type of regular chapel exercise held in the schools of your system?

	U.S. as a Whole	**West**	**Midwest**	**South**	**East**
YES	**22.07%**	1.35%	14.69%	70.86%	12.62%
NO	**77.93%**	98.65%	85.31%	29.14%	87.38%

Is Bible reading conducted in the schools of your system?

	U.S. as a Whole	**West**	**Midwest**	**South**	**East**
YES	**41.74%**	11.03%	18.26%	76.84%	67.56%
NO	**58.26%**	88.97%	81.74%	23.16%	32.44%

Are religious holidays observed by any kind
of activities in the schools of your system?

U.S. as a Whole	Yes	U.S. as a Whole	Yes
Christmas	87.92%	Passover	2.17%
Hanukah	5.39%	Thanksgiving	76.75%
Easter	57.82%	Other	0.48%

*Non-curricular activities refer to programs and practices provided by the school in addition to formal classwork.

8c. The Public Schools and Religious Groups

Does your school system cooperate in a program of released time instruction?

	U.S. as a Whole	West	Midwest	South	East
YES	29.66%	29.32%	27.39%	10.74%	44.46%
NO	70.43%	70.68%	72.61%	89.26%	55.54%

Does your school system provide bus transportation for students attending parochial schools?

	U.S. as a Whole	West	Midwest	South	East
YES	19.86%	11.39%	16.79%	3.59%	37.96%
NO	80.14%	88.61%	83.21%	96.41%	62.04%

Are there any members of religious orders teaching in the public schools of your system?

	U.S. as a Whole
YES	5.76%
NO	94.24%

8d. The School Administrator and Religion in the Public Schools

What is your opinion regarding the celebration of religious holidays by school activities?

U.S. as a Whole	14.46%	Not proper
	61.96%	Can be done if care is used
	23.58%	School has the right to do this

Do you favor the distribution of Gideon Bibles in the public school?

	U.S. as a Whole	West	Midwest	South	East
YES	54.80%	49.44%	56.56%	83.20%	38.41%
NO	45.20%	50.56%	43.44%	17.70%	61.59%

Do you believe your school system is dealing in an adequate way with religion?

	U.S. as a Whole
YES	77.47%
NO	22.53%

9. *ATTITUDES TOWARD FEDERAL AID TO EDUCATION*

From American Institute of Public Opinion (Gallup Poll), March 30, 1961.

THESE questions were put to a national cross section of 1,608 adults—with persons of major religious faiths represented in their correct proportion to the population.

Some members of Congress believe that the government should give Catholic schools long-term loans at low interest to build more school buildings. Would you approve or disapprove of this?

All faiths		Catholics only		Protestants only	
Approve	42%	Approve	76%	Approve	34%
Disapprove	46%	Disapprove	17%	Disapprove	52%
No opinion	12%	No opinion	7%	No opinion	14%

If the federal government in Washington decides to give money to aid education, should this money go only to public schools, or should money go to help Catholic and other private schools as well?

All faiths		Catholics only		Protestants only	
Public schools only	57%	Public schools only	28%	Public schools only	63%
Catholic and private as well	36%	Catholic and private as well	66%	Catholic and private as well	29%
No opinion	7%	No opinion	6%	No opinion	8%

Religion in American History

1. SOME HIGHLIGHTS: A CHRONOLOGY

Condensed from *Encyclopedia of American History*, Richard B. Morris, ed., New York, Harper and Bros., 1961, pp. 579–86.

1609. Church of England was established by law in Virginia. A statute (1610), re-enacted when Virginia became a royal colony, but never rigidly enforced, provided for compulsory church attendance. The Anglican Church was also established in the lower counties of New York (1693), and in Maryland (1702), South Carolina (1706), North Carolina (nominally, 1711), and Georgia (1758). . . . After the first quarter of the eighteenth century the Anglican Church gained ground as a result of a split among Calvinists. . . . The first bishop in America was *Samuel Seabury* (1729–96), consecrated in Aberdeen (1784).

1620. Congregational Churches were introduced by the Pilgrims in Plymouth (1620) and by the Puritans in Massachusetts Bay (1630). The principal difference was that the former (Independents) repudiated the Church of England; the latter (Nonconformists) did not openly break with the Established Church. . . . The *Halfway Covenant* (1657–62), which admitted to baptism the children of baptized persons who themselves had not experienced conversion, served to erase the distinction between the "elect" and all others.

1628. Dutch Reformed Church (a Calvinist, Presbyterian group) was organized in New Amsterdam, by Reverend *Jonas Michaëlius* (1628), placed under the jurisdiction of the Classis of Amsterdam, and established by the Freedoms and Exemptions (1640).

1633. Roman Catholic Church has previously been established in North America as a result of Spanish and French missionary activity, but the first group of Catholics to arrive in the English colonies came to Maryland, which had been founded (1632) to provide refuge for that denomination. . . . The Revolution of 1689 in Maryland, leading to Protestant ascendancy, resulted in the passage of anti-Catholic legislation (1) imposing poll tax on Irish Catholic immigrant servants; (2) requiring that children of mixed marriages be reared as Protestants; (3) imposing a fine for sending children to Catholic schools abroad. . . . In the beginning of the eighteenth century, Rhode Island and Pennsylvania were the only colonies in which Roman Catholics enjoyed religious and civil rights. . . . By 1775, public worship by Roman Catholics was confined to Pennsylvania.

1639. Baptists (opposed to infant baptism and stressing the separation of Church and State) were organized as a church by *Roger Williams* at Providence, Rhode Island, followed by Newport (1644). . . .

1640. Lutheran Church. Reverend *Reorus Torkillus,* first Lutheran minister to serve in the New World, arrived in New Sweden (spring 1640). The first synod was not organized until 1748. . . .

1654. Jews. Despite the efforts of Stuyvesant to deprive them of civil rights, the first group of Jews, arriving in New Amsterdam (1654) from Curaçao, induced the Dutch West India Company (7 Jews were among the 167 stockholders) to permit them to reside and engage in wholesale trade (1655-56). In 1657, they were admitted to the retail trades. In 1685, they demanded the right of public worship, denied under Dutch rule, and a synogogue (Shearith Israel, "Remnant of Israel") was known to exist in New York City in 1695. . . . The Jews prior to 1789 were mainly *Sephardim* (of Spanish, Portuguese and Dutch origin).

1656. Quakers (Society of Friends), founded by *George Fox*, stressed "inner light," separation of Church and State, opposition to war and oaths. Except in Rhode Island, they were persecuted in the period 1656-70. Expansion of this sect is attributed to the visit of Fox to America (1671) and to Penn's "Holy Experiment" (1681). . . .

1683. Mennonites, led by *Francis Daniel Pastorius* (1651-c.1720), settled in Germantown, Pennsylvania. They advocated separation of Church and State, religious liberty, adult baptism, a church of the elect, pacifism, refusal to take oaths, and drew up the first protest against slavery (1688). Most conservative of this group were the *Amish.*

1706. Presbyterians. The first presbytery was organized in Philadelphia by *Francis Makemie* (1658-1708); the first synod in 1718. The Adoption Act, the first constitution of American Presbyterianism, was adopted (1729).

1723. Dunkards, or German Baptists, were organized under the leadership of *Alexander Mack*. Their distinctive features were triple immersion, pacifism and agape feasts.

1726-56. Great Awakening, a series of revivals. . . . In New England, undisputed leadership in the movement was assumed by *Jonathan Edwards,* beginning with his sermons of 1734. . . . The Methodist phase, under Reverend *Devereux Jarrett,* reached its climax, 1775-85. Among Presbyterians, the Great Awakening led to a schism between "New Side" (revivalists, who organized an independent synod, 1745) and "Old Side" (conservatives), which was healed in 1758. Among Congregationalists a similar devision developed, with the more conservative joining the Anglican Church.

1735. Moravians, or United Brethren, comprising Hussites and German Pietists, came to Georgia in 1735, and . . . founded a settlement at Bethlehem, Pennsylvania (1741).

1766. Methodism began in America, as in England, as a movement within the Church of England. It appeared first in New York City (1766).

1775-83. Churches and the Revolution. The Anglican clergy throughout the colonies were Loyalist, the Southern laity overwhelmingly Patriot. The Congregational and Presbyterian clergy took a Patriot stand. The Methodist missionaries were Loyalist. Lutherans and Roman Catholics were divided in loyalty. The Quakers, officially neutral, leaned toward the Loyalists, as did the Shakers.

1776-89. Disestablishment. Under the leadership of Baptists and Presbyterians the movement for religious freedom and separation of Church and State gained headway in Virginia in the Revolutionary period. . . . An Act of 1776 suspending payment of tithes . . . really disestablished the Church of England [in Virginia]. Elsewhere the church was disestablished: 1776—Pennsylvania, Delaware and New Jersey; 1777—New York, North Carolina, and Georgia (partially, completely in 1789); 1790—South Carolina. (1818—Connecticut constitution disestablished the Congregational Church; 1833—Massachusetts disestablished the [Congregational] Church.)

1780. Universalists. The first American Universalist church, built . . . in Gloucester, Massachusetts, favored separation of Church and State.

1782. First Parochial School erected by St. Mary's Church, Philadelphia ("Mother School"). The system was officially sanctioned in Baltimore (1829). By 1840, there were 200 parochial schools in the U.S.

1784. Theological Schools. The first theological college in the U.S. was established at New Brunswick, New Jersey. Other important seminaries were Andover (founded to oppose Unitarian trends at Harvard, 1808), Princeton (1812), General (1817), Auburn (1818), Virginia (1823), Hartford (1834), and Union Theological (1836).

1789. Protestant Episcopal Church, depleted by Loyalist emigration, now independent of the Church of England, was organized at its first triennial convention in Philadelphia. . . . By 1792, five bishops had been named.

1790. Roman Catholic Episcopate was established with the consecration of Reverend *John Carroll* (1735-1815); nominated, 1788. . . . Political discrimination against Catholics continued until 1835 (North Carolina).

1792. Russian Orthodox Church began missionary activities in Alaska, with a resident bishop at Sitka, 1798. The episcopal see was moved to San Francisco (1872), and in 1905 to New York City.

1794. Deism gained ground after the publication of Tom Paine's *Age of Reason.* . . . Deism's most influential exponent in America was *Elihu Palmer,* ex-Baptist preacher, whose *Principles of Nature* (1797) attacked the orthodox tenets of Christianity. Deists established ties with pro-Jacobin democratic societies after 1794.

1797. Great Revivals began on the frontier with the preaching of *James McGready* (c. 1758-1817). . . . In New England the revival was led by the *Edwardeans* who were opposed by (1) the *old covenant theologians (Timothy Dwight* [1752-1817] and *Lyman Beecher* [1775-1863], and (2) by the *rationalists and Unitarians.*

1808. Methodist Church adopted a constitution.

1810. Organization of the *American Board of Commissioners for Foreign Missions* (Congregational), which became interdenominational (1812), marked the beginning of American missionary interest. The American Bible Society (1816), the Home Missionary Society (1826) and the American Tract Society (1825) followed.

Disciples of Christ, a group of progressive Presbyterians opposed to open communion, founded the Independent Church of Christ at *Brush Run,* Pennsylvania.

1813-17. Large Negro groups formed independent churches, including African Methodist Episcopal Church (Philadelphia, 1816). The first Negro Baptist church was founded in Georgia (1773). In 1861, there were 200,000 Negro members of the Methodist Episcopal Church, South; 150,000 Negro Baptists.

1819. Unitarian Church (stressing unity of God and denying Trinitarianism) founded by *William Ellery Channing.*

1824-50. Revivalism in Pennsylvania, New York and Massachusetts led by *Charles G. Finney* (1792-1875), licensed to preach as a Presbyterian. The Broadway Tabernacle was established for him in New York City (1834).

1829-54. Anti-Catholic Agitation, following the founding of the Society for the Propagation of the Faith (Lyons, France, 1822) and the Leopold Association (Vienna, 1829) to promote Roman Catholic missions in America, resulted in . . . anti-Catholic sermons by Reverend *Lyman Beecher* and writings by *Samuel F. B. Morse* and acts of violence, such as the burning of the Ursuline Convent at Charlestown, Massachusetts (August 11, 1834).

1830. Latter-day Saints, or Mormons owe their origin to the publication of the *Book of Mormon,* based on a revelation claimed by *Joseph Smith* (1805-44), followed by the founding of the Church at Fayette, New York, the same year. As a result of opposition, the Mormons left New York (1831) for Kirkland, Ohio, and Independence, Missouri. Expelled from Missouri, they settled at Nauvoo, Illinois. Violence followed them, culminating in the lynching of Smith in the jail at Carthage. Driven from Nauvoo (1846), the Saints settled in the valley of the Great Salt Lake in Utah (1848) under the leadership of *Brigham Young.*

1832-69. Slavery and the Churches. The issue of abolitionism came to a head when *Theodore Dwight Weld,* a student at Lane Theological Seminary, Cincinnati, withdrew from that institution when the trustees suppressed an anti-slavery society. In the North abolitionism quickly became part of revivalism. The issue divided the Protestant churches. The Southern Baptists withdrew (1843) to organize the Southern Baptist Convention. The Methodist Church, South, set up a separate organization (1844). An abolitionist group of New School Presbyterians organized the Synod of Free Presbyterian Churches, Ohio (1847), followed by a major schism in the New School (1857), when the United Synod of the South was established. Old School Presbyterians split (1861), and the Presbyterian Church in the Confederate States was founded. The Ohio Synod and the New School Presbyterians united in 1862. In 1864, the Southern groups united as the Presbyterian Church in the U.S. The Northern groups united as the Presbyterian Church in the U.S.A. (1869). Division on this issue was avoided in the Protestant Episcopal Church.

1840-60. Reform and Conservative Judaism. Rabbi *Isaac Mayer Wise* . . . advocated the idea of reform. In 1873, he organized the Union of American Hebrew Congregations, followed (1875) by Hebrew Union College in Cincinnati. . . . A conservative movement in opposition was headed by Rabbis *Isaac Leeser* (1806-68) and *Sabato Morais* (1823-97) of Philadelphia. The Jewish Theological Seminary (conservative) was founded (1886).

1843. Millerism, an Adventist movement, resulted from the preaching of *William Miller* (1782-1849), who prophesied the second coming of Christ between 1843-44. His followers founded the Adventist Church (1845). The *Seventh-Day Adventists* separated from the parent body (1846).

1874. The publication of *Outlines of Cosmic Philosophy* by *John Fiske* with its attempt to reconcile theism with Darwinian evolution, brought theological liberalism . . . into open conflict with orthodoxy.

1875-86. Archbishop *John McClosky* became the first American cardinal. Archbishop *James Gibbons* was elected to the same rank (1886). The Catholic University of America was founded at Washington, D.C. (1884).

1875-92. Christian Science textbook, *Science and Health,* by *Mary Baker Eddy* was published and the Christian Science Association organized. The first church was established at Boston, 1879; reorganized, 1892.

1876. Society for Ethical Culture established in New York by *Felix Adler.*

1880. Salvation Army, evangelistic organization, after being first established by General *William Booth* in England, was organized in the U.S.

1895. National Baptist Convention of the U.S.A., representing merger of Negro Baptist groups, formed at Atlanta; incorporated (1915). The National Baptist Convention of America separated (1916).

1905. The Federal Council of Churches of Christ in America, first major interdenominational organization, was founded; succeeded (1950) by the National Council of Churches of Christ in the U.S.A.

1907. Social Gospel. Publication of *Christianity and the Social Crisis* by *Walter Rauschenbusch* (1861-1918), with its criticism of capitalism and the industrial revolution and its stress on co-operation rather than competition.

1908. Home Missions Council established to direct noncompetitive missionary activity.

1909-25. Fundamentalist Reaction, inspired by such traveling evangelists as *William Jennings Bryan, William A. ("Billy") Sunday,* and *John Alexander Dowie,* reached its climax at Dayton, Tennessee (July 10-21, 1925), in the trial and conviction of *John Scopes,* a Tennessee schoolteacher, for teaching evolution. Scopes was opposed by Bryan; defended by Clarence Darrow and Dudley Field Malone.

1918. United Lutheran Church in U.S. formed, placing 45 synods on the same doctrinal basis.

1931. Jehovah's Witnesses, under the leadership of Judge *J. F. Rutherford* . . . were incorporated (1939) as The Watch Tower Bible and Tract Society.

c.1935. Neo-Orthodoxy, a synthesis of the socio-economic liberalism of the Social Gospel and a rediscovery of Biblical theology, with stress on the fall of man and the judgment of God, secured a wide following among American Protestants under the leadership of *Reinhold Niebuhr.*

1939. Methodist Episcopal Church, Methodist Episcopal Church, South, and the Methodist Protestant Church were reunited.

1952. Bible, Revised Standard Version (National Council, Churches of Christ, U.S.A.), best seller; also Roman Catholic Confraternity translation, vol. 1.

1950-60. Protestant Church Unity Trend. National Council of the Churches of Christ in the U.S.A. formed November 29, 1950 by 25 Protestant denominations and 5 Eastern Orthodox bodies embracing 37 million church members. Congregational Christian Churches and the Evangelical Reformed Church united (June 1957) to form the United Church of Christ. Presbyterian Church in the U.S.A. and United Presbyterian Church joined May 28, 1958 to form the United Presbyterian Church in the U.S.A. On December 4, 1960 the chief executive officer of the United Presbyterian Church proposed a merger into a new church of the Methodist, Protestant Episcopal, and United Presbyterian Churches and the United Church of Christ, with total membership of 12,250,000 for the 4 churches.

2. EARLY HISTORY OF THE INDEPENDENT NEGRO CHURCHES

From *Protestant—Catholic—Jew,* by Will Herberg, New York, Doubleday Anchor Books, 1960, pp. 112-13.

BEFORE the Civil War, Negro slaves, as they became Christians, found themselves in the same churches as the whites, though of course segregated from them. Such was the case, too, with most of the free Negroes in the North. Considerations of Christian unity in Christ and the patriarchal responsibility of master for slave, combined with a natural reluctance to allow Negro slaves to develop independent institutions, helped bring about a very limited kind of fellowship in worship. The revival movement reached the Negroes in large numbers and swept them into the Methodist and Baptist churches as these spread in the South and Southwest.

Even before the Civil War, however, there were here and there beginnings of separate Negro churches, usually the result of resentment of free Negroes in the North at segregation and other discriminatory practices. But it was not until after the war that independent Negro churches emerged on a large scale. The Civil War and Emancipation removed restrictions which had fettered independent Negro organization and released the energies of the former slaves. At the same time, the war and postwar conflicts exacerbated the bitterness between the races and intensified the "color" consciousness of the whites. The newly emancipated Negroes carried out the work of separation and independent organization with astounding energy and success. The colored members of the Methodist Episcopal Church, South, left in vast numbers to join the African M.E. and African M.E. Zion churches, which had been formed as small groups in the North in 1816 and 1821 respectively. Of the 208,000 Negro members of the Southern Methodist Church in 1860, only 49,000 remained in 1866, and these soon departed to form the Colored Methodist Episcopal Church. Another Negro church came into being with the division of the Presbyterians, and still another with the separation of the Baptists, both in the decade and a half after the Civil War. The Northern Methodist Church and the Episcopal Church resisted division but could not avoid a great measure of inner segregation.

3. RELIGIOUS AFFILIATION OF PRESIDENTS OF THE UNITED STATES

The listing of Presidents is from *Facts about the Presidents,* by Joseph Nathan Kane, New York, H. W. Wilson, 1959, p. 235. President Kennedy's name has been added to the list.

Baptist
Warren Gamaliel Harding
Harry S. Truman

Congregational
Calvin Coolidge

Disciples of Christ
James Abram Garfield

Dutch Reformed
Martin Van Buren
Theodore Roosevelt

Episcopalian
George Washington
James Madison
James Monroe
William Henry Harrison
John Tyler
Zachary Taylor
Franklin Pierce
Chester Alan Arthur
Franklin Delano Roosevelt

Friends (Quaker)
Herbert Clark Hoover

Methodist
Ulysses Simpson Grant
Rutherford Birchard Hayes
William McKinley

Presbyterian
Andrew Jackson
James Knox Polk
James Buchanan
Grover Cleveland
Benjamin Harrison
Woodrow Wilson
Dwight David Eisenhower

Roman Catholic
John Fitzgerald Kennedy

Unitarian
John Adams
John Quincy Adams
Millard Fillmore
William Howard Taft

No Specific Denomination
Thomas Jefferson
Andrew Johnson

No Religious Affiliation
Abraham Lincoln

Editor's Note: Some exceptions and amplifications of the above list follow: (1) Madison was not a church member, according to William W. Sweet. Madison "accepted the ministrations of the Episcopal Church, but was never a communicant."[a] (2) Hayes attended the Methodist Church but never joined it, according to the 1962 *World Almanac.*[b] (3) According to the *Dictionary of American Biography,* Polk's "wife was an ardent Presbyterian, and he accompanied her regularly to the church of her choice. But his 'opinions and predilections' were in favor of the Methodists, with whom he united just before his death."[c] Polk is listed as a Methodist in the 1962 *Information Please Almanac.*[d] (4) Jefferson is listed as a "deist" in the 1962 *Information Please Almanac.*[e] Sweet describes him in the same terms as Madison (see note 1 above). The 1962 *World Almanac* says: "Jefferson was a member of the Episcopal Church, but in later life became a deist, described himself as 'a disciple of the doctrines of Jesus,' and commended Unitarianism."[f] (5) Johnson, according to the 1962 *Information Please Almanac,* "was not a professed church member; however, he admired the Baptist principles of church government."[g] Johnson is listed as a Methodist by the 1962 *World Almanac.*[h] (6) The Dictionary of American Biography makes two relevant statements concerning Lincoln. As a youth, he "shunned the vociferous camp meetings of his time, and avoided member-ship in the church." "Though never identifying himself with any ecclesi-astical denomination, he was not lacking in the religious sense; and in his public papers he expressed with sincerity the spiritual aspirations of his people."[i] Lincoln is listed as a "liberal" by the 1962 *Information Please Almanac*.[j] The 1962 *World Almanac* gives this note: "Lincoln attended Presbyterian services in Washington but was not a member."[k]

[a] *Religion in Colonial America*, New York, Charles Scribner's Sons, 1942, p. 337.
[b] 1962 *World Almanac*, New York, N.Y. *World Telegram and The Sun*, 1962, p. 162.
[c] *Dictionary of American Biography*, edited by Allen Johnson and Dumas Malone, New York, Scribner's, 1928-1937.
[d] 1962 *Information Please Almanac*, edited by Dan Golenpaul Associates, New York, Simon and Schuster, 1961, p. 542.
[e] *ibid.*, p. 542.
[f] *ibid.*, p. 162.
[g] *ibid.*, p. 542.
[h] *ibid.*, p. 162.
[i] *ibid.*
[j] *ibid.*, p. 542.
[k] *ibid.*, p. 162.

4. RELIGIOUS AFFILIATION OF JUSTICES OF THE SUPREME COURT OF THE UNITED STATES

The listing of justices is from the 1962 *Information Please Almanac*, edited by Dan Golenpaul Associates, New York, Simon and Schuster, 1961, pp. 524-26.

THE RELIGIOUS affiliation of the 13 men who have served as Chief Justices is as follows:

Baptist	2	Protestant	1
Congregational	1	Roman Catholic*	2
Episcopalian	5	Unitarian	1
Methodist	1		

The religious affiliation of the 82 Associate Justices appointed before 1962 is as follows:

Protestant	73	Jewish	3
Catholic	5	No denomination	1

*The first Catholic Chief Justice was Roger B. Taney (served 1836-64) who presided over the Court in the Dred Scott case (1857).

5. *RELIGIOUS AFFILIATION OF COLONIAL LEADERS*

Quoted from *Religion in the Development of American Culture, 1765–1840,* by William W. Sweet, New York, Charles Scribner's Sons, 1952, p. 85.

THE FRAMERS of the Constitution represented a cross-section of the American religious bodies of that day. Of them, nineteen were Episcopalians, eight were Congregationalists, seven were Presbyterians, two were Roman Catholics, two were Quakers, one a Methodist, one a Dutch Reformed while Edmund Randolph was a deist, though he later became a communicant of the Episcopal Church.

Quoted from *Religion in Colonial America* by William W. Sweet, New York, Charles Scribner's Sons, 1942, pp. 336–39.

A CONSIDERABLE proportion of the most important leaders in the fight for religious liberty in America were not church members; Madison, Jefferson and Franklin serve as good examples. None of them were communicants of a church; all of them were interested in religion as such; all were philosophical liberals, with little in common with the orthodox churches of their time. Madison was a graduate of the College of New Jersey and remained a year after graduation to pursue further study in Hebrew and Ethics under the sturdy Presbyterian president John Witherspoon, who not only presided over his formal studies, but imbued him with his own antipathy for a state-controlled church. Madison had been reared as an Episcopalian, but was never a communicant. Jefferson had little liking for formal Christianity as expressed in the priesthood and dogma, though he was a believer in deity and accepted the ministrations of the Episcopal Church. He was a liberal contributor to many denominations and many clergymen of various churches were his friends, but he abhorred any connection between church and state. . . . Certain it is that the principal leaders of Revolutionary America were latitudinarian in their religious views, with no strong predilection for any one religious body. . . . Thus, the political and religious liberalism of seventeenth- and eighteenth-century England and France was mediated to the American Colonies through a group of unchurched leaders, whose unattached position made them the more responsive to these liberal voices.

Religion in Contemporary American Life: Sociological Data and Polls

1. A SOCIOLOGICAL COMPARISON OF MAJOR UNITED STATES RELIGIOUS GROUPS

Quoted from an article by that title by Bernard Lazerwitz, *Journal of the American Statistical Association*, September, 1961, vol. 56, pp. 568-79.

RELIGIOUS, demographic, and economic data gathered [in 1957 and 1958] on three Survey Research Center [University of Michigan] studies have been analyzed by major religious groups.*

The analysis indicates only slight differences in sex composition, marital status, and age structure among Protestants, Roman Catholics and Jews except for a middle-aged concentration among Episcopalians and Presbyterians.

People who report they are without a religion are heavily male and have a larger percentage single than does the nation as a whole.

The number of children in Jewish, Episcopalian and Presbyterian families is similar, but smaller than the number in other religious groups.

On education, occupation and income, the religious groups can be separated into three descending ranks: (1) a top rank, having large percentages of college graduates and white collar workers, and enjoying high incomes, composed of Episcopalians, Jews and Presbyterians; (2) a middle rank, containing smaller percentages of college graduates and white collar workers, and earning less income, consisting of Methodists, Lutherans, Roman Catholics and the "no religion" group; and (3) the bottom ranked Baptists with few college graduates or white collar workers and low family incomes.

*Editor's Note: Religious classification was determined by respondents' answers to a question about their religious preference. In the following tables, N = number of persons in each category and Nation = total number of persons in the survey.

Sex Composition and Marital Status for Adults of Major
United States Religious Groups, December, 1957 (in percentages)

Religious Groups	N	Men	Women	Single	Mar-ried	Wid-owed	Di-vorced	Sepa-rated	Total
Nation	5,827	46	54	6	82	8	2	2	100%
Protestants	4,185	45	55	5	82	8	3	2	100
Baptists	939	42	58	5	80	9	4	2	100
Whites	713	44	56	5	83	8	3	1	100
Negroes	226	34	66	5	68	12	6	9	100
Methodists	730	44	56	5	81	10	2	2	100
Lutherans	328	46	54	9	81	8	1	1	100
Presbyterians	272	42	58	8	78	9	4	1	100
Episcopalians	119	35	65	9	79	9	1	2	100
Roman Catholics	1,270	46	54	8	82	7	2	1	100
Jews	188	42	58	8	85	5	1	1	100
No Religion	125	81	19	11	77	5	6	1	100

Age Composition of Adults of Major United
States Religious Groups, December, 1957 (in percentages)

Religious Groups	N	21 to 24	25 to 29	30 to 34	35 to 39	40 to 44	45 to 49	50 to 54	55 to 59	60 to 64	65 or over	Total
Nation	5,827	6	12	12	12	13	10	9	8	6	12	100%
Protestants	4,185	6	12	12	11	12	11	10	8	6	12	100
Baptists	939	8	11	13	12	12	11	9	6	6	12	100
Whites	713	9	12	13	11	12	12	9	6	5	11	100
Negroes	226	7	10	15	14	10	10	11	7	7	9	100
Methodists	730	6	10	12	11	11	10	10	8	6	16	100
Lutherans	328	6	13	13	9	12	11	10	6	6	14	100
Presbyterians	272	5	10	13	9	13	8	9	11	8	14	100
Episcopalians	119	4	6	12	13	17	12	11	4	9	12	100
Roman Catholics	1,270	7	13	13	12	15	9	8	7	5	11	100
Jews	188	5	9	13	16	16	8	10	9	4	10	100
No Religion	125	9	5	10	12	12	15	11	6	5	15	100

Number of Children in the Homes of Major United
States Religious Groups, December, 1957 (in percentages)

Religious Groups	N	No Children	1 Child	2 Children	3 or more Children	Total
Nation	5,827	44	16	18	22	100%
Protestants	4,185	43	16	19	22	100
Baptists	939	42	16	17	25	100
Whites	713	41	15	19	25	100
Negroes	226	41	19	11	29	100
Methodists	730	46	14	19	21	100
Lutherans	328	43	13	20	24	100
Presbyterians	272	48	15	21	16	100
Episcopalians	119	53	13	19	15	100
Roman Catholics	1.270	39	15	19	27	100
Jews	188	40	17	27	16	100
No Religion	125	48	16	13	23	100

Amount of Education for Adults of Major United
States Religious Groups, December, 1957 (in percentages)

Religious Groups	N	0–8 Grades	Some High School	4 Yrs. High School	1–3 Yrs. College	4 Yrs. or More of College	Total
Nation	**5,827**	**33**	**20**	**28**	**10**	**9**	**100%**
Protestants	**4,185**	**33**	**21**	**27**	**10**	**9**	**100**
Baptists	939	44	24	21	7	4	100
Whites	713	39	26	24	7	4	100
Negroes	226	63	20	11	3	3	100
Methodists	730	31	20	28	10	11	100
Lutherans	328	35	22	29	9	5	100
Presbyterians	272	18	17	29	20	16	100
Episcopalians	119	8	14	25	25	28	100
Roman Catholics	**1,270**	**34**	**20**	**32**	**9**	**5**	**100**
Jews	**188**	**21**	**13**	**33**	**17**	**16**	**100**
No Religion	**125**	**40**	**20**	**18**	**10**	**12**	**100**

Occupation of Family Heads for Major
United States Religious Groups,
December, 1957 (in percentages)

Religious Groups	N	Professions	Owners, Managers and Officials	Clerical and Sales	Skilled	Semi-skilled	Unskilled	Farmers	Without an Occupation	Total
Nation	**5,827**	**9**	**12**	**10**	**18**	**15**	**9**	**9**	**18**	**100%**
Protestants	**4,185**	**9**	**12**	**10**	**17**	**15**	**10**	**10**	**17**	**100**
Baptists	939	5	8	7	16	20	15	11	18	100
Whites	713	6	11	9	19	19	8	12	16	100
Negroes	226	4	1	4	10	21	34	8	18	100
Methodist	730	10	11	11	16	14	8	9	21	100
Lutherans	328	7	11	13	18	14	8	15	14	100
Presbyterians	272	13	20	14	17	7	8	4	17	100
Episcopalians	119	23	23	17	12	6	4	2	13	100
Roman Catholics	**1,270**	**8**	**11**	**10**	**22**	**20**	**10**	**4**	**15**	**100**
Jews	**188**	**19**	**32**	**16**	**9**	**9**	**1**	**0**	**14**	**100**
No Religion	**125**	**15**	**10**	**5**	**10**	**20**	**7**	**11**	**22**	**100**

Total Family Income in 1956 for Major United States Religious Groups (in percentages)

Religious Groups	N	Under $1,000	$1,000–$1,999	$2,000–$2,999	$3,000–$3,999	$4,000–$4,999	$5,000–$5,999	$6,000–$7,499	$7,500–$14,999	$15,000 or more	Total
Nation	**5,827**	**7**	**8**	**10**	**13**	**15**	**15**	**13**	**16**	**3**	**100%**
Protestants	**4,185**	**8**	**9**	**11**	**13**	**14**	**15**	**12**	**15**	**3**	**100**
Baptists	939	17	13	14	15	14	11	9	6	1	100
Whites	713	10	9	13	15	16	14	12	9	2	100
Negroes	226	27	20	17	15	9	5	5	1	1	100
Methodists	730	7	10	14	10	15	17	12	13	2	100
Lutherans	328	6	9	11	10	18	16	14	14	2	100
Presbyterians	272	5	6	9	12	14	14	14	20	6	100
Episcopalians	119	1	1	4	7	12	13	16	35	11	100
Roman Catholics	**1,270**	**4**	**7**	**8**	**12**	**17**	**17**	**17**	**16**	**2**	**100**
Jews	**188**	**1**	**2**	**5**	**9**	**10**	**15**	**16**	**31**	**11**	**100**
No Religion	**125**	**10**	**11**	**11**	**11**	**17**	**11**	**7**	**15**	**7**	**100**

2. *RELIGION, VOTING AND PUBLIC OPINION*

2a. *Analyses of 1960 Presidential Election Vote*

Quoted from American Institute of Public Opinion (Gallup Poll) releases of
December 3 and 6, 1960.

The Catholic Vote With the election of Senator John F. Kennedy as
the first Roman Catholic to occupy the White House, the question arises
as to just how big a role his fellow Catholic voters played in giving Kennedy
his razor-thin victory margin. From pre-election and post-election surveys,
it is possible to study not only the Catholic vote as a whole, but also various
voting patterns of sub-groups among Catholic voters. Some highlights of
this analysis:

(1) On a national basis, Catholics shifted sharply back to the Democratic party in 1960 after defections on the part of many to President
Eisenhower in 1952 and 1956.

Some 62 per cent of Catholics who said they voted for Eisenhower
in 1956 this year were supporting Kennedy.

Here is a comparison of the Catholic presidential vote in the last three
elections:

Catholic Vote	1952	1956	1960
Democratic	56%	51%	78%
Republican	44%	49%	22%

(2) Catholic Independent voters went to Kennedy by an overwhelming
majority in the November election. In addition, there was a defection to
the Senator on the part of nearly one Catholic Republican in five.

(3) Although the Catholic vote was solidly in the Kennedy column, it
could by no means be described as monolithic. Some of the sharpest
differences, for example, are noted in the vote of Catholics from various
education levels. Generally speaking in this country, more education
means more income. Better-educated Catholics, with higher incomes,
gave Nixon a higher proportion of their vote than did Catholics with
less education. In this respect, the Catholic voting pattern resembled the
electorate as a whole where better-educated, higher-income groups tend
to vote Republican, voters with less education and lower down the
economic scale tend to vote Democratic.

(4) While most commentators noted the wide defections among Eastern
Catholics from their 1956 vote, the Catholic vote in other areas was also
heavily for Kennedy. In these states—where Catholics make up a smaller
proportion of the total population—Catholics voted as heavily Democratic if not more so than did Catholics in the East where they make up
a large proportion of the population.

The accompanying table gives the complete breakdown of the Catholic vote—based on the 3,312 interviews among Catholic voters conducted by the Gallup Poll before and after the 1960 election:

The Catholic Vote in the 1960 Election

	Kennedy	Nixon		Kennedy	Nixon
Catholic Democrats	95%	5%	**Catholic Voters by Education:**		
Catholic Republicans	18	82	College	65%	75%
Catholic Independents	72	28	High School	80	20
Catholics for Eisenhower in 1956	62	38	Grade School	83	17
Catholics for Stevenson in 1956	97	3	**Catholic Voters by Age:**		
Catholic Voters by Region:			21 to 29 years	78	22
East	77	23	30 to 49 years	78	22
Midwest	81	19	50 years and over	77	23
South	75	25	**Catholic Voters by Occupation:**		
Far West	74	26	Professional and Business	69	31
Catholic Voters by City Size:			White-collar	75	25
500,000 and over	75	25	Skilled workers	81	19
50,000 to 500,000	82	18	Unskilled workers	83	17
2,500 to 50,000	79	21	Farmers	84	16
Under 2,500	80	20	Union members	85	15
Farms	86	14	**Catholic Voters by Sex:**		
			Men	77	23
			Women	78	22

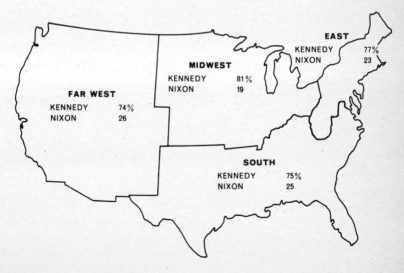

VOTE OF CATHOLICS

EAST		
KENNEDY	77%	
NIXON	23	

MIDWEST		
KENNEDY	81%	
NIXON	19	

FAR WEST		
KENNEDY	74%	
NIXON	26	

SOUTH		
KENNEDY	75%	
NIXON	25	

The Protestant Vote The Protestant vote remained solidly in the Republican column in the 1960 election.

In contrast to the nation's Catholic voters who shifted sharply back to
the Democrats this year, voters of Protestant faith gave about the same
majority of their vote to Vice-President Nixon as they did to President
Eisenhower in both 1952 and 1956.

In those years, many Protestants who had voted Democratic in the past
switched to Eisenhower and have now remained in the GOP column for
three successive elections.

The Gallup Poll's comprehensive analysis of the 1960 vote reveals this
about the voting behavior of the 8,575 Protestants who were interviewed
in these surveys:

(1) Just over six out of ten Protestants voted for Nixon in the 1960
election. This compares with about eight out of ten Catholics who cast
their ballots for Senator Kennedy.

There was little or no shift in the Protestant vote since 1956. Here is
how members of that faith have voted for President in the last three
elections:

Protestant Vote	1952	1956	1960
Republican	63%	63%	62%
Democratic	37%	37%	38%

(2) Nixon's support from Protestant Independents exactly parallels the
support Kennedy got from Catholic Independents. Each man drew a
heavy majority from the respective members of his own faith in this
all-important "switch voting" group. In addition to his support from
Protestant Independents, Nixon got the vote of nearly one Protestant
Democrat in four.

(3) The Vice-President ran best among members of the Protestant
faith who live in the heavily-populated Eastern states. In that same region,
however, where Catholics make up a large proportion of the population,
Kennedy had an even bigger majority of the Catholic vote. In the South,
Nixon polled a slim majority of the vote of Protestants.

(4) Protestant women gave a substantially heavier vote to Nixon than
did Protestant men. Among Catholics, there was little difference between
the heavy majorities for Kennedy registered by both Catholic men and
women.

(5) The support for Senator Kennedy among younger voters, which many observers noted, was apparently due in large part to younger voters of his own Catholic faith. Nixon had the vote of about six out of ten Protestant voters between the ages of 21 and 29.

The accompanying table gives the complete breakdown of the Protestant vote—based on 8,575 interviews among Protestant voters conducted by the Gallup Poll:

The Protestant Vote in the 1960 Election

	Nixon	Kennedy		Nixon	Kennedy
Protestant Republicans	97%	3%	**Protestant Voters by Education:**		
Protestant Democrats	23	77			
Protestant Independents	72	28	College	73%	27%
Protestants for Eisenhower in 1956	85	15	High School	61	39
			Grade School	55	45
Protestants for Stevenson in 1956	16	84	**Protestant Voters by Age:**		
Protestant Voters by Region:			21 to 29 years	59	41
			30 to 49 years	58	42
East	72	28	50 years and over	66	34
Midwest	62	38	**Protestant Voters by Occupation:**		
South	53	47			
Far West	63	37	Professional and Business	73	27
Protestant Voters by City-size:			White-collar	68	32
			Skilled workers	56	44
500,000 and over	63	37	Unskilled workers	48	52
50,000 to 500,000	66	34	Farmers	55	45
2,500 to 50,000	65	35	Union members	48	52
Under 2,500	60	40	**Protestant Voters by Sex:**		
Farms	55	45	Men	59	41
			Women	65	35

VOTE OF PROTESTANTS

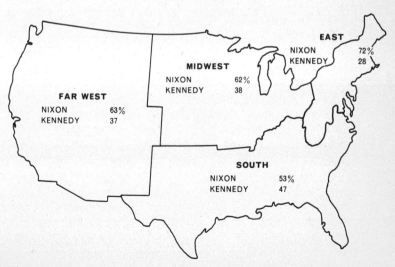

EAST
NIXON   72%
KENNEDY   28

MIDWEST
NIXON   62%
KENNEDY   38

FAR WEST
NIXON   63%
KENNEDY   37

SOUTH
NIXON   53%
KENNEDY   47

The Jewish Vote Jewish voters of the nation went heavily Democratic in the November election. Senator Kennedy had slightly greater support from this religious group in the 1960 race than Adlai Stevenson had in either 1952 or 1956.

Here is a comparison of the Jewish vote for President in the last three elections:

Jewish Vote	1952	1956	1960
Democratic	77%	75%	81%
Republican	23%	25%	19%

Quoted from *The Public Pulse*, Elmo Roper and Associates, January 1961, no. 11, p. 2.

ANOTHER key factor in the Kennedy victory last November was the Democratic candidate's religion. Analysts may debate for years the precise impact of the religious issue, and Nixon may have been the net gainer—in the *popular* vote; that's a moot point. But *electorally,* there seems little question that Kennedy's religion actually helped him, since he was able to hold much of the presumably anti-Catholic but strongly Democratic South by narrow margins, while a strong Catholic vote helped to win him the populous states of the industrial North. In recent years, many Catholics had deserted their traditional Democratic allegiance to vote for Eisenhower; Kennedy's religion helped to turn these Republican defections back to the Democrats—and added many more.

Excerpts quoted from "Religious Affiliation and the Election" in *Information Service,* published by Bureau of Research and Survey, National Council of Churches of Christ in the U. S. A., New York, March 4, 1961, p. 4.

SENATOR KENNEDY'S religious affiliation may have handicapped him, Louis Harris, who heads an organization making surveys, is quoted in *The New York Times,* November 23, 1960. His study indicated that Senator Kennedy's popular vote ran about 7 per cent behind the votes of Democrats for seats in Congress in the nation. Mr. Harris believed that the Kennedy victory came about largely because he was able to restore the traditional big-city Democratic majorities and because he was able to appeal to younger voters in the suburbs. Even in those states where the Roman Catholic population is equal to over 30 per cent of the total population, Senator Kennedy ran almost 3 per cent behind the Democratic Congressional vote. The Senator's close triumph, Mr. Harris stated, may be attributed to his victory in the three states of New Jersey, Michigan and Minnesota, where he ran by small proportions ahead of the votes for Democratic nominees for seats in Congress.

On the other hand Louis H. Bean, a long-time student of election results, wrote in *The Nation,* New York, November 26, 1960: "The overriding feature in this election is extremely similar to that of 1928: states where Catholics are relatively numerous gave Kennedy more support than he would have had were he not a Catholic. In other states his support was reduced."

Of nine "heavily Roman Catholic states," Senator Kennedy carried six, with 121 electoral votes *(Newsweek,* New York, November 14); Mr. Nixon carried three with 41 electoral votes. Specifically, the Vice President carried Wisconsin, New Hampshire and Ohio, among the "heavily Roman Catholic states."

Of nine "heavily Protestant states" (*i.e.* those with small, statistically insignificant proportions of Catholics) Mr. Kennedy carried five (all regarded as Southern), with 50 electoral votes, and Mr. Nixon carried 4 with 35 electoral votes. (*Newsweek,* November 14.)

The President-elect carried 7 out of 11 states in which Roman Catholic membership officially reported makes up 30 per cent or more of the population; in 1956 Adlai Stevenson carried none of these *(U. S. News and World Report,* Washington, November 21, 1960). "Kennedy's share of the vote was smaller than Stevenson's in only six states, all with relatively heavy Protestant population. He lost only two of these six, however: Tennessee and Oklahoma." (In both of these states there were frequent press reports of Protestant officials advising that no Roman Catholic should be elected President.)

U. S. News and World Report sums up: There was a massive shift of votes from Eisenhower in 1956 to Kennedy in 1960 in heavily urban and Catholic states; Kennedy fared better than either Stevenson or Truman in the Catholic states; Protestants voting against having a Roman Catholic in the White House "saved some states for Nixon."

The public declarations of officials of the Latter-day Saints in favor of Vice-President Nixon undoubtedly were influential in the several Western states where that church has many adherents.

Labor union members and Jews are reported to have voted Democratic by large majorities—as in previous elections. In the Middle West, Senator Kennedy carried the same states that President Roosevelt won in 1944. *U. S. News and World Report* alleges that there was little change from 1956 in the "heavily farm counties" of the Middle West. Former President Truman, however, noted that Mr. Kennedy's church affiliation turned many farm votes to Mr. Nixon in that region.

2b. Religious Prejudice and Politics

Quoted from American Institute of Public Opinion (Gallup Poll) release of November 19, 1960.

OVERLOOKED in all the discussion about the role of the "religious issue" in the 1960 election is the fact that the long-time trend in opinion surveys clearly showed a decline in prejudice against a Roman Catholic in the White House.

On this evidence alone, in fact, Senator John Kennedy should have been expected to fare better with the U. S. electorate in 1960 than Governor Alfred Smith did over 30 years ago.

And with younger voters showing the least amount of resistance to a member of the Catholic faith becoming President, the indication is that this decline in prejudice will likely continue.

In 1940, when James Farley's name figured in political speculation in the event President Roosevelt did not run for a third term, the Gallup Poll asked voters for their views on a Catholic nominee. The question was repeated on several occasions in recent years as Senator Kennedy's candidacy became a possibility. Voters were asked: *If your party nominated a generally well-qualified man for President, and he happened to be a Catholic, would you vote for him?*

This was the vote 20 years ago compared with results obtained up to the time of Kennedy's nomination:

Vote for Catholic for President?	Yes	No	DK
1940	62%	31%	7%
1958	68%	24%	8%
1959	69%	20%	11%
1960	71%	20%	9%

In the most recent survey, these were the results by various age groups:

Vote for Catholic for President?	Yes	No	DK
21-29 years	77%	13%	10%
30-49 years	77%	17%	6%
50 years and over	62%	27%	11%

Quoted from American Institute of Public Opinion (Gallup Poll) release of September 26, 1961.

THE DECLINE in anti-Catholic sentiment as it affects the Presidency is paralleled by a decline in prejudice toward two other minority groups.

In the three years since 1958—during which time a Catholic has been elected President—the proportion of U. S. citizens who say they would not vote for a Catholic has declined from 25 to 13 per cent.

During this three-year period, a decrease in the number of persons opposed to voting for a Jew or a Negro for President has been registered in Gallup Poll surveys.

In order to gain insight into the touchy and difficult-to-ascertain area of prejudices, a concrete situation was presented to a representative sample of U. S. adults, as follows:

If your party nominated a generally well-qualified man for President, and he happened to be a Jew, would you vote for him?

Here are the results to this question when asked in 1958 and again in the latest survey:

Vote for Jew for President? (3-Year Trend)	Yes	No	DK
1958	62%	28%	10%
1961	68%	23%	9%

An interim survey, reported in early 1960, at the time of synagogue defacings and other anti-Jewish acts, found 72 per cent who said they would vote for a Jew for President, 22 per cent opposed, and 6 per cent in the "no opinion" category.

If your party nominated a generally well-qualified man for President, and he happened to be a Negro, would you vote for him?

The results, showing the trend:

Vote for Negro for President?	Yes	No	DK
1958	38%	53%	9%
1961	50%	41%	9%

Decline in Prejudice by Population Groups

Younger persons show less prejudice than older people. Persons with a college background are more tolerant than those who attended only grade school.

Here are the figures by educational background of respondents:

Vote for Jew for President?	Yes	No	DK
College	83%	11%	6%
High School	73%	20%	7%
Grade School	55%	33%	12%

Vote for Negro for President?	Yes	No	DK
College	60%	31%	9%
High School	52%	39%	9%
Grade School	43%	49%	8%

Following are the figures by age group:

Vote for Jew for President? (By age group)	Yes	No	DK
21-29 years	76%	16%	8%
30-49 years	71%	21%	8%
50 years and over	62%	28%	10%

Vote for Negro for President? (By age group)	Yes	No	DK
21-29 years	54%	34%	12%
30-49 years	58%	37%	5%
50 years and over	42%	48%	10%

Only negligible differences were found between men and women in respect to voting for a Jew or a Negro for the Presidency.

Catholics were more likely than Protestants to say they would vote for a Jew or a Negro for President.

2c. Comparison of Attitudes Toward a Catholic President

Quoted from American Institute of Public Opinion (Gallup Poll) release of September 23, 1961.

THE FEARS of many Americans about a Roman Catholic in the Presidency have been largely allayed during the early months in office of the country's first Chief Executive of that faith.

Three years ago—before the emergence of the then Senator John F. Kennedy as a contender for the Democratic Presidential nomination— one person in four (25 per cent) was against voting for his party's nominee if he were a Catholic.

Today—eight months after Kennedy became the first President of that faith—only one person in eight (13 per cent) maintains this opposition to voting for a Catholic.

During this same period, the proportion willing to vote for a Catholic has gone from 68 per cent to 82 per cent.

This important, but little talked about aspect of Kennedy's Presidency thus far comes to light in a nationwide Gallup Poll in which a representative sample of adults was asked this question:

If your party nominated a generally well-qualified man for President, and he happened to be a Catholic, would you vote for him?

The latest vote:

Vote for Catholic for President?	(1961)
Yes, would	82%
No, would not	13%
Don't know	5%

The current survey is actually further evidence of a long-term decline in prejudice against a Catholic President over the last two decades. The following table shows the trend of the public's thinking about a Catholic for President since the Gallup Poll first asked this question in 1940:

Vote for Catholic for President?	Yes	No	DK
1940	62%	31%	7%
1958	68%	25%	7%
1959	69%	20%	11%
*1960	71%	20%	9%
1961	82%	13%	5%

*Before Kennedy's nomination.

1960 Vote

As the above table indicates, the decline in prejudice against a Catholic has been particularly marked during the last year. Further analysis suggests, moreover, that much of the decline has occurred since Kennedy took over the Presidency.

Gallup Poll studies some eighteen months before the November, 1960 election indicated that if Kennedy were nominated, the fact of his religion would both help and hurt him.

On the one hand, many Catholics who voted for Eisenhower in 1952 and 1956 indicated that they might swing to the Democrats with a member of their own faith heading that ticket.

At the same time, some normally Democratic Protestants evidenced that they would vote Republican if the Democrats nominated a Catholic.

The net effect of both the "anti" and "pro" Catholic votes pointed to about a 4-point loss for Kennedy at that time if he were running against Vice-President Nixon.

In the election itself, Kennedy trailed his party's candidates for Congress by about 5 percentage points. He received just over 50 per cent of the popular vote, Democratic candidates for the House of Representatives got just over 55 per cent of the vote.

It should be pointed out, however, that Adlai Stevenson ran behind his party by 8 points in 1956 and by 5 points in 1952.

As might be expected, the decline in prejudice against a Catholic over the last year has come largely from Protestant voters. Catholics, themselves, show almost no opposition to voting for a member of their own faith in either survey.

The decline is most marked among older persons in the population—those over 50 years of age—and among persons with the least amount of formal education.

Both of these groups previously had evidenced the greatest degree of "anti-Catholic" sentiment regarding the Presidency.

3. NEGROES AS CHURCH MEMBERS

3a. The Negro Churches

Quoted from "Religion Among Ethnic and Racial Minorities" by J. Oscar Lee, *Annals of the American Academy of Political and Social Science,* November 1960, vol. 332, pp. 113-14, 116.

The largest non-white minority group in the United States is the Negro-American group. In 1950, the United States Census indicated that there were 15,482,000 non-whites in the United States and that Negroes constituted more than 95 per cent of this group. Negroes are mainly found in separate Negro denominations. These denominations are the National Baptist Convention, United States of America, Incorporated; the National Baptist Convention of America; the African Methodist Episcopal Church; the African Methodist Episcopal Zion Church, and the Christian Methodist Episcopal Church. While accurate membership figures for these denominations are not available, it is estimated that the five Negro denominations have approximately ten million members.* Comparisons of this estimate with estimates made in previous years would seem to indicate that these denominations are growing in membership. There are approximately 600,000 Negro members in the predominantly white Protestant denominations of which about 366,000 are in the Methodist Church.† According to the *National Catholic Almanac* for 1960, there were, as of January 1959, about

---

* *Yearbook of the American Churches, 1960* (New York: The National Council of Churches, 1960), pp. 253, 257.
† "Proceedings of the General Conference of the Methodist Church, 1960," *Daily Christian Advocate* vol. 1, no. 3 (April 29, 1960), p. 105.

595,155 Roman Catholic Negroes in the United States. This is an increase of 20,000 over the preceding year.*

These figures indicate that a high proportion of the Negro population are members of churches belonging to the five Negro denominations. But they reflect more than this. They point to the central place that the churches have occupied and continue to occupy in the life of the Negro community. In a very real sense, it is the Negro's own institution in that it is organized, led, developed, owned and controlled by Negroes.

Even though Negro communities have developed many types of organizations to serve various social, political and civic purposes, the Negro church still occupies a central place. It is to the churches that these organizations turn when they need to communicate with the entire Negro community or desire mass support for a program or project. The Negro churches are not only composed of the masses of the people, but the churches are also an important medium through which these masses shape and express their aspirations. Moreover, the Negro minister has the historic role of leader in the community. In the days after slavery, he was the principal if not only leader in many communities. While this has changed as teachers, medical doctors, lawyers, and other professional and business people assume a share of the leadership burden, the Negro minister still occupies an important place of leadership. He still has direct contact with the masses of the people who are members of his congregation and who look to him for counsel and guidance on many problems.

Negro churches play an important role in the shaping and the expression of the aspirations of the masses of Negro people, and these aspirations are important in shaping the goals, functions and programs of the churches which must attempt to meet the felt needs which confront people in a period of rapid social change.

There appears to be substantial agreement among many Negroes that in addition to worship and religious education the church should be active in promoting the social advancement of the race. There is an expectation among an increasing number of Negroes that the churches should be active in the improvement of the community, cooperate with community welfare and civic organizations, and engage in social action to correct injustice, particularly in race relations.

---

*National Catholic Almanac, 1960 (Garden City, N. Y.: Doubleday and Co., 1960), p. 473.

3b. Integration in Protestant Churches

Quoted from "Ecological Changes and the Church," by Truman B. Douglass, *Annals of the American Academy of Political and Social Science,* November 1960, vol. 332, pp. 83–85.

THE DENOMINATIONS which have been known as churches of the proletariat have made slower progress toward the integration of Negroes into their membership than have some of the longer established and presumably more socially conservative bodies. In 1950 a survey of Presbyterian, United States of America churches disclosed that out of 2,706 reporting congregations, 832 were integrated. A 1958 study of Congregational Christian churches in metropolitan areas found that 12 per cent included Negro members and that 49 per cent were willing to accept Negroes as members. The Protestant Council of New York City asserts on the basis of a recent study that half the churches in that city have an interracial membership. Liston Pope estimates that about 10 per cent of the total number of Protestant churches in the nation are interracial.* This figure is five times as large as the corresponding figure for ten years ago. There is no evidence that the Pentecostal sects have shown any similar disposition toward integration. This is probably due, in the first place, to their tendency to make a radical separation between faith and social ethics and, in the second place, to the fact that many of these sects have their greatest strength in the South.

The most intensive study yet made of the attitudes and practices of a single denomination respecting racial integration covered the Congregational Christian churches in standard metropolitan areas. Questionnaires were sent to all the churches of that denomination in such areas. When congregations showed themselves willing to participate in the study, interviews were held with the minister and at least one lay official. Of the 1,500 churches of the denomination located in standard metropolitan areas, 1,054 took part in the study.

Two significant and encouraging facts were disclosed. First, some modest gains in racial inclusiveness were revealed. The survey showed that 26.6 per cent of the churches in metropolitan communities included in their membership representatives of at least one minority group. A less thorough study made twelve years previously revealed that only 17 per cent of these churches could be classified as inclusive.

*Liston Pope, *The Kingdom Beyond Caste* (New York: Friendship Press, 1957).

Second, in the opinion of ministers and lay leaders, well over half the congregations studied—63.4 per cent of them—would support their pastors in implementing a policy of racial inclusiveness.

There were some disheartening findings. Nearly half the local churches that were studied had no definite policy for receiving members of racial minorities. Approximately 70 per cent said they had never confronted a situation that required decision in that area of policy. Since the study was limited to highly urbanized communities where the size of racial minorities has rapidly increased in recent years, it is evident that the churches are not aggressively pressing toward a policy of racial inclusiveness.

In the opinion of a large number of lay officers of churches, the pastors would have more support for programs of desegregation in the community than in their own churches. Dr. Herman Long, the director of the study, considered this the most negative finding.

A majority—51.4 per cent—of the lay respondents from the Midwest believed that there are exceptions to the denomination's announced policy of unconditional hospitality to members of all racial groups. It is alarming that what has been considered the southern pattern may also be the midwestern pattern.

A general result of the study was to indicate that in a period of history when events in the realm of human relations move with lethal swiftness the churches proceed with glacial slowness. The extent of integration in the churches compares unfavorably with accomplishments in other areas such as employment in federal and state governments, the armed services, professional sports, labor unions, institutions of higher education, and so on.*

---

*Herman H. Long, *Fellowship for Whom? A Study of Racial Inclusiveness in Congregational Christian Churches* (New York: Department of Race Relations, the Board of Home Missions, 1958).

3c. Negroes in Roman Catholic Parishes

From *Information Service,* published by Bureau of Research and Survey, National Council of Churches of Christ in the U.S.A., New York, May 12, 1962, vol. 41, no. 10, p. 4.

THE ANNUAL report of the Commission for Catholic Missions Among the Colored People and the Indians, released 1961, in Washington, states that 653,217 of the more than 18,000,000 Negroes in the country are Roman Catholics. This is an increase of 37,000, or 6 per cent, over 1960 figures. A third of the Negro gain is accounted for by a record number of converts, 12,248. This compares with 12,066 in 1960, 11,802 in 1959, and 11,374 in 1958.

The report notes that one of every eight U. S. converts to Catholicism in 1960 was a Negro. In the city of New Orleans, two out of five converts were Negroes. In St. Louis, the proportion was one out of five. Gains in the missionary South add to "a remarkable 9 per cent," though increase in actual numbers, 6,345, was comparatively small.

Ten dioceses with Negro Catholic populations over 20,000 are listed in the report. They are: Lafayette, La., 80,500; New Orleans, 72,000; Washington, D. C., 58,582; New York, 45,324; Chicago, 45,000; Philadelphia, 42,759; Galveston, Tex., 40,188; Los Angeles, 31,796; Baltimore, 25,862; and Brooklyn, 21,000.

The report also states a record high of 93,292 children are enrolled in 348 schools conducted for Negroes, taught by slightly more than 2,000 sisters and 600 lay teachers. A total of 702 priests now minister exclusively to Negroes. (From a press release of the Bureau of Information, National Catholic Welfare Conference, Washington.)

4. RELIGION AND YOUNG AMERICANS

4a. Beliefs and Opinions of High School Students

Condensed from *The American Teenager,* by H. H. Remmers and D. H. Radler, Indianapolis and New York, Bobbs-Merrill Co. Inc., 1957, pp. 167-73.

Editor's Note: This book is based on the answers given by a national sample of high school students to polls prepared and analyzed by the Purdue Opinion Panel, under the direction of Dr. H. H. Remmers. A few of the many questions and answers on religion follow:

	Religion			
	Prot.	**Cath.**	**Jew**	**Other**
The more I learn about science the more I doubt my religious beliefs	%	%	%	%
Yes	13	10	19	18
No	84	86	69	73
No response	3	3	12	9
Man has evolved from lower forms of animals				
Yes	36	32	58	38
No	40	45	12	32
Don't know	24	21	27	30
No response	0	2	3	0
My religious beliefs have made me:				
Very happy	34	46	5	23
Happy	38	36	34	31
Neither happy nor unhappy	24	14	45	35
Unhappy	2	1	5	3
Very unhappy	1	2	11	3
No response	1	1	0	5
Religious faith is better than logic for solving life's important problems				
Yes	57	63	23	48
No	18	14	44	24
Don't know	23	20	33	24
No response	2	3	0	4
Our fate in the hereafter depends on how we behave on earth				
Yes	69	77	23	55
No	9	6	27	13
Don't know	17	12	46	26
No response	5	5	4	6
God knows our every thought and movement				
Yes	84	88	38	74
No	3	3	12	8
Don't know	10	6	50	16
No response	3	3	0	2
God controls everything that happens everywhere				
Yes	59	69	31	50
No	20	14	23	17
Don't know	17	10	39	23
No response	4	7	7	10
Men working and thinking together can build a good society without any divine or supernatural help				
Yes	34	24	50	40
No	45	55	31	29
Don't know	18	18	19	19
No response	3	3	0	3
The one group of people I think can do most to promote peace in the world:				
Politicians	5	5	8	11
Religious leaders	50	55	15	40
Military leaders	9	9	4	13
Educators	23	20	50	24
Statesmen	5	5	15	4
Leaders in science	8	6	8	8

4b. Gallup Poll of Youth: 1961

Excerpts quoted from "Youth," by George Gallup and Evan Hill, *Saturday Evening Post*, December 23, 1961, p. 70.

Editor's Note: A special survey of more than 3,000 young Americans, age 14 through 22, was made by the Gallup Poll for the above-named article.

EIGHTY-FOUR per cent of them are church members, and more than half attend church regularly.

Seventy-four per cent of our youth believe in God "very firmly"; 76 per cent think of God as an omnipresent judge who observes all individual human actions and rewards or punishes them; 78 per cent believe in a hereafter; almost two-thirds of the high-school and working youth believe the Bible is "completely true," and 22 per cent of our college youth believe every word of the Testaments. Nine per cent of the college boys and 5 per cent of the college girls say they don't believe in God, but nearly two-thirds of our collegians are "very firm" believers.

Yet youth as a whole, while quite religious, is quite critical of the church as an institution. The girls, who are much more religious, have more criticism than the boys . . . Fifty-four per cent of the youth expressed dissatisfaction with religion, and their comments cut through all religious sects. The most frequent complaints are that the church fails to explain itself and its precepts, that it fails to stress its true meaning fervently enough, that it is not reaching the people, and that sermons are too vague and muddy. Many charge that "the church is not keeping pace with a changing world" and express disgust with what they call "too much ritual and mysticism."

4c. Youth's Attitudes Toward Religious Leaders

Quoted from "Youth's Attitudes *Re* Elections, Competition, Discipline, Status, Spare Time, Driving, Grandparents, and Health," Report of Poll no. 57 of the Purdue Opinion Panel, Purdue University, January, 1960, pp. 13a and 14a.

Which ONE of the following would you rather talk to about a personal problem?

	Total Sample*	Religion			Region			
		Prot.	Cath.	Other	East	Mid-West	South	West
	%	%	%	%	%	%	%	%
A psychiatrist	8	7	8	11	6	7	9	9
A psychologist	5	4	6	6	3	4	4	8
A teacher	13	13	11	11	11	14	12	12
A school counselor	14	13	15	17	16	16	7	17
A minister	46	49	45	34	49	43	51	35
A doctor	14	13	12	17	13	12	15	14

*Total number in sample—2,000: 70.1% Protestant, 15.7% Catholic, 1.4% Jewish and 12.8% Other.

4d. Opinions of High School Students About Birth Control

Quoted from *Planned Parenthood News,* Fall, 1960, p. 3.

High School Students Favor Birth Control, U.S. Aid on Family Planning

AN OVERWHELMING majority of American high school students—including Catholic students—believe in birth control and intend to try to control the size of their families when they get married. And a smaller, but still large, majority of them believe the United States should give scientific information and foreign aid funds to other countries for birth control programs.

These were the results of a poll conducted earlier this year among a nationally representative sample of high school students by the Purdue Opinion Panel, under the direction of Dr. H. H. Remmers.

The poll showed that:

85 per cent of all students—and 71 per cent of Catholics—believe couples are justified in controlling family size.

81 per cent of all students—and 63 per cent of Catholics—say they will try to control family size after marriage.

70 per cent of all students—and 58 per cent of Catholics—believe the United States government should give other countries scientific data on birth control.

60 per cent of all students believe the United States should give foreign aid funds to other countries for birth control research. On this question, the proportion of Catholic students favoring birth control was 47 per cent.

Asked how many children they would like to have, 76 per cent of all students—and 69 per cent of Catholics—said either two, three or four.

4e. College Students and Religion

Quoted from *What College Students Think,* by Rose K. Goldsen, Morris Rosenberg, Robin M. Williams, Jr. and Edward Suchman, Princeton, New Jersey, D. Van Nostrand Inc., 1960, pp. 153–54.

THEY TOLD us that they believe in God. Some of them described Him as a Divine, Omniscient, Omnipresent, and vigilant kind of Being; others visualized Him as a more mystical Power; but in either case, they said they believed.

They told us that they go to religious services, many of them with a high degree of regularity. Some said that they derived from their church attendance, or simply from being part of an identifiable religious group, certain strong feelings of identification and belongingness.

They said that they were aware of a need for some kind of religious faith or personal philosophy. They told us that they talk about it, grope for it, and some of them eagerly seize upon this or that organizational means of finding it.

We were struck, too, by the observation that even in this allegedly secular society of ours, certain students nevertheless declared (some solemnly, some quite casually) that their religious beliefs and activities constituted for them a sort of focal point around which their major life-goals and life-satisfactions, they thought, would ultimately revolve.

College Students' Conceptions of Deity (Responses of 2,975 Men Undergraduates at 11 Colleges)

Which of the following statements most closely describes your ideas about the deity?

I believe in a Divine God, Creator of the Universe, Who knows my innermost thoughts and feelings, and to Whom one day I shall be accountable	48%
I believe in a power greater than myself, which some people call God and some people call Nature	27%
I believe in the worth of humanity but not in God or a Supreme Being	5%
I believe in natural law, and that the so-called universal mysteries are ultimately knowable according to scientific method	7%
I am not quite sure what I believe	12%
I am an athiest	1%
All other responses	3%

4f. Early Religious Experience of College Students

From *Religion and the College Student,* by W. Seward Salisbury, a pamphlet published by The Research Foundation, State University of New York, Albany, N. Y., September 1957, p. 31, Table 5.

As you look back on your childhood, was your religious training and experience constructive and positive, incidental, or negative and frustrating?

	Male					Female					Total Males and Females
	Cath-olic	Jew	Prot-estant	No pref-erence	Total males	Cath-olic	Jew	Prot-estant	No pref-erence	Total fe-males	
	N-281	N-47	N-273	N-53	N-654	N-339	N-112	N-523	N-44	N-1018	N-1672
	%	%	%	%	%	%	%	%	%	%	%
Constructive and positive	76.9	40.5	65.9	13.2	64.5	84.1	47.3	81.1	34.1	76.3	71.8
Incidental	15.6	46.8	31.5	64.1	28.4	10.9	47.3	16.8	47.7	19.6	23.0
Negative and frustrating	4.3	10.6	1.8	15.1	4.6	4.1	4.5	2.1	13.6	3.5	3.9
No answer	3.2	2.1	.8	7.6	2.5	.9	.9	.0	4.6	.6	1.3
Total	100.0	100.0	100.0	100.0	100.0	100.0	100.0	100.0	100.0	100.0	100

5. *RELIGION AND MARRIAGE*

5a. *Religion Reported by Married Couples*

Data from U. S. Bureau of Census, "Religion Reported by the Civilian Population of the U. S.: March 1957," *Current Population Reports*, February 2, 1958, Series P-20, no. 79, pp. 2 and 8, Table 6.

Editor's Note: Only the state of Iowa requires information regarding religious affiliation on marriage license applications. Therefore, no official count of intermarriages in the United States is available. However, when the U.S. Bureau of Census surveyed 35,000 households in all parts of the nation in March, 1957, some information was gathered relating to intermarriage or mixed marriage:

AMONG all married couples in which one partner was reported as Protestant, Roman Catholic or Jewish, in 93.6% of the cases the husband or wife was in the same religious group. *In other words, 6.4% of the marriages were mixed marriages.*

Among couples where at least one spouse was Protestant:

    in 91.4% of the cases, the partner was also Protestant;

    in 8.4% of the cases, the partner was Roman Catholic;

    in 0.2% of the cases, the partner was Jewish.

Thus, 8.6% of the marriages involving Protestants were intermarriages.

Among couples where at least one spouse was Roman Catholic:

    in 78.5% of the cases, the partner was also Roman Catholic;

    in 21.2% of the cases, the partner was Protestant;

    in 0.4% of the cases, the partner was Jewish.

Thus, 21.6% of the marriages involving Roman Catholics were intermarriages.

Among couples where at least one spouse was Jewish:

    in 29.8% of the cases, the partner was also Jewish;

    in 4.2% of the cases, the partner was Protestant;

    in 3.0% of the cases, the partner was Roman Catholic.

Thus, 7.2% of the marriages involving Jews were intermarriages.

5b. *Mixed Marriages*

Excerpts quoted from "Mixed Marriages—Research Finding," by Judson T. Landis and Mary G. Landis in *Sex Ways—in Fact and Faith: Bases for Christian Family Policy,* Evelyn M. Duvall and Sylvanus M. Duvall, ed., New York, Association Press, 1961, pp. 84–86, 87–89.

Catholic-Protestant Marriages The most common type of mixed religious marriage in the United States is the marriage of Catholic to Protestant. Early in the twentieth century most Catholics, numerically speaking, came as immigrants to the United States; therefore, in many cases Catholic-Protestant marriages were mixed also by nationality and involved differences in ways of living. With the nearly complete assimilation of nationality groups within the American culture today, nationality background differences are not so important in such marriages.

In spite of the fact that Protestants as well as Catholics oppose interfaith marriages, such marriages are very common. *Studies show that today from one-fourth of the Catholics in some dioceses to three-fourths in other dioceses marry outside their faith.* [our italics.—Ed.] These figures are surprising to many Protestants who know of the Catholic policy of putting strong pressure on their young people to marry within their own faith. Protestant pressure against mixed marriages is not so strong nor so consistent as is the Catholic.

When university students are questioned about whether they would be willing to marry outside their own faith, Catholic young people report greater willingness than either Protestant or Jewish young people to marry one of a different religion. Jews report less willingness than either Catholics or Protestants. Moreover, Catholic young people report that although they would be willing to marry a Protestant, they would not be willing to change to the faith of the mate. Young Protestants express less willingness to make a mixed marriage. But a higher proportion of them report that if they should marry a Catholic, they would be willing also to change to the faith of the mate (from a study of 3,000 University of California students, 1955).

Perhaps one factor underlying the attitude of the Catholic young people is their confidence in the Catholic policy dealing with mixed marriages. The Catholic Church requires that parties to a mixed marriage sign the Antenuptial Agreement, and if the marriage is to be ecclesiastically valid the non-Catholic member must, in addition, take instruction in the Catholic faith. Protestants and Jews have no similar requirements. ....

Sociologists interested in the success or failure rate of mixed marriages have made several studies of Catholic-Protestant marriages. The studies have found the following:

> All studies showed that the divorce rate is lowest when Catholics and Protestants marry within their faith group. The divorce rate is three to four times higher in Catholic-Protestant mixed marriages which have produced children.

> There is strong evidence to show that spousal differences over the religious training of the children is a major factor causing disharmony in Catholic-Protestant marriages.

> Although couples sign the Antenuptial Agreement, in which they promise to bring up the children in the Catholic faith, in actual practice the children are more often brought up in the faith of the mother, whether she is Catholic or Protestant.

The divorce rate is by far the highest in mixed marriages in which the wife is Protestant and the husband is Catholic.

There is some evidence to indicate that the best solution, as far as marital success is concerned, is for one of the couple to accept the faith of the other.

As to what happens to the religious life of people who make mixed marriages, the studies reveal that these couples seem to follow one of three patterns: one or both drop out of church; both go to their individual churches and try to maintain their separate faiths; or one gives up his faith and accepts the faith of the other. The predominant pattern seems to be the first mentioned, whereby the parents and their children tend to have little to do with organized religion.

Some recent studies of young people add further light to the above findings. Studies show that young people who are strong in their faith and who come from families devout in their religious beliefs are less willing to state that they would make a mixed marriage. This applies to all major faith groups. Catholic, Protestant or Jewish young people who are indifferent religiously are most likely to report that they would be willing to marry outside the faith.

Other studies show that those who rate high in religiousness in all of the faith groups have a high happiness rating in marriage and a low divorce rate. Success in marriage is closely related to whether the married couple have religious or non-religious families. In other words, the non-religious are more willing to enter mixed marriages, but the non-religious also have characteristics that are associated with less successful marriage even if their marriages are not across faith lines. Research at the present time does not tell us how much of the failure in mixed marriages is due to problems arising from the mixture and how much is due to the other factors often present in the lives of those who are willing to enter mixed marriages.

Successful marriages tend to run in families. Children tend to marry into families who have values similar to their own family values; they tend to marry those who come from the same socio-economic-educational-religious backgrounds. Thus, young people who rate high in marriageability tend to marry their own kind; they are not so likely to make mixed marriages.

Jewish-Gentile Marriages The Jewish-Gentile marriage is mixed not only in religion but also in other aspects of culture. Differences in food habits, holidays, and days of rest are involved. Because of these cultural differences and because the Jews strongly urge their people to marry within their group, relatively few Jewish-Gentile marriages take place. Various studies have shown that approximately 95 per cent of Jewish marriages are within the faith. In the interfaith marriages that do occur, the Jewish man is much more likely to marry outside the faith than the Jewish woman. Jewish family pressure is very strong toward preventing interfaith marriages, and Jewish girls' marriage choices are more strictly controlled than are the choices of Jewish boys.

5c. Divorce and Desertion

Data from "Divorce and Desertion by Religious and Mixed-Religious Groups," by Thomas P. Monahan and William M. Kephart, *American Journal of Sociology*, March, 1954, pp. 454–65.

Editor's Note: Monahan and Kephart analyzed over 1,300 cases in Philadelphia for marriages, divorces and separations. Some highlights of that study may be given here:

Protestants in Philadelphia (and in three areas studied by other scholars—Maryland, Washington and Michigan) show a higher incidence of divorce than Catholics.

Divorce is increasing among the Catholic population.

Catholics figure in a disproportionately high number of desertions and non-support cases.

Jews appear least often (of the three major religious groups) in both the divorce and desertion categories.

Mixed religious marriages are not a factor in desertion—but do appear to account for a higher percentage of divorces.

Monahan and Kephart concluded that "the sizable proportion of divorces among Catholics . . . is surprising. A prior or present divorce for both parties was found in many of the Catholic-Catholic marriages in Philadelphia's desertion cases . . ." Further: ". . . while Catholics were found to contribute less than their share of divorce" they appear "much more frequently than their relative number in the population" in desertion cases.

5d. Fertility of Religious Groups: Census Materials

Quoted from *The Population of the United States,* by Donald J. Bogue, Glencoe, Illinois, Free Press, pp. 695–97.

DEMOGRAPHERS have long been interested in the differences between religious groups with respect to fertility, because of the different attitudes toward family size and family planning that are expressed or implied by the ideologies of the various groups. [The table of cumulative fertility rate— on P. 310] reports measures of fertility of each of the leading religious groups, in terms of the number of children ever born per 1,000 women of each group who are married and living with their husbands. Data are reported separately for women still in the childbearing ages (15 to 44), and for women past the ages of fertility (45 years old and over).

Comparison of these measures with the corresponding measures for earlier periods of American history, and with those of other nations that have high fertility, makes it very obvious that no one of the religious groups is subject to uncontrolled fertility. The practices of family planning and family limitation have evidently become widely diffused throughout the population. Although the fertility of every religious group is above the replacement level, no group is characterized by rates of children ever born that imply an average of 5 or 6 children per married woman, an average which is typical of high fertility groups. Thus, fertility control is a widely-accomplished fact throughout all major American religious groups. . . . .

In reviewing the census materials on fertility recently, Paul C. Glick, census expert on family and fertility statistics, concluded, . . . the differences between the major religious groups with respect to fertility patterns reflect differences in the age, color, geographic and socio-economic distributions of these groups—perhaps as much as, or more than, they reflect differences in religious doctrines with regard to family behavior. . . . Differences between rates for those under and over childbearing age suggest a trend toward convergence of fertility levels among women in the major religious groups.* There is also unmistakable evidence that differences in religious doctrines *do* stimulate fertility differences, independently of these other traits. One of the unfinished and important tasks of demography is to measure and analyze the independent effect of religious affiliation upon fertility. It is hoped that the necessary data will be made available soon—if not by the Bureau of the Census, then by private research organizations.

*"Intermarriage and Fertility Patterns among Persons in the Major Religious Groups," unpublished paper presented at the annual meeting of the American Sociological Society held in Seattle, Washington, August, 1958.

5e. Do Fertility Patterns Differ by Religious Groups?

Quoted from "Jewish Fertility in the United States," by Erich Rosenthal, *American Jewish Year Book,* edited by Morris Fine and Milton Himmelfarb, American Jewish Committee, New York, and The Jewish Publication Society of America, Philadelphia, 1961, vol. 62, p. 10.

THERE ARE considerable variations of fertility patterns within each group at a given point in time, as shown in the following table. Among Protestants, Baptists are the most fertile group. Their current and completed fertilities* are 6 and 11 per cent, respectively, higher than the average for the country as a whole. Lutherans and Presbyterians are the least fertile Protestant groups recorded. The completed fertility of the Presbyterians is 1 per cent below that of the Jews. The above-average fertility of the Baptists has been attributed to two factors: the first, that about one-third of the Baptists are Negroes, whose fertility is considerably higher than that of whites, and the second, that a large number of white Baptists are rural. By contrast, the low fertility of the Presbyterians has been attributed to urban residence, combined with a high level of education, occupation and income.

Cumulative Fertility Rate (Number of Children Ever Born Per 1,000 Women Ever Married), by Religion Reported, March 1957

Religion	15 to 44	45 and Over
Total	2,218	2,798
Jewish	1,749	2,218
Roman Catholic	2,282	3,056
Protestant	2,220	2,753
Baptist	2,359	3,275
Lutheran	2,013	2,382
Methodist	2,155	2,638
Presbyterian	2,001	2,188
Other Protestant	2,237	2,702
Other, none, and not reported	2,069	2,674

Source: "Statistical Abstract of the United States," 1958, p. 41, Table 40.

Current fertility applies to women between the ages of 15 and 44. *Completed* fertility applies to women 45 years and older.

5f. How Many Children Do Catholics, Jews and Protestants Want?

From *Family Growth in Metropolitan America,* by Charles Westoff, Robert Potter, Jr., Philip Sagi and Elliott Mishler, Princeton, N. J., Princeton University Press, 1961, p. 187, Table 43.

Number of Children Desired by Wives and Husbands, by Religion and Class*

Religious Preference	Wives			Husbands		
	White Collar	Blue Collar	Total	White Collar	Blue Collar	Total
Protestant	3.0	2.9	3.0	2.9	2.8	2.8
Mixed Catholic	3.2	3.4	3.3	3.4	3.4	3.4
Catholic	3.8	3.5	3.6	3.7	3.5	3.6
Jewish	2.8	2.7	2.8	2.9	2.9	2.9
All Couples	3.3	3.2	3.2	3.2	3.2	3.2

*1,165 metropolitan couples who had a second child in September, 1956. Areas included New York-New Jersey, Camden-Philadelphia, Pittsburgh, Detroit, Chicago, Los Angeles and San Francisco-Oakland.

5g. How Many Children Do Catholics, Jews and Protestants Expect to Have?

Quoted from *Population Bulletin,* Population Reference Bureau Inc., Washington, D. C., June 1960, vol. 16, no. 4, pp. 76–78.

Editor's Note: The GAF Study (Growth of American Families) was based on interviews with a scientifically selected sample of 2,713 white married women between the ages of 18 and 37. This research is reported at length in Family Planning, Sterility and Population Growth *by Ronald Freedman, Pascal K. Whelpton and Arthur A. Campbell, New York, McGraw Hill, 1959.*

THE GAF STUDY reveals interesting birth-expectation differentials on the basis of religion. Roman Catholic wives expect the largest number of children, 3.4; Jewish wives the smallest, 2.4; and Protestant wives expect 2.9. As educational achievement increases, the differential between Catholic and Protestant widens:

	Protestant	Catholic
College	2.7	3.9
High School Graduates	2.7	3.9
High School (1-3 Years)	2.9	3.1
Grade School	3.6	3.7

The fact that Roman Catholic women within virtually all of the socio-economic groups consistently reported higher birth-expectations than Protestant women indicates that religious birth-expectation differences cannot be explained by variations in educational achievement, income or residence.

Both Catholic and Protestant wives had borne an equal number of children (2.1) at the time the study was conducted. This similarity was found among wives of various ages, including the 35 to 39 year olds whose families were almost completed. The Catholic wives had no more children than the Protestants primarily because they were slightly older— an average of 1.5 years older—at the time of marriage. Thus they had fewer years in marriage to bear children. But when Protestant and Catholic wives in the same cohort [*i.e.* born in the same year] who were married at the same age were compared, the Catholic women consistently had higher fertility. When wives were grouped by duration of marriage, the same differences were revealed.

In view of the reports of the older Catholic women, it is likely that the younger Catholic wives will reduce their expectations as they have more experience with bearing and raising children. Catholic women aged 35 to 39, for example, said that they wanted 3.5 children when they were married, but only 3.1 at the time of the interview. In contrast, Protestant women 35 to 39 years old wanted 2.9 children when they were married and again at the time of the interview.

5h. Adult Attitudes Toward Family Limitation

Quoted from *Family Planning, Sterility, and Population Growth,* by Ronald Freedman, Pascal K. Whelpton and Arthur A. Campbell, New York, McGraw Hill, 1959, pp. 154, 156.

BASIC TO the widespread use of some method of contraception by American married couples is a strong concensus of opinion supporting the general idea of spacing children and preventing excessively large families. The use of contraception is, in itself, indirect behavioral evidence of the existence of these underlying attitudes. To measure them directly all wives were asked the following question:

"Many married couples do something to limit the size of their families and to control when their children come. How do you feel about that?"

. . . . The words birth control and contraception were avoided in these questions, since we were interested in attitudes toward the general idea of family limitation and child spacing rather than attitudes toward specific methods. Nevertheless, it is likely that some respondents, especially Catholics, identified the phrase "family limitation" with particular disapproved methods and expressed less favorable attitudes than they would have done in answer to a separate question about the use of rhythm (periodic continence). In consequence, the results . . . probably underestimate the degree of approval of family limitation practices as defined in this report (*i.e.,* including rhythm).

Per Cent Distribution by Attitude Toward Family Limitation, for All Wives, by Religion of Wife and Husband

Religion of Wife and Husband (no. of wives)	Total	Wife's Attitude Toward Family Limitation					
		Unqualified Approval	Qualified Approval	Pro-con	Qualified Disapproval	Unqualified Disapproval	N.A.*
Total (2,713)	100%	62%	12%	4%	16%	5%	1%
†Wife Protestant (1817)	100	72	13	4	9	1	1
Husband Protestant (1684)	100	73	13	3	9	1	1
Husband Catholic (91)	100	62	11	7	14	2	4
†Wife Catholic (787)	100	33	12	5	35	13	2
Husband Catholic (628)	100	32	12	6	35	13	2
Husband Protestant (133)	100	35	12	5	34	13	1
Wife Jewish (74)	100	88	4	3	4	—	1
Wife Other (35)	100	69	11	6	—	9	5

*N. A. = not ascertained.
†Includes wives with husbands of other religious preference than Protestant or Catholic.
The dash indicates a percentage below 0.5% in all tables.

6. RELIGION AND MENTAL HEALTH

6a. Differing Characteristics of Religious Groups

Excerpted from *The Churches and Mental Health,* by Richard V. McCann, Joint Commission on Mental Illness and Health, Monograph Series, no. 8, New York, Basic Books, Inc., 1962, pp. 219–220, 222, 225, 226.

TWO QUESTIONS are often asked: whether one religious group shows higher mental illness rates than another; and whether any differences exist as to symptom choice—*i.e.,* does one religious group show for example, high suicide rates, while another shows high alcoholism rates? Rates of illness and type of illness have a great deal to do with factors other than religious affiliation. Education, income, occupation, ethnicity, place of residence and age distribution are some of the factors that would have to be controlled and their influences understood for each religious group before a meaningful answer could be obtained.

Religious groups show great differences by education, occupation and income, in other words, by social class. . . . And what is said about the mental health or illness of these groups must take these differences into account. In many instances it is impossible to separate the religious component from other components.

Distribution by Religious Groups of Answers to the Question, "Have You Ever Felt You Were Going to Have a Nervous Breakdown?"

	Yes	No		Yes	No
Fundamentalist*	26%	74%	Methodist	17%	83%
Other Protestant†	25	75	Lutheran	16	84
Baptist	22	78	Roman Catholic	16	84
Jewish	21	79	Congregational	16	84
Protestant (total)	20	80	Episcopalian	13	87
Presbyterian	20	80			

Extent of Happiness as Reported by Religious Groups

	Not too happy	Pretty happy	Very happy	Not Ascertained
Baptist	15%	53%	31%	1%
Jewish	15	51	32	2
Presbyterian	14	50	36	
Roman Catholic	12	53	35	
Protestant (total)	11	54	35	
Fundamentalist*	9	51	40	
Methodist	8	53	39	
Other Protestant†	7	55	38	
Lutheran	6	64	30	
Episcopalian	4	47	49	
Congregational	2	49	49	

Percentage of Persons, by Religious Group, Who Have Had Professional Help for a Mental Health Problem

Episcopalian	10%	Lutheran	14%
Baptist	11	Roman Catholic	16
Presbyterian	12	Congregationalist	16
Fundamentalist*	13	Jewish	20
Protestant (total)	13	Other Protestant†	21
Methodist	13		

The Number of Persons, by Religious Group, Who Mentioned Clergy Only As a Potential Source of Help for Every 100 Who Mentioned Psychiatrist Only

Roman Catholic	2,020	Methodist	540
Lutheran	1,030	Presbyterian	310
Baptist	1,000	Other Protestant†	260
Congregationalist	1,000	Episcopalian	240
Fundamentalist*	790	Jewish	40
Protestant (total)	620		

*Fundamentalist: includes members of Protestant Fundamentalist sect groups
†Other Protestant: includes members of Protestant denominations other than the six for which tabulations were made, but not members of Fundamentalist groups and small sects.

6b. Religious Origins and Mental Health

From *Mental Health in the Metropolis,* The Midtown Manhattan Study, vol. I., by Leo Strole, Thomas S. Langner, Stanley T. Michael, Marvin K. Opler and Thomas A. C. Rennie, New York, McGraw-Hill Book Co., 1962.

Editor's Note: The Midtown Manhattan Study represents one of the most intensive metropolitan surveys ever attempted in the field of mental health. The data were gathered by a team of psychiatrists and social scientists who conducted 1,660 interviews with residents aged 20 to 59, selected at random from a population of 175,000, in an unspecified neighborhood in the borough of Manhattan, New York City, where homes ranged from luxury apartments to congested slum tenements.

THE RESEARCH operations consisted of a Treatment Census and a Home Interview Survey. The former analyzed Midtown's psychiatric patients and "treatment destination"—in hospitals, clinics and private therapy offices. The Home Interview Survey involved the sample of 1,660 adults. "Each of these was interrogated for two hours, on the average, by a professional person trained and experienced in the intimate interviewing role. The interviewer was guided by a questionnaire that was about one year in preparation."

The study concluded:

Only one out of every five—or about 20 per cent—of the non-Puerto Rican white adults living in this area could be described as well (that is, free of symptoms) in terms of mental health.

The majority—close to 60 per cent—of the residents of this community were found to have symptoms of tension and anxiety, in varying degrees.

The remaining 20 per cent showed impaired mental health, with marked, severe or incapacitating symptoms.

Some of the findings concerning religious origins and mental health are as follows:

The Protestants present a more favorable mental health picture than the Catholics; the Jewish group the most favorable of all. However, when socio-economic status, origin and age are standardized, Protestants and Catholics emerge quite similar in mental health composition.

The Jews, by comparison, retain a heavier concentration in the sub-clinical Mild-Moderate symptom range of the mental health spectrum, and a significantly lower Impaired rate. At the same time, paradoxically, Jews were the highest of the three religious groups in Total Patient rates.

The Midtown data seem to imply that "readiness for psychotherapy," or the "pro-psychiatry" attitude among Jews, contributes to their high patient rates.

"While there are fewer Jews than Catholics or Protestants who are completely well, there are also fewer Jews who are so mentally sick that their social functioning is impaired.

"Among Jews, mental illness clusters in the mild and moderate symptom groups. Perhaps this is the reason that more Jews go to psycho-therapists for treatment than do members of the other two groups. Half the Jews said they would go to such a professional, while only 23 per cent of the Catholics and 31 per cent of the Protestants elected this type of therapy. The two Christian groups relied more on physicians and non-professionals —principally clergymen—for help in emotional and mental crises."

Converts, from one religion to another, showed a favorable "mental health outlook." Those who say they have "no religion" presented a relatively unfavorable picture of mental health.

Another significant finding in *Mental Health in the Metropolis: Concerning sex and marital status:* "In the Midtown sample as a whole there are no significant differences between married males and married females in their mental health composition." Among single people, however, "the impairment frequencies of bachelors are higher by wide margins" than those of single women. The Midtown divorced of both sexes, however, "have the highest mental morbidity rates of all four marital status categories."

The authors of "Mental Health in the Metropolis" believe there is "a likely net effect of large-scale *improvement* in the over-all mental health composition of the American people."

A number of other popular assumptions are challenged by the data in the book. The groups with the largest proportion of disturbed people have the fewest *in treatment,* whereas the groups with the fewest sick people have the largest proportion of patients in treatment.

6c. Distribution of Psychiatric Illness

Quoted and table adapted from "Some Relationships Between Religion, Ethnic Origin and Mental Illness," by Jerome K. Myers and Bertram H. Roberts in *The Jews: Social Patterns of an American Group,* Marshall Sklare, ed., Glencoe, Ill., Free Press, 1958, pp. 551 and 553, table 1.

A SURVEY was made of all patients residing in the metropolitan area of New Haven, Connecticut, who were under the treatment of a psychiatrist on December 1, 1950. . . . A total of 1,963 cases were found with 1,393 located in public hospitals, 37 in private hospitals, 159 in clinics, and 374 being treated by private practitioners.

Distribution of Psychiatric and General Population
According to Diagnosis and Religious Affiliation

	Catholic		Protestant		Jewish		Total	
	No.	%	No.	%	No.	%	No.	%
General population (5% sample)	6,736	57.5	3,869	33.0	1,108	9.5	11,713	100
Psychiatric population	1,059	57.0	576	31.0	223	12.0	1,858	100
Psychoneurotic disorders	189	46.2	122	29.8	98	24.0	409	100
Alcohol and drug addiction	61	68.5	28	31.5	0	00.0	89	100
Schizophrenia	506	60.8	245	29.4	81	9.7	832	100
Affective disorders	86	55.1	53	34.0	17	10.9	156	100
Psychosis with mental deficiency	56	61.5	23	25.3	12	13.2	91	100
Disorders of senescence	100	55.9	67	37.4	12	6.8	179	100
Epilepsy	25	71.5	9	25.7	1	2.9	35	100
Other organic	36	53.8	29	43.4	2	2.8	67	100

6d. Incidence of Drinking and Religious Affiliation

Excerpted from "Who, What and How Often?" by John Riley, Jr., and Charles F. Marden in *Drinking and Intoxication*, Raymond G. McCarthy, ed., Publications Division: Yale Center of Alcohol Studies, New Haven, Connecticut, and Glencoe, Illinois, The Free Press, 1959, pp. 186–87, Table 3.

SINCE organized religion has traditionally been more or less concerned with the problems of alcohol, it is also interesting to note that the proportions of drinkers and abstainers according to broad religious groupings appear to reflect the differences in outlook or emphasis on this question. Only 59 per cent of the Protestant respondents [in a national survey of public attitudes toward alcohol and alcoholism], but 79 per cent of the Catholics and as high as 87 per cent of the Jewish respondents said they drank alcoholic beverages.

Incidence and Frequency of
Drinking, by Religious Affiliation

	Percent Abstainers	Percent Occasional Drinkers	Percent Regular Drinkers
Protestant	41%	46%	13%
Catholic	21	52	27
Jewish	13	64	23

The high percentage of drinkers among Jews is of especial interest in connection with the question of the relationship of the prevalence of drinking to the incidence of alcoholism, a subject deserving of intensive research. Numerous studies agree that Jews as a group have a lower rate of alcoholism than any other ethnic group. The majority of explanations which have been offered for this phenomenon have stressed either the realization of danger and the necessity of avoiding social scandal of all kinds, or the religious and ritualistic factors connected with the use of wine among Jews.

Whatever the reason for this particular drinking pattern coupled with conspicuous lack of excess, it tends to support the hypothesis that the incidence of alcoholism within any specific cultural group is not necessarily related to the proportion of the group which drinks.

Excerpted from *Drinking and Intoxication,* Raymond G. McCarthy, ed., Publications Division: Yale Center of Alcohol Studies, New Haven, Connecticut, and Glencoe, Illinois, The Free Press, 1959, pp. 219, 220, Table 2.

THE STRAUS AND BACON study* is the most comprehensive analysis of the use of alcohol by young people available in the literature at present. However, it is concerned only with a college-age group. Questionnaires were administered to 17,000 students in 27 public, private, and sectarian colleges.

*Robert Straus and Seldon D. Bacon, *Drinking in College,* Yale University Press, 1953.

Incidence of Drinking, by Religious Affiliation

	College Men, Percent Drinking	College Women, Percent Drinking
Jewish	94%	94%
Catholic	90	78
Protestant	77	60
Mormon	54	23

The Jews have no sanctions against moderate drinking. The Catholic Church, while encouraging abstinence for young people, particularly by a pledge at confirmation, does not prohibit drinking among adults. Protestant denominations are divided on the issue, some opposing vigorously any association with drinking, others being less stringent.

7. *POLLS CONCERNING RELIGIOUS BELIEFS AND OPINIONS*

7a. *Attitudes on the Importance of Religion in America: Public's Views Show Religious "Revival" Has Passed High Mark*

Quoted from American Institute of Public Opinion (Gallup Poll), April 17, 1962.

At the present time, do you think religion as a whole is increasing its influence on American life, or losing its influence?

In March, 1957—in a period which was probably near the apex of the current "revival"—69 per cent of those interviewed thought religion was increasing its influence on American life. Only 14 per cent at that time believed religion to be losing its influence.

Today, five years later, 45 per cent say religion is gaining ground, while the proportion who think religion is losing its influence has more than doubled (31 per cent).

The following table shows the change between 1957 and 1962:

Religion Increasing, or Losing Influence?	1957	1962
Increasing	69%	45%
Losing	14	31
About same	10	17
No opinion	7	7

History of Revivals   The most recent upsurge of interest in religion started in the U. S. following World War II. The war itself undoubtedly provided the momentum for the revival which appears to have reached its highest point about 1958.

According to historians, the current mid-twentieth-century revival is the seventh in a series of "re-awakenings" which have swept this continent, starting with the Great Awakening of 1730, associated with the names of Jonathan Edwards and George Whitefield.

The last revival, previous to the current one, was in the 1920s and is associated with the name of Billy Sunday and his "old-time religion."

Church-Going   The Gallup Poll's yearly audits of church attendance give further evidence that the peak period of church interest and activity has been passed.

The following table (which records the highlights of the 21-year trend) shows that there has been a general leveling off in average church attendance, after an upward trend over the first 15 years:

Percentage of All Adults Attending Church in a Typical Week

1940	1955	1958	1961
37%	49%	49%	47%

Contrast to the Netherlands Compared to other Christian nations, the United States stands out markedly in its church interest.

For example, when people in the Netherlands were recently asked the same question on the influence of religion, by the Gallup-affiliated organization in that country, opinions contrasted sharply with those in the U.S.

Only 9 per cent thought religion to be increasing its influence on life in the Netherlands. More than six times as many as this—57 per cent—said religion was losing its influence.

Religious Leaders as National Leaders

Quoted from *The Public Pulse,* Elmo Roper and Associates, December 21, 1957.

THE following table shows how the American people have evaluated their leaders since 1942:

Which one of these groups do you feel is doing the MOST good for the country at the present time?	1957	1948	1942
	%	%	%
Religious leaders	46	34	18
Government leaders	17	11	28
Business leaders	12	20	19
Congress	8	4	6
Labor leaders	4	12	6
Express no opinion	13	19	24

7b. Attitudes to the Return of Christ and Life After Death

Quoted from American Institute of Public Opinion (Gallup Poll) releases of (1) April 14, 1960, and (2) December 23, 1961.

(1) The Gallup Poll had its reporters interview a cross section of persons of all faiths in all areas of the nation.

Here is the first question asked and the results:

Do you think Jesus Christ will ever return to earth?

Yes	No	No opinion
55%	31%	14%

The expectation of the early Christians was that the return of Christ was close at hand.

Since that day various interpretations have been made among religious groups as to when this would occur. Some maintain that Jesus has returned already—in the hearts of believers. Other groups have designated exact dates for the return of Christ in person.

To determine what people in present-day America believe concerning the Second Coming, the Gallup Poll asked the following question of those who stated a belief in the Reappearance:

When do you think this will happen?

Of those persons who selected a specific point in time, about one-half expected the return of Christ to be within the next one hundred years.

Life After Death   An overwhelming majority of Americans profess a belief in some form of life after death. Here is the question asked, and the results:

Do you believe there is, or is not, a life after death?

Is	Is not	Can't say
74%	14%	12%

More Doubt Among Men   Analysis of today's survey reveals that more women than men hold to these basic Christian beliefs of the Second Coming and life after death.

Here are the results by men and women:

Christ Return to Earth?	Men	Women	Life After Death?	Men	Women
Yes	53%	58%	Is	68%	78%
No	33	29	Is not	17	12
No opinion	14	13	Can't say	15	10

(2) In this nuclear age, more people in the U.S. could turn to a belief in an afterlife for comfort and support than is the case in six other nations where this basic Christian tenet was tested.

Here is a comparison:

Belief in Life After Death	Yes	No	D.K.
U.S.	74%	14%	12%
Norway	71	15	14
Canada	68	19	13
Holland	63	27	10
Great Britain	56	18	26
Switzerland	55	27	18
West Germany	38	29	33

*7c. Views of Catholics and Protestants Toward Each Other:
Catholics, Protestants Both Pessimistic About Uniting*

Quoted from American Institute of Public Opinion (Gallup Poll), March 19, 1959.

CHANCES of the Catholic and Protestant Churches ever uniting—as suggested in Pope John XXIII's plan for a world conference on Christian unity—are exceedingly slim in the opinion of America's Catholics and Protestants.

Undoubtedly because of their Pontiff's proposed study of ways in which Christian groups might draw closer together, U. S. Catholics are significantly more optimistic than are Protestants about the possibility of eventual unification into one church.

But the fact remains that sizable majorities of both Catholics and Protestants in this country today are pessimistic about the chances of the two groups ever forming one church.

With the Vatican's plan for an Ecumenical Conference within the next few years causing world-wide speculation about the possibility of Catholics and Protestants forming one church, the Gallup Poll had its nationwide corps of reporters put to a cross section of U. S. Catholics and Protestants a series of questions on the issue of Christian unification—ranging from views on mixed marriages to opinions about who leads a more Christian life, to the things the two groups would find hardest to accept in each other's church.

The first question asked was:

Do you think the day will ever come when all Christians of the world— including all Catholic and Protestant groups—will be united into one church?

Here are the views of both groups:

Eventual Unification?	Protestants	Catholics
Yes, will	13%	23%
No, will not	77	62
No opinion	10	15

(The initial Vatican announcement concerned itself more with the possibility of some move toward unification of the Roman Catholic church with the Eastern Orthodox church—the third major branch of Christianity. The proposed world council, however, has caused speculation and comment from leading Protestant churchmen about the question on Protestant-Catholic unification.)

One Must "Give In"

For most U. S. Catholics and Protestants the more than four-century-old split between the two groups has grown too wide to hold out much hope of "patching up" differences.

With both groups, it is often a case of "your move first." As Protestants tend to see it, the chief stumbling blocks would be something "the Catholics wouldn't do"; Catholics, in turn, view a Protestant refusal to compromise as the main hindrance.

"I don't think Catholics would change their beliefs enough to unite," was the way one Protestant put it.

"The Protestants wouldn't accept our beliefs," was the comment of one Catholic interviewed.

For both groups, unification could be accomplished only by each forsaking doctrines that they hold to be essential to their beliefs.

Protestants, for example, view the Catholic belief that the Church of Rome is "the one, true Church" as one of the main stumbling blocks.

Catholics, on the other hand, feel that the great diversity of Protestant denominations would hinder any move toward forming one church—a diversity described by one leading Protestant theologian as "a testimony to the greatness and manifoldness of God's disclosures of Himself to men."

Papal Infallibility   Many Protestants and Catholics agree as to one of the major items of "disunity." Protestants charge, and many Catholics admit, that the Catholic doctrine of Papal infallibility (that the Pope, when speaking as the head of the Church on matters of faith or morals, cannot be in error) would be one of the toughest hurdles for Protestants to overcome.

Who Leads More Christian Life?   Catholics, as a whole, are more convinced than are Protestants that they follow Christian principles more closely in their everyday lives.

When asked which of the two groups tended to be better Christians in their daily lives, one Protestant in nine says he believes that Catholics are. This compares with only one Catholic in 33 who feels that Protestants lead more Christian lives than Catholics do.

The results:

Who Follows Christian Principles More Closely?	Protestants say	Catholics say
Catholics do	11%	58%
Protestants do	45	3
No difference	26	26
No opinion	18	13

Catholics Less Opposed Than Protestants to Mixed Marriage

Quoted from American Institute of Public Opinion (Gallup Poll), March 21, 1959.

As PART of its study of Catholic-Protestant relations in the U. S. and their implications in the Vatican's proposed study of ways in which all Christians might unite, the Gallup Poll assigned its reporters to ask U. S. members of the two major branches of Christianity about the mixed marriages that they personally have known about, as well as their feelings on a son or daughter marrying a member of the opposite faith.

(The U. S. Census Bureau estimates that about one Protestant in twelve who is married has a Catholic spouse; about one married Catholic in five has a Protestant spouse—or a total of 4,510,000 persons who are partners in a mixed marriage.)

Although majorities of both Catholics and Protestants would have no serious objection to their child marrying a member of the other church, Catholics show significantly less objection to the idea than do Protestants.

Catholics, whose church imposes strict conditions under which a Catholic may marry a non-Catholic, tend to feel that most of the mixed marriages they have known of personally have worked out as well as marriages between members of the same faith.

Protestants, on the other hand, for whom marriage to a Catholic under Catholic stipulations would mean raising all children in the Catholic faith, tend to feel that the mixed marriages they have known have not worked out.

From comments recorded by Gallup Poll reporters, it is apparent that much of the Protestant and Catholic misgivings about intermarriage stems from the conditions which Catholics impose on a marriage with a non-Catholic.

A Protestant interviewed felt that most mixed marriages he knew of did not work out well "because there's the dispute over the children."

A Catholic admitted that in many such marriages, "the children cause conflicts."

Paralleling this, however, was the comment of a Protestant mother who said:

"They work out. My son married a Catholic and it's very harmonious."

All Catholics and Protestants interviewed across the country were asked this question:

"*In the cases you have known or heard about, have marriages between Catholics and Protestants worked out as well as marriages between members of the same religion?*"

The views of the two groups:

Mixed Marriage Worked?	Catholics	Protestants
Yes, have	55%	38%
No, have not	36	46
No opinion	9	16

All Catholics and Protestants were next asked if they would have a serious objection to a daughter or son of theirs marrying a member of the opposite faith. The views of both groups:

Object to Mixed Marriage?	Catholics	Protestants
Yes, would	23%	35%
No, would not	72	58
No opinion	5	7

Few Protestants, Catholics Have Thought of "Switching"

Quoted from American Institute of Public Opinion (Gallup Poll), March 24, 1959.

IN THE speculation touched off in religious circles by Pope John XXIII's call for Christian unity, one key issue centers on just how much of their doctrine the Protestant and Catholic churches would have to reconcile in order to form one church.

How many Protestants and Catholics have felt that there was sufficient appeal in the other faith to seriously consider "switching" their religion?

What things about the other's church would Catholics and Protestants find hardest to accept?

On the first of these two questions, Gallup Poll reporters questioning Catholics and Protestants across the country found a "stand-off." The small minorities who have thought of changing their religion are identical in proportion.

As the following table shows, the vast majority of the U. S. members of the two Christian churches have never given serious thought to becoming a member of the opposite faith.

The question asked of Catholics:
Have you ever seriously considered becoming a Protestant?

Catholics Only	Yes 6%	No 94%

Protestants were asked:
Have you ever seriously considered becoming a Catholic?

Protestants Only	Yes 6%	No 94%

A Gallup Poll study in 1955 on the subject of Protestant-Catholic conversions revealed that an identical number of the two faiths had actually taken the step of joining the other's church—approximately 1,400,000 Protestants had become Catholics, while the same number of Catholics had become Protestants.

Beliefs Most Difficult to Accept? What is it about the respective doctrines of the two faiths that might have kept the vast majority of Protestants and Catholics from changing their beliefs? What things, for example, would a Protestant find hardest to accept in Catholicism?

When Gallup Poll reporters asked that question of a cross section of the nation's Protestants, many criticisms of Catholic doctrine and liturgy were cited.

One thing frequently named by Protestants was the Catholic practice of confessing sins to a priest (to Catholics, one of the seven sacraments known as Penance).

"I wouldn't like confession," was the way one Protestant put it, "only God can forgive, not a priest."

Another major item of criticism was the Catholic belief in the infallibility of the Pope.

Still other Protestant criticisms dealt with what was felt to be an undue emphasis by Catholics on the Virgin Mary and various Catholic saints, with the Catholic restrictions on eating meat on Friday, and with Catholic services being held in Latin.

Catholics' View on Protestantism   The aspects of Protestantism which Catholics would find hardest to accept tend to be of a negative nature, *i.e.,* the things that Protestants *don't* do.

Mentioned frequently was what Catholics feel is a lax attitude on the part of Protestants toward divorce and re-marriage. "I just can't see their beliefs about divorce," was the way one Catholic put it.

Many Catholics criticized the fact that there are so many different Protestant services, or, as one Catholic commented, "they all don't have the same set of rules."

Other Catholics interviewed objected to Protestant attitudes toward birth control, lack of a formal confession, and the fact that Protestant ministers are allowed to marry.

8.   FACTS ABOUT BIBLE READING IN AMERICA

Opinions on Revised Bible

Quoted from American Institute of Public Opinion (Gallup Poll), December 25, 1952.

Have you heard or read about the changes in wording in the new revised edition of the Bible?
The vote:

Yes 67%   **No** 33%

Those who said "yes" were then asked:
From what you have heard or read, do you approve or disapprove of the changes in wordings which have been made in the new edition of the Bible?

Approve	28%
Disapprove	22
No opinion	17
Have not heard or read about it	33
	———
	100%

Persons with the greatest amount of formal education are more likely to approve of the revised Bible than are persons with a limited education.

	College	High School	Grade School
Approve	47%	31%	15%
Disapprove	20	21	24
No opinion	17	19	14
Have not heard or read about it	16	29	47
	100%	100%	100%

Women are more inclined to approve of the new Bible than men are.

Protestants questioned in the survey had much more favorable views of the new Bible, from what they had heard or read about it, than Catholics had.

Among Protestants the vote was: approve 32 per cent, disapprove 24 per cent, and no opinion 17 per cent. 27 per cent had not heard or read about the new Bible.

Among Catholics the vote divided: approve 19 per cent, disapprove 18 per cent, and no opinion 17 per cent. 46 per cent had not heard or read about the new Bible.

Revision of Bible—Controversy

Quoted from American Institute of Public Opinion (Gallup Poll), December 26, 1952.

THE NEW revised Bible, which modernizes the language used in the King James Version, has brought a mixture of praise and criticism from clergymen and lay members of the Protestant churches.

An Institute survey found that two out of every three persons (67 per cent) have heard or read about the new Bible and that 28 per cent approve of it, while 22 per cent disapprove and the rest have no opinion.

Do you plan to buy a copy of the new Bible?

A total of 4 per cent said they had already bought a copy—a figure which checks closely with sales to date.

Another 19 per cent, or nearly one out of five, said they intended to buy a copy.

Nearly two persons out of every three questioned in the survey said they had read some part of the Bible at home within this last year. Here are the figures:

Have you, yourself, read any part of the Bible at home within the last year?

Yes 67%   No 33%

Of all sections of the country, the South showed the highest proportion of Bible readers—81 per cent. The New England and Middle Atlantic sections showed the lowest—59 per cent.

Editor's Note: In the light of the data in the above polls, it is interesting to note that during the decade from 1952 to 1962 in which the Revised Standard Version of the Bible has been on sale, about 10,000,000 copies have been sold, in addition to 4,000,000 copies of the Revised Standard Version New Testament which appeared in 1946. (Publisher's Weekly, *January 29, 1962*)

How Many Can Name First Four Books of New Testament?

Quoted from American Institute of Public Opinion (Gallup Poll), March 30, 1950.

Will you tell me the names of any of the first four books of the New Testament of the Bible—that is, the first four Gospels?

Named 4 Gospels correctly	35%
Named 3 correctly	4
Named 2 correctly	4
Named 1 correctly	4
	47
Could not name *any*	53
	100%

Americans are put to shame by the British when it comes to remembering the names of the Gospels.

A survey by the British Institute of Public Opinion found that three out of every five (61 per cent) were able to rattle off Matthew, Mark, Luke and John and one in seven could name some. One-fourth of the British adults could not name any, as compared to more than one-half in the United States.

The British survey found young people more ignorant about the names of the Gospels than older people, with one-third unable to name any of the four books. A similar situation was found in the American survey. Here are the results by age:

By Age:	21-29 Years	30-49 Years	50 Years and Over
Named all four Gospels	26%	36%	39%
Named one, two, or three	16	13	10
Could not name *any*	58	51	51
	100%	100%	100%

The American survey found that knowledge of the Gospels is a function of degree of school education, as follows:

By Education:	College	High School	Grade School
Named all four Gospels	59%	36%	27%
Named one, two, or three	11	14	11
Could not name *any*	30	50	62
	100%	100%	100%

part three

Selected Reading List and Reference Aids

Selected Reading List of Books on Religion

COMPILED BY *Beryl E. Hoyt, Publications Librarian, Racine (Wisconsin) Public Library; Elvera Lake, Librarian's Assistant, Waukegan (Illinois) Public Library, and Ruth W. Gregory, Chairman, Coordinating Committee on Materials (American Library Association—Adult Services Division), Waukegan (Illinois) Public Library.*

1. HISTORY OF RELIGIONS

Bach, Marcus. *Had You Been Born in Another Faith; the story of religion as it is lived and loved by those who follow the path of their parental faith.* Prentice-Hall, 1961.

> INTRODUCTION to the basic beliefs of the Hindu, Parsi, Buddhist, Confucianist, Shintoist, Jewish, Moslem, Roman Catholic and Protestant faiths.

Ballou, Robert O., ed. *The Bible of the World.* Viking, 1939.

> "THE SCRIPTURAL essence" of the Hindu, Buddhist, Confucionist, Taoist, Zoroastrian, Jewish, Christian and Mohammedan religions.

Braden, Charles S. *The World's Religions, a short history.* Rev. ed. Abingdon, 1954.

> A READABLE standard work in comparative religion.

Hume, Robert E. *The World's Living Religions; with special reference to their sacred scriptures and in comparison to Christianity; an historical sketch.* Completely rev. Scribner, 1959.

> SURVEY of the origins, the sacred documents, and the significance of eleven religions which have been in existence for more than a century.

Hutchinson, Paul, and Garrison, Winifred E. *20 Centuries of Christianity; a concise history.* Harcourt, 1959.

> A GENERAL history of the Christian faith expanding the Hutchinson article in *Life's* "the world's great religions" series.

Latourette, Kenneth S. *A History of Christianity.* Harper, 1953.

> THE RECORD of the spread of Christianity from the time of Christ to about 1950.

Life (Periodical) *The World's Great Religions.* Time, Inc., 1957.

> ILLUSTRATED articles on Hinduism, Buddhism, the Chinese religions, Islamism, Judaism and Christianity.

Smith, James W., ed. *Religion in American Life.* 3 vols. in 4. Princeton University Press, 1961.

> SCHOLARLY, readable essays by specialists on various aspects of the history, the structure and the impact of Protestantism, Catholicism and Judaism on American life.

Soper, Edmund D. *Religions of Mankind.* 3d ed. rev. Abingdon, 1951.

> A CLASSIC introduction to the religions of the world.

Walker, Williston. *History of the Christian Church.* Rev. ed. Scribner, 1959.

> GENERAL history which traces developments from the beginnings to the modern era.

2. LEADING FAITHS IN AMERICA

Baptist

Newton, Louis D. *Why I Am a Baptist*. Nelson, 1957.

A PERSONAL affirmation of a religious way of life including information on the history and organization of the Baptist Church.

Stealey, Sydnor L., comp. and ed. *A Baptist Treasury*. Crowell, 1958.

SELECTIONS from writings which include history, principles, sermons and prayers.

Torbet, Robert G. *History of the Baptists*. Judson Press, 1950.

COMPREHENSIVE summary of the Baptist heritage, history and contributions.

Catholic (Roman)

De Wohl, Louis. *Founded on a Rock; a history of the Catholic Church*. Lippincott, 1961.

POPULAR history of the Roman Catholic Church, its leading personalities, and important events from its founding to 1958.

Folliet, Joseph. *World Catholicism Today*. Newman, 1961.

REPORT on contemporary Catholicism around the world.

Higgins, Rev. Thomas J., S. J. *Dogma for the Layman*. Bruce, 1961.

WELL WRITTEN explanation of basic tenets of Roman Catholic theology for laymen of all faiths.

Thomson, Paul V. *Why I Am a Catholic*. Nelson, 1959.

A CONVERT'S statement of belief in the significance of the doctrines, sacraments and organization of the Roman Catholic Church.

Christian Scientist

DeWitt, John, and Canham, Erwin D. *The Christian Science Way of Life*. Prentice-Hall, 1962.

PRESENTATION of the Christian Science way of life from its beginning to the present day with an interpretation of its founder and her teachings as they affect personal lives.

Leishman, Thomas L. *Why I Am a Christian Scientist*. Nelson, 1958.

A STATEMENT of belief in the values of Christian Science from the standpoint of a trained theologian.

Congregationalist

Jenkins, Daniel T. *Congregationalism: a restatement*. Harper, 1954.

AN EXAMINATION of the meaning of Congregationalism.

Rouner, Arthur A. *The Congregational Way of Life*. Prentice-Hall, 1960.

HISTORY of the founding of Congregationalism in England, its growth and changes in the United States, and an interpretation of its belief and form of worship.

Disciple of Christ

Adams, Hampton. *Why I Am a Disciple of Christ*. Nels n, 1957.

A STATEMENT which reviews history and discusses the theological attitudes, the congregational type of church government, social concerns, and steps toward mergers.

Whitley, Oliver R. *Trumpet Call of Reformation*. Bethany Press, 1959.

A GENERAL study of the Disciples of Christ.

Eastern (Greek) Orthodox

Callincos, Constantine. *The Greek Orthodox Catechism*. Greek Archdiocese of North and South America, 1953.

"A MANUAL of instruction on faith, morals and worship"—subtitle.

Carlson, Stanley, and Soroka, Leonid. *Faith of Our Father*. Rev. ed. Olympic Press, 1954.

A HISTORY and interpretation of the Eastern Orthodox Church.

Le Guillou, M. J. *The Spirit of Eastern Orthodoxy*. Hawthorn, 1962.

A STUDY of the fundamental characteristics of the Byzantine tradition and a commentary on its relations with Rome.

Episcopalian

Addison, James Thayer. *The Episcopal Church in the United States, 1789-1931*. Scribner, 1951.

DETAILED history which cites major developments and important leaders.

Pittenger, William N. *The Episcopalian Way of Life*. Prentice-Hall, 1957.

AN AUTHORITATIVE presentation of Episcopal history, dogma and ways of worship.

Simcox, Carroll E. *Approach to the Episcopal Church*. Morehouse, 1961.

AN INTRODUCTION which is particularly useful for the inquirer interested in the beliefs of the Episcopal faith.

Jehovah's Witness

Cole, Marley. *Jehovah's Witnesses; the new world society*. Vantage Press, 1955.

A JOURNALISTIC report based on interviews with leaders on various phases of doctrine and practice. Appendix gives information on court cases, biographies of leaders and statistics.

Pike, Edgar R. *Jehovah's Witnesses*. Philosophical, 1954.

"WHO they are, what they teach, what they do"—subtitle.

Jew

Bamberger, Bernard J. *The Story of Judaism*. Union of American Hebrew Congregations, 1957.

A COMPREHENSIVE popular history of the religious and intellectual life of the Jewish people from the time of Moses to modern times.

Hertzberg, Arthur, ed. *Judaism*. Braziller, 1961.

AN ANTHOLOGY of spiritual literature revealing the unity which characterizes the Jewish faith.

Roth, Leon. *Judaism: A Portrait*. Viking, 1961.

A PHILOSOPHER'S explanation of the nature and significance of Jewish thought and tradition.

Wouk, Herman. *This Is My God*. Doubleday, 1959.

A PROVOCATIVE examination of the significance of beliefs, customs and sacred literature of Orthodox Judaism for the modern world.

Lutheran

Beck, Victor E. *Why I Am a Lutheran*. Nelson, 1956.

A BRIEF account of the Lutheran Church in the U. S. with an explanation of its teachings, worship service and music.

Lueker, Erwin L., editor-in-chief. *Lutheran Cyclopedia*. Concordia, 1954.

AN ENCYCLOPEDIC compilation of information on the Bible, systematized theology, church history, and life and worship in the church.

Wentz, Abdel R. *A Basic History of Lutheranism in America*. Muhlenberg Press, 1955.

COMPREHENSIVE study of Lutherans in the U.S.

Methodist

Luccock, Halford E., and Hutchinson, Paul. *Story of Methodism*. Abingdon, 1949.

HISTORY of John Wesley, his associates and the Methodist Church.

Smith, Roy L. *Why I Am a Methodist*. Hermitage House, 1955.

AUTOBIOGRAPHICAL approach to the history, convictions and activities of the Methodist Church.

Sweet, William Warren. *Methodism in American History*. Abingdon, 1954.

HISTORY of the Methodist Church from pre-Revolutionary days to mid-twentieth century.

Mormon

Bennett, Wallace F. *Why I Am a Mormon*. Nelson, 1958.

AN OUTLINE of history, essential doctrines, church organization and a personal statement of faith.

Smith, Joseph F. *Essentials in Church History*. Deseret News Press, 1950.

"A HISTORY of the church from the birth of Joseph Smith to the present time" —subtitle.

West, Ray Benedict. *Kingdom of the Saints; the story of Brigham Young and the Mormons*. Viking, 1957.

HISTORY of Mormonism since its establishment by Joseph Smith in 1830.

Presbyterian

Mackay, John A. *The Presbyterian Way of Life*. Prentice-Hall, 1960.

AN INTERPRETATION of Presbyterian history, theology, organization, worship services, and relationship to the ecumenical movement and secular society.

Miller, Park H. *Why I Am a Presbyterian*. Nelson, 1956.

AN INTERPRETATION of the Westminster confession of faith, the organization of the church, and its work in educational and mission fields.

Protestant

Brown, Robert M. *The Spirit of Protestantism*. Oxford, 1961.

A DEFINITION and interpretation of Protestant faith and theology which analyzes strengths, weaknesses and the challenges which face it.

Cobb, John. *Varieties of Protestantism*. Westminster, 1960.

A REVIEW of the diversity of principles and practices within various Protestant movements with an exploration of approaches to unity.

Hudson, Winthrop S. *American Protestantism*. University of Chicago Press, 1961.

HISTORY of the development of Protestant churches in the U. S. from 1607 to 1960.

Quaker

Lucas, Sidney. *The Quaker Story*. Harper, 1949.

EXPLANATION of the history, organization, doctrines and behavioral standards of the Quaker movement.

Sykes, John. *The Quakers: A New Look at Their Society*. Lippincott, 1959 (*c.* 1958).

EXPLANATION of basic Quaker beliefs, their stand on peace and reconciliation, types of meetings and methods of prayer.

West, Jessamyn, ed. *The Quaker Reader*. Viking, 1962.

ANTHOLOGY of 61 selections by or about Quakers interpreting Quaker beliefs and humanitarian spirit.

Seventh-day Adventist

Herndon, Booton. *The Seventh Day; the story of the Seventh-day Adventists*. McGraw-Hill, 1960.

A REVIEW of the history and organization of the Seventh-day Adventist Church, its welfare and missionary functions, and the influence of its beliefs on its members.

Seventh-day Adventists Answer Questions on Doctrines (prepared by a group of Seventh-day Adventist leaders, Bible teachers, and editors). Review and Herald Publishing Association, 1957.

"AN EXPLANATION of certain major aspects of Seventh-day Adventist belief"— subtitle.

Unitarian

Mendelsohn, Jack. *Why I Am a Unitarian*. Nelson, 1960.

EXPLANATION of Unitarianism as an ethical religion with an interpretation of fundamental beliefs.

Parke, David B., ed. *The Epic of Unitarianism*. Starr King Press, 1957.

"ORIGINAL writings from the history of liberal religions"—subtitle.

3. VARIETIES IN AMERICAN RELIGION

Bach, Marcus. *Strange Sects and Curious Cults*. Dodd, 1961.

SYMPATHETIC account of beliefs and rituals practiced by "sex cults," "conscience groups" and utopian movements.

————. *They Have Found a Faith*. Bobbs, 1946.

EXAMINATION of such little known groups as Jehovah's Witnesses, Four-square Gospel, Spiritualism, the Oxford group, Kingdoms of Father Divine, Baháí Faith, Unity and Psychiona.

Braden, Charles Samuel. *These Also Believe; a study of modern American cults and minority religious movements*. Macmillan, 1949.

EXAMINATION of 13 minority groups which either originated or experienced a prime impetus in the United States.

Clark, Elmer T. *The Small Sects in America*. Rev. ed. Abingdon, 1949.

REVIEW of the doctrines and practices of two hundred little known groups and the reasons for their establishment.

Mathison, Richard R. *Faiths, Cults, and Sects of America: from Atheism to Zen*. Bobbs, 1960.

STUDY of small religious groups, their leaders and their significance in the periods in which they developed in American life.

Mead, Frank S. *Handbook of Denominations in the United States*. 2d rev. ed. Abingdon, 1961.

USEFUL reference volume of factual information on the majority of religious bodies in the U. S.

Olmstead, Clifton E. *History of Religion in the United States*. Prentice-Hall, 1960.

SURVEY of major denominations and their development in relation to intellectual, political and social backgrounds from colonial times to the present.

Spence, Hartzell. *The Story of America's Religions;* published in co-operation with the editors of *Look* magazine. Holt, 1960.

SURVEY of 14 religions "which have made great sociological impacts upon the American scene."

Stuber, Stanley I. *How We Got Our Denominations; a primer on church history*. Rev. ed. Association Press, 1959.

CONCISE information on religious movements, schisms and mergers.

Wiegel, Gustave, S. J. *Churches in North America*. Helicon, 1961.

BACKGROUND material developed for intelligent understanding of differences among principal churches.

4. MEN AND WOMEN AND RELIGIOUS MOVEMENTS

Albright, Raymond Wolf. *Focus on Infinity*. Macmillan, 1961.

LIFE OF Phillips Brooks, Episcopal bishop and composer of "O Little Town of Bethlehem," which also illuminates the religious climate of nineteenth-century America.

Anderson, Leila W., and Dexter, Harriet Harmon. *Pilgrim Circuit Rider*. Harper, 1960.

UNUSUAL personal story of a woman minister serving rural churches for the Congregational Christian Church.

Bainton, Roland Herbert. *Here I Stand*. Abingdon, 1950.

BIOGRAPHY of Luther interpreting his problems, work and writings and the significance of his role in the sixteenth century.

Bowie, Walter Russell. *Men of Fire*. Harper, 1961.

SHORT biographical sketches of religious men of action from the time of Saint Paul to Thomas Dooley and Albert Schweitzer.

Brodie, Fawn M. *No Man Knows My History; the life of Joseph Smith, the Mormon prophet*. Knopf, 1945.

FULL-LENGTH biography of the founder of the Mormon Church.

Deen, Edith. *Great Women of the Christian Faith*. Harper, 1959.

BIOGRAPHICAL sketches of women leaders throughout Christian history.

Di Donato, Pietro. *Immigrant Saint*. McGraw-Hill, 1960.

LIFE OF Saint Frances Xavier Cabrini, foundress of the Missionary Sisters of the Sacred Heart and of schools, orphanages and hospitals throughout the U. S.

Fox, George. *Journal*. A rev. ed. by John L. Nickalls; with an epilogue by Henry J. Cadbury and an introduction by Geoffrey F. Nuttall. Cambridge, 1952.

JOURNAL of the founder of the Society of Friends. Introduction and epilogue provide biographical interpretation of Fox, the man, and Fox, the mystic.

Grailsford, Mabel Richmond. *Tale of Two Brothers: John and Charles Wesley*. Oxford, 1954.

JOINT biography of the Wesleys as religious leaders, with background material on the church they founded and on the events which separated them.

McCorry, Vincent P. *Everyman's St. Paul*. Farrar, 1961.

INTRODUCTION to life and teaching of Saint Paul with commentaries on Pauline epistles.

Powell, Lyman Pierson. *Mary Baker Eddy: A Life-Size Portrait*. Christian Science Publishers, 1950.

A DOCUMENTED biography of the founder of the Christian Science movement.

Schweitzer, Albert. *Mysticism of Paul the Apostle.* Macmillan, 1955 (*c.* 1931).

FAMOUS and provocative study of Saint Paul's life, thought and influence.

Sugrue, Francis. *Popes in the Modern World.* Crowell, 1961.

READABLE biographical sketches of Leo XIII, Pius X, Benedict XV, Pius XI, Pius XII and John XXIII.

Vining, Elizabeth Gray. *Friend of Life: The Biography of Rufus M. Jones.* Lippincott, 1958.

BIOGRAPHY of Quaker leader and founder of the American Friends Service Committee.

Winslow, Ola. *Master Roger Williams.* Macmillan, 1957.

BIOGRAPHY of a vigorous defender of religious freedom and founder of Rhode Island.

5. *FICTION ABOUT GREAT RELIGIOUS FIGURES*

Barr, Gladys H. *Master of Geneva.* Holt, 1962.

A NOVEL based on the life of John Calvin, onetime aspirant for the priesthood who became a champion of the Protestant faith.

————. *Monk in Armour.* Abingdon, 1950.

A STORY of the conflicts and physical peril endured by Martin Luther, founder of Protestantism, in his search for God.

Brady, C. A. *Stage of Fools.* Dutton, 1953.

AN HISTORICAL novel centered around Sir Thomas More, canonized in 1935, and his struggles for a "pure" Roman Catholic Church during the Reformation.

Caldwell, Taylor. *Dear and Glorious Physician.* Doubleday, 1959.

A STORY of Saint Luke, the physician, and his travels in the ancient world until he is finally brought to service to God.

De Wohl, Louis. *Citadel of God.* Lippincott, 1959.

STORY of Saint Benedict, from his boyhood in sixth-century Rome to his founding of religious communities which lighted the Dark Ages.

————. *The Glorious Folly.* Lippincott, 1957.

A NOVEL of Saint Paul and his conversion, woven into the political intrigue of Rome and Palestine in the first century A.D.

Fisher, Vardis. *Children of God.* Vanguard, 1939.

A NOVEL which tells the whole story of Mormonism, from its founding by Joseph Smith to its disintegration after the death of Brigham Young.

Oliver, Jane. *Flame of Fire.* Putnam, 1961.

FICTIONIZED life of William Tyndale, translator of first English Bible, and his contacts with Erasmus, Luther, Sir Thomas More, and other religious figures.

Rohrbach, Peter-Thomas. *Bold Encounter.* Bruce, 1960.

A NOVEL of Saint John of the Cross and his struggles which eventually brought about the triumph of the Carmelite Reform.

Slaughter, Frank G. *Warrior and King.* World, 1962.

STORY of the boy David, who grew up to unite the many nations of Israel into one splendid kingdom.

Facts About the Bible

Adapted from *The Bible and the American Bible Society* (pamphlet), American Bible Society, New York.

IN WHAT LANGUAGES WAS THE BIBLE FIRST WRITTEN?

Hebrew, Aramaic and Greek.

HOW MANY VERSES, CHAPTERS AND BOOKS ARE THERE IN THE BIBLE?

	Old Testament	New Testament	Total
Verses	23,214	7,959	31,173
Chapters	929	260	1,189
Books	39	27	66

The Bible was divided into *chapters* by Cardinal Hugo de Sancto-Caro about 1250.

The Greek New Testament was divided into *verses* by Robert Stephens, a French printer, in 1551. He is said to have done this work while riding on horseback between Paris and Lyons.

The first English Bible to carry both chapters and verse numbers was the Geneva Bible, published in 1560. The Bibles published today still use the same divisions for chapters and verses.

WHERE ARE THE ORIGINAL COPIES OF THE BIBLE?

The original manuscripts of the Hebrew Old Testament and of the Greek Gospels and Epistles, etc., were long thought to have been worn out or discarded long ago. Copies were made by hand, and were copied and discarded over and over again.

But in 1947 the entire book of Isaiah, with the exception of two very small breaks, was discovered in a cave northwest of the Dead Sea. The parchment had been hidden in an earthenware jar, wrapped in yards of cloth and covered with pitch. This book is considered by experts to have been written during the first century B.C., fully 1,000 years before the oldest previously-known Hebrew manuscript of a book of the Bible. The evidence points to the fact that this manuscript of Isaiah was in use while Christ was living. A few manuscripts since discovered may be even older.

The oldest Greek manuscripts of larger parts of the Bible are the *Codex Sinaiticus,* now in the British Museum, and the *Codex Vaticanus,* now in the Vatican. These were probably written in the fourth century and contain the Greek text of nearly the whole Bible. Older papyrus fragments exist in Greek.

WHAT WERE THE DATE AND PLACE OF THE FIRST PRINTED BIBLE?

The Bible was first printed between 1450-56 at Mainz, Germany, from type devised by Johann Gutenberg. It was printed in Latin, from a contemporary manuscript of the Vulgate. Between forty and fifty copies of this Bible are known to be in existence. One copy, owned by the Congressional Library, Washington, D.C., is said to be one of only three perfect copies, and one of several printed on vellum. The cost of the Congressional Library copy was nearly $400,000.

WHEN WAS THE FIRST BIBLE PRINTED IN AMERICA?

The first Bible was printed in America in 1663 for the Indians of Massachusetts, in their language. It was translated by John Eliot, a missionary.

WHAT WAS THE FIRST BIBLE TO BE PRINTED IN AMERICA IN A EUROPEAN LANGUAGE?

A German Bible was printed by Christopher Saur in Germantown, Pennsylvania, in 1743.

WHEN WAS THE FIRST ENGLISH BIBLE PRINTED IN THIS COUNTRY?

An English Bible was first printed in this country in 1782 by Robert Aitken in Philadelphia, with the approval and recommendation of the Congress.

IS ANY TRANSLATION WORK BEING DONE NOW?

Every year, the Gospels and other portions of the Bible are translated into languages which formerly possessed no part of the Bible. The entire New Testament or the whole Bible appear from time to time in languages in which only a lesser portion of the Bible has previously been translated and published.

WHY ARE REVISIONS NECESSARY?

Because of changes in language, and because scholars become better acquainted with the original Hebrew and Greek texts and acquire a better understanding of the languages in which they have been working. Revisions in translations become necessary as local scholarship develops and the Christian community grows.

Condensed from news release, *The Bible in 1,181 Languages,* by Margaret T. Hills, Librarian, American Bible Society, New York.

SOME PART of the Bible has been published in 1,181 languages (as of December, 1961), according to the records of the American Bible Society.

Languages in which the whole Bible has been published	226
Languages in which the whole Testament has been published	281
Languages in which at least a complete Gospel or other book has been published	674
Total languages in which some part of the Bible has been published	1,181

In 1961, complete Bibles were published for the first time in Bali (Mengaka), Bambara, Teso and Sukuma for Africa, and Sadan Toradja for Indonesia. In 1961, first New Testaments were published in Kekchi (Guatemala), Maya and Mazateco (Mexico), Piro (Peru), Ogoni (Nigeria), Kwara'ae Mwala (Solomon Islands), Mao Naga (Assam), Kambera (Indonesia) and Hindustani (India).

New languages are added to the list at the rate of about ten a year. Scriptures were published for the first time as follows:

Language	Country	Part	Year
Baure	(Bolivia)	Mark	1960
Bawm	(East Pakistan)	Mark	1961
Diola	(Senegal, Gabon)	Mark	1961
Ghetsogo	(Gabon)	John	1955
Guaica	(Venezuela)	Mark	1961
Hallam	(Assam)	Mark	1960
Huitoto: Muinana	(Peru)	Mark	1961
Ixil	(Guatemala)	Mark	1961
Kabre	(Togoland)	Luke	1961
Kyaka	(New Guinea)	Mark, I John	1961
Manobe: Ilianen	(Philippines)	Mark	1961
Mixe de Coatlan	(Mexico)	Luke	1961
Nambya	(Southern Rhodesia)	Mark	1961
Phom Naga	(Assam)	Gospels, Acts	1961
Piro: Manchineri	(Peru)	Mark	1961
Toma	(Guinea)	Mark	1961

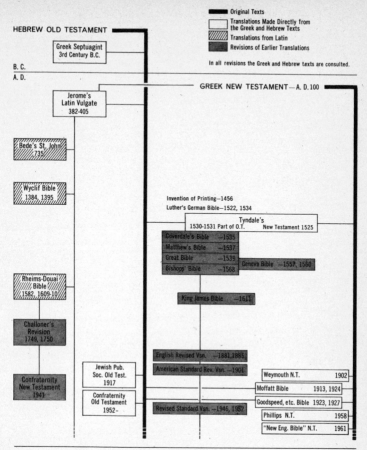

HEBREW OLD TESTAMENT

■■■	Original Texts
☐	Translations Made Directly from the Greek and Hebrew Texts
▨	Translations from Latin
▨	Revisions of Earlier Translations

In all revisions the Greek and Hebrew texts are consulted.

Greek Septuagint
3rd Century B.C.

B. C.
A. D.

GREEK NEW TESTAMENT—A. D. 100

Jerome's
Latin Vulgate
382-405

Bede's St. John
735

Wyclif Bible
1384, 1395

Invention of Printing—1456
Luther's German Bible—1522, 1534

Tyndale's
1530-1531 Part of O.T.   New Testament 1525

Coverdale's Bible —1535
Matthew's Bible —1537
Great Bible —1539
Bishops' Bible —1568   Geneva Bible —1557, 1560

Rheims-Douai
Bible
1582, 1609-10

King James Bible —1611

Challoner's
Revision
1749, 1750

English Revised Vsn. —1881, 1885
American Standard Rev. Vsn. —1901

Jewish Pub.
Soc. Old Test.
1917

Confraternity
Old Testament
1952-

Confraternity
New Testament
1941

Revised Standard Vsn. —1946, 1952

Weymouth N.T.   1902
Moffatt Bible   1913, 1924
Goodspeed, etc. Bible 1923, 1927
Phillips N.T.   1958
"New Eng. Bible" N.T. 1961

SOURCE: AMERICAN BIBLE SOCIETY

Greek Septuagint: The Old Testament was translated into Greek in the third century B.C. for those Jews who lived outside of Palestine. Called Septuagint (meaning "of the seventy") because it was said to have been translated by 70 elders in 70 sessions in Egypt, it was used constantly by the early Christians.

Greek New Testament: Paul wrote his letters for early Christians in Greek. The sayings of Jesus were perhaps written in Aramaic, the language Jesus spoke, but soon the whole New Testament was written in Greek and circulated throughout the Mediterranean world. By the fourth century the Old and New Testaments in Greek were used by the Church as one collection of writings.

Vulgate Bible: About 382 the Bishop of Rome asked Jerome to make a new translation of the Bible into Latin. He went to Palestine and worked for twenty-five years to make a Bible for the common people. It was therefore called the vulgar or Vulgate Bible and is still the official Bible of the Roman Catholic Church.

Bede: Bede, the great historian of Anglo-Saxon England, started to translate the Vulgate (Latin) Bible into the English of his day because only the scholars could understand Latin. Legend says he died as he finished the translation of the Gospel of John in 735. In the 10th and 11th centuries there were other translations of the Psalms and the Gospels.

Wyclif: John Wyclif sent out poor priests, called Lollards, to preach to the people in their own language instead of in Latin, which was used in the churches. He realized that a Bible in English was needed, and, under his inspiration, the first translation of the entire Bible was made from Latin in 1384.

Luther: The Reformation needed a Bible in the language of the people, so Luther himself made a German translation, completed in the years 1522–1534. It was the first Western European Bible based, not on the official Latin Vulgate Bible, but on the original Hebrew and Greek.

Tyndale: Church authorities in England prohibited a new English translation, so Tyndale went to Germany and translated the New Testament from the original Greek. This was the first printed English New Testament, 1525. Copies were smuggled into England in shipments of grain and cloth, even though many of them were confiscated. He also translated parts of the Old Testament. Soon after, Tyndale was betrayed, strangled and burned near Brussels. But so excellent was his work that almost every English version since is indebted to it.

Coverdale: Coverdale, like Tyndale, fled to Germany to complete the translation of the Bible. He used Latin and German versions and Tyndale's New Testament, Pentateuch, and Jonah. This was the first printed English Bible, 1535. Matthew's Bible, 1537, containing additional sections of Tyndale's work on the Old Testament, was revised by Coverdale. The result was known as the Great Bible, 1539. Its Psalms are still in the Book of Common Prayer. The Bishops' Bible, 1568, was a revision of the Great Bible, and the King James (see below) was ordered as a revision of the Bishops' Bible. The Geneva Bible, 1560, also a revision of the Great Bible, was produced by English Puritans in Geneva and strongly influenced the King James Bible also.

Roman Catholic Versions: The New Testament published in Rheims in 1582, followed in 1609–1610 by the Old Testament at Douai, was a translation from the Latin Vulgate. This was revised by Bishop Challoner in 1749 and 1750. The Confraternity New Testament, 1941, although strongly influenced by contemporary Greek scholarship, was based on the Vulgate, but the Confraternity Old Testament, 1952, on the Hebrew text.

King James: The various versions of the Bible aroused so many arguments that James I, after the Hampton Court Conference, appointed fifty-four scholars to make a new version. It took about seven years, for all the known copies of oldest manuscripts and later translations were studied. Despite the great variety of men who worked on it, the book was harmonious in style and beauty. It was first published in 1611 and became the most popular English Bible.

Later Revisions: For more than 250 years the King James Bible was supreme among English-speaking people. During the last one hundred years, the knowledge from newly-discovered manuscripts, archeological discoveries and recent scholarship had led to its revision. The first "Revised Version" was published in England, 1881–1885; a modification of this, the American Standard Revised Version, was issued in 1901. The most recent is the Revised Standard Version, 1946- 1952. There were also translations by individual scholars and groups of scholars: Weymouth, Moffat, Goodspeed, Phillips, etc. The "New English Bible," (New Testament, 1961), a group translation, is not a revision but an entirely new translation.

What Catholics, Jews and Protestants Believe: A Comparison Chart*

Reprinted by permission from the February, 1954, issue of the *International Journal of Religious Education;* revised as of 1962. (Reprints of this chart are available from the National Council of Churches, 475 Riverside Drive, New York 27, N. Y.)

The statements listed below are drawn by the author from authentic sources within the faiths concerned, and represent the analysis of each faith by authorities within that faith, not the opinion of one about others.

Protestants	Jews	Catholics

GOD

God is one; manifested as Father, Son and Holy Spirit. Protestants believe in a much more individual and direct approach to God than do Roman Catholics. More stress is placed on the love of God, as revealed in Christ, than in a God of law and justice.	One God, personal and universal, whose ways are beyond understanding, yet whose reality gives purpose to man and to the world. No one can serve as an intermediary between God and man.	Supreme Being, infinitely perfect, who made all things and keeps them in existence. God is the only one God, but has three divine Persons—Father, Son, and Holy Ghost. Revealed through Jesus Christ, the Son of God, who teaches through the Catholic Church.

CHRIST

Accept Christ as divine Son of God. Believe in direct, personal relationship, rather than through Church institutionalism, including Virgin Mary. He is elder brother, moral leader, as well as Messiah and Savior.	Many accept Jesus as a child of God, as a Jew, and as a prophet or inspired teacher, with no supernatural powers. They do not accept the Divinity and Atonement of Christ.	Christ is God made man. Born of the Virgin Mary, incarnation of God, atonement for sin, bodily resurrection. Second. Person of Trinity. Both man and God. Salvation through his sacrifice on the Cross, manifested in the Mass.

ONE TRUE RELIGION

Protestantism has never claimed to be the one and only true religion; but that Christ is the only true way to salvation—not the Church. Recognize Roman Catholics and members of the Eastern Orthodox churches as Christians. Desire the same recognition from others.	Jews do not claim that their religion alone is the true one. They are content that others have their own faith, as long as it has elements of decency, kindliness, justice and integrity. However, Jews regard *Judaism* as the only religion for Jews.	"We know that the Catholic Church is the one true Church established by Christ because it alone has the marks of the true Church." (One, holy, universal, apostolic.) "We know that no other church but the Catholic Church is the true Church of Christ because no other church has these four marks." *(Catechism of Christian Doctrine)*

CHURCH

Protestants believe that the Church belongs to all true Christians, and is a community of forgiven sinners. Christ the only head. Voluntary attendance and financial support. Make a difference between Kingdom of God and the Church as an institution.	Jews are permitted to attend Christian churches as visitors, not as worshipers. They have their own synagogues and temples. These are self-governing. Most Jews will join interfaith services when Bible readings, prayers, hymns are acceptable to all concerned.	Christ founded the Roman Catholic Church. It is the Body of Christ. The congregation of all baptized persons united in the same faith, sacrifice, sacraments, Pope and bishops. Peter the first pope. Chief attributes of the Church: authority, infallibility, indefectibility. Saving institution represented in Papacy and priesthood.

Protestants	Jews	Catholics

CHURCH MEMBERSHIP

No one is automatically born into the Protestant faith. Baptism the usual way to membership. Both infant and adult baptism practiced. Infant baptism followed by confirmation. Stress is placed upon active, not formal, membership.

Jews are born into Judaism. Converts accepted upon commitment to faith. (Circumcision the outward sign for males.) Confirmation personal reocgnition of membership.

Baptism is the gateway to the Church. Each remains a member (from infancy) so long as he professes the "one true faith"; does not withdraw through schism or heresy, or is not excommunicated.

BIBLE

Accept Old and New Testaments as inspired, but not *Apocrypha*. Individual right of interpretation. Final authority for faith and life.

Accept the Old Testament, but not the *Apocrypha* or New Testament. First five books of Moses called *Torah* are considered basic to the faith. Wide range of interpretation.

Inspired Word of God. Interpreted by the Church, which preceded it. 72 books, including *Apocrypha*. Not sufficient guide; tradition of Church added.

SACRAMENTS

Two: baptism and the Lord's Supper. Wide variation of meaning from a saving sacrament to mere symbol. Protestants are not "sacramentalists."

No sacraments, but many rites and ceremonies such as circumcision, bar mitzvah, confirmation. Reject all imagery.

Seven: baptism, confirmation, holy eucharist, penance, extreme unction, holy orders, matrimony. All instituted by Christ and all give grace.

PRAYER

Honor is paid to saints, but prayers never directed to them. Emphasis placed upon direct approach to God through prayer. No beads or rosary used. Informal, individual prayers encouraged. Worship must be in spirit and in truth.

Great stress placed upon prayer: petitions, adoration, confession of sin, expression of joyful fellowship, thanksgiving. Found both in daily personal devotions and in public worship.

Largely formal prayers not only for themselves personally, but for others (such as those in purgatory). Prayers through Virgin Mary and saints. Use of the rosary as aid to prayer. Not all prayers answered.

SIN

Original sin through Adam usually accepted, and plan of salvation through Christ's death on the Cross. All in need of redemption. But salvation comes through Christ and not Church; forgiveness comes from Christ and not through priest.

Recognize two kinds of sin: against man; against God. Must seek forgiveness of the first from those sinned against. Sin against God expiated by "a return to God."

Original sin due to Adam's "fall". Baptism removes this, but sins after baptism must be removed through penance and absolution of the priest. Sins are carefully catalogued, along with penalties.

HEAVEN AND HELL

Believe in both heaven and hell, but not purgatory. Wide differences in interpretation. General belief in some form of punishment for sin, and eternal reward for righteousness.

Most Jews no longer accept any literal conception of heaven and hell. More concerned with leading a good life in this world, rather than reward or punishment in the next (which they do not reject).

Accept literal heaven and hell, plus temporal place of punishment known as purgatory.

Protestants	Jews	Catholics

EVANGELISM

Protestants	Jews	Catholics
A basic principle and practice with Protestants, linked closely to church extension, world missions and salvation.	Not a proselytizing religion, although sincere converts are welcomed.	Mostly conducted by the priesthood, although laity now being encouraged to be evangelists and win converts.

CONFESSION

Protestants	Jews	Catholics
Confession of sins directed to Christ. He alone has power of forgiveness (along with God). Counseling services of pastors now encouraged, but no absolution.	Confess sins directly to God. Have no intermediary. Day of Atonement on collective as well as individual basis. Personal confession also before marriage and just prior to death.	All must go to confession. Confession tied directly to penance and power of priest to forgive sins.

MARRIAGE

Protestants	Jews	Catholics
While secular (civil) marriage contract is recognized, the sacredness of the marriage bond is stressed. Love basis of marriage. Beautiful ceremony either at home or church the usual practice.	Marriage much more than a personal matter; part of entire Jewish community. Usually elaborate marriage rites and symbols.	A sacrament binding a baptized man and a baptized woman for life. Parties actually perform ceremony, conferring on each other the sacrament.

DIVORCE

Protestants	Jews	Catholics
Divorce is allowed under certain conditions such as adultery and willful desertion, but is held as a last resort. Will remarry the innocent party.	Divorce is permitted when living together is intolerable. Emphasis on reconciliation and better understanding.	Not allowed. Separation permitted. Annulment, when there has been "no true marriage," is sometimes granted.

BIRTH CONTROL

Protestants	Jews	Catholics
Not thought of as a sin. Permitted when not abused. May be employed for health purposes.	Permitted and even advocated when it is for the welfare of all concerned.	Not permitted under any circumstances by any artificial means, and birth prevention is considered a grave sin.

INDIVIDUAL RESPONSIBILITY

Protestants	Jews	Catholics
Individual supreme; salvation a very personal matter. Priesthood of all believers stressed. Nothing can be substituted for personal responsibility.	All Jews completely free as individuals. Rabbis have no authority over individuals. No religious hierarchy.	Roman Catholicism stresses individual responsibility for sin and salvation, but power is placed in Church and priesthood—not in the individual.

SOCIAL RESPONSIBILITY

Protestants	Jews	Catholics
While salvation is thought of as an individual affair, Protestants have always applied their faith in good works to all areas of life. Have responsibility to community. Along with missions goes the desire to build as much of the Kingdom of God into the world as possible.	Have a marked sense of community relationships and service. Charity basic tenet. Inspired by Old Testament prophets. Human rights, freedom and equality paramount in Jewish practice.	Parents responsible for well-being of children. Taught to love country and obey all laws. Charity basic principle. Social teaching of Pope Leo XIII now championed by Church, and emphasized by the recent encyclical of Pope John XXIII.

Comparison of Religious Beliefs: 16 American Denominations

This summary-comparison of religious beliefs (of the 16 denominations whose creeds have been presented in the main body of this book) is designed solely as a cross-reference aid.

The material which follows is not to be construed as representing official doctrine—except where the articles in *Look* magazine, from which these extracts are taken, were themselves approved by a denomination. Nor does this summary attempt to include the variations in creed and practice of groups within any individual denomination.

The material has been arranged by points of creed or practice: under each point, the position of the religious groups is listed in alphabetical order.

BAPTISM

Baptists. Baptism is by immersion. It is limited to adults and to such children as have reached an age when they can understand the meaning of the ceremony. Baptists look upon immersion as realistic symbolism, through which the life of sin is buried and the new life of faith emerges.

Christian Scientists. Baptism means purification from all material sense and is not practiced in the material form.

Congregationalists. Baptism is the rite by which the Church takes a child or an adult to itself. The mode is usually "sprinkling," though other forms may be used if desired.

Disciples of Christ. Baptism is by immersion as an act of obedience and surrender, a symbol of the death, burial and resurrection of the Lord Jesus. Only those who are adult enough to know what they are doing when they stand up to confess Christ are baptized.

Eastern Orthodox. The baptismal rite is performed by a triple immersion into water. It is followed by chrismation, the anointment of the baptized with holy oils, which symbolizes a confirmation of the faith.

Episcopalians. All who are baptized (whether by Episcopalian or other baptism, provided it is with water and in the name of the Holy Trinity) are members of the Church of Christ. Even those who are not actually baptized, but by intention would be baptized if they were able, are believed to be "saved."

Jehovah's Witnesses. Baptism is complete submersion. It is not for infants but for persons of responsible age who have the ability to learn. It is a symbol of dedication to God to do His will.

Jews. In traditional Judaism, baptism is required only for those converted from another faith.

Lutherans. In baptism a person is born into the Kingdom of God and becomes an heir of salvation.

Methodists. Baptism is usually by sprinkling. It is a sign not only of profession but also of regeneration, or a new birth. The church assumes responsibility for her baptized children and awaits the time when they will be mature enough to appreciate and assume for themselves the vows made at baptism.

Mormons. Baptism is by immersion and performed by those having authority. It is only for those who have become "accountable" for their actions, at the age of eight years and over.

Presbyterians. Ordinarily performed by sprinkling, this rite is an outward symbol of inward regeneration. While baptism is urgently recommended, it is not held to be necessary for salvation. It is customary to baptize children, but those children who die without baptism are not excluded from heaven.

Quakers. Friends believe in baptism of the Spirit but practice no form of baptism. At birth, the infant's name is recorded on the official books of the meeting to which his parents belong.

Roman Catholics. Baptism restores supernatural life. Without that life, man does not have the capacity to enjoy heaven. Adults may gain the life of grace by an act of perfect contrition or pure love of God ("baptism of desire"). Infants are incapable of such an act of the will; unbaptized babies cannot go to heaven but in their state of "limbo" do not suffer in any way.

Seventh-day Adventists. All who would enter the Church are required to be baptized by immersion, the method followed by the Church of New Testament times.

Unitarians. While many Unitarians do practice baptism of infants and, more rarely, of adults, they prefer to look upon baptism as an act of dedication which has only symbolic meaning. It is possible to become a Unitarian without being baptized.

THE BIBLE

Baptists. All Baptists believe in the inspiration of the Bible, but only the extreme fundamentalists accept it literally or regard it as infallible in every detail. All Baptists accept the Bible as infallible in religious teachings and as a trustworthy record of the progressive revelation of God, climaxed by the supreme revelation of Himself in Jesus Christ. No official dogma prescribes how an individual Baptist shall interpret the Bible.

Christian Scientists. Each person, of any religion, can find what is satisfying to him as the spiritual meaning in the Bible. But Christian Scientists feel that Mary Baker Eddy's book, *Science and Health with Key to the Scriptures,* offers the complete spiritual meaning of the Bible.

Congregationalists. The Bible reveals God in a way which will never be superseded. Christ shows that God is love; all subsequent knowledge, imparted to men by God through the Scriptures, merely elaborates this fundamental truth. Congregationalists apply methods of science to Bible study; thus, they feel they know what God is saying in the Bible better than their fathers who lived in a pre-scientific age.

Disciples of Christ. Disciples share the common Protestant belief that the Bible (except for the Apocryphal Books) is the inspired Word of God, written at different times under the inspiration of the Holy Spirit. Many Disciples accept the New Testament as a third and purely Christian dispensation, following the Old Testament which represents two dispensations.

Fundamentalist Disciples accept the Authorized Version of the Bible as the final and infallible word of God. The liberals believe newer translations and studies of inspired scholars have thrown new light on many passages of the Scriptures.

Episcopalians. The Holy Scriptures are the great source and testing ground of Christian doctrine. But the Episcopal Church does not hold to the literal inerrancy of the Scriptures. The Bible is considered sacred for its general inspiration, as the record of God's revelation.

Jehovah's Witnesses. The Bible is followed all the way, not half the way. The Hebrew and Greek Scriptures are considered entirely consistent and practical for our day.

Jews. Orthodox Jews accept the Bible as the revealed Will of God. Reform Jews accept as binding only the moral laws of the Bible. Conservative Jews follow the pattern of traditional Judaism but regard it as an evolving, ever-growing religion.

Lutherans. God's Word is recorded in the Bible, but the Word itself is a living, active thing through which the Holy Spirit stirs us to growth in understanding and obedience to God's will.

Methodists. Methodists look upon the Bible as a library of inspired books containing the progressive revelation of God. They believe in the "open Bible" and encourage the individual to read it for himself, leaving him free to make his own interpretation under the guidance of the Holy Spirit.

Mormons. The Bible is basic to Mormon belief. The King James Version is used officially and is believed "to be the word of God as far as it is translated correctly." (8th Article of Faith.) The Book of Mormon is a complementary work accepted by Mormons as Scripture.

Presbyterians. Presbyterians believe the Scriptures of the Old and New Testaments to be the Word of God and "the only infallible rule of faith and practice," and that they are the source of those truths by which men live. They believe that God spoke through men whose minds and hearts He had touched. They therefore emphasize inspired men, not inspired words.

Quakers. Friends have always believed that the Truth is found in the Bible, rather than holding that what has been written is true *because* it is in the Bible.

Roman Catholics. The Church is the divinely appointed custodian of the Bible and has the final word on what is meant in any specific passage. The Church guards orthodoxy (including interpretation of the Scriptures) and passes down essential Christian tradition from one generation to another.

Seventh-day Adventists. Seventh-day Adventists accept the Bible literally and believe that the authors were inspired by God. There have been many translations but the original intent of the authors has come down unimpaired through the centuries, the original message is clearly discernible, and "the word of the Lord endureth forever." The record of creation in the first chapter of Genesis is considered not fable but literal fact.

Unitarians. The doctrine of "revelation," of the absolute and indisputable authority of the Bible, is alien to Unitarian faith and teaching. Unitarians hold the Bible very dear, but they reserve the prerogative of critical appreciation.

BIRTH CONTROL

Baptists. No parish Baptist Church and no ecclesiastical convention of Baptists has ever by resolution expressed approval or disapproval of birth control. Most Baptists would resent and repudiate such a resolution as an unwarranted intrusion into the private life of husband and wife.

Christian Scientists. Married couples are free to follow their own judgment as to having children and as to the number they will have.

Congregationalists. There is no official statement on birth control from the churches. In general, Congregationalists believe that the use by man of the brains which God has given him to invent means of preventing conception is not contrary to God's will.

Disciples of Christ. A majority of Disciple ministers believe that birth control is justifiable under certain circumstances. In general, Disciples are content to leave such matters to the individual consciences of husband and wife.

Eastern Orthodox. Though birth control is not mentioned in the binding doctrinal decisions of the seven ecumenical councils, it has been repeatedly disapproved of by Orthodox synodical and patriarchal pronouncements and encyclicals.

Episcopalians. When birth control is practiced without selfish motives, it is permissible.

Jehovah's Witnesses. Birth control is regarded as an entirely personal matter.

Jews. The Jewish religion has traditionally been opposed to birth control when practiced for purely selfish reasons. It sanctions birth control if pregnancy represents a health hazard or if previous children have been born defective; modern Judaism extends this to cases of extreme poverty, inadequate living conditions.

Lutherans. There is no general objection to birth control. The United Lutheran Church in America has stated that irresponsible conception of children up to the limit of biological capacity and selfish limitation of the number of children are equally detrimental.

Methodists. The General Conference of the Methodist Church has stated that parenthood is a Christian privilege and responsibility, and that planned parenthood practiced in Christian conscience fulfills rather than violates the will of God. The justifying motive must be unselfish. The spacing of children, the health of parents and adequate economic support are factors to be considered.

Mormons. The Church has always advocated rearing large families; birth control, as commonly understood, is contrary to its teachings.

Presbyterians. The Presbyterian Church does not legislate for its people on personal issues. Nothing in the Church's teaching can be construed as forbidding an intelligent, conservative and unselfish employment of birth control.

Quakers. Birth control is a matter for the individual conscience. Education for marriage and parenthood has long been a concern of Quakers.

Roman Catholics. The Church is opposed to birth control in the belief that artificial contraception is against the law of God and that because it is immoral, it cannot be employed as a means, even to a good end. Birth prevention is regarded as an evil in itself—circumstances cannot change it into something morally good or indifferent. "Natural" birth control—the so-called rhythm theory—is permitted (as Pope Pius XII stated) in cases where undue medical or economic hardship makes family limitation imperative.

Seventh-day Adventists. Seventh-day Adventists, as a denomination, have never taken an official position on the matter of birth control.

Unitarians. Most Unitarians are strong advocates of birth control in a world that is threatened with a population explosion.

CREED

Baptists. There is no single, official creed. The nearest statement is the so-called "Grand Rapids Affirmation," adopted by the American Baptist Convention on May 23, 1946. It resolves that faith be reaffirmed in the New Testament as a divinely inspired record and therefore an all-sufficient rule of faith and practice. It also calls all its churches to the common task of sharing the whole Gospel with the whole world.

Christian Scientists. Christian Scientists have no formal creed. They have six brief religious tenets to which all members of the Church of Christ, Scientist, subscribe. (These are found in *Science and Health with Key to the Scriptures,* by Mary Baker Eddy.)

Congregationalists. Each particular congregation is accustomed to write its own creed. A few churches use the Apostles' Creed.

Disciples of Christ. Disciples of Christ have no creed but Christ and no doctrines save those which are found in the New Testament or are reasonably to be inferred therefrom.

Eastern Orthodox. The official creed accepted by Orthodoxy is the Nicene Creed, formulated and adopted by the First Ecumenical Council of Nicaea (325 A.D.) and the Second Ecumenical Council of Constantinople (381 A.D.).

Episcopalians. Basic Episcopalian beliefs are affirmed in the Apostles' Creed and the Nicene Creed.

Jehovah's Witnesses. The Witnesses have no creed. They follow the Bible completely.

Jews. There is no formal creed. However, the *Talmud* speaks of three central principles in life: Torah—or learning; service of God; and the performance of good deeds, or charity. This represents the core of Judaism.

Lutherans. Lutheran teachings are based on the common Christian faith described in the New Testament and first summarized in the Apostles' Creed.

Methodists. Methodists are not required to sign any formal creed. Those joining the church are asked to affirm allegiance to Christ and the New Testament faith.

Mormons. Basic Latter-day Saint beliefs are to be found in the Mormon Articles of Faith, and in the "standard works" of the Church, including the Bible.

Presbyterians. The Westminster Confession of Faith is the creed of English-speaking Presbyterians. Most adherents accept also the Nicene and Apostles' Creeds.

Quakers. There is no written or formal creed. Serving as a substitute are the "Queries," a set of questions designed to encourage the faithfulness of the members in their religious life.

Roman Catholics. The chief articles of faith are summed up in the creeds. There are four great creeds: The Apostles', the Nicene, the Athanasian, and that of Pius IV. Equally essential to Catholic belief are the doctrines and dogmas proclaimed infallibly true by the teaching authority of the Church —e.g., the Immaculate Conception of the Blessed Virgin Mary, her assumption into heaven after death, the real presence of Jesus Christ in the Blessed Sacrament, and so forth.

Seventh-day Adventists. Seventh-day Adventists do not make use of a formal creed. They hold certain fundamental beliefs based, they claim, upon the Bible.

Unitarians. Unitarians follow no formal or central creed. Freedom of belief among Unitarians is broad enough to include agnosticism, humanism, even atheism, on the one hand, and, on the other, a belief in God which can be manifested in a wide range of definitions from that of a "personal God" to an "Ultimate Reality."

DIVORCE

Baptists. Baptists do not approve of divorce except on grounds of adultery. But there is no regulation among Baptist churches regarding divorce. Each clergyman depends on his conscience in deciding whether or not to officiate at the marriage of divorced persons.

Christian Scientists. The Church of Christ, Scientist, takes no doctrinaire position on such social questions as divorce, but leaves it members free to work out their salvation on the basis of their highest understanding of moral and spiritual law.

Congregationalists. Though the churches have never made a joint official pronouncement on divorce, they frown upon current divorce habits of Americans. They do not oppose legal divorce after a couple has been "spiritually" divorced.

Disciples of Christ. There is no central church authority on this subject. Some ministers and congregations oppose any remarriage of divorced persons. Others will remarry the innocent party to a divorce obtained on the ground of adultery. Others, perhaps a majority, believe that divorce has become a legal function of the state and will remarry anyone to whom the civil government accords the right of remarriage.

Eastern Orthodox. Though Orthodox churches believe in the essential indissolubility of marriage, divorce is permitted as a last resort, in certain cases, and after all attempts for reconciliation by the clergy have failed. Remarriage of the innocent party is permitted, though not more than three marriages are allowed.

Episcopalians. In America, the "canons" (church law) do not recognize divorce but do provide a number of grounds for annulment. A bishop may permit a divorced person to remarry if certain conditions are met.

Jehovah's Witnesses. Divorce may be obtained only on the ground of marital unfaithfulness.

Jews. Divorce is permitted when love and harmony have ceased to exist between a man and a woman, and their marriage has become empty and meaningless.

Lutherans. Following the New Testament, Lutherans agree that adultery and desertion may be grounds for divorce. They feel that Christians should not legislate general principles to apply to all cases; every case must be considered individually.

Methodists. No Methodist minister should remarry a divorced person whose mate is living and unmarried, unless the person is the innocent party to a divorce on the grounds of adultery or other vicious conditions invalidating the marriage vow.

Mormons. Divorce is deplored and discouraged. "Temple divorces" (as distinguished from civil divorces) may be granted only by the president of the Church, for serious cause, including infidelity.

Presbyterians. Divorce is permitted to the innocent party on scriptural grounds (adultery), and that party may remarry. Divorce is also permitted in cases of willful desertion. In cases of doubt, the minister can consult his Presbytery's Committee on Divorce. However, no minister may remarry persons who have been divorced less than twelve months.

Quakers. Divorce is contrary to the "Discipline of Friends." Friends' Meetings are urged not to permit weddings of divorced persons as long as one of the divorced couple is still alive.

Roman Catholics. The Church does not recognize any absolute divorce between a couple who are validly married, where one or the other would be free to marry again. Separation from bed and board may be approved.

Seventh-day Adventists. Seventh-day Adventists follow the Biblical position that adultery is the only possible ground for divorce.

Unitarians. Unitarianism recognizes no specifically theological doctrines as regards divorce. It is referred to the individual's conscience, intelligence and common sense. The church is always ready to offer counsel and advice in keeping with its ethical and spiritual ideals.

HEAVEN AND HELL

Baptists. Most Baptists believe in some form of life beyond the grave. Ideas range from a nebulous, indefinable existence to a definite place, like a city of golden streets or a region of everlasting torment. Some Baptists find it difficult to reconcile the fact of an all-merciful God with endless punishment for sins committed within the short span of a lifetime on earth.

Christian Scientists. Christian Scientists believe in heaven and hell but not in a geographical sense. In the words of Mrs. Eddy: "The sinner makes his own hell by doing evil, and the saint his own heaven by doing right."

Congregationalists. Heaven and hell are not viewed as places of bliss and torment. God's justice cannot be escaped; it will be heaven to be with God and hell to be without Him.

Disciples of Christ. Practically all Disciples believe in the immortality of the soul and in a blissful reunion hereafter for all the faithful who have died in the Lord. Many doubtless believe in a literal paradise and hell. Many others are content to leave the details of future rewards and punishments in the hands of Divine mercy. Disciple faith in general is a matter of deep personal conviction.

Eastern Orthodox. Eastern Orthodoxy believes there is a heaven and a hell, and also an intermediate state between heaven and hell where souls experience a foretaste of the bliss or the punishment that will eventually be theirs.

Episcopalians. Heaven is a state in which the vision of God is enjoyed in a "life of perfect service" of God; hell is alienation from God. Episcopalians do not believe in a physical heaven or hell; these are "states of being."

Jehovah's Witnesses. Hell is a place of rest, in hope of resurrection, not an inescapable place of torture. Heaven is the habitation of spirit creatures. The reward of spiritual life with Christ Jesus in heaven for men on earth is limited to exactly 144,000. The rest of mankind who gain life in God's new world will live forever in the paradise earth. The Devil and the willfully wicked will be permanently destroyed.

Jews. Jews believe in the immortality of the soul—an immortality whose nature is known only to God—but they no longer accept the literal idea of heaven and hell.

Lutherans. Those who live and die in faith in Christ will live with Him eternally, freed from the limitations of time and space. Predictions about this eternal life must necessarily be in picture language, for it is beyond the range of finite minds. Naive descriptions of heaven and hell are inadequate, but victory over death is the certain destiny of God's people.

Methodists. Methodists believe in divine judgment after death. Goodness will be rewarded and evil punished. Concepts of heaven and hell vary from the concrete idea of golden streets and fiery furnaces to the more prevalent spiritual idea that heaven is the realm where the redeemed keep company with God and His Risen Son and hell is the state where such fellowship is absent.

Mormons. Heaven is looked to and lived for as a real place of eternal progress, with endless association with loved ones, with families and friends. For those willfully indifferent to their opportunities on earth, the knowledge that they have fallen short of their highest possible happiness will be part of the penalty of the "hell" of hereafter.

Presbyterians. Heaven and hell are not only places; they are also states of mind and character. The Bible and human experience teach us that we are living in a moral universe; therefore, sin carries its own appropriate penalty, and righteousness is its own reward, including the vision of God.

Quakers. Friends consider heaven and hell as matters for individual interpretation. They do, nonetheless, believe in life after this life.

Roman Catholics. Heaven is both a place and a state of being. The state consists essentially in seeing God "face to face." We have no knowledge of the place beyond the fact that it exists. Hell is both a place and a state of punishment. Purgatory exists to purge those souls who are not yet pure enough for heaven but have not died in a state of serious (mortal) sin.

Seventh-day Adventists. The ancient supposition that people go to heaven or hell immediately upon death is held to be an infiltration of pagan mythology into Christian theology. The dead are merely asleep until the glorious return of Christ. Then and only then will final rewards and punishments be meted out.

Unitarians. The idea that a God of Love and Mercy would want to consign a human being to eternal damnation because of wrongdoing during a relatively brief spell of mortal existence, or that God will reward the mortal doers of good with everlasting happiness appears to most Unitarians as entirely inconsistent with any moral concept of our Deity. Unitarians repudiate literal interpretations of heaven and hell as places of eternal bliss or damnation.

LORD'S SUPPER

Baptists. Sacraments are regarded by Baptists as simple, dignified ordinances with no supernatural significance and no sacramental value. The communion service is usually observed on the first Sunday of the month.

Christian Scientists. A communion service is held in all branch Churches of Christ, Scientist, twice a year. The communion celebrated is wholly spiritual, without visible elements of bread and wine.

Congregationalists. The holy communion is the ritual meal at which Christ is the host, and through which the Church's faith is confirmed and increased.

Disciples of Christ. Disciples hold to the weekly observance of the Lord's Supper. Communion is never omitted from the Sunday service.

Eastern Orthodox. Each communicant may decide for himself when he is worthy to receive holy communion. Custom holds that every member of the church should have communion at least four times a year, after proper fasting and adequate spiritual preparation: on Christmas, Easter, the Commemoration of the Apostles on June 30, and the Assumption of the Virgin Mary on August 15.

Episcopalians. Holy communion, or holy eucharist, is the chief service of worship in the Episcopal Church, though it may not always have chief place in the Sunday service. "The sacrament of the Lord's Supper was ordained for the continual remembrance of the sacrifice of the death of Christ, and of the benefits which we receive thereby."

Jehovah's Witnesses. Witnesses celebrate the memorial of Christ's death annually on the day corresponding to *Nisan* 14 of the Jewish calendar—the day Christ instituted the celebration. They consider it unscriptural to celebrate this occasion more often than once a year.

Jews. Jews cannot accept the principle of incarnation. A cardinal tenet of Judaism is that God is purely spiritual; He admits no human attributes.

Lutherans. The Lord's Supper is an encounter of the believer with the living Lord, Who is truly present in the holy communion to forgive sins and renew the spiritual life of believers. But no physical change takes place in the bread and wine.

Methodists. Methodists do not regard the Lord's Supper as the "real presence" of Christ in body and soul. God is a spirit; the body of Christ is given, taken and eaten only in a "heavenly and spiritual manner."

Mormons. The sacrament of the Lord's Supper is administered in a simple manner "in remembrance" of the Savior and as witness that "they are willing to keep His commandments."

Presbyterians. Christ is spiritually and not physically present in holy communion. The sacrament is only a commemoration of the sacrifice of Christ.

Quakers. There is no necessity for any ritual to establish relationship between man and God. Friends believe in all the sacraments but only in their inward and spiritual revelation of the Divine presence.

Roman Catholics. Catholics believe that Christ is truly and substantially present in the eucharist, body and soul, humanity and divinity, after the priest pronounces the words of consecration in the Mass. The whole substance of the bread becomes the Body of Christ, the whole substance of the wine becomes the Blood of Christ.

Seventh-day Adventists. Seventh-day Adventists celebrate the Lord's Supper in their churches about once a quarter. The consecrated bread and wine are regarded as symbols of Christ's body and blood and "show forth the Lord's death till He come."

Unitarians. Communion in Unitarian churches is a symbolic rite of remembrance and fellowship. No supernatural power of "grace" resides in this sacrament, nor does its observance automatically convey any special spiritual gift.

POSITION REGARDING OTHER RELIGIONS

Baptists. Baptists are stanch believers in the historic Baptist principle of full, complete, unrestricted religious freedom, and demand it for other religions, as well as for the adherents of no religion, just as zealously as for themselves.

Christian Scientists. The Christian Scientist does not feel superior to the adherents of any denomination. Every man is free to demonstrate the efficacy of his own faith; each is entitled to encouragement in his pursuit of spiritual objectives.

Congregationalists. Congregationalists believe in co-operation among the Christian denominations and encourage exchanges of ideas with Jewish groups. In any community they oppose religious isolationism and denominational exclusiveness.

Disciples of Christ. Disciples do not believe theirs is the only true religion; they do believe it is most nearly in accord with the practices of the early Christian churches. They never doubt the right of any man to go directly to God, by prayer, for guidance in all problems of conscience. They have no sense of rivalry among the denominations.

Episcopalians. The Church is Christ's instrument for fulfilling His purpose in the world and the means by which His continuing presence is made available. Of that one Church, Episcopalians believe they are a part; they have never claimed they are the *only* part.

Jehovah's Witnesses. Witnesses believe that theirs is the only true faith and that there is only one way to gain salvation. They do not believe that the the majority of people will meet the strict requirements of true faith.

Jews. Jews do not presume to judge the honest worshiper of any faith. "The righteous of *all* nations are worthy of immortality."

Lutherans. Lutherans believe there is only one church, but it is not any visible institution. It consists of all the congregations of believers "among whom the Gospel is preached in its purity and the holy sacraments are administered according to the Gospel." Lutherans are eager for better understanding and co-operation among Christians everywhere.

Methodists. Methodist leaders encourage tolerance and understanding toward all other religious bodies.

Mormons. The Mormon believes his is the "right way." The Church of Jesus Christ of Latter-day Saints affirms it is the "restored" Church of Jesus Christ, with the same authority, organization, and ordinances that Jesus established on earth but which were lost by centuries of change and apostasy. However, he believes in freedom of worship, as expressed in the 11th Article of Faith. "We claim the privilege of worshiping Almighty God according to the dictates of our own conscience, and allow all men the same privilege, let them worship how, where, or what they may."

Presbyterians. Presbyterians believe that every man has the right to choose and practice the faith that he personally accepts.

Quakers. To Friends, all those who do the will of the Father are brethren of Jesus in the Spirit. In their attitude toward other religions, Friends have considered that they are members of one household in the family of God.

Roman Catholics. American Catholics believe in and practice religious tolerance. However, Catholics believe that theirs is the only true religion.

Seventh-day Adventists. Seventh-day Adventists are ardent champions of religious liberty. They are opposed to all religious legislation such as "blue" laws and support the principle of separation of church and state.

Unitarians. Unitarians believe that the church should be universal in its appeal, and should welcome all men and women, of every race, color and creed, who wish to share the quest for the good life and to serve their fellow man. Every individual has the right to approach ultimate values in his own way; every religious community has the duties of creating such patterns of worship as best serve its needs.

PROPAGATION OF THE FAITH

Baptists. The historic Baptist view holds that *every* church member and every professing Christian is an evangelist. Throughout their history, Baptists have engaged in very active missionary effort at home and abroad.

Christian Scientists. The Church of Christ, Scientist, engages in no formal missionary activities. However, its Board of Lectureship, its periodicals, and its radio programs are important elements in its preaching of the gospel to all men.

Congregationalists. Missionary work is carried on in the name of Christianity through preaching of the gospel. It is not carried on to propagate Congregationalism *per se*.

Disciples of Christ. Disciples of Christ invite but do not proselytize. An offer of fellowship to any adult who wishes to take his stand by the Cross of the Risen Lord is given at the close of Sunday morning service.

Eastern Orthodox. Eastern Orthodoxy has been, from its beginnings, a missionary church. Recently, the Greek Orthodox Church has initiated missionary activities in Africa and Asia. Orthodoxy does not approve of the practice of proselytizing other Christian denominations, but genuine converts are accepted and welcomed.

Episcopalians. The Church has been active in propagation of the faith, carrying missionary work throughout the world.

Jehovah's Witnesses. Witnesses believe they have the most urgent message of all time and believe they must preach to people around the world before this generation passes away. Witnesses enter people's homes to try to convert them and they distribute literature on street corners.

Jews. Modern Judaism is not a proselytizing creed.

Lutherans. Lutherans believe that Christians are under compulsion to seek to convert all people to the Christian faith. This is a matter of doctrinal conviction.

Methodists. Methodists put much emphasis on missionary expansion and evangelistic sharing of the Gospel.

Mormons. Missionaries have been active since the 1830s in proselytizing.

Presbyterians. Presbyterianism is a decidedly missionary faith. The central core of the missionary effort is evangelistic.

Quakers. Friends do not try to make converts; they discover those who are in unity with them and nurture them until they are accorded full membership, following a written request of the applicant to become a member.

Roman Catholics. The Catholic Church from its very beginning has sent out missionaries to all nations to make known to all men the Gospel of Christ and incorporate them into His Church. Catholicism is a world-wide religion meant for all men of all races at all times.

Seventh-day Adventists. Seventh-day Adventists have missionaries all over the world and publications are issued in 228 languages. Seventh-day Adventists carry on a large health and medical work alongside their evangelistic activities.

Unitarians. Unitarians do not proselytize and do not send out missionaries.

SIN AND SALVATION

Baptists. Every true believer in Christ as personal Savior is saved—without the intervention of preacher or church. The confession of sin is a personal matter between the individual and God. Each individual must give evidence of his personal redemption by faith, good works and the Christian way of life.

Christian Scientists. Sin is the belief in the real existence of a mind or minds other than the Divine Mind, God. Christian Scientists hold that sin is unreal. If the sinner knew this, his capacity for sinning would be destroyed. Salvation consists of being saved from the illusions and delusions of mortal sense—the sense of being capable of becoming sick and dying.

Congregationalists. Sin is opposition or indifference to the will of God. God, however, is willing to forgive. When a person repents in faith, God accepts him—then he need have no fear of any future in this world or the next. He is "saved."

Disciples of Christ. Disciples, as a rule, reject the doctrine of original sin, but most believe we are all sinful creatures unless and until redeemed by the saving sacrifice of the Lord Jesus.

Episcopalians. In man, sinner because he is ridiculously proud and self-centered, there is no real "health"; by fellowship with God in Christ, he is brought into the sphere of healthy and whole life. Salvation, therefore, means that one is given the wholeness which is God's will for man, and is delivered from arrogance and selfishness. Salvation has to do not only with the "hereafter" but also with man's present earthly existence.

Jehovah's Witnesses. Sin is lawlessness. The human race was born in sin because Adam and Eve rebelled against God and His law. Salvation is only possible through the ransom sacrifice of Christ Jesus. It will come to those who conform to the conditions upon which it is offered. All must accept Christ Jesus and obey. Those who believe will be saved but the wicked will be destroyed.

Jews. Judaism does not accept the doctrine of original sin. Nor can Judaism accept the principle of vicarious atonement—the idea of salvation *through* Christ. Every man is responsible for his own salvation. Jews approach God —each man after his own fashion—without a mediator.

Lutherans. Sin is the word describing the situation of all people as disobedient to God. Sin is not specific wrongdoing (this is the result of sin), but the basic condition of our personality. Salvation is a gift from God; even the desire for salvation comes from God, and only God can save human beings.

Methodists. When men truly and earnestly repent of their sins, God forgives them. Man's salvation comes by faith and through the grace of God. Salvation means not only security in heaven after death but a present experience of God's grace and power.

Mormons. "Salvation," according to Latter-day Saints, is universal. However, "exaltation" (with the highest eternal opportunities) must be earned by obedience to laws, ordinances and commandments of the Kingdom.

Presbyterians. God pardons our sins and accepts us, not for any merit of our own, but because of our faith in the perfect obedience of Christ and His sacrificial death. Forgiveness, grace and salvation are obtained through a direct personal relationship to God. Salvation is not earned by good works but is the gift of God. Good works are the *fruits* of salvation, evidence that we are growing in grace and in the knowledge of Christ.

Quakers. Friends point to the inherent goodness in men and women, instead of emphasizing the inheritance of sin. The term "original sin" overemphasizes the power of evil. Even when he is fallen, man still belongs to God, who continues to appeal to the goodness within him.

Roman Catholics. Catholics believe in original sin and in the possibility of a man's damning himself for all eternity by deliberately and knowingly disobeying the law of God. Catholics believe that men are saved by faith and good works. Salvation comes through the Church but is not limited to visible members of the Church, in the case of those who are invincibly ignorant of the Church's divine authority.

Seventh-day Adventists. Salvation is by grace alone. Keeping the commandments is the result, the evidence of salvation.

Unitarians. Unitarians recognize the evil in our world and man's responsibility for much of it. They do not believe in original sin. Man has innate capacities for both good and evil. His natural tendency for good can grow through proper environment, effective education and spiritual awareness. Unitarians believe in "salvation by character." If a man is to be "saved," his God-given mental capacity and his potential for good will will save him—here, and hereafter.

THE TRINITY

Baptists. The doctrine of the Trinity is accepted by Baptists, who leave its sublime mystery to interpretation by theologians.

Christian Scientists. By the Trinity, Christian Scientists mean the unity of Father, Son, and Holy Spirit, but do not accept the Trinity as three persons in one. Life, Truth and Love are "the triune Principle called God."

Congregationalists. Congregationalists believe fully in the Holy Trinity.

Disciples of Christ. Disciples are not bothered by speculation about the Holy Trinity and the nature of a triune God. They baptize into the name of the Father, Son, and Holy Spirit, as Christ commanded. They believe that the Holy Spirit is the Comforter promised in the New Testament, but they do not worry over its constitution or the nature of its operation, accepting its guidance as constantly enlarging the horizons of Christian thought.

Eastern Orthodox. God is one in substance and a trinity in persons. Orthodoxy worships one God in the Trinity and the trinity in unity, neither confusing the persons nor dividing the substance. The Orthodox believe that our Lord Jesus Christ, while truly God, begotten of the same substance as the Father and consubstantial with Him, is also truly a man in every respect except sin.

Episcopalians. In light of man's experience of God's working in the world, it is seen that God *is* as He *reveals* Himself. He is Creative Reality (God the Father); He is Expressive Act (God the Son); He is Responsive Power (God the Holy Spirit). He is one God experienced in a "trinitarian" fashion.

Jehovah's Witnesses. Witnesses believe that Jehovah God and Christ Jesus are two distinct persons and are not combined with a so-called "Holy Ghost" in one godhead called a Trinity.

Jews. Jews do not accept the divinity of Christ and therefore cannot accept the concept of the Trinity. The Lord is One.

Lutherans. Lutherans believe in the Trinity as one God in three personalities.

Methodists. The meaning of the Trinity is not fully understood. The doctrine is the expression of the three aspects in our experience of God: the Creator, the Father; the historical personality of Christ, the Son; a pervading and continuing presence and power in our lives, the Holy Spirit. The Trinity is also the formula for understanding the personality of God. God is Love, Love must have an object. Before Creation God must have loved Christ. The divine activity linking the Father with the object of his love is the Holy Spirit.

Mormons. The Latter-day Saint accepts the Godhead as three literal, distinct personalities: God the Father; His Son, Jesus the Christ (who is one with the Father in purpose and in thought, but separate from Him in physical fact); and the Holy Ghost, a Personage of Spirit. This interpretation is derived from literal scriptural language.

Presbyterians. Presbyterians think of God not as three individuals, but as three manifestations of One.

Quakers. There is wide freedom for personal opinion regarding the Trinity. Friends tend to believe in the immanence of God rather than His transcendence.

Roman Catholics. Catholics believe in one God, in whom there are three Divine Persons co-equal in all things. The doctrine of the Holy Trinity is a central mystery of the Catholic faith.

Seventh-day Adventists. Seventh-day Adventists worship Father, Son and Holy Spirit—"three Persons in one God."

Unitarians. Unitarians do not believe in the Trinity but in one God.

VIRGIN BIRTH

Baptists. A great majority undoubtedly accept the Virgin Birth. A substantial minority do not. Since Baptists have no authoritarian creed to control their faith and practice, each local parish has the right to decide whether or not to make acceptance of the doctrine of the Virgin Birth a condition of church membership.

Christian Scientists. Christian Scientists accept completely the Virgin Birth.

Congregationalists. Probably the majority do not accept the doctrine of the Virgin Birth; undoubtedly many do. The fact of Christ, and not the manner in which he was born, is held to be of dominant importance.

Disciples of Christ. It is probable that a vast majority believe in the Virgin Birth; it is possible that others have doubts. There is no ecclesiastical or denominational authority that can declare one belief to be orthodox and reject the other as heretical.

Eastern Orthodox. The Orthodoxy hold that Christ was conceived and born without original sin.

Episcopalians. The creeds and the liturgy of the Episcopal Church assert the traditional belief that Jesus was born of Mary without human father. There is disagreement within the Church, not on the *theological* meaning of the Virgin Birth, but on its biological detail. Most Episcopalians probably accept it as literally true; some regard it as symbolic in character.

Jehovah's Witnesses. Witnesses believe that Jesus was born miraculously, a virgin birth in fulfillment of the prophecy of Isaiah 7:14.

Jews. Jews do not believe in the doctrine of the Virgin Birth.

Lutherans. Lutherans affirm the Apostles' Creed as a basic summary of belief, including "born of the Virgin Mary." However, Lutherans do not go on to the extra-Biblical doctrines regarding the perpetual virginity of Mary.

Methodists. The great majority accept the Virgin Birth literally. Some would distinguish the biological aspects from the theological implications. As long as a Methodist believes in the Deity of Christ, it is not necessary for him to believe that Christ was begotten without a human father.

Mormons. The Latter-day Saint accepts the miraculous conception of Jesus the Christ.

Presbyterians. A majority of Presbyterians undoubtedly believe in the Virgin Birth. Some find a symbolic rather than a physical meaning in the accounts of the birth of Jesus.

Quakers. The question of the Virgin Birth does not seem as important a problem for Quakers as the meaning and teaching of Christ's life on earth and His continuing power to reveal Himself at all times and to all seekers.

Roman Catholics. Catholics believe in the Virgin Birth and believe that Mary remained a virgin throughout her life.

Seventh-day Adventists. Seventh-day Adventists accept the Virgin Birth as one of the vital truths of the Christian faith, foretold in the Old Testament and confirmed in the New.

Unitarians. Unitarians repudiate the dogma or doctrine of the Virgin Birth.

Church Holy Days and Religious Observances

1. CALENDAR AND DESCRIPTION OF RELIGIOUS OBSERVANCES: ALL FAITHS

Compiled from the following sources: the *Information Please Almanac, 1962,* Dan Golenpaul Associates, New York, N. Y., pp. 326-28; the *School Calendar; indicating Holidays and Holy Days,* prepared by Community Relations Service, The American Jewish Committee, 165 East 56 Street, New York, N. Y.

Editor's Note: In determining church holidays, both the lunar and the solar calendars are used. Dates determined by the lunar calendar are generally movable; *those determined by the solar calendar are* fixed. *Movable holidays are indicated by an asterisk(*).*

New Year's Day—January 1—Protestant and Catholic Holy Day. Ecclesiastically the New Year celebrates the Feast of Circumcision.

Feast of Epiphany—January 6—Falls the twelfth day after Christmas and commemorates the manifestation of Jesus as the Son of God, as represented by the adoration of the Magi, the baptism of Jesus, and the miracle of the wine at the marriage feast at Cana. Epiphany originally marked the beginning of the carnival season preceding Lent, and the evening (sometimes the eve) is known as Twelfth Night.

***Shrove Tuesday**—Falls the day before Ash Wednesday and marks the end of the carnival season, which once began on Epiphany but is now usually celebrated the last three days before Lent. In France, the day is known as Mardi Gras (Fat Tuesday), and Mardi Gras celebrations are also held in several American cities, particularly in New Orleans. The day is sometimes called Pancake Tuesday by the English because fats, which were prohibited during Lent, had to be used up.

***Ash Wednesday**—The first day of the Lenten season, which lasts forty days. Having its origin sometime before A.D. 1000, it is a day of public penance and is marked in the Roman Catholic Church by the burning of the palms blessed on the previous Palm Sunday. With his thumb, the priest then marks a cross upon the forehead of each worshiper. The Anglican Church and a few Protestant groups in the United States also observe the day, but generally without the use of ashes.

***Purim (Feast of Esther)**—The Biblical Book of Esther is read in the synagogue and there is general merry-making in the home. Gifts are exchanged and also distributed to the poor.

***Palm Sunday**—Is observed the Sunday before Easter to commemorate the entry of Jesus into Jerusalem. The procession and the ceremonies introducing the benediction of palms probably had their origin in Jerusalem.

***Holy Week**—All the days of the week preceding Easter have special connotation as they relate to the events of the last days in Jesus's life. Beginning with Palm Sunday, each of these days takes on a special importance.

***Holy Thursday (in Holy Week)**—This day is marked by the sacrament of holy communion in remembrance of the Last Supper which Jesus had with His disciples.

***Good Friday**—This day commemorates the Crucifixion, which is retold during services from the Gospel according to Saint John. A feature in Roman Catholic churches is the Liturgy of the Passion: there is no Consecration, the Host having been consecrated the previous day. The eating of hot cross buns on this day is said to have started in England.

***Easter Sunday**—Observed in all Christian churches, Easter commemorates the Resurrection of Jesus. It is celebrated on the first Sunday after the full moon which occurs on or next after March 21 and is therefore celebrated between March 22 and April 25 inclusive. This date was fixed by the Council of Nicaea in 325.

***First Day of Passover** *(Pesach)—(Nisan* 15)—The Feast of the Passover, also called the Feast of Unleavened Bread, commemorates the escape of the first-born of the Jews from the Angel of Death. As the Jews fled Egypt, they ate unleavened bread, and from that time the Jews have allowed no leavening in the houses during Passover, bread being replaced by matzoth.

***Second Day of Passover.**

***Conclusion and Last Day of Passover** (8th Day).

***Greek Orthodox Palm Sunday**—Commemorates the triumphal entry of Jesus into Jerusalem. First day of Greek Orthodox Holy Week.

***Greek Orthodox Holy Thursday**—Commemorates the Last Supper at which Jesus instituted the sacrament of holy communion.

***Greek Orthodox Holy Friday** (Good Friday)—Commemorates the Passion and Crucifixion of Jesus.

***Greek Orthodox Easter.**

***Ascension Day**—Took place in the presence of His apostles 40 days after the Resurrection of Jesus. It is traditionally held to have occurred on Mount Olivet in Bethany.

***Pentecost** (Whitsunday)—This day commemorates the descent of the Holy Ghost upon the apostles fifty days after the Resurrection. The sermon by the apostle Peter, which led to the baptism of 3,000 who professed belief, originated the ceremonies that have since been followed. "Whitsunday" is believed to have come from "white Sunday" when, among the English, white robes were worn by those baptized on the day.

***First Day of Shabuoth** (Hebrew Pentecost)—(*Sivan* 6)—This festival, sometimes called the Feast of Weeks, or of Harvest, or of the First Fruits, falls fifty days after Passover and originally celebrated the end of the seven-week grain-harvesting season. In later tradition, it also celebrated the giving of the law to Moses on Mt. Sinai, and both aspects have come down to the present.

***Fast of Ab** (*Tishah B'ab*)—A day of mourning in memory of the destruction of the Temple.

Feast of the Assumption—August 15—The principal feast of the Blessed Virgin, this holy day commemorates two events: the happy departure of Mary from this life and the assumption of her body into heaven.

***First Day of Rosh Hashanah** (Jewish New Year)—(*Tishri* 1)—This day marks the beginning of the Jewish year and opens the Ten Days of Penitence, closing with Yom Kippur.

***Yom Kippur** (Day of Atonement)—(*Tishri* 10)—This day marks the end of the Ten Days of Penitence that began with Rosh Hashanah and is the holiest day of the Jewish year. It is described in *Leviticus* as the "Sabbath of Sabbaths," and synagogue services begin the preceding sundown, resume the following morning, and continue through the day to sundown.

***First Day of Sukkoth** (Feast of Tabernacles)—(*Tishri* 15)—This festival, also known as the Feast of the Ingathering, originally celebrated the fruit harvest; the name comes from the booths or tabernacles in which the Jews lived during the harvest, although one tradition traces it to the shelters used by the Jews in their wandering through the wilderness. During the festival many Jews build small huts in their back yards or on the roofs of houses.

***Eighth Day of the Feast of Tabernacles**—This marks the climax of the Jewish Holy Day season. Prayers for rain are recited in the synagogue.

***Simhath Torah** (Rejoicing of the Law)—The Reading of the Law is concluded and re-commenced. Gaiety is the characteristic mood of the day combined with a spirit of reverence.

Reformation Day—October 31—The date which is regarded as the beginning of the Protestant Reformation observed in many Protestant churches.

All Saints' Day—November 1—This is a Roman Catholic and Anglican holiday celebrating all saints, known and unknown.

*****First Sunday in Advent**—Advent is the season in which the faithful must prepare themselves for the advent of the Savior on Christmas. The four Sundays before Christmas are marked by special church services.

Feast of the Immaculate Conception—December 8—Catholic Holy Day of Obligation. Celebrating Mary's privilege of freedom from sin from the first moment of her conception as the child of Saint Joachim and Saint Anne.

*****First Day of Hanukkah** (Festival of Lights)—*(Kisler* 25*)*—This festival was instituted by Judas Maccabaeus in 165 B.C. to celebrate the purification of the Temple of Jerusalem, which had been desecrated three years earlier by Antiochus Epiphanes, who set up a pagan altar and offered sacrifices to Zeus Olympius. In Jewish homes, a light is lighted the first night, and on each succeeding night of the eight-day festival, another is lighted.

Christmas (Feast of the Nativity)—December 25—The most widely celebrated holiday of the Christian year, Christmas is observed as the anniversary of the birth of Jesus. Christmas customs are centuries old. The mistletoe, for example, comes from the Druids, who, in hanging the mistletoe, hoped for peace and good fortune. Use of such plants as holly comes from the ancient belief that such plants blossomed at Christmas. Comparatively recent is the Christmas tree, first set up in Germany in the seventeenth century, and the use of candles on trees developed from the belief that candles appeared by miracle on the trees at Christmas. Colonial Manhattan Islanders introduced the name Santa Claus, a corruption of the Dutch name for the fourth-century Asia Minor St. Nicholas.

2. TABLES OF MOVABLE HOLIDAYS: CHRISTIAN AND JEWISH

Adapted from 1962 *Information Please Almanac,* Dan Golenpaul Associates, eds., Simon and Schuster, New York, 1962, p. 326.

Movable Holidays, 1962 to 1971

CHRISTIAN AND SECULAR

Year	Ash Wed.	Easter	Pentecost	1st Sunday Advent
1962	Mar. 7	Apr. 22	June 10	Dec. 2
1963	Feb. 27	Apr. 14	June 2	Dec. 1
1964	Feb. 12	Mar. 29	May 17	Nov. 29
1965	Mar. 3	Apr. 18	June 6	Nov. 28
1966	Feb. 23	Apr. 10	May 29	Nov. 27
1967	Feb. 8	Mar. 26	May 14	Dec. 3
1968	Feb. 28	Apr. 14	June 2	Dec. 1
1969	Feb. 19	Apr. 6	May 25	Nov. 30
1970	Feb. 11	Mar. 29	May 17	Nov. 29
1971	Feb. 24	Apr. 11	May 30	Nov. 28

Shrove Tuesday: 1 day before Ash Wednesday.
Palm Sunday: 7 days before Easter.
Maundy Thursday: 3 days before Easter.
Good Friday: 2 days before Easter.

Holy Saturday: 1 day before Easter.
Ascension Day: 10 days before Pentecost.
Trinity Sunday: 7 days after Pentecost.
Corpus Christi: 11 days after Pentecost.

JEWISH

Year	Purim	1st day Passover	1st day Shabuoth	1st day Rosh Hashanah	Yom Kippur	1st day Sukkoth	Simhath Torah	1st day Hanukkah
1962	Mar. 20	Apr. 19	June 8	Sept. 29	Oct. 8	Oct. 13	Oct 21	Dec. 22
1963	Mar. 10	Apr. 9	May 29	Sept. 19	Sept. 28	Oct. 3	Oct. 11	Dec. 11
1964	Feb. 27	Mar. 28	May 17	Sept. 7	Sept. 16	Sept. 21	Sept. 29	Nov. 30
1965	Mar. 18	Apr. 17	June 6	Sept. 27	Oct. 6	Oct. 11	Oct. 19	Dec. 19
1966	Mar. 6	Apr. 5	May 25	Sept. 15	Sept. 24	Sept. 29	Oct. 7	Dec. 8
1967	Mar. 26	Apr. 25	June 14	Oct. 5	Oct. 14	Oct. 19	Oct. 27	Dec. 27
1968	Mar. 14	Apr. 13	June 2	Sept. 23	Oct. 2	Oct. 7	Oct. 15	Dec. 16
1969	Mar. 4	Apr. 3	May 23	Sept. 13	Sept. 22	Sept. 27	Oct. 5	Dec. 5
1970	Mar. 14	Apr. 15	June 6	Oct. 1	Oct. 10	Oct. 15	Oct. 30	Oct. 25
1971	Mar. 10	Apr. 10	May 30	Sept. 20	Sept. 29	Oct. 4	Oct. 12	Dec. 13

Length of Jewish holidays (O = Orthodox, C = Conservative, R = Reform)

Passover: O & C, 8 days (holy days: first 2 and last 2); R, 7 days (holy days: first and last).
Shabuoth: O & C, 2 days; R, 1st day.
Rosh Hashanah: O & C, 2 days; R, 1 day.
Yom Kippur: All groups, 1 day.
Sukkoth: All groups, 7 days (holy days: O & C, first 2; R, first only). O & C observe two additional days:

Shemini Atsereth (Eighth Day of the Feast) and Simhath Torah (Rejoicing of the Law). R observes Shemini Atsereth but not Simhath Torah.
Hanukkah: All groups, 8 days.

NOTE: All holidays begin at sundown on the even-before the date given.

3. CATHOLIC HOLY DAYS, OBSERVANCES AND FEASTS

3a. Holy Days of Obligation for the United States

From the *National Catholic Almanac, 1955,* St. Anthony's Guild, Paterson, New Jersey.

Every Catholic who has attained the age of reason, and is not prevented by sickness or other sufficient cause, is obliged to rest from servile work and attend Holy Mass on the following days:

All Sundays of the year.
The Circumcision of Our Lord (New Year's Day), January 1.
The Ascension of Our Lord (40 days after Easter).
The Assumption of the Blessed Virgin Mary, August 15.
All Saints' Day, November 1.
The Immaculate Conception of the Blessed Virgin Mary (Patronal Feast of the United States), December 8.
Christmas, the Nativity of Our Lord, December 25.

3b. Principal Catholic Devotions

From the *National Catholic Almanac, 1955,* St. Anthony's Guild, Paterson, New Jersey.

Angelus, The, commemorates the Incarnation of Christ. It consists of three versicles, three Hail Marys, and a special prayer, and recalls the announcement to Mary by the Archangel Gabriel that she was chosen to be the Mother of Christ, her acceptance of the divine will, and the Incarnation. The practice of reciting the Hail Mary in honor of the Incarnation was introduced by the Franciscans in 1263. The Regina Caeli, commemorating the joy of Mary at Christ's Resurrection, replaces the Angelus during the Easter season.

Benediction is a short exposition of the Blessed Sacrament for adoration by the faithful. At the close of the exposition, the priest makes the Sign of the Cross with the Blessed Sacrament over the people. Benediction closes with recitation of the Divine Praises.

Enthronement of the Sacred Heart, The, in the home is the acknowledgment of the sovereignty of Jesus Christ over the Christian family, expressed by installation of an image or picture of the Sacred Heart in a place of honor, accompanied by a prescribed act of consecration. **Night Adoration** in the home, which consists of one hour of adoration once a month between the hours of 9 P.M. and 6 A.M. by one or more persons, or even the entire family, is connected with the Enthronement, though distinct from it. Its purpose is to make reparation for the sins of families.

First Friday devotion is the practice of receiving holy communion on the first Friday of nine consecutive months in honor of the Sacred Heart of Jesus and in reparation for sin. Christ promised the grace of final penitence to those who would make the nine First Fridays.

First Saturday devotion had its origin in the promise of Mary at Fatima in 1917 to obtain the graces necessary to salvation for those who, besides going to confession, would on the first Saturday of five consecutive months receive holy communion, recite five decades of the Rosary, and meditate on the mysteries for fifteen minutes.

Five Wounds, The, of Christ are honored as the channels through which His Precious Blood flowed for the redemption of mankind.

Forty Hours Adoration, The, is the solemn exposition of the Blessed Sacrament for forty hours, in memory of the time Christ's Body lay in the tomb, and for the purpose of making reparation for sin and begging God's graces. The devotion, which includes the celebration of special Masses, the holding of processions and recitation of the Litany of the Saints, was first instituted in Milan in 1534.

Immaculate Heart of Mary, The, devotion was first propagated by Saint John Eudes (d. 1680), and was revived and increased after the apparitions of Mary at Fatima in 1917. In keeping with her expressed wishes there, Pope Pius XII consecrated the world to the Immaculate Heart of Mary in 1942; three years later he extended the feast of this title to the universal Church. Recitation of the Rosary and observance of the five First Saturdays are elements of this devotion. (*See above.*)

Infant Jesus of Prague, The, devotion began in the early seventeenth century in Prague, Bohemia. Princess Polixena of Prague presented the Carmelites there with a statue of the Infant which was lost and forgotten when war and persecution befell the city. After recovery of the statue some years later devotions were instituted and became widespread.

Little Office of the Blessed Virgin, The, consists of psalms, lessons, hymns, and prayers in honor of the Blessed Virgin, arranged in seven hours like the Divine Office. The Little Office was probably written about the middle of the eighth century. It is recited by most religious communities of women, other religious, and many lay persons.

Miraculous Medal, The, devotion owes its origin to apparitions made by Mary to Saint Catharine Laboure in 1830. In the course of the apparitions the Blessed Virgin revealed the form and elements of the Miraculous

Medal, which was first struck in 1832. Wearing of the medal is indulgenced. Devotion to Mary under the title of Our Lady of the Miraculous Medal is widespread. The feast of this title is observed November 27.

Mother of Sorrows, The, devotion consists of the recitation of approved prayers, a sermon on the Blessed Virgin, the Via Matris and Benediction of the Most Blessed Sacrament. The **Via Matris,** or Stations of the Cross of Our Sorrowful Mother, represents her seven Sorrows.

Precious Blood, The, devotion honors the Blood of Christ as the price of His redemption of mankind. The feast is observed July 1.

Rosary, The, is a form of prayer in honor of Our Lady made up of a series of ten "Hail Marys" or decades, each beginning with an "Our Father" and ending with a "Glory be to the Father." The Apostles' Creed and the Hail, Holy Queen are also recited in the Rosary. The complete Rosary is made up of fifteen decades. While reciting the prayers of each decade a person meditates on **Mysteries of the Rosary,** which commemorate events in the life of Mary and Christ. The mysteries are **Joyful**—Annunciation, Visitation, Nativity of Christ, Presentation, Finding of the Christ Child in the Temple; **Sorrowful**—Agony in the Garden, Scourging at the Pillar, Crowning with Thorns, Carrying the Cross, Crucifixion; **Glorious**—Resurrection, Ascension, Descent of the Holy Spirit upon the Apostles, Assumption, Coronation of Mary as Queen of Heaven. Rosary beads are used to aid in counting the prayers without distraction. Recitation of the Rosary is highly indulgenced. A common practice is the recitation of five decades daily. The Blessed Virgin confirmed the efficacy of this devotion by an appearance to Saint Dominic in the thirteenth century when he was preaching in opposition to the Albigensian heresy.

Sacred Heart, The, devotion is directed to the humanity of Christ which is personally united with His divinity. In adoring the Heart of Christ, persons adore Christ Himself. The devotion was revealed by Christ to Saint Margaret Mary Alacoque in the seventeenth century. He asked that a feast of reparation (now the feast of the Sacred Heart) be instituted. The Holy Hour and the Communion of Reparation on the first Friday of each month are special manifestations of the devotion. Christ made the **12 Promises of the Sacred Heart** to Saint Margaret Mary: I will give them all the graces necessary in their state of life.—I will establish peace in their homes.—I will comfort them in all their afflictions.—I will be their secure refuge during life and above all in death.—I will bestow abundant blessing upon all their undertakings.—Sinners shall find in My Heart the source and the infinite ocean of mercy.—By devotion to My Heart tepid souls shall grow fervent.—Fervent souls shall quickly mount to high perfection.—I will bless every place where a picture of My Heart shall be set up and honored.—I will give to priests the gift of touching the most hardened hearts.—Those who promote this devotion shall have their names written in My Heart, never to be blotted out.—I will grant the grace of final penitence to those who communicate on the first Friday of nine consecutive months. (*See* Enthronement of, *above*.)

Seven Sorrows or **Seven Dolors** of the Blessed Virgin Mary is a form of prayer in honor of the seven Sorrows: prophecy of Simeon, flight into Egypt, loss of Jesus in the temple of Jerusalem, meeting Jesus on the way to Calvary, crucifixion, removal of the sacred Body from the Cross, burial of Jesus. Seven Hail Marys are said during a meditation on each of these Sorrows. A chaplet of beads is used to count the prayers.

Stations of the Cross, The, is a series of meditations on the sufferings endured by Christ during His Passion. The subjects of the meditations: Jesus is condemned to death by Pilate, Jesus carries His Cross, Jesus falls the first time, Jesus meets His Mother Mary, Simon of Cyrene helps Jesus carry the Cross, Veronica wipes the face of Jesus, Jesus falls the second time, Jesus speaks to the women of Jerusalem, Jesus falls the third time, Jesus is stripped of His garments, Jesus is nailed to the Cross, Jesus dies upon the Cross, Jesus is taken down from the Cross, Jesus is buried in the tomb. Depictions of these scenes (pictures or sculptured-pieces surmounted by crosses) are mounted in most churches and chapels. The person making the Way of the Cross passes in succession before each of these stations, pausing at each for the required meditations. Pilgrims to the Holy Land make the Stations by visiting places at which these events of the Passion occurred. The Stations of the Cross is highly indulgenced.

Those at sea, prisoners, the sick, residents of pagan countries, and others who are unable to make the Stations in their ordinary form, may gain all the indulgences provided they hold in their hand a crucifix blessed for this purpose **(Stations Crucifix),** and recite with the proper sentiments Our Father, Hail Mary, and Glory once for each Station, five times in honor of the Wounds of Our Lord, and once for the Pope's intention.

Those whose grave bodily infirmity prevents their making even the shorter Way of the Cross described above, may gain all the indulgences if they contritely kiss, or at least fix their eyes upon, a crucifix blessed for this purpose, and recite if possible some short prayer or ejaculation in memory of the Passion and Death of Christ.

Three Hours' Agony, The, is a devotion practiced on Good Friday in memory of the three hours Christ hung upon the Cross. It usually begins at twelve o'clock, when Christ was nailed to the Cross, includes prayers, hymns, and meditations upon His sufferings and His seven last words, and ends at three o'clock, the hour of His death.

Vespers and Compline are parts of the Divine Office which must be said daily by priests, men in major orders, and solemnly professed religious.

The order of Vespers is as follows: (1) five psalms, each with an antiphon; (2) capitulum, or little chapter; (3) a hymn; (4) versicle and response; (5) the Magnificat, with its antiphon; (6) the prayer; (7) conclusion, after which comes an anthem to the Blessed Virgin. There are four anthems, sung according to the season.

The order of Compline is as follows: (1) Confiteor, followed by three psalms with antiphon; (2) hymn "Te Lucis ante Terminum"; (3) a little chapter, with responses; (4) the canticle of Simeon, "Nunc Dimittis"; (5) the prayer, "Visita, Quaesumus"; (6) one of the four anthems used at Vespers.

3c. Principal Catholic Feasts

From the *National Catholic Almanac, 1955,* St. Anthony's Guild, Paterson, New Jersey.

The Circumcision, January 1, commemorates the circumcision of Christ eight days after His birth, according to the Jewish law, His initiation into the Jewish religion, and His reception of the name Jesus which Archangel Gabriel had made known to Mary at the Annunciation. It is a holy day of obligation in the U.S.

The Epiphany, January 6, commemorates Christ's manifestation of Himself to the Gentiles as represented by the Three Kings of the East who, guided by a star, came to adore Him in His infancy. It also marks Christ's manifestations of Himself near the beginning of His public life, when He was baptized by John the Baptist and when He performed His first recorded miracle at the marriage feast in Cana.

The Purification, February 2, commemorates the purification of the Blessed Mother forty days after the birth of Christ and the presentation of Christ in the Temple according to the prescriptions of Leviticus 12:2-8; Exodus 13:2. The feast is also called **Candlemas,** because candles for use during the year are blessed on this day and commemoration is made of the fact that Christ is, in the words of Simeon, "A light to the revelation of the Gentiles and the glory of His people Israel."

Ash Wednesday, first day of the penitential season of Lent, is so called because of the blessing of ashes and their use to remind the faithful: "Remember, man, that thou art dust and unto dust thou shalt return." The priest says these words as, with ashes, he makes the sign of the cross on each person's forehead.

The Annunciation, March 25, commemorates the announcement by the Archangel Gabriel to Mary that she was to become the Mother of Christ, the Second Person of the Blessed Trinity made Man.

Holy Week and Easter

Palm Sunday, the first day of Holy Week, commemorates Christ's triumphant entry into Jerusalem. It receives its name from the palm branches which the people spread under the feet of Jesus, crying out, "Hosanna to the Son of David! Blessed is He Who comes in the name of the Lord!" On this day palms are blessed and distributed to the faithful.

Holy Thursday, or **Maundy Thursday,** occurs in Holy Week and commemorates the institution of the holy eucharist by Christ at the Last Supper the night before He died. There is only one Mass in each church on this day; white vestments are used because of the joyful commemoration, but at the same time there are certain signs of the mourning proper to Holy Week, such as the silencing of the bells. The celebrant consecrates two Hosts, one of which he receives, while the other is placed in a chalice and carried in solemn procession to an altar prepared for Its reception, called the **Altar of Repose or Repository.** Here It remains for the adoration of the faithful until Good Friday when It is taken back to the high altar and received by the priest at the communion in the Mass of the Presanctified. After the procession of the Blessed Sacrament on Holy Thursday, the altars are stripped to recall the fact that Christ was stripped of His garments. Then follows the washing of the feet, known as the "Mandatum," from the first word of the antiphon recited during the ceremony; whence the name "Maundy" Thursday. Christ washed the feet of the apostles at the Last Supper.

Good Friday commemorates the Passion and Crucifixion of Christ. The liturgy is in every way of an exceptional character, befitting the day of the Great Atonement. The distinctive feature is the **Mass of the Presanctified,** in which there is no Consecration, the Host having been consecrated in the Mass the day before. The service consists of (1) lessons from Holy Scripture and prayers, terminating with the chanting of the Passion; (2) solemn supplication for all conditions of men; (3) veneration of the Holy Cross; (4) procession of the Blessed Sacrament from the Repository and the priest's communion, or the Mass of the Presanctified proper.

Holy Saturday is the day before Easter. During the eighth century the custom began of anticipating the Saturday night liturgy, which originally continued into Easter day and hence is full of the Resurrection spirit. This explains the joyous character of the Mass, and the fact that the history of the Resurrection is sung in the Gospel. The ceremonies begin early in the morning with the blessing of the new fire and the Paschal Candle, which is followed by the reading of the twelve prophecies. The priest then goes in procession to bless the baptismal font, and the water is scattered toward the four quarters of the world to indicate the catholicity of the Church and the world-wide efficacy of her sacraments. Solemn High Mass is then sung, white vestments are used, flowers and candles are set upon the altar, statues are unveiled, the organ is heard, and the bells, silent since Holy Thursday, are joyfully rung. Lent ends officially at noon on this day.

Easter Sunday or **The Resurrection** commemorates Christ's rising from the dead by His own power on the third day after His Crucifixion. The feast occurs on the first Sunday after the first full moon after the vernal equinox, or March 21.

The Invention or **Finding of the Holy Cross,** May 3, commemorates the finding of the true Cross by Saint Helena, in 326, after it had been hidden by the infidels and buried for 180 years.

The Patronage of Saint Joseph, on the third Wednesday after Easter, honors Saint Joseph as the Patron of the Universal Church. Saint Joseph is also commemorated by a special feast observed on March 19.

The Ascension, forty days after Easter, commemorates Christ's Ascension into heaven from Mount Olivet, in the presence of His Blessed Mother and His Apostles and disciples. It is a holy day of obligation in the United States.

Pentecost or **Whitsunday,** fifty days after Easter, commemorates the descent of the Holy Spirit upon the apostles, in the form of fiery tongues. It is the birthday of the Catholic Church. The word "Pentecost" means "fiftieth." The name Whitsunday recalls the white garments worn by catechumens who were admitted to baptism on the eve of Pentecost.

Trinity Sunday, the first Sunday after Pentecost, commemorates the mystery of One God in Three Divine Persons.

Corpus Christi, the Thursday after Trinity Sunday, is the feast day of the holy eucharist, on which special honor is paid to Christ truly present in this sacrament under the appearances of bread and wine. The purpose of the feast is to make reparation for sins committed against the Blessed Sacrament and to kindle devotion to the eucharist. Solemn ceremonies include a procession of the Blessed Sacrament, which may be held on the following Sunday.

Sacred Heart, the Friday after the Octave of Corpus Christi, commemorates the love of the God-Man Christ for men. An act of reparation is recited in all churches on this feast.

SS. Peter and Paul, June 29, honors the Prince of the Apostles and the great Apostle of the Gentiles who were both martyred on this day at Rome.

The Precious Blood, July 1, honors the Blood of Christ shed for the redemption of mankind.

The Visitation, July 2, commemorates Mary's visit to her cousin Saint Elizabeth after the Annunciation.

The Assumption, August 15, commemorates the taking into heaven of the Blessed Virgin, soul and body, at the end of her life on earth. It is a holy day of obligation in the United States.

The Immaculate Heart of Mary, August 22, honors the Blessed Virgin and commemorates the consecration of the world to her Immaculate Heart by Pope Pius XII in 1942. The feast also urges remembrance of the message of Our Lady of Fatima.

The Nativity of the Blessed Virgin, September 8, commemorates the birth of Mary.

The Exaltation of the Holy Cross, September 14, commemorates the recovery of the Cross from the Persians by Heraclius, King of Judea.

Saint Michael or **Michaelmas,** September 29, honors the Archangel Michael, prince of the angels and patron of the Church.

Christ the King, the last Sunday of October, commemorates the Kingship of Christ and His rule over the world.

All Saints, November 1, honors all the saints in heaven, especially those who have no set feasts during the year. It is a holy day of obligation in the United States.

All Souls' Day, November 2, is a day set apart for the Church to pray for all the faithful departed in purgatory. All priests may say three Masses on this day.

The Presentation of the Blessed Virgin Mary, November 21, commemorates Mary's presentation in the Temple of Jerusalem by her parents, SS. Joachim and Anne.

The Immaculate Conception, December 8, commemorates the preservation of the Blessed Virgin from the stain of original sin from the moment of her conception. It is the patronal feast of the United States, and a holy day of obligation.

Christmas or **The Nativity,** December 25, commemorates the birth of Christ. It is a holy day of obligation. Priests may say three Masses on this day.

3d. Formula for Unified Regulations on Fast and Abstinence

[The regulations below are the official text submitted to Catholics. These regulations were drawn from the report of the Bishop's Committee on Fast and Abstinence, and were submitted to the Catholic hierarchy at the annual meeting in Washington, D.C., November 14–16, 1951.]

Regulations on Fast and Abstinence To foster the spirit of penance and of reparation for sin, to encourage self-denial and mortification, and to guide her children in the footsteps of Our Divine Savior, Holy Mother Church imposes by law the observance of fast and abstinence.

In accordance with the provisions of Canon Law, as modified through the use of special faculties granted by the Holy See, we herewith publish the following regulations:

On Abstinence Everyone over 7 years of age is bound to observe the law of abstinence.

Complete abstinence is to be observed on Fridays, Ash Wednesday, the Vigils of the Assumption and Christmas, and on Holy Saturday morning. On days of complete abstinence meat and soup or gravy made from meat may not be used at all.

Partial abstinence is to be observed on Ember Wednesdays and Saturdays and on the Vigils of Pentecost and All Saints. On days of partial abstinence meat and soup or gravy made from meat may be taken only *once* a day at the principal meal.

On Fast Everyone over 21 and under 59 years of age is also bound to observe the law of fast.

The days of fast are the weekdays of Lent, Ember Days, the Vigils of Pentecost, the Assumption, All Saints and Christmas.

On days of fast only one full meal is allowed. Two other meatless meals, sufficient to maintain strength, may be taken according to each one's needs; but together they should not equal another full meal. Meat may be taken at the principal meal on a day of fast except on Fridays, Ash Wednesday and the Vigils of the Assumption and Christmas.

Eating between meals is not permitted; but liquids, including milk and fruit juices, are allowed.

When health or ability to work would be seriously affected, the law does not oblige. In doubt concerning fast or abstinence, a parish priest or confessor should be consulted.

We earnestly exhort the faithful during the periods of fast and abstinence to attend daily Mass; to receive holy communion often; to take part more frequently in exercises of piety; to give generously to works of religion and charity; to perform acts of kindness toward the sick, the aged and the poor; to practice voluntary self-denial especially regarding alcoholic drink and worldly amusements; and to pray more frequently, particularly for the intentions of the Holy Father.

4. JEWISH HOLIDAYS

Extracts from a pamphlet by Mordecai Soltes, The National Jewish Welfare Board, New York, 1952.

A DISTINGUISHING characteristic of the Jewish religion is its emphasis on conduct and character rather than on belief, faith or dogma. Judaism is synonymous with life and its ceremonial expression therefore embraces cultural and sociological as well as ritualistic elements. This is true particularly of the symbols and customs associated with the observance of the holidays which afford the Jew an opportunity to relive symbolically, yet vividly, significant experiences of his ancestors, and to commemorate their historic struggles for a fuller and richer life.

The Jewish calendar differs from the secular in that the former is based on the revolutions of the moon around the earth (lunar), while the latter is solar in character. The day begins and ends with sunset. The day preceding the Sabbath or a Jewish holiday is designated as *Ereb Shabbat* and *Ereb Yom Tob*.

There are twelve months in a normal year consisting of 29 or 30 days each, and their Hebrew names are: *Nisan* (falls about April), *Iyar* (May), *Sivan* (June), *Tammuz* (July), *Ab* (August), *Elul* (September), *Tishri* (October), *Heshvan* (November), *Kislev* (December), *Tebet* (January), *Shebat* (February), *Adar* (March). In a leap year, which occurs seven times in nineteen years, *i.e.,* the third, sixth, eighth, eleventh, fourteenth, seventeenth and nineteenth, a thirteenth month is added, known as *Adar Sheni,* Second *Adar*. By means of this additional month, the lunar year (consisting of 354 days) is periodically brought into conformity with the solar year (365 days).

Rosh Hashanah *Rosh Hashanah* (literally, "head of the year") is observed in the beginning of the seventh month (*Tishri*), as the Jewish New Year.

Nisan is regarded as the first month of the Jewish calendar, and all the festivals are arranged according to this reckoning.

The first of *Tishri* marks the anniversary of the creation of the world, which occurred, according to tradition, over 5,700 years ago. Hence Jewish chronology begins the year with this day.

The name "*Rosh Hashanah*" does not occur in the Bible. Instead, it is referred to as the Day of the Blowing of the Trumpet, the Day of Memorial or Remembrance, and the Memorial of the Blowing of the *Shofar*.

It is also considered the Day of Judgment (*Yom Hadin*), when all mankind is judged by the Creator, and the fate of each individual is inscribed in the Book of Life.

Rosh Hashanah inaugurates the Ten Days of Penitence, the most solemn season in the Jewish calendar, which has been set apart for retrospection and self-examination.

The observance of the High Holy Days is characterized by a feeling of solemnity. Jews generally abstain from their daily occupations and participate in communal worship.

The home customs and ceremonies also reflect concern over the fate for the New Year. In addition to the recital of the *Kiddush* (the sanctification prayer) and the kindling of the festive lights, a piece of sweet apple is dipped in honey on the eve of *Rosh Hashanah,* the person performing this symbolic act saying, "May it be God's will to grant us a good and sweet year." The bread, too, is dipped in honey, symbolizing the hope that, as the bread is sweet, so may the experiences during the approaching year be only of the most pleasant.

On the second night some kind of fruit is tasted which has not yet been eaten during the year, and an appropriate benediction is recited.

An outstanding feature of the synagogue service is the blowing of the *Shofar,* which serves to intensify the spirit of reverence and contributes toward the creation of an atmosphere of solemnity.

Sixty to one hundred distinct sounds, arranged in various combinations, are blown, the exact number varying with different congregations.

The *Shofar* is blown during the morning service before the Scroll is returned to the Holy Ark, and during the Additional Service.

If the first day of *Rosh Hashanah* falls on a Sabbath, the blowing of the *Shofar* is usually deferred to the second day.

The *Shofar* is made of the horn of a ram, or of some other clean animal except a cow or an ox.

In the afternoon of the first day of *Rosh Hashanah* (if it does not fall on a Sabbath), pious Jews assemble along the banks of a stream, river or seashore, and recite verses from the prophets and appropriate prayers.

The Sabbath which falls during the ten days of repentance is called "*Shabbat Shubah*" (the Sabbath of Repentance), because the prophetic portion read at the morning service, which is taken from Hosea, begins with the word "*Shubah*" (literally, Return). It is an exhortation to Israel to return to God.

The penitential days reach their culmination on the Day of Atonement (*Yom Kippur*), which is ushered in on the eve of the tenth of *Tishri,* and is regarded as the most sacred day in the Jewish year. It is frequently referred to as the Sabbath of Sabbaths.

In conformity with the Biblical injunction, "Ye shall afflict your souls," it is customary to abstain from all food and drink from sunset on the eve of the Day of Atonement until the beginning of night of the following day.

A large taper, sufficient to burn throughout the twenty-four hours of the fast, is kindled on the eve of *Yom Kippur,* in memory of the departed ones.

It is deemed appropriate to wear white shrouds on this solemn day, since white is a symbol of purity. The High Priest, in ancient times, wore white garments on *Yom Kippur.*

Yom Kippur—Synagogue Service The evening service of the Day of Atonement is preceded by the chanting of *Kol Nidre* (literally "all vows") which is repeated three times. It is a formal abrogation of all vows made under the influence of great emotional strain, and is intended to guard against oaths which may remain unfulfilled through negligence or forgetfulness.

The dispensation from vows refers only to those which an individual voluntarily assumes for himself alone, and concerns his relation to his conscience and Heavenly Judge. No oath or promise involving another person, a community, or a court of justice is implied in the *Kol Nidre.*

The ritual of the Day of Atonement is replete with petitions for forgiveness for sins committed by all the worshipers present. In the "Confessions," transgressions are enumerated of which a particular individual may not be guilty. The prayers for pardon are uttered in behalf of all Israel.

According to Jewish tradition, a person will not be forgiven on the Day of Atonement for any sins committed against a fellow being unless he rights the wrong and makes amends to the individual involved.

Sukkoth, the Festival of Booths or **Tabernacles** *Sukkoth* is the third of the three pilgrimage feasts—the other two being *Pesach* and *Shabuoth*—on which Jews from all parts of Palestine used to make pilgrimages to the Temple in Jerusalem.

This festival was originally pastoral in nature and occurred during the time of the fruit harvest. It was also generally observed as thanksgiving at the completion of the entire harvest, "for the bounties of nature during the previous year."

Sukkoth are temporary structures, especially built either in the yard or on the roof of a home, for the festival, and serve as a protection against the sun. They are not covered from above with board, but with detached branches, sparsely laid, "to allow the stars to shine through the roof."

The construction and decoration of the *Sukkah* are usually family functions. The mother blesses the candles and the father and children recite the *Kiddush* and sometimes partake of the meals in the *Sukkah*.

The *Sukkah* is the emblem of the *Galut* (Exile)—a temporary dwelling, dependent upon God's protection.

During the Spanish Inquisition, when to be found observing the Jewish religion meant death, the Jews used to build subterranean *Sukkoth*, so anxious were they to perform the precept of "dwelling in a *Sukkah*."

Hanukkah, the Festival of Dedication   *Hanukkah* is one of the two minor festivals, the observance of which is not enjoined in the Pentateuch. It was instituted by the early rabbis for the purpose of strengthening the Jewish historic consciousness.

Hanukkah commemorates the successful struggle for religious liberty carried on by a small band of Israelites, led by the brave Maccabees, against the vast army of their Syrian oppressors, under the leadership of Antiochus, which culminated in the recapture of Jerusalem and the rededication of the Holy Temple (165 B.C.).

The celebration of *Hanukkah* begins on the twenty-fifth day of *Kislev*, the day on which the Temple was consecrated anew to the service of God, and lasts for eight days, because the ceremony of rededication and festivities continued for that length of time.

This holiday is also called the Feast of Lights or Illumination, since it is customary to kindle the *Hanukkah* lamp throughout the eight days of the festival. One light is kindled on the first night, and an additional one is lit on each succeeding evening until the last day, when eight lights are burned, exclusive of the "*Shamas*," which is a special candle used in lighting the others. ("Thus do the pious grow in the service of praise and duty from strength to strength.")

Little yellow wax candles or wells of oil with threads folded together are used, as a rule, and the lamp is generally placed on the window sill or in some other conspicuous place where it may be seen from the outside. (Symbol of freedom.)

Because it is not permitted to do any work by the light of the *Hanukkah* candles, it has become customary to indulge in games, riddles and other pastimes, especially during the evenings of the festival.

Purim   *Purim* is one of the minor historical festivals of the Jewish calendar, and occurs on the 14th day of *Adar*. Its observance is based on the narrative recorded in one of the five small Biblical scrolls or *Megillot*, known as the Book of Esther.

The events associated with the Feast of *Purim* occurred in Persia during the reign of Ahasuerus (Xerxes, 485-464 B.C.). Haman, haughty prime minister and arch anti-Semite, plotted to exterminate the entire Jewish people because a Jew, Mordecai, refused to bow down to him. His sinister designs were frustrated by the timely intervention of Queen Esther. The observance of this festival was ordained by the Great Men of the Synod, of which Mordecai was said to have been a member.

It is customary to read *Megillat Esther* (the Scroll of Esther) in the synagogue and at home on the eve of the *Purim* festival, as well as on the following morning. Because of the important part played by Esther, women are required to attend the *Purim* service. Whenever the reader mentions the name of Haman, the children are permitted to stamp their feet, whirl their "greggers" or rattles, and resort to other noise-making devices.

Two important customs prevalent on this holiday are the giving of alms to the poor and the mutual exchange of presents between friends and relatives. The latter custom gave rise to the interesting character known as the "*Shalah Manot Tregger*" (the messenger who carried the gifts from home to home on *Purim*).

Exuberant joy is the keynote of the *Purim* festival. It is marked by unbounded festivity and offers opportunities for participation of both parents and children in the domestic celebration. Special dainties and sweets are consumed, including the triangular cakes known as *Haman Taschen* (Haman's hat). All kinds of merry-making are indulged in, culminating in the evening with the jovial party, at which all the members of the household are gathered.

Masquerading by both young and old has been a general practice on this holiday. Companies of amateurs *(Purim Shpieler)* used to go from house to house to dance, sing and produce episodes of the *Purim* story, usually concluding with the comic ditty, "*Heint is Purim, morgen is ois, git uns a groshen, und varft uns arois.*" ("Today is *Purim,* tomorrow is not, give us a penny, and throw us out.")

Pesach, the Festival of Freedom   Passover *(Pesach)* is associated with the birth of the Jewish nation, the redemption of its ancestors from Egyptian bondage (1200 B.C.)—an epoch-making event in the early history of its people.

Pesach also marked the early barley harvest in Palestine, when the Jewish farmers used to make a pilgrimage to the Temple in Jerusalem to offer sacrifices upon the altar.

During the Passover festival week Jews abstain from partaking of leavened bread or of any food prepared with leaven. Special sets of utensils and dishes are used, and *matzoth* or unleavened cakes are eaten, as a reminder of the Israelites' hurried departure from Egypt, when they had to bake their bread in haste, without permitting the dough to rise. It is customary for the head of the household to search for "*hometz*" or "leaven" on the evening preceding the festival, and to remove or burn it the following morning.

A special service known as the *Pesach Seder* is conducted at home on the first two evenings of the Passover festival. "*Seder*" means "order," and refers to the order of the service arranged. It is considered a holy and solemn occasion and one of the most beautiful Jewish ceremonies.

The symbols included in the "*Seder*" are arranged in a special dish, and consist of the following: three *matzoth*, bitter herbs *(marror)*, other vegetables—parsley, celery, lettuce *(karpas)*, salt water, a combination made of nuts, apples, raisins and wine *(haroset)*, a roasted lamb bone *(z'roa)*, and a roasted egg.

Four cups of wine are drunk by every member of the family seated around the table, during the *Seder* service.

The *Haggadah* (literally, narrative), which contains the special ritual service of the evening, the story of Israel's exodus from Egypt, as well as some folk songs and ditties *(Had Gadya, Addir Hu*, etc.), is read aloud and sung.

Various phases of the *Seder* have been introduced primarily for the benefit of the children: They ask the "Four Questions" to which the narrative of the *Haggadah* is a reply.

A special goblet or a cup of wine is prepared for Elijah, the Prophet, mysterious emissary of hope and faith, and a child opens the door to admit the eagerly-awaited guest.

Matzoth recalls the haste which characterized our ancestors' deliverance from Egyptian slavery. The Bible also calls the *matzoth* "Bread of Affliction," reminding us of the affliction of the Israelites while under Pharaoh's yoke. Thus the unleavened bread is a symbol of both slavery and freedom.

Marror symbolizes the bitter hardships endured in Egypt.

Haroset resembles the brick and mortar used in Egypt (Exodus 1:14).

Roasted Shank Bone and Egg. In the Temple days, the offering of the *paschal* lamb on the evening of Passover was an annual institution, which was observed with great detail. Some of the elements included in this ceremony have been retained in the *Seder* service, the roasted shank bone and egg on the *Seder* plate, symbolizing the *paschal* and festival offerings, respectively.

Shabuoth, the Festival of Weeks *Shabuoth* (literally "Weeks") falls on the sixth day of *Sivan*, the third month of the Jewish calendar, which is exactly seven weeks after *Pesach*. It is the second of the three major festivals of the Jewish year, the other two being *Pesach*, which precedes, and

Sukkoth, which follows it. Together they are known as the *Shalosh Regalim,* or the Three Pilgrimage Feasts.

Originally *Shabuoth* was observed as an agricultural feast, and marked the beginning of the wheat harvest. Later, *Shabuoth* served to commemorate an important event in the early history of our people—the proclamation of the Ten Commandments at Mount Sinai. Since the destruction of the Temple, when the Jews ceased to be primarily an agricultural people, the historical aspect has assumed greater significance.

Shabuoth is observed one day in Palestine and for two days by all pious Jews in other countries. It is called by the following names, each of which suggests a different phase of its significance or refers to some ceremony in its celebration: Pentecost, *Hag Ha-Kazir* ("Feast of Harvest"), *Yom Ha-Bikhurin* ("Day of First Fruits"), and *Z'man Matan Toratenu* ("Season of the giving of Our Law").

Pesach marks the time when Israel received its *physical* freedom, while *Shabuoth* commemorates the occasion when Israel received *spiritual* freedom, the consummation of the purpose for which Israel was led forth from Egyptian bondage.

It is customary to display greens and to decorate the synagogue and home with flowers, plants and even trees. The greens serve to commemorate the harvest festival of former times and to symbolize the freshness of the verdure which covered Mount Sinai, when the Law was given to Israel.

Another custom which is usually followed is that of partaking of dairy food. Special cheese cakes *(blintzes)* are eaten as significant of the Torah, which is compared in the Bible to milk.

The Scroll of Ruth is read in the synagogue at the *Shabuoth* services, because the story of Ruth embracing Judaism and the charming description of agricultural life in ancient Palestine, particularly the treatment accorded the poor during the harvest season, furnish a proper background for the *Shabuoth* festival. Another reason is that King David, who was a descendant of Ruth, was born and passed away, according to tradition, on this holiday.

Pious Jews stay up until midnight or during the entire first night of *Shabuoth,* devoting their time in the synagogue to the study and reading of excerpts from the Pentateuch, Prophets, and rabbinic literature. These selections have been assembled and arranged in a collection called "*Tikkun Shabuoth.*"

Tishah B'Ab   *Tishah B'Ab,* the ninth day in the Hebrew month of *Ab,* is observed as a fast day. It marks the anniversary of the destruction of the First and Second Temples in Jerusalem by the Babylonians under Nebuchadnezzar (586 B.C.) and the Romans under Titus (70 A.D.), respectively, and the loss of Jewish independence.

Other sad episodes in the life of the Jewish people are associated with this mournful day, among them the suppression of Bar Kokhba's revolt by the Romans in 135 A.D., and the expulsion of the Jews from Spain in 1492.

Grief is the keynote of *Tishah B'Ab,* and the traditional mourning code governs this day. Pious Jews refrain from eating, drinking, bathing, or participating in festive occasions, from sunset to sunset, following the *Taanit S'udah* (the last repast before the fast), and study only melancholy phases of the Torah, such as the Book of Job, the prophecies of misfortune in Jeremiah, the laws of mourning, and similar subjects which tend to sadden the heart.

Some of the external features of the synagogue are brought into consonance with the gloomy character of the day. Thus, the curtain in front of the Holy Ark is removed, the latter being draped in black or remaining bare. Worshipers remove their shoes and seat themselves on boxes, low stools, or turned-over chairs or benches, as do mourners observing *Shib'ah* (seven days of mourning for the deceased). The *talit* (prayer shawl) and *tefillin* (phylacteries) are put on at the afternoon service, instead of in the morning, and all prayers and scriptural readings are chanted in a low tone, with a weeping intonation.

In the synagogue *Tishah B'Ab* is ushered in at the evening service with the reading of the prophet Jeremiah's Book of Lamentations, in depressed, mournful tones. This also constitutes the central feature of the service the following morning, when, in addition, the *Kinot,* a collection of plaintive hymns of poetic beauty, heartrending dirges and laments are chanted.

Sabbath   The observance of the Sabbath is a fundamental precept of Judaism, and for thousands of years has exerted a dominant influence in Jewish life. The admonition to set aside a weekly day of rest from labor is included among the Ten Commandments ("Remember the Seventh day, to keep it holy"), and applies alike to masters, servants and beasts of burden.

The Sabbath is ushered in at the home Friday before sunset with the kindling of candles by the housewife, with an appropriate benediction and ceremony, and at the synagogue with the recital of the *Kabbalat Shabbat* (welcoming the Sabbath) prayers.

While observant Jews refrain from carrying on their usual work or business on the Sabbath, the traditional rest on that holy day does not imply mere idleness, but rather a change in occupation. Invested by Scripture with a uniquely religious connotation, the Sabbath is dedicated to physical and spiritual relaxation and replenishment. Biblical readings, discussions of contemporary Jewish affairs, the study of *The Ethics of The Fathers,* and other intellectual activities are indulged in, which are in accord with the religious nature of the Sabbath and reflect a reverential concern for its sanctity.

On the other hand, strenuous, excessive, or boisterous exercise, mourning, fasting, weeping, and other practices which would detract from the quiet contemplation, dignified cheerfulness, and pleasure that should characterize the Sabbath, are scrupulously avoided.

Among the Sabbath ceremonies which contribute toward the creation of a distinctive atmosphere in the home and synagogue are the recital of the *Kiddush* (sanctification) prayer over sacramental wine or Sabbath white bread before the Friday evening and Sabbath noon repasts, and the *Habdalah* (distinction) blessings at the conclusion of the Sabbath, the singing of Sabbath hymns and melodies at the family table, attendance at public services, central features of which are the reading of the weekly portion of the Pentateuch, as well as a corresponding selection from the Prophets, and a discourse by the rabbi. In recent decades it has become customary to conduct, in addition, late Friday evening services and forums.

SUMMARY JEWISH CALENDAR, 5721-30 (1960-70)

Quoted from American Jewish Year Book 1960, vol. 61.

Month	Day	HOLIDAY	5721 (1960)	5722 (1961)	5723 (1962)	5724 (1963)	5725 (1964)	5726 (1965)	5727 (1966)	5728 (1967)	5729 (1968)	5730 (1969)
Tishri	1	Rosh Hashanah	Sept. 22 Th	Sept. 11 M	Sept. 29 Sa	Sept. 19 Th	Sept. 7 M	Sept. 27 M	Sept. 15 Th	Oct. 5 Th	Sept. 23 M	Sept. 13 Sa
	3	Fast of Gedaliah	*Sept. 24 Sa	Sept. 13 W	Oct. 1 M	*Sept. 21 Sa	Sept. 9 W	Sept. 29 W	*Sept. 17 Sa	*Oct. 7 Sa	Sept. 25 W	Sept. 15 M
	10	Yom Kippur	Oct. 1 Sa	Sept. 20 W	Oct. 8 M	Sept. 28 Sa	Sept. 16 W	Oct. 6 W	Sept. 24 Sa	Oct. 14 Sa	Oct. 2 W	Sept. 22 M
	15	Sukkoth	Oct. 6 Th	Sept. 25 M	Oct. 13 Sa	Oct. 3 Th	Sept. 21 M	Oct. 11 M	Sept. 29 Th	Oct. 19 Th	Oct. 7 M	Sept. 27 Sa
	21	Hosha 'na Rabbah	Oct. 12 W	Oct. 1 S	Oct. 19 F	Oct. 9 W	Sept. 27 S	Oct. 17 S	Oct. 5 W	Oct. 25 W	Oct. 13 S	Oct. 3 F
	22	Shemini 'Azeret	Oct. 13 Th	Oct. 2 M	Oct. 20 Sa	Oct. 10 Th	Sept. 28 M	Oct. 18 M	Oct. 6 Th	Oct. 26 Th	Oct. 14 M	Oct. 4 Sa
	23	Simhat Torah	Oct. 14 F	Oct. 3 T	Oct. 21 S	Oct. 11 F	Sept. 29 T	Oct. 19 T	Oct. 7 F	Oct. 27 F	Oct. 15 T	Oct. 5 S
Heshvan	1	New Moon	†Oct. 22 Sa	†Oct. 11 W	†Oct. 29 M	†Oct. 19 Sa	†Oct. 7 W	†Oct. 27 W	†Oct. 15 Sa	†Nov. 4 Sa	†Oct. 23 W	†Oct. 13 M
Kislev	1	New Moon	Nov. 20 S	Nov. 9 Th	†Nov. 28 W	Nov. 17 S	†Nov. 6 F	Nov. 25 Th	†Nov. 14 M	Dec. 3 S	†Nov. 22 F	Nov. 11 T
	25	Hanukkah	Dec. 14 W	Dec. 3 S	Dec. 22 Sa	Dec. 11 W	Nov. 30 M	Dec. 19 S	Dec. 8 Th	Dec. 27 W	Dec. 16 M	Dec. 5 F
Tebet	1	New Moon	†Dec. 20 T	Dec. 8 F	†Dec. 28 F	†Dec. 17 T	†Dec. 6 S	Dec. 24 F	†Dec. 14 W	**1968** †Jan. 2 T	†Dec. 22 S	Dec. 10 W
	10	Fast of the 10th of Tebet	Dec. 29 Th	Dec. 17 S	**1963** Jan. 6 S	Dec. 26 Th	Dec. 15 T	**1966** Jan. 2 S	Dec. 23 F	Jan. 11 Th	Dec. 31 T	Dec. 19 F
Shebat	1	New Moon	**1961** Jan. 18 W	**1962** Jan. 6 Sa	Jan. 26 Sa	**1964** Jan. 15 W	**1965** Jan. 4 M	Jan. 22 Sa	**1967** Jan. 12 Th	Jan. 31 W	**1969** Jan. 20 M	**1970** Jan. 8 Th
	15	Hamishshah-'asar bi-Shebat	Feb. 1 W	Jan. 20 Sa	Feb. 9 Sa	Jan. 29 W	Jan. 18 M	Feb. 5 Sa	Jan. 26 Th	Feb. 14 W	Feb. 3 M	Jan. 22 Th
Adar I	1	New Moon		Feb. 5 M			†Feb. 3 W		†Feb. 11 Sa			†Feb. 7 Sa
Adar II	1	New Moon	†Feb. 17 F	†Mar. 7 W	†Feb. 25 M	†Feb. 14 F	†Mar. 5 F	†Feb. 21 M	†Mar. 13 M	†Mar. 1 F	†Feb. 19 W	†Mar. 9 M
	13	Fast of Esther	Mar. 1 W	Mar. 19 M	‡Mar. 9 Sa	Feb. 26 W	Mar. 17 W	‡Mar. 5 Sa	‡Mar. 25 Sa	Mar. 13 W	Mar. 3 M	‡Mar. 21 Sa
	14	Purim	Mar. 2 Th	Mar. 20 T	Mar. 10 S	Feb. 27 Th	Mar. 18 Th	Mar. 6 S	Mar. 26 S	Mar. 14 Th	Mar. 4 T	Mar. 22 S
Nisan	1	New Moon	Mar. 18 Sa	Apr. 5 Th	Mar. 26 T	Mar. 14 Sa	Apr. 3 Sa	Mar. 22 T	Apr. 11 T	Mar. 30 Sa	Mar. 20 Th	Apr. 7 T
	15	Passover	Apr. 1 Sa	Apr. 19 Th	Apr. 9 T	Mar. 28 Sa	Apr. 17 M	Apr. 5 T	Apr. 25 T	Apr. 13 Sa	Apr. 3 Th	Apr. 21 T
Iyar	1	New Moon	†Apr. 17 M	†May 5 Sa	†Apr. 25 Th	†Apr. 13 M	†May 3 M	†Apr. 21 Th	†May 11 Th	†Apr. 29 M	†Apr. 19 Sa	†May 7 Th
	18	Lag ba-'Omer	May 4 Th	May 22 T	May 12 S	Apr. 30 Th	May 20 Th	May 8 S	May 28 S	May 16 Th	May 6 T	May 24 S
Sivan	1	New Moon	May 16 T	June 3 S	May 24 F	May 12 T	June 1 T	May 20 F	June 9 F	May 28 T	May 18 S	June 5 F
	6	Shabouth	May 21 S	June 8 F	May 29 W	May 17 S	June 6 S	May 25 W	June 14 W	June 2 S	May 23 F	June 10 W
Tammuz	1	New Moon	†June 15 Th	†July 3 T	†June 23 S	†June 11 Th	†July 1 Th	†June 19 S	†July 9 S	†June 27 Th	†June 17 T	†July 5 S
	17	Fast of the 17th of Tammuz	*July 1 Sa	July 19 W	July 9 T	*June 27 Sa	*July 17 Sa	July 5 T	July 25 T	*July 13 Sa	July 3 Th	July 21 T
Ab	1	New Moon	July 14 F	Aug. 1 W	July 22 M	July 10 F	July 30 F	July 18 M	Aug. 7 M	July 26 F	July 16 W	Aug. 3 M
	9	Fast of the 9th of Av	*July 22 Sa	Aug. 9 Th	July 30 T	*July 18 Sa	*Aug. 7 Sa	July 26 T	Aug. 15 T	*Aug. 3 Sa	July 24 Th	Aug. 11 T
Elul	1	New Moon	†Aug. 13 S	†Aug. 31 F	†Aug. 21 W	†Aug. 9 S	†Aug. 29 S	†Aug. 17 W	†Sept. 6 W	†Aug. 25 S	†Aug. 15 F	†Sept. 2 W

*Fast observed on following day. †Second day of New Moon. ‡Fast observed two days before.

Headquarters of Denominations

with Membership of 100,000 or More

Condensed from the 1962 *Yearbook of American Churches,* Benson Y. Landis, ed., National Council of the Churches of Christ in the U.S.A., New York, 1961, pp. 12-104.

*Address of presiding officer.

Adventists, Seventh-day
6840 Eastern Avenue, N. W.
Takoma Park
Washington 12, D.C.

Armenian Church:
DIOCESE OF AMERICA
630 Second Avenue
New York 16, New York
DIOCESE OF CALIFORNIA
3200 West Adams Boulevard
Los Angeles 18, California

Assemblies of God
434 West Pacific Street
Springfield 1, Missouri

Baptist Groups:
AMERICAN BAPTIST ASSOCIATION
214 East Broad Street
Texarkana, Arkansas-Texas
AMERICAN BAPTIST CONVENTION
152 Madison Avenue
New York 16, New York
CONSERVATIVE BAPTIST ASSOCIATION
OF AMERICA
44 East Genesee Street
Auburn, New York*
FREE WILL BAPTISTS
3801 Richland Avenue
Nashville 5, Tennessee
GENERAL ASSOCIATION OF REGULAR
BAPTIST CHURCHES
608 South Dearborn Street
Suite 1246, Transportation Building
Chicago 5, Illinois

NATIONAL BAPTIST CONVENTION OF
AMERICA
714 West 10th Street
Little Rock, Arkansas*
NATIONAL BAPTIST CONVENTION,
U.S.A., INC.
3101 South Parkway
Chicago, Illinois*
NORTH AMERICAN BAPTIST ASSOCIATION
Conway
Arkansas*
SOUTHERN BAPTIST CONVENTION
127 9th Avenue, North
Nashville 3, Tennessee
UNITED FREE WILL BAPTIST CHURCH
Kinston College
1000 University Street
Kinston, North Carolina

Christian Churches (Disciples of Christ) International Convention
P.O. Box 19136
221 Ohmer Avenue
Indianapolis, 19, Indiana

Church of the Brethren
22 South State Street
Elgin, Illinois

Church of Christ, Scientist
107 Falmouth Street
Boston 15, Massachusetts

Church of God in Christ
958 Mason Street
Memphis, Tennessee

Church of the Nazarene
6401 The Paseo
Kansas City 10, Missouri

Churches of Christ
(strictly congregational with no
general headquarters)

Churches of God:
CHURCH OF GOD (Anderson, Indiana)
Box 430
Anderson, Indiana
CHURCH OF GOD (Cleveland, Tennessee)
922-1080 Montgomery Avenue
Cleveland, Tennessee

Eastern Orthodox Churches:
AMERICAN CARPATHO–RUSSIAN ORTHO-
DOX GREEK CATHOLIC CHURCH
Johnstown, Pennsylvania
GREEK ARCHDIOCESE OF NORTH AND
SOUTH AMERICA
10 East 79th Street
New York 21, New York
RUSSIAN ORTHODOX GREEK CATHOLIC
CHURCH OF AMERICA
59 East 2nd Street
New York 3, New York
SERBIAN EASTERN ORTHODOX CHURCH
Saint Sava Monastery
Libertyville, Illinois
SYRIAN ANTIOCHIAN ORTHODOX
CHURCH
239 85th Street
Brooklyn 9, New York

**Evangelical United Brethren
Church**
601 West Riverview Avenue
Dayton 6, Ohio

Friends
AMERICAN FRIENDS SERVICE
COMMITTEE, INC.
15th and Race Street
Philadelphia 2, Pennsylvania

Jehovah's Witnesses
124 Columbia Heights
Brooklyn 1, New York

Jewish Congregations:
UNION OF AMERICAN HEBREW
CONGREGATIONS
838 Fifth Avenue
New York 21, New York
UNITED SYNAGOGUE OF AMERICA
3080 Broadway
New York 27, New York
UNION OF ORTHODOX JEWISH
CONGREGATIONS OF AMERICA
84 Fifth Avenue
New York 11, New York
CENTRAL CONFERENCE OF AMERICAN
RABBIS
40 West 68th Street
New York 23, New York
RABBINICAL ALLIANCE OF AMERICA
154 Nassau Street
New York 38, New York
RABBINICAL ASSEMBLY OF AMERICA, INC.
3080 Broadway
New York 27, New York
RABBINICAL COUNCIL OF AMERICA, INC.
84 Fifth Avenue
New York 11, New York
SYNAGOGUE COUNCIL OF AMERICA
110 West 42nd Street
New York 36, New York
UNION OF ORTHODOX RABBIS OF THE
UNITED STATES AND CANADA
132 Nassau Street
New York 38, New York

Latter-day Saints:
CHURCH OF JESUS CHRIST OF LATTER–DAY
SAINTS
47 East South Temple Street
Salt Lake City 1, Utah
REORGANIZED CHURCH OF JESUS CHRIST
OF LATTER–DAY SAINTS
The Auditorium
Independence, Missouri

Lutheran Churches:
AMERICAN LUTHERAN CHURCH
422 South 5th Street
Minneapolis 15, Minnesota
AUGUSTANA EVANGELICAL LUTHERAN
CHURCH
2445 Park Avenue
Minneapolis 4, Minnesota★

LUTHERAN CHURCH–MISSOURI SYNOD
The Lutheran Building
210 North Broadway
St. Louis 2, Missouri

UNITED LUTHERAN CHURCH IN AMERICA
231 Madison Avenue
New York 16, New York

WISCONSIN EVANGELICAL LUTHERAN
SYNOD
3624 West North Avenue
Milwaukee 8, Wisconsin

Methodist Bodies:
AFRICAN METHODIST EPISCOPAL CHURCH
Daniel Payne College
Birmingham, Alabama★
AFRICAN METHODIST EPISCOPAL ZION
CHURCH
4736 South Parkway
Chicago 15, Illinois★
CHRISTIAN METHODIST EPISCOPAL
CHURCH
6432 South Green Street, Apt. 1
Chicago 21, Illinois★
METHODIST CHURCH
475 Riverside Drive
New York 27, New York

Pentecostal Assemblies:
PENTECOSTAL CHURCH OF GOD OF
AMERICA, INC.
312–316 Joplin Street
Joplin, Missouri
UNITED PENTECOSTAL CHURCH, INC.
3645 South Grand Boulevard
St. Louis 18, Missouri

**Polish National Catholic Church
of America**
529 East Locust Street
Scranton 5, Pennsylvania

Presbyterian Bodies:
PRESBYTERIAN CHURCH IN THE U.S.
341 Ponce de Leon Avenue, N.E.
Atlanta 8, Georgia
UNITED PRESBYTERIAN CHURCH IN
THE U.S.A.
510 Witherspoon Building
Philadelphia 7, Pennsylvania

Protestant Episcopal Church
281 Park Avenue South
New York 10, New York

Reformed Bodies:
CHRISTIAN REFORMED CHURCH
2850 Kalamazoo Avenue
Grand Rapids, Michigan

REFORMED CHURCH IN AMERICA
475 Riverside Drive
New York 27, New York

Roman Catholic Church:
APOSTOLIC DELEGATION
3339 Massachusetts Avenue, N.W.
Washington, D.C.
ARCHDIOCESE OF BOSTON
2101 Commonwealth Avenue
Brighton, Massachusetts
ARCHDIOCESE OF CHICAGO
1555 North State Parkway
Chicago 10, Illinois
ARCHDIOCESE OF LOS ANGELES
1531 West 9th Street
Los Angeles, California
ARCHDIOCESE OF NEW YORK
452 Madison Avenue
New York 22, New York
ARCHDIOCESE OF ST. LOUIS
3810 Lindell Boulevard
St. Louis, Missouri

Salvation Army
120–130 West 14th Street
New York 11, New York

**Spiritualists, International General
Assembly**
1915 Omohundro Avenue
Norfolk, Virginia

Unitarian Universalist Association
25 Beacon Street
Boston 8, Massachusetts

United Church of Christ
297 Park Avenue South
New York 10, New York

Glossary of Religious Terms

The following definitions are adapted from two sources: *Handbook of Denominations in the U. S.* by Frank S. Mead, Abingdon-Cokesbury Press, Nashville, 1961; and *Webster's New International Dictionary of the English Language*, G. & C. Merriam Company, Springfield, 1940.

absolution — *The remission of guilt and penalty for sin, by a priest, following confession.*

Adventism — *The doctrine that the second coming of Christ and the end of the world (or age) are near at hand.*

agnostic — *One who believes in the doctrine that neither the existence nor the nature of God, nor the ultimate origin of the universe, is known or knowable.*

Anabaptist — *One of a party arising in 1523 in Zurich which rejected infant baptism, held the church to be composed of true Christians baptized on confession of faith, and advocated separation of church and state.*

anathema — *A solemn ban or curse pronounced by ecclesiastical authority, and accompanied by excommunication.*

Annunciation — *The announcement by the angel Gabriel to the Virgin Mary that she was to be the mother of Christ.*

anointing — *The act of consecrating by the application of oil, used in consecrating sacred objects or persons, as preparation for death or in completing the efficacy of baptism.*

Apocalypse — *The last book of the New Testament, otherwise called* The Revelation of Saint *John the Divine.*

apocalyptical — *Anything viewed as a prophetic revelation.*

Apocrypha —
(1) Commonly, the fourteen books of the Old Testament in the Vulgate (Latin) that were taken from the Septuagint (Greek version) but are not found in Hebrew; now excluded from the Authorized Version.
(2) Christian gospels, epistles and apocalypses of fictitious authorship, not admitted to the New Testament.

apocryphal — *Not canonical, unauthentic, spurious.*

apologetics — *Systematic argumentative discourse in defense, especially of the divine origin and authority of Christianity.*

apostle — *One of the twelve disciples of Christ sent forth to preach the gospel. The original twelve included: Simon Peter, Andrew, James and John (sons of Zebedee), Philip, Bartholomew, Matthew (or Levi), Thomas (or Didymus), James (son of Alphaeus), Jude (or Thaddeus), Simon the Cananaean and Judas Iscariot. Matthias was chosen by lot to take the place of Judas. Paul, though not one of the twelve, was equal with them in office and dignity. Barnabas, the companion of Paul on his first missionary journey, is sometimes called an apostle.*

Apostles' Creed — *A widely used creed, formerly ascribed to the Twelve Apostles, beginning "I believe in God the Father Almighty, maker (creator) of heaven and earth: and in Jesus Christ his only Son our Lord."*

apostolic succession — *The doctrine of an unbroken line of succession in the episcopacy from the apostles to the present time, maintained in Greek, Roman and Anglican churches.*

Arminian — *A follower of Arminius (1560-1609), a Dutch Protestant theologian. Arminius denied Calvin's doctrine of unconditional predestination, limited atonement, and irresistible grace, and stood for universal salvation for all. The theology of the Wesleyans of Great Britain and the Methodists of America is Arminian.*

Athanasian — *A follower of Athanasius (293-373), who defended the orthodox view of the divinity of Christ: that the son of God was of the same essence or substance with the Father. He opposed and won over Arius at the council of Nicaea; Arius held that Christ was created by, but was essentially different from, the Father.*

atheist —
(1) One who holds to atheism, disbelief in or denial of the existence of a God, or Supreme Being.
(2) A godless person.

atonement — *The reconciliation of the sinner with God through the sufferings of Jesus Christ.*

ban — *A sentence by the church, which amounts to excommunication or outlawry, upon those guilty of an act or speech forbidden by the church.*

baptism — *Act or ceremony of baptizing; specifically, a sacrament by whose reception one becomes a Christian or a member of a Christian church.*

Bible —
(1) The book of writings accepted by Christians as inspired by God and of divine authority.
(2) Also, the book made up of writings similarly accepted by the Jews.
(3) The Scriptures of the Old and New Testament.

Calvary —
(1) The place outside the ancient city of Jerusalem where Christ was crucified.
(2) A representation of the crucifixion of Christ.

Calvinism — *The doctrines of the French theologian John Calvin (1509-1564), including election or predestination, limited atonement, total depravity, irresistibility of grace, and the perseverance of the saints. Calvinism especially emphasizes the sovereignty of God in the bestowal of grace.*

canon — *An ecclesiastical decree, code or constitution.*

catechism   *A manual or guide for catechizing or oral instruction, especially for moral and religious instruction.*

Christ —
(1) The Messiah, or (Lord's) Anointed, whose coming was prophesied and expected by the Jews.
(2) Jesus; Christ as the person who fulfilled this prophecy and expectation.

Communion —
(1) The sacrament of the Eucharist; the celebration of the Lord's Supper.
(2) The act of partaking of the sacrament.

communion — *A body of Christians having one common faith and discipline.*

concordance — *An alphabetical index of the principal words in a book, citing the passages in which they occur.*

concordat — *An agreement made between the Pope and a sovereign or government for the regulation of ecclesiastical matters.*

confession —
(1) Acknowledgment of sins or sinfulness, especially in a prescribed form in public worship; specifically, the act of disclosing sins or faults to a priest or minister to obtain sacramental absolution.
(2) A confession of faith.

confirmation — *The initiatory rite by which persons are inducted into the church.*

consecrate — *To set apart as sacred certain persons, animals, places, objects or times.*

covenant — *A solemn compact between members of a church to maintain its faith, discipline, etc.*

creed — *An authoritative summary or formula of the essential articles of a faith; for the Christian faith, especially the Apostles' Creed, the Nicene Creed and the Athanasian Creed.*

deism — *Belief in a personal God who exerts no influence on men or on the world he has created.*

denomination — *A class, or society of individuals, called by the same name; a sect.*

diocese —
(1) The territory of a church under the jurisdiction of a bishop.
(2) An archdiocese is the diocese of an archbishop.

disciple — *One who receives instruction from another; specifically, a professed follower of Christ in his lifetime, especially one of the twelve apostles.*

doctrine — *That which is taught as the belief of a church.*

dogma —
(1) That which is held as an opinion, especially, a definite tenet; also a code of such tenets.
(2) A doctrine or body of doctrines of theology and religion formally stated and authoritatively proclaimed by a church or sect, especially the Roman Catholic Church.

ecclesiastical — *Pertaining to the church or the clergy.*

ecumenical (*or* oecumenical) — *General; universal; representing the whole Christian Church.*

episcopal — *Having to do with bishops, or governed by bishops.*

Eucharist — *The sacrament of the Lord's Supper; the solemn act or ceremony of commemorating the death of Christ, in the use of bread and wine as the symbols.*

evangelical — *A word used to denote primary loyalty to the gospel of Christ, in contrast to ecclesiastical or rationalistic types of Christianity; spiritual-mindedness and zeal for Christian living, as distinguished from ritualism, etc.*

excommunication — *An ecclesiastical censure whereby one is, for the time, cast out of the communion of the church.*

fundamentalist — *One who believes in the infallibility of the Bible as inspired by God, and that it should be accepted literally, as distinguished from the modernist, who interprets the Bible in accordance with more modern scholarship or scientific knowledge.*

Gospel — *The story or record of Christ's life and doctrines, contained in the first four books of the New Testament; especially, one of the four New Testament books containing narratives of the life and death of Jesus Christ ascribed respectively to Matthew, Mark, Luke and John.*

gospel   *The good news concerning Christ, the Kingdom of God, and salvation; hence, the teachings of Christ and the apostles; the Christian faith, revelation, or dispensation.*

grace — *The gift of God to man of the Divine favor and inner power necessary to salvation.*

hierarchy   *Government by priests or prelates, as in the Roman Catholic Church.*

Holy Ghost — *The third person of the Trinity.*

holy orders — *The ranks, or orders, of the Christian ministry.*

homiletics — *The art of preaching; that branch of theology which treats of homilies or sermons.*

icon —
    (1) An image or representation.
    (2) In the Eastern church, an image of Christ, the Virgin Mary or a saint.

Immaculate Conception — *In the Roman Catholic Church, the miraculous conception by which the Virgin Mary was herself conceived, without original sin; or the doctrine proclaimed a dogma in 1854, which affirms this.*

immersion — *Baptism by complete submersion in water.*

impanation — *A doctrine that the body of Christ is present in the eucharistic bread and wine without any change in their substance.*

infallibility — *The authority of the Scriptures as incapable of error.*

kosher — *Sanctioned by Jewish law, especially designating food that may be eaten as ritually clean.*

laity — *The people, as distinguished from the clergy; laymen.*

lay — *Of or pertaining to the laity, as distinct from the clergy.*

laying on of hands — *A form used in consecrating to office, in the rite of confirmation, and in blessing persons. The hands are put upon the head of the recipient.*

liturgy, liturgical —
> *(1) A prescribed form or collection of forms for public worship; in "liturgical" churches rite and ceremony are more prominent than the emphasis on preaching or evangelism.*
> *(2) The public rites and services of the Christian church, specifically, the eucharistic rite called the Liturgy (also Divine Liturgy) in the Eastern, the Mass in the Western, church.*

Mass — *The central worship service of the Roman Catholic Church, consisting of prayers and ceremonies.*

Messiah —
> *(1) The expected king and deliverer of the Hebrews.*
> *(2) The Christ, the divinely sent Savior of the world.*

mezuzah — *A tiny piece of parchment bearing the passages Deuteronomy 6:4–9 and 11:13–21 written in twenty-two lines. It is rolled up in a wooden, metal or glass case or tube and attached to the doorpost, by Orthodox Jews, as both the passages command.*

missal — *The book containing that which is said or sung at Mass for each and every day of the year.*

monotheism — *The doctrine or belief that there is but one God.*

New Testament — *The covenant of God with man embodied in the coming of Christ and the teaching of Christ and his followers as set forth in the Bible. Hence, usually, that portion of the Bible in which this covenant is contained.*

Nicene (Nicaean) Creed —
> *(1) A confession formulated and decreed by the First Council of Nicaea, A.D. 325, settling the controversy concerning the persons of the Trinity.*
> *(2) An expanded form of the foregoing read at the Council of Chalcedon (A.D. 451) as the creed of the Council of Constantinople—hence, also called the Niceno-Constantinopolitan Creed.*
> *(3) A form now in use in the Western church identical with the preceding except for one extra clause inserted at a church council in A.D. 589.*

Old Testament — *The covenant of God with the Hebrews as set forth in the Bible. Also the canonical books including the Law, Prophets, and Hagiographa, and (Roman Catholic Church) the books except two of the Apocrypha of Protestants.*

ordain, ordination — *To invest with ministerial or sacerdotal functions; to introduce into the office of Christian ministry.*

order — *To admit to holy orders; to ordain.*

original sin — *In theology, the innate sin, or depravity, inherited from our parents, and the source of all actual sins. It originated in the first sin of Adam, the father of the human race.*

orthodoxy — *Belief in doctrine considered correct and sound, or holding the commonly accepted faith.*

papal infallibility — *In the Roman Catholic Church, the dogma adopted by the Ecumenical Council in Rome in 1870, that the Pope cannot, when speaking in his official character of supreme pontiff, err in defining a doctrine of Christian faith or rule of morals to be held by the Church.*

parochial — *Of or pertaining to a parish; as, parochial clergy, or parochial school.*

patriarch — *A bishop of highest rank, standing above metropolitans and ruling patriarchates.*

penance — *An ecclesiastical punishment inflicted for sin, or a sacrament of the Christian Church.*

Pentecost —
(1) A solemn festival of the Jews celebrated on the fiftieth day (seven weeks) after the second day of the Passover.
(2) A Christian festival commemorating on the seventh Sunday after Easter the descent of the Holy Spirit on the apostles; hence, Whitsunday.

Pentecostal — *The religious experience of conversion based upon the descent of the Holy Ghost upon the apostles at the Jewish Pentecost.*

polity — *Form or constitution of the government of a state, or of any institution or organization, such as a church, similarly administered.*

presbytery — *A church court or assembly having the ecclesiastical or spiritual rule and oversight of a district, or the district itself.*

proselyte, proselytize — *To convert, especially to some religious sect.*

reredos — *A screen or partition wall, usually ornamental, behind an altar.*

Resurrection — *The rising of Christ from the dead.*

revelation —
(1) God's disclosure or manifestation of himself or of his will to man, as through some act, oracular words, signs, laws, etc.; that which is revealed by God to man.
(2) The Revelation of Saint John The Divine: the last of the canonical books of the Bible; the Apocalypse.

rubric — *A rule for the conduct of a liturgical service; as, the rubrics of the Mass.*

sabbatarian — *One who favors a strict observance of the Sabbath; specifically, one who would make compulsory by law abstinence on the Sabbath from all secular occupations or recreations.*

Sabbath — *A season or day of rest from labor, specifically;*
(1) The seventh day of the week in the Jewish calendar, now called Saturday, *the observance of which as a day of rest was enjoined in the Decalogue.*
(2) The first day of the week, Sunday, kept by most Christians as a day of rest and worship.

sacerdotal — *A term denoting a religious system in which everything is valued in relation to the ministrations of the priestly order.*

sacrament — *One of certain religious ceremonies distinguished in Christian rites as instituted or recognized by Christ. The Roman Catholic and the Eastern churches recognize seven sacraments, viz., baptism, confirmation, the Eucharist, penance, extreme unction, holy orders and matrimony; Protestants, only baptism and the Lord's Supper.*

salvation — *The rescue of man from evil or guilt by God's power, that he may obtain blessedness.*

sanctify —
(1) To set apart to a sacred office or to religious use or observance; to hallow.
(2) To render productive of holiness or piety.

Scripture — *The books of the Old and the New Testament, or of either of them; the Bible.*

sect —
(1) A group having in common a leader or a distinctive doctrine.
(2) In religion, (a) a party dissenting from an established or parent church; (b) one of the organized bodies of Christians, a denomination.

sectarian —
(1) Of or pertaining to, or characteristic of a sect; one of a sect, especially a religious sect.
(2) A narrow or bigoted denominationalist.

secular — *Of or pertaining to the wordly or temporal, as distinguished from the spiritual or eternal; specifically, (a) not under church control; non-ecclesiastical; (b) not sacred; profane, as secular music.*

see — *The local seat from which a bishop, archbishop, or the Pope exercises jurisdiction.*

Septuagint — *The Greek version of the Old Testament, still in use in the Eastern Church.*

synagogue —
(1) A local assembly of Jews organized for public worship.
(2) The building or place of assembly used by Jewish communities primarily for religious worship.

syncretism —
(1) The reconciliation or union of conflicting beliefs, especially religious beliefs, or a movement or effort intending such.
(2) In the development of a religion, the process of growth through coalescence of different forms of faith and worship or through accretions of tenets, rites, etc. from those religions which are being superseded.

synod — *An ecclesiastical council, either of regular standing or appointed as needed.*

Talmud — *The collected body of Jewish civil and canonical law, consisting of the combined* <u>Mishnah</u>, *or text, and* <u>Gemara</u>, *or commentary.*

tithe — *To pay or give a tenth part of, especially for the support of the church.*

torah, Torah —
(1) In Jewish literature, a law; precept; divine instruction; revelation.
(2) The Pentateuch, or "Law of Moses" (Torah).

total depravity — *The equivalent of original sin, every human faculty having an innate evil taint.*

trine immersion — *A form of baptism in which the candidate is immersed three successive times, in the name of the Father, Son and Holy Ghost.*

Trinitarian — *A believer in the Trinity—that there is a union of Father, Son and Holy Ghost in one divine nature.*

unction — *A ceremonial anointing with oil, as in extreme unction, in case of death or imminent death.*

Uniat — *Persons or churches acknowledging the supremacy of the Pope, but maintaining their own liturgies or rites.*

Unitarian — *One who denies the doctrine of the Trinity, believing that God exists only in one person; also one of a denomination of Christians holding this belief.*

Virgin Birth — *The doctrine that Jesus was miraculously begotten of God and born of a virgin mother.*

Vulgate — *A Latin version of the Scriptures, in the main, the work of Saint Jerome in the fourth century, used as a standard for services of the Roman Catholic Church.*

Acknowledgments

A GREAT many persons, organizations and church officials provided invaluable help with the research and vast range of materials which have gone into making this book.

The series on religion (Part One), published in *Look* Magazine, benefited at all stages from the encouragement and support of Gardner Cowles, Editor. The editors and staff of *Look* deserve thanks for the judgment and skill with which the articles were first presented to the public. William J. Burke, director of editorial research, was of unfailing assistance, as were Katherine Hartley, Robinette Nixon and Frank Latham. Hazel Harvest guided the project through its many stages with great competence and good sense.

I am indebted to the excellent and unflagging research conducted for this new edition by Research, Writing, Editing Associates: Elizabeth B. Barnes, in charge, supervised the researches of Joy Dryfoos and Carol Ascher; all three deserve high praise for the diligence and intelligence with which they pursued their investigations.

Our innumerable requests for information met with generous response from the following, who are listed in alphabetical order: the Rev. C. Rankin Barnes, of the National Council of the Protestant Episcopal Church; the Rev. David W. Barry, of the National Council of the Churches of Christ in the U.S.A.; Mrs. Dorothy Dunbar Bromley, of the American Civil Liberties Union; Dr. Uriah Engelman, of the American Association for Jewish Education; John Fenton, of the American Institute of Public Opinion; Dr. Robert Goldenson, of Hunter College; Naomi Grand, of the American Jewish Committee; Dr. Robert Handy, of Union Theological Seminary; Rabbi Wolfe Kelman, of the Jewish Theological Seminary; Rabbi Morris N. Kertzer, of the American Jewish Committee; Helen Knubel, of the National Luthern Council; Dr. Benson Y. Landis, editor of the *Yearbook of American Churches,* and his colleagues on the staff of the National Council of the Churches of Christ in the U.S.A.; J. Louis Meyer, of *The Official Catholic Directory;* Dr. Cyril Richardson, of Union Theological Seminary; Elmo Roper, of Elmo Roper Associates; Dr. Paul Scherer, of Union Theological Seminary; Helen F. Smith, of the General Conference of Seventh-day Adventists; Dr. Henry P. Van Dusen, of Union Theological Seminary.

Grateful acknowledgment is made to the following for official permission to reprint valuable material, in part or in whole, from their publications:

The American Bible Society, New York, for permission to reprint the "Chart of the English Bible" and material from pamphlets about the Bible;

The American Jewish Committee and the Jewish Publication Society of

America, New York, for permission to reprint data from the *American Jewish Year Book, 1961;*

The *Annals of the American Academy of Political and Social Science,* Philadelphia, for permission to reprint excerpts from "Trends in Church Membership in the U.S." by Benson Y. Landis, "Religion Among Ethnic and Racial Minorities" by J. Oscar Lee, and "Ecological Changes and the Church" by Truman B. Douglass;

The *Annals of the Association of American Geographers,* Washington, D. C., for permission to reprint excerpts from "An Approach to the Religious Geography of the U.S.: Patterns of Church Membership in 1952" by Wilbur Zelinsky;

The Association Press, New York, for permission to reprint extracts from "Mixed Marriages—Research Finding" by Judson T. Landis and Mary G. Landis in *Sex Ways—In Fact and Faith: Bases for Christian Family Policy* edited by Duvall and Duvall;

Basic Books Publishing Co., Inc., New York, for permission to reprint data from *The Churches and Mental Illness* by Richard V. McCann;

The Bureau of Labor Statistics, Washington, D. C., for permission to reprint excerpts from *Occupational Outlook Handbook,* 1961 edition;

Christianity Today, Washington, D. C., for permission to reprint data from "Religious Trends in the United States" by Richard C. Wolf;

Daedalus and the American Academy of Arts and Sciences, Cambridge, Mass., for permission to reprint material from "Some Effects of Parochial School Education in America" by Peter H. and Alice S. Rossi;

Doubleday & Company, Inc., New York, for permission to reprint excerpts from *Protestant—Catholic—Jew* by Will Herberg, 1955;

The Free Press of Glencoe, New York, for permission to reprint material from *Drinking and Intoxication* edited by Raymond G. McCarthy, from *Social Patterns of an American Group* edited by Marshall Sklare, and from *The Population of the United States* by Donald J. Bogue;

George Gallup for permission to reprint opinion polls by the American Institute of Public Opinion, Princeton, N. J., and excerpts from "Youth" by George Gallup and Evan Hill, *Saturday Evening Post;*

The *Georgetown Law Journal,* Washington, D.C., for permission to reprint data from "The Constitutionality of the Inclusion of Church-Related Schools in Federal Aid to Education" by the Legal Department, National Catholic Welfare Conference;

Dan Golenpaul Associates, New York, for permission to reprint data from the *1962 Information Please Almanac;*

Harper & Row, Publishers, Inc., New York, for permission to reprint excerpts from *Encyclopedia of American History* edited by Richard B. Morris, and from *The Church as Employer, Money Raiser, and Investor* by Johnson and Ackerman;

Health, Education, and Welfare Trends, Washington, D.C., for permission to reprint excerpts from the 1962 edition;

Journal of the American Statistical Association, Washington, D.C., for permission to reprint data from "A Comparison of Major United States Religious

Groups" by Bernard Lazerwitz;

P. J. Kenedy & Sons, New York, for permission to reprint data from the *Official Catholic Directory*, 1961;

The McGraw-Hill Book Co., Inc., New York, for permission to reprint material from *Family Planning, Sterility, and Population Growth* by Freedman, Whelpton, and Campbell;

The National Council of the Churches of Christ in the U. S. A., New York, for permission to reprint material from the *1962 Yearbook of American Churches,* the National Council *Outlook, Churches and Church Membership in the United States,* and the *Information Service;*

The Planned Parenthood Federation of America, Inc., New York, and H. H. Remmers, Director of the Purdue Opinion Panel, Lafayette, Ind., for permission to reprint excerpts from the "Report of Poll 57" and the "Report of Poll 58," Purdue Opinion Panel;

The Population Reference Bureau, Inc., Washington, D. C., for permission to reprint extracts from the *Population Bulletin;*

Princeton University Press, Princeton, N. J., for permission to reprint data from *Family Growth in Metropolitan America* by Westoff, Potter, Sage and Mishler;

The Public Affairs Press, Washington, D. C., for permission to reprint excerpts from *Religion in American Schools* by R. B. Dierenfeld;

Elmo Roper and Associates, New York, for permission to reprint excerpts from *The Public Pulse;*

St. Anthony's Guild, Paterson, N. J., for permission to reprint material from *The National Catholic Almanac,* 1955;

Charles Scribner's Sons, New York, for permission to reprint excerpts from *Religion in the Development of American Culture* and *Religion in Colonial America* by William W. Sweet;

The State University of New York, College at Oswego, New York, for permission to reprint data from "Religion and the College Student" by W. Seward Salisbury;

Dr. Stanley I. Stuber and the *International Journal of Religious Education,* New York, for permission to reprint Dr. Stuber's chart;

The University of Notre Dame Press, Notre Dame, Ind., for permission to reprint data from *Parochial School* by Joseph H. Fichter, S. J.;

The U. S. Bureau of the Census, Washington, D. C., for permission to reprint data from *Current Population Reports;*

The U. S. Department of Health, Education, and Welfare, Social Security Administration, Washington, D. C., for permission to reprint data from "Coverage of Ministers Under Old-age, Survivors and Disability Insurance" by Saul Waldman in the *Social Security Bulletin;*

D. Van Nostrand Company, Inc., Princeton, N. J., for permission to reprint excerpts from *What College Students Think* by Goldsen, Rosenberg, Williams and Suchman;

H. W. Wilson Co., New York, for permission to reprint data from *Facts About the Presidents* by Joseph Nathan Kane;

The World Almanac, New York, for permission to reprint census data from the *1962 World Almanac;*

The World Council of Churches, Inc., New York, for permission to reprint data from *Summary of Facts about the Ordination of Women in the Member Churches of the World Council of Churches.*

None of the above is to be held responsible, of course, for my notes, comments, footnotes, interpretations, or errors of judgment.

—LEO ROSTEN

December 14, 1962
New York, N. Y.

Index

About the Editor

LEO ROSTEN, *one of the most versatile and stimulating minds of our time, is the author of* Captain Newman, M.D., The Education of H*Y*M*A*N K*A*P*L*A*N, The Return of H*Y*M*A*N K*A*P*L*A*N, The Story Behind the Painting, The Washington Correspondents, Hollywood: The Movie Colony, *and many essays on politics and life, short stories, melodramas and screenplays.*

A Ph.D. from the University of Chicago, he has taught at Yale, is a faculty associate at Columbia University, and was Visiting Professor of Political Science at the University of California at Berkeley.

During the war he was Deputy Director of the Office of War Information and Special Consultant to the Secretary of War. He recently served as consultant to the President's Commission on National Goals.

He has won the Commonwealth Medal for Literature, the George Polk Memorial Award and the Freedoms Foundation Award.

He serves as Special Editorial Adviser to Look *Magazine.*